Seth Low

The Reformer in an Urban and Industrial Age

Seth Low
The Reformer in an Urban and Industrial Age

by GERALD KURLAND

Brooklyn College of the City University of New York

Twayne Publishers, Inc. :: New York

Dedicated to My Parents
Sophia and Carl Kurland

Acknowledgments

The author has in the course of researching and writing this study incurred many intellectual debts. Professor Dean Albertson of the University of Massachusetts originally inspired my work on Seth Low, and sponsored my master's essay on Low's tenure as mayor of New York. Professors John H. Cox and Benjamin J. Klebaner of the City College of New York offered helpful criticism, as did Dean Milton M. Klein of the State University of New York at Fredonia. My dissertation sponsor, Professor Sidney I. Pomerantz of City College gave careful attention to my manuscript, and guided me through the pitfalls of New York City politics. Finally, Professor Hans L. Trefousse of Brooklyn College provided useful stylistic criticisms, and extended the author invaluable assistance. The author, however, retains responsibility for errors of fact or interpretation.

I also wish to thank the staff of Columbia University Library's Special Collections Department for cheerful and efficient service. Lastly, I am indebted to *The New York Historical Society Quarterly* for permission to reprint chapter 5 of this book.

Contents

Acknowledgments

PART ONE
The Patrician as Social Reformer

Foreword to The Patrician as Social Reformer   9

I. "After All We Are the 'Knickerbockers' of New York"   11

II. "The Brooklyn Idea" in Municipal Government   25

III. Interlude: Seth Low as President of Columbia, 1890–1901   50

IV. From Mugwump to Progressive: Seth Low and the Problem of Urban Government   63

V. The Citizens' Union and the Greater New York Mayoralty Campaign of 1897   82

VI. The Fusion Crusade of 1901   107

VII. "The Best Administration New York Ever Had"   140

VIII. "The Dog Has Returned to His Vomit"   169

IX. The Patrician as Reformer vs. the Democrat as Villain   193

PART TWO
The Patrician as Social Architect

Foreword to the Patrician as Social Architect   215

X. The National Civic Federation to 1905   218

XI. The Industrial Philosophy of Seth Low   239

XII. The Effort to Regulate the American Economy, 1908–1911   258

XIII. The National Civic Federation between Scylla and Charybdis   281

XIV. From the New Nationalism to the New Freedom   302

XV. The Measure of a Man and a Movement   323

XVI. The National Civic Federation, the Progressives, and the Historians   340

Notes and References   357

Bibliography   397

Index   409

The Patrician as Social Reformer

Foreword to The Patrician as Social Reformer

Born in the cities of America, the Progressive movement in the first decade of this century took firm hold of municipal government in the eastern, mid-western, and western sections of the United States. Almost everywhere it realized its objectives of giving to the people an honest, efficient civic administration of which they could be proud—an administration which would work for them, not for the special interests. The one notable failure in the Progressive record was the City of New York. By examining the character of Seth Low, the nature of the fusion movement in New York City, and the temper of the people, this work shall try to advance some tentative answers to the question of why Progressive reform failed to take roots in the nation's largest city.

Unfortunately, the personal and intimate side of Seth Low's life, the "flesh and blood" of any good biography, cannot be reconstructed. He left no personal letters or papers, and his private life cannot be recreated. Only those documents pertaining to Low's public career have been preserved, and even they contain serious and severely limiting deletions. As a result, it is only possible to relate the details of Seth Low's public life, and as a biographical subject, he must forever remain a paper skeleton devoid of those human features which are needed to bring history to life. Historians, as a consequence of this dearth of personal material about his life, have tended to shy away from a consideration of Seth Low's place in American history. This is most unfortunate, for Seth Low was one of the leading figures in the Progressive movement in New York State. An understanding of the nuances of Progressive thought and goals is greatly increased by an examination of Seth Low's career, and it is to be regretted that he has become almost a forgotten man in recent American political history.[1]

Seth Low's life lends itself to a division into two parts. The first (The Patrician as Social Reformer) deals with his active political career as a municipal reformer, the second (The Patrician as Social Architect) begins after Low's defeat in the 1903 New York Mayoralty. After stepping down as mayor of New York, Low withdrew from active political life, and became increasingly more involved with labor-capital relations. Losing his once abiding interest in municipal reform, he devoted the last years of his life to the improvement of the conditions of labor, and to the attempt to regulate America's great industries so that the public interest might better be served.

---

[1]. The Seth Low Papers at Columbia University are in the process of being refiled according to sender and recipient. The re-classification has been in progress for a number of years, and, consequently, the author's citations may no longer correspond to the present arrangement of the papers. The author's citations, therefore, refer to the documents as they were filed when he last used them.

CHAPTER I

"After All We Are the 'Knickerbockers' of New York"

"Old Low, old Low's son,
Never saw so many Lows
Since the world begun."

THE REVEREND NATHANIEL ROGERS, FINDING ENGLAND'S CLI-
mate harsh on religious nonconformists, determined to join
his brethren in the great migration to the Puritan's "Zion in the
wilderness." Setting out from Gravesend, England, on the 1st
of June, 1636, the Reverend Rogers and his band of pilgrims
reached the shores of Massachusetts Bay the following November. The grip of winter was beginning to close over New England. The hilly, rocky land of eastern Massachusetts was becoming increasingly barren of vegetation, the branches of the trees,
bare of leaves now, bent with the wind, swaying in response to
the chilling blasts sweeping over the landscape. Along the shore-
line, a whistling wind whipped the surface of the ocean, tearing
the waves asunder and hurtling white sprays of foam across the
top of the water.

To this cold, forbidding land the Reverend Rogers' party
came. Seeking to live in accordance with the laws of their God,
they were a stern people, who, while not immune to the pleasures of the senses or the allure of beauty, remembered that theirs'
was a God of wrath and jealousy, a God who demanded much
from his "Chosen People." They came to set a city upon a hill
and to be a light unto the world; and if life was enjoyable, they
realized that joy must take second place to God's work, that they
were here on a sacred mission. Never were men and climate better matched. The fleeting beauty of the New England summer
and the momentary rapture of the Puritan soul were both subordinate to the drab death-inspiring winter and the dark fore-
bodings of everlasting damnation and hell-fire which warped
the spirit and haunted the mind of the early settlers.

Among the Reverend Rogers' party was one Thomas Low, a young man of thirty-one who had been born somewhere near Colchester in Essex County.[1] The founder of the Low family in America, Thomas was granted ten acres of upland at Chebacco Parish, now Essex County. Taking a wife, he devoted his energies to the land with all the fervor the Puritan gave to his God, and on his death in 1677, he left his son an increased patrimony.

The second Thomas Low was born in 1631, becoming a Deacon of the Chebacco Parish church in 1679. In the absence of the Reverend John Wise, who had taken part in the Phipps expedition against Quebec, Deacon Low acted as the parish clerk. He took part in the Great Swamp Fight against King Philip; and, in 1692, when the suppressed fears and terrors which surged through and warped the Puritan psyche finally broke to the surface of consciousness and expressed itself in the disgraceful Salem witch hunt, Thomas Low retained his reason. Joining with Rev. Wise, he condemned the madness, and petitioned for the acquittal of John Proctor and his wife who were being duly tried for witchcraft. He died April 12, 1712, at the age of eighty, leaving a wife and seven children.

One of Thomas Low's sons, David (1667–1746), was the first of four David Lows in the direct line. A carpenter by trade, he built his house with his own hands. He was known to have participated in Sir William Phipps' expedition, but otherwise led a quiet life. The second David (1700–1771) commanded the Essex Militia, having the rank of Captain. The third David Low (1728–1782) was a Lieutenant in an Ipswich Minute Company, and was among those responding to the Lexington alarm. Commissioned a Captain of the Third Massachusetts Regiment, he was sent, in 1777, to re-enforce General Gates at Saratoga. The fourth and last David Low (1753–1797) was a Sergeant in Dodge's Company of Little's Massachusetts Regiment. He fought at Bunker Hill, helped to build the breastworks for the Battle of Long Island, and later engaged in the battles of Trenton and Princeton. It was believed that he may have wintered with Washington at Valley Forge. Marrying Hannah Haskell, a Gloucester woman who was the great-granddaughter of the Reverend John Wise, he became a sea captain after the Revolutionary War and was lost at sea in 1797.

Six generations of Lows had sunk their roots deep into the tenacious and stony New England soil, stubbornly wresting a living from the infertile clods. They were a hardy race of men, of rugged physique, never out of hearing of the sea, and while as devoted to the soil as were their yeoman ancestors, they could not quite resist the lure of the ocean. Each generation participated in military service, none achieving a brilliant record, but all giving testimony to their devotion to the public service. Literate but not learned, godly in their church duties but not slavish, obedient to orders but with enough of the Cromwellian in them to stand up to a good fight, the Lows lived quietly in the same localities as their fathers. As far as we are able to tell, they lived peacefully and happily with their wives and obeyed the Biblical injunction to beget large families.

Seth Low, the elder, was born on March 29, 1782 in the Haskell family home on Lincoln Road in West Gloucester, Cape Ann.[2] Upon the death at sea of his father, the family moved to Haverhill where Seth was prepared for Harvard under the Unitarian minister, Abiel Abbot. Planning to enter the ministry, he matriculated at Harvard in 1800 but due to a severe case of ophthalmia brought on by an attack of the measles, he was forced to leave college in his junior year without taking a degree. Settling in Salem, he went to work as a clerk in a drug store and, in 1807, married Mary Porter. A descendant of General Israel Putnam, and a relative of Nathaniel Hawthorn and Joseph Choate, she was a devoutly pious woman who bore her husband twelve children, all but one of whom survived to maturity. Seth Low eventually went into the drug business for himself, but failed. Finally, in 1828, with Salem's harbor silting up and with new ships of deeper drafts seeking better harbors, Seth Low determined to leave the home of his fathers and seek his fortune in a more prosperous clime. The Erie Canal was opening the Western heartland of America to the merchants of New York, and seeing an opportunity to reap the profits of the wide new market created by the canal, Low and his eldest son, Abiel Abbot, moved to New York Harbor and began importing drugs from South America and the Orient.

Opening a wholesale house on Manhattan's Fletcher Street, Seth Low and Company imported "myrrh and aloes from Africa, musk in pods, gum benzoin, peppers, asafetida, Bombay arrowroot, Mocha gum arabic," to mention but a few items, and prospered mightily.[3] In September 1829, the remainder of the family came down from Salem, and crossing the East River settled into the family's new home on Brooklyn Heights' Nassau Street where pigs still wallowed in the rich muck of the village's streets.

Seth Low took a vigorous part in the development of Brooklyn Heights. Using the profits from his importing business, he built two blocks of houses on Concord and Washington Streets, and behind the houses he constructed a classical school, manned by teachers imported from "civilized" Salem, for the children of his middle-class neighbors, many of whom were themselves expatriate sons of New England. When the first City of Brooklyn was incorporated in 1834, Seth Low was among the incorporators, and for many years he served his adopted city as an Alderman from the Fourth Ward. Becoming the first President of the new city's Board of Education, he worked to develop the community's public school system, and he also served Brooklyn as a county supervisor.

Never forgetting his Puritan ethical heritage, he helped, in 1843 to organize the Brooklyn Association for Improving the Condition of the Poor—a group dedicated to erasing poverty by curtailing intemperence, and by instilling into the poverty-stricken the Puritan virtues of thrift, sobriety, and hard work as an unfailing cure for all the ills and problems besetting them. With many other sons of Puritan New England, Seth Low was both attracted to the poor by their obvious need and repelled by their condition. It was, of course, his clear Christian duty to aid his distressed fellows, but there was also the firm belief that poverty was a providential punishment for vice—a warning from God against indolence and intemperance. The Association for Improving the Condition of the Poor always found it necessary to lecture the poor on their moral failings before aiding them. and this patrician self-righteousness would not be quickly dissipated. Formal religion itself was not to be neglected. In 1844 Seth Low was one of the founders of Brooklyn's first Unitarian Church of the Saviour.

Seth Low died in 1853, a prosperous and honored Brooklyn merchant. According to family legend, the dying patriarch called for Abiel Abbot's youngest son to be brought to him, the grandson who had been named for him. The three-year-old child was hoisted onto his grandfather's bed, and the old man—placing his hands on the shoulders of the young Seth—admonished him, in what was almost his dying breath, "Be kind to the poor."[4] The youngster would not disappoint the old man, and would far surpass his grandfather's record of public service.

With the elder Seth Low's death, Abiel Abbot Low took over as patriarch of the Low clan. Born in Salem, Massachusetts on

February 7, 1811, he had attended the public schools of his native town, but did not seek a higher education. He began his business career as a clerk with Howard and Company, a Salem drug firm specializing in the South American trade. Accompanying his father to New York in 1828, he worked for him for five years, when, heeding the call of his uncle William Henry Low, a partner in Russell and Company, he set sail for Canton to assume a clerkship in that firm.

An engaging young man, Abiel Abbot quickly became a favorite of Wu Ping Ch'ien, better known as Houqua, the wealthiest merchant of the Canton Cohong. Houqua virtually adopted the young American as a son, and threw Russell and Company all of his considerable business dealings. Abiel Abbot used his influence with Houqua to develop a profitable side trade between his father's firm and Wu's. Father Seth Low expanded the market for Houqua's teas and silks in New York, and in return Houqua purchased the goods of Seth Low and Company, whose stock-in-trade included an occasional bit of opium. It was, indeed, fortunate that Abiel Abbot built up a vigorous China trade, for Seth Low and Company found itself caught short in the panic of 1837 and on the first of May was forced to suspend payment to its creditors. It was only with his son's help that Seth Low was able to settle his debts the following year for seventy cents on the dollar while retaining his Brooklyn properties. It was also in 1837 that Abiel Abbot was admitted to partnership in Russell and Company.[5]

It was Abiel Abbot's intention to remain with Russell and Company only long enough to amass a profit sufficient to begin his own mercantile venture. He made $25,000 in his first year as a Russell partner, and told his father that if his income remained constant he would leave the firm in October 1840.[6] In the meantime, a crisis struck the Western community at Canton. In March 1839, Commissioner Lin determined to crack down on the opium trade. Demanding that the Western traders surrender their opium stocks, Commissioner Lin ordered them confined to their compounds until they complied with his request, and to add injury to insult, he withdrew the merchants' Chinese servants forcing the Westerners to do their own cooking and cleaning. At Russell and Company's factory, Abiel Abbot Low found himself elected head cook, but after serving his first meal, a Sunday breakfast of ham and eggs, was, amid the hisses of his compatriots, promptly dismissed from his newly-occupied office. Warren Delano was selected to fill the post vacated by him, while Abiel Abbot endured the remainder of the forty-five day siege in the ignominious position of chief table setter for the company.[7] Finally, necessity forced compliance with Commissioner Lin's edict and the Western merchants surrendered their opium, Russell and Company alone giving up 1,407 chests.

"I am glad," Abiel Abbot wrote his sister, "we are done irrevocably with a branch of business, that of late has seemed actually disreputable, a trade which has brought us into contact with the most degraded Chinese, and consequently served to sink us in the estimation of the better classes.[8]

Man's greed being far stronger than his altruism, the opium trade was far from being ended; Commissioner Lin had merely won a skirmish, but Abiel Abbot Low, true to his intention, resigned his partnership in Russell and Company, and in the fall of 1840 returned home to America.

Once again back in Brooklyn, Abiel Abbot Low bestowed a great honor on Ellen Almira Dow by allowing her to become his wife, for, as one relative put it, "I think the young lady may consider herself one of Fortune's favorites to obtain such an excellent young gentleman as your brother Abbot."[9] Besides getting married, he also entered the China trade on his own account, laying the foundation for what would become A. A. Low and Brothers which, in the judgment of the historian of New York Port, was the foremost American house in the China trade.[10]

The Lows were an extremely lucky family who had an uncanny habit of being in the right place at the right time. Even apparent disaster was turned into profit at their hands. In January 1848, 4° south of the Cape of Good Hope, a Low clipper, captained by Abiel Abbot's younger brother, Charles Porter Low, was caught in a furious storm, lashed by gale force winds and nearly inundated by a hard, driving rain. Badly battered by wind and water, its cargo inundated, the clipper limped to Hong Kong, its voyage seemingly a financial failure. Selling its cargo at a damaged goods auction, the clipper was repaired at Hong Kong, a load of teas taken on board, and the ship's course set for home. Abiel Abbot Low later calculated that had the ship not been caught in the storm, and put in at its original port of call—Shanghai—it would have lost forty or fifty thousand dollars on the voyage, due to a drop in the price of the market. But this way, bringing home the first of the new tea crop, it made a sixty thousand dollar profit.[11] The Lows' good fortune would be repeated over and over in the years to come.

Low clippers, famed the world over for their grace and speed, sailed the world's oceans, taking on tea and silk in the Orient, and speeding them to New York, London and Paris. The Low family claimed to be the first American firm to bring home a cargo of Japanese silk, and they boasted that their commercial paper was as good as gold throughout the world. With the opening of the California gold fields, Low clippers made the fantastically profitable California run. As profits mounted, the Low partners, descendants of sturdy but hardly wealthy New England yeoman, took on the accoutrements of merchant princes.

When the agony of Civil War convulsed the American nation. Abiel Abbot Low rallied to the Union's defense. Becoming Treasurer of the New York Union Defence Committee, he helped raise funds to outfit Union regiments, and as a Director of the New York Bank of Commerce, he was a valued financial supporter of the federal government. Elected President of the New York State Chamber of Commerce in 1863, he organized mercantile opposition to Great Britain's construction of commerce raiders for the Confederate navy. His own *Jacob Bell* and *Constant,* it should be noted, were lost to Confederate raiders. His vigorous pronouncements, in the opinion of American Ambassador John Bigelow, did much to help dissuade France from following England in supplying the Confederates with warships.[12] With the end of the war, A. A. Low became a major investor in the Atlantic Cable, the Chesapeake and Ohio Railoard, and Virginia iron foundries as well.

He showed no inclination to enter politics though he was not devoid of the instinct for public service. He was among the founders of the Brooklyn Public Library system, served as President of the Packer Collegiate Institute, which pioneered in the higher education of women, and was one of the incorporators of the Long Island Historical Society. Dedicated to commerce and to the development of the Port of New York, he was an articulate and vocal proponent of federal subsidies for the American merchant marine, as well as for the early resumption of specie payments by the national government. He was also a strong opponent of organized labor, for as he told the Chamber of Commerce, "The prosperity of our port and city appear to be endangered rather by the combinations of men who seek continually to advance the prices of labor beyond what employers can afford to pay.... "[13] It was an attitude his son was not to share. He was, nonetheless, an honored member of the New York mercantile aristocracy at a time when they counted for much in the social and political life of the city. As Henry Ward Beecher put it:

> I honor a man, not merely because he is the architect of his fortune, but because he has not forgotten to be a MAN, and maintains the love of things good and just and true and beautiful. A man who . . . stands in the midst of the community, after the rivalries and strifes of a long commercial life, without a spot and without a stain....[14]

Abiel Abbot Low passed on to his younger son the family tradition of devotion to the public service. On January 18, 1850, in the City of Brooklyn, at the family home at 165 Washington Street, a large brick structure with a spacious garden overlooking his grandfather's home at 40 Concord Street, Seth Low was born. It was Ellen Low's fourth confinement in ten years, one from which she was not to recover. On January 25, as an old historian of Brooklyn affirms, "With her hands devoutly laid upon his [Seth's] head, she, in almost her last breath, commanded him to the blessing of God and died serenely.... "[15] The baby was frail and sickly and was not expected to live; in fact, it was remembered in the family that a stewardess on the Fall River boat opined that the child was not worth the trouble of raising.[16] However, carefully nursed by Ann Davison Bedell Low, the widow of his uncle William H. Low, Seth thrived. Moving into Abbot's new mansion at 3 Pierrepont Street, Ann Low soon became indispensable to Abbot's household, and shortly after Seth's second birthday, they were married.

Summers spent at the Dow farm in New Hampshire helped to strengthen the child, but still considered delicate, he was kept from school until past the age of seven. His half-brother asserted that Seth taught himself to read while playing with alphabet blocks on the floor of his playroom.[17] In the light of his subsequent academic career, the story seems not improbable. Eventually. though, he was sent to a day school kept by the Misses Dobbin and Rogers, and he promptly assumed the position as the school's first scholar, a position which he was to retain throughout his academic career. He was by all accounts a sensitive child who demanded constant attention. Vacationing in New England in the summer of his twelfth year, he complained to his sister Harriette that, "I am very much disappointed that I have not had a letter from home since I have been here. Please write soon and often."[18] It was a habitual complaint with Seth. A year later, accompanying his father to London, he confided to his sister that he felt, "very badly at receiving no letter this afternoon . . . ," and added. "I should not have cared so much had it not been the first day of separation."[19]

He was prepared for college at Brooklyn Polytechnic Institute, where, of course, he added to his reputation for academic excellence. Reporting that he was getting along "splendidly in French," he declared that his average of 89 and 11/12 percent, "just puts me on the best merit roll and I think it will lead the school."[20] It did. The French came in handy also, for on the voyage to London there was a Frenchman of secessionist proclivities who knew no English, and this gave Seth a chance to test and improve his French. "It is in giving him fits," he told Harriette, "that I have made so much progress."[21] He graduated from Brooklyn Polytechnic Institute in 1866 at the head of his class, and went on to Columbia College.

A Columbia classmate remembered Seth as, "young and ruddy, he was vigorous and plucky, he was joyous and natural. We expected that he would stand for something. . . ."[22] Apparently there were no traces of his childhood fragility remaining, for Oscar S. Straus recalled that Low went, "on the coldest winter days without an overcoat."[23] He also participated vigorously in a wide range of college athletics, playing football, golf, and billiards, and took up bicycle racing as well. It was reported that he attained no great distinction at any sport, though he did play a fair game of golf.[24] Looking to him as a class leader, one of Seth's classmates declared that, "he was no prig and he had his faults like the rest of us. . . ."[25] Unfortunately, no evidence is extant which would substantiate Professor Sloane's most comforting assurance.

Academically, Seth impressed Columbia's President Frederick A. P. Barnard as "the first scholar in college, and the most manly young man we have had here for many years."[26] The young man was under considerable, albeit tacit, pressure to excel. After all, there was a family tradition, going back two and a half centuries, to maintain, and Seth himself had his name to live up to. "The manner in which Grandpa Low was named both by Mr. Putnam himself and by the Reverend Dr. Holland in a letter to the pastor made me feel," he wrote his sister, "that I will have to struggle hard to be worthy of being called after such a man, but with God's help I shall do my best."[27] And struggle hard he did. Determined to win a Greek prize, he realized that more study was required to achieve his goal. Consequently, he rose at six every morning and studied Greek an hour before breakfast. "I sincerely believe that I feel brighter the whole day for so doing," he told Harriette.[28] His determination paid off, for, "He was an admirable Grecian and he made it appear a trifle to repeat the complicated choruses of Aeschylus and Sophocles as if they were welling up from out his own mind."[29] He was graduated from Columbia College as valedictorian in 1870, and as befitted a young man of station, he made the grand tour of Europe before entering his father's countinghouse at Manhattan's 31 Burling Slip as a clerk.

In the early 1870s, Seth Low underwent a crisis of religious identity. Living in an age when religion still bore relevancy to human life, it seemed imperative to Seth Low that he identify himself in some form with organized religion. His grandfather and father had been prominent Unitarians, but his stepmother was a devout Episcopalian and he was torn between the two sects. "As you know," he told Harriette:

> I have long felt that I could not join the Unitarian Church while it was the harbor of so much that seemed to me terrible, in the way of theological views: & yet you know that I have been very desirous of uniting myself with the Church of Christ in some one of its branches. Naturally, therefore, I would like to join that branch which contains those with whom I would best love to work, & with the spirit of which I feel myself in perfect symathy [sic].

"I spoke to father," he continued, "& told him of my feeling towards the Unitarian Church, & received his full permission to join whichever Church I pleased, and his admonition [sic] to follow the dictates of my own conscience." Seth felt ill-at-ease with the Unitarians and inclined towards the Episcopalians, but he "could not give a reason satisfactory to my own mind for a belief in the Trinity...."[30] For many months he wavered between the two faiths, when, finally. in September of 1872, he made his decision. "Henceforth I consider myself an Episcopalian," he announced to Harriette:

> I feel conscious I have done right, and my mind is entirely at rest; but Father's broad and loving charity makes the apparent difference between us a fearful trial, altho' he has told

me he would far rather see me united with the Episcopal Church at once than longer wavering between two opinions.[31]

He was never truly satisfied with Episcopalianism, but he remained with that Church for the rest of his life. "I really drifted into the Episcopal Church because my Stepmother was an Episcopalian . . . . " he told the Reverend David H. Greer years later. "If I were doing today what I did then," he added, "I should join the Congregational Church; for, in matters of polity, I am really a Congregationalist rather than an Episcopalian."[32] Seth Low's religious faith was deep and genuine, but he was repelled and appalled by doctrinal niceties and theological hair-splitting. He never felt completely at home in any organized religion, and as a consequence, his Puritan instinct to perform good works manifested itself in the field of public service rather than in the confines of institutional religion.

In 1875, Seth Low was admitted as a junior partner in A. A. Low and Brothers. Though he told his father, "It will be my constant aim to be more worthy of your abounding kindness," he did not enjoy the life of a businessman—the call of public service beckoned strongly.[33] Three years later. he told one of the firm's senior partners, "Speaking personally, I wish to look forward to a time when I shall be at liberty to continue in business or not as may seem good to me then. I am not clear in my mind that I wish to pass my whole career in business, should my life be prolonged."[34] He was eventually admitted to fullpartnership, and remained with the firm until its liquidation in 1888. But, after 1879, with his interests elsewhere, he was only a parttime member of the company. In 1887, Seth Low, having stepped down as Brooklyn's mayor and not yet elected president of Columbia College, returned to the family business and attempted to corner the market in Amoy tea. He purchased sixty thousand bags of Amoy, the third cheapest grade of Oolong tea, and did, indeed, corner the market. However, instead of buying the Low's Amoy tea at an inflated price, the tea merchants simply substituted other varieties in their tea blends, and A. A. Low and Brothers found itself with thirty-five thousand bags of Amoy tea which it was unable to sell.[35] The next year, A. A. Low and Brothers was liquidated, not on account of Seth's Amoy fiasco, but because the steamship had made the clipper obsolete. From this point on, Seth Low would live off invested capital—principally from Virginia real estate and iron foundries which he acquired as his share in the liquidation of the family's business.

In 1876, drawn by the call of public service, Seth Low became a volunteer visitor to the poor for the County Commission of Charities. His primary function was to ascertain whether
applicants for outdoor relief (that is, welfare given to the family in its home rather than at an eleemosynary institution) were,
in fact, in need of aid, and whether those already receiving public assistance were legitimate recipients. Brooklyn's system of
outdoor relief, under the administration of Hugh McLaughlin's
Democratic machine, had, as an early historian declared, "become a sink of corruption."[36] There were numerous instances of
families collecting relief under several different names; people
with political connection, who were not in need of assistance,
were also enjoying the public's largesse. The entire outdoor relief system had been turned into an auxiliary of the McLaughlin machine, and had become nothing more than a political
slush fund.[37] Then, too, the city was plagued by applicants who,
while not in need, wanted something for nothing. "In the course
of one of my calls," Low recalled:

> I visited a woman who had an apple stand near the ferry.
> Her room gave every evidence of comfort. It was neat as a
> pin, and there was no outward suggestion that she was in any
> need. I suggested that, as neatly as I could, for she had been
> an applicant for aid, and, as her eloquence did not seem per-
> suasive, she went to the closet and handed me an apple. I
> said, "Madam, if you are rich enough to give me an apple,
> you are not poor enough to be helped by the county." Her
> daugter who was there said, "Mother, he has got you." Her
> whole attitude—and she very frankly expressed it—was that
> if anything was going she wanted her share.[38]

To prevent corruption, and to eliminate a source of political
spoilsmanship, Seth Low urged the abolition of Brooklyn's system of outdoor relief, which was finally ended in 1879. The
County now confined its charitable operations to eleemosynary
institutions with private charity taking over the burden of giving direct aid to individuals. Declaring that it was the act of a
heartless aristocrat, which would condemn the poor to starva-
tion, the advocates of outdoor relief charged that its abolition
would work needless hardship on many of the worthy poor, and
that economy was being placed above human need. Seth Low,
however, "pledged his personal honor that no poor person in
the city shoold [sic] go hungry if they would only let him know

of their condition," and to make certain that the poor would not be injured, he, in conjunction with Alfred T. White, established the Brooklyn Bureau of Charities.[39]

Serving as its first president, Low organized the Brooklyn Bureau of Charities as a clearinghouse for the many private and church charitable oganizations in the city. Each charitable group sent the Brooklyn Bureau a list of the people receiving its aid, the names were placed in a master index and by this means those collecting from numerous organizations—the professional welfare recipient who made a living by defrauding charitable associations—could be weeded out. Eliminating duplication, the Bureau made it possible for existing private charities to effectively meet their new burdens and to efficiently serve those who were in genuine need of assistance. Low's attitude towards charity was the typical Puritan view. He opposed the giving of alms, "without securing from the recipient some labor or service in return," as emasculating, as tending toward the destruction of self-respect and independence.[40] People should be made to work for the assistance they received, he argued, even if the service they were required to perform was only nominal, in order to enable them to feel that they were entitled to the aid they received and to preserve their sense of human worth. "The condition of the poor," he pointed out, "can be improved only by helping them to help themselves," and not by placing them on a permanent dole.[41] Social welfare workers might condemn this attitude as puritanical in the worst sense of the term, but, perhaps, the Puritans knew better of human nature than they.

His tenure as president of the Brooklyn Bureau of Charities was but the beginning of Seth Low's long career of public service. On December 9, 1880, just prior to the dawn of his political career, Seth Low married. Annie Wroe Scollay Curtis, the sister-in-law of his half-brother William Gilman Low, was the daugter of Supreme Court Justice Benjamin Robbins Curtis, and according to Low's ward and nephew, she was, "A woman of rare mind, poise and sagacity," who gave her husband, "without stint, and with complete self-effacement, her constant and devoted sympathy, companionship and advice."[42] It was to prove to be a childless marriage, but an apparently happy one, nonetheless. His nephew declared that upon his marriage, "the fulness of [his] life began there and then."[43] Content in his marriage, enjoying ample means, and a rich family heritage, this scion of an old house, accustomed to receiving the respect of the community, and prepared to shoulder the responsibilities of his social station, Seth Low was set to commence his public career in earnest. "After all," he told William M. Sloane, "we are the 'Knickerbockers' of New York."[44] But the 'Knickerbockers' of New York were entering a time of troubles.

CHAPTER II

"The Brooklyn Idea" in Municipal Government

... There are some of us who can remember the thrill of hope and expectation, like the breath of a fresh wind from the hills, that spread over the land, confined not at all by the boundaries of his State, when the young man in Brooklyn, against the devices and purposes of political organizations, was chosen for the mayor of that city. . . . It seemed that then a new day was dawning for municipal politics in our country, a day when public service would be exalted, and the high principles on which public service could be most perfectly attained would be advocated and sustained.

RUSH RHEES[1]

When the twentieth century was in its infancy, a great political storm, spawned in the cities of the nation, raged fiercely across the American landscape. Picking up the impulse of reform from a moribund Populism, the Progressive ferment gave an air of respectability and sophistication to attempts at altering the superstructure of American society. For almost two decades, the Progressive movement would dominate the political life of America, and by the time it had spent its last energies, the nation's political, economic, and social life would be materially improved. With all its shortcomings, arising, perhaps, from the personality failings of its patrician leadership, Progressivism was successful in helping to make America a better and happier land in which to live. While Progressivism occupied the nation's attention in the first two decades of the new century, its genesis was a product of the late nineteenth century, and, indeed, its period of gestation, which has been all too little studied, was of a duration equal to the life of the mature movement. The intellectual and moral characteristics of the Progressive movement were shaped in the "Gilded Age," and its leaders received their training in the political realm battling the corruption and depravity plaguing American society in the post-Civil War era.

The Progressive movement was conceived in the 1870s and early 1880s.

With the end of the Civil War, and the concomitant decline of the idealistic crusade of the Radical Republicans, American political life entered upon a period of twilight—if not of absolute darkness—in which the ideal of public service was subordinated to personal aggrandizement; official honesty gave way to organized and systematic plunder of the public treasury, and the old Yankee-Protestant political aristocracy fell before the awesome vote-getting power of the immigrant-based political machine. The decline in the nation's political morality was general and all-pervasive, but nowhere was it more obvious and gross than in America's great cities.

In the latter half of the nineteenth century, the United States witnessed an astounding growth in its urban population. Brooklyn, for example, was a sleepy little village of 2,370 souls according to the census of 1800, and after fifty years of growth and development its population still had not reached the one hundred thousand mark. However, from 1850 to 1860, the city's population jumped from ninety-six thousand to two hundred ninefive thousand and ten years later Brooklyn had added another one hundred and five thousand to its population. By 1880, with a population approaching five hundred seventy-five thousand, Brooklyn was the nation's third largest city. Of course, some of this rapid population growth can be accounted for by Brooklyn's geographic expansion which saw the city incorporate the outlying villages and townships of Williamsburg, New Lots, Flatlands, and others. But the prime factor in Brooklyn's growth was the rapid development of industry which in a few decades had transformed the city from a residential suburb of New York City into a modern industrial city. With 5,154 manufacturing establishments capitalized at $69,000,000 and employing forty-five thousand people, Brooklyn, by 1880, ranked among the nation's leading industrial centers. This phenomenal urban growth outstripped the ability of America's agrarian-based and negatively-oriented sociopolitical institutions to adequately deal with the new problems posed by an emergent urban-industrial society.[2] America was too inexperienced with the problems of the industrial order to provide the positive services essential to the new urban society, and the spoilsman was able to exploit this governmental vacuum to his own advantage, much to the bewilderment of the Yankee middle class.

As the nation became ever more urbanized and industrial, corruption seemed to grow apace, leading many to fear that the democratic values of an agrarian America were unsuited to a society of large cities. It appeared to many that in the rise of the municipality and its attendant political machine, America was witnessing the death of her cherished democratic and individualistic social order. Others, however, were more optimistic, and confidently clung to the belief that the ills besetting urban America were curable, that what was needed was not breast-beating and lamentation, but knowledge of the factors causing them and a practical program of amelioration. It was such a spirit which engendered the urban reform movements which, beginning in the early 1880s, eventually spawned the larger Progressive movement. Among the earliest, and one of the most important, of the urban reform movements of the "Gilded Age" arose in the city of Brooklyn and was led by Seth Low.

Having organized the Brooklyn Bureau of Charities in 1878, and after serving as its first President, Seth Low, in the fall of 1880, turned his attention to the political scene. James A. Garfield was the Republican party's Presidential candidate that year, and to assist in the election of the G.O.P.'s national ticket, Seth Low, as the first act of his political career, organized and headed a Garfield and Arthur Campaign Club. There was little to distinguish it from the countless ad hoc committees now and then formed to work for some particular cause, except that most of its members were young men in their twenties and thirties, and were, moreover, scions of Brooklyn's "best" families. Low's campaign club printed and distributed great quantities of campaign literature, undertook a sustained speaking program to convince Brooklynites of Garfield's sterling qualifications for the high and esteemed office of President of the United States, and lastly, conducted a vigorous house-to-house canvass to bring out the voters. The club soon had an enrolled membership of over eight hundred young men, and on election day, it aided the undermanned Republican party by supplying poll watchers.[3] The election campaign successfully concluded, and having earned the gratitude of the regular Republican party, the club's members, resolving not to allow so much hard work to be forgotten, decided to reorganize as a permanent political organization.

In the spring of 1881, the Brooklyn Young Republican Club was formally established. Despite its title, it was not in any sense an appendage of the Grand Old Party, for while the young men who founded the club were Republicans, they were all of the independent variety, and the organization quickly demonstrated its Mugwump proclivities. "Its members," proclaimed a flyer announcing the birth of the Young Republican Club, "utterly disclaim any sympathy with the current supercilious expressions of contempt for political positions and political work. We believe in the honorableness of public office. No station is higher or more to be esteemed than that of a servant of the people."[4]

The club went on to declare that it would concern itself only with local political affairs, and would seek to promote honesty in the public service of Brooklyn by championing non-partisanship in municipal affairs and by divorcing the politics of the city from that of the State and nation. Arguing that city affairs resembled business problems far more closely than they did political questions, the Young Republican Club branded partisan considerations as irrelevant to the efficient administration of municipal government. It pledged itself to the support of all capable officials regardless of their convictions as to national political issues. The founder of the original Garfield and Arthur Campaign Club, however, declaring that the Young Republican Club's decision to confine itself to purely local questions was neither practicable nor desirable, resigned from the club upon its reorganization.[5] In any event, the Young Republicans proceeded to assess the records of all candidates for political office in Brooklyn, and did not hesitate to condemn unfit or incompetent officials—even if they happened to be Republicans.

Brooklyn, in the fall of 1881, was slated to elect a new mayor, and because the State legislature had given the city a radically new charter, the biennial mayoralty race took on critical importance. Determined to give the "Schroeder" charter a good chance for success, the Brooklyn Young Republican Club resolved to force the nomination, by the regular G.O.P. organization, of a capable mayoral candidate able to effectively implement the new instrument of government. As an early historian of the city of Brooklyn pointed out, "Under the new theory, or 'idea,' everything depended upon the mayor who should be entrusted with the administration."[6] But, aside from wanting to see the new form of government succeed, the charter scheduled to come into effect on January 1, 1882 gave the mayor far too much power to allow the city to fall into the clutches of Democratic "Boss" Hugh McLaughlin. At all costs a McLaughin victory must not be permitted.

Like many major American cities in the years immediately following the Civil War, Brooklyn was a victim of political corruption, and while the city never sank to the depths of depravity reached by New York City under the guidance of William Marcy Tweed, Hugh McLaughlin appeared to many observers as an able student of the master corruptionist. In an effort to root out the boodlers from the government of the city of Brooklyn, the State legislature in 1873 framed a new charter for the "City of Churches" which was based on the premise that a city was a miniature state or nation, and that what was needed to guarantee honest and democratic government was a municipal system of checks and balances. Consequently, to prevent the concentration of power in the hands of a man who might be negligent or under the control of a political boss, the charter specified that each city department was to be administered by a three-man commission appointed by the mayor with the approval of the Board of Aldermen. Indeed, virtually all of the mayor's official acts were subject to confirmation by the aldermen. Rather than producing an honest and efficient government, the charter of 1873 quickly resulted in administrative paralysis. It led to "confusion, an endless hunt for spoils, and public servants who could not be held accountable."[7] With three men running each city department, with the mayor's powers fettered by the Board of Aldermen, and with a large aldermanic board manned by political drones, it was impossible to fix responsibility for wrongdoing, since accused officials could always declare that they had neither the authority nor the jurisdiction to correct or prevent the abuse. Whoever controlled the Board of Aldermen was master of Brooklyn, and as the city was normally Democratic, the charter of 1873 served only to tighten Hugh McLaughlin's iron grip over the municipal government.

By 1880, it was obvious that the charter of 1873 was a dismal failure, and it became apparent that while a system of checks and balances might preserve political liberty on the state or national level, it was not a concept applicable to cities because, it was argued, municipal government did not actually concern itself with political questions affecting individual freedom. Instead, city government was properly concerned with the removal of garbage, the provision of a clean and adequate water supply, safe and efficient transportation services, and the maintenance of a public school system serving the needs of the community. In short, the government of a city was fundamentally different from

that of a state or nation; it was, in effect, far more similar to
the internal functioning of a great corporation than to a political entity. A city's government should be placed in the hands
of an efficient administrator who would oversee the affairs of
the municipality in the same way that a corporation president
conducted the business of his concern, and since the mayor would
have adequate powers, he, and he alone, would be accountable
for corruption. In line with this new theory, the Albany Legislature, under the prodding of Assembly Frederick A. Schroeder,
in May of 1880 granted Brooklyn a new charter to go into effect
at the expiration of the current mayor's term of office.

Under Brooklyn's new charter, the comptroller and auditor
would be popularly elected, but all other executive officers would
be appointed solely by the mayor without confirmation by the
aldermen. All departments would be administered by a single
commissioner responsible to the mayor, who would serve a two-
year term commencing one month after the mayor assumed office, and terminating one month after the expiration of the
mayor's term. A commissioner could be suspended at any time
by the mayor, but the removal would have to be confirmed by
the State's Supreme Court. In addition, the mayor could block,
by refusing to sign the necessary warrants and vouchers, all expenditures of public funds of which he did not approve, and
could command an investigation into the propriety of every
appropriation voted by the common council. Moreover, the may-
or had the controlling voice in the Board of Estimate. Also the
charter permitted the mayor to introduce, at his discretion, an
extensive civil service system in the city's bureaucracy. Whoever
became Brooklyn's mayor on January 1, 1882, would possess
more authority than any other municipal chief executive in the
United States.[8] No longer could responsibility for malfeasance
be disclaimed by the mayor; he would be responsible in all respects for the conduct of his administration. The charter offered
great hope for the establishment of an efficient municipal government, but if Hugh McLaughlin's candidate won control of
the mayor's office, a reign of corruption might ensue which
would rival Tweed's. To demonstrate the charter's effectiveness,
McLaughlin had to be defeated, for, as the *New York Times* observed:

> The chance now offered them [the people of Brooklyn] to
> secure a practical and substantial improvement in local gov-

ernment is one that they have never before had, and one which they may not have again in a long time.

If they allow the Mayor's office, with its largely extended powers, to be seized by an agent of the ring, or by a representative of the class of politicians who in both parties have so long made a spoil of the City Government, they will have only themselves to blame for the consequences which will surely follow, and which will be harder to bear than anything they have hitherto suffered.[9]

For the "goo-goos" (good government advocates), the election of 1881 assumed crisis proportions.

In the fall of 1881, prospects were favorable that "Boss" McLaughlin's control over Brooklyn's government would soon come to an end. His iron grip over the city had weakened, and his hold over the Democratic organization was no longer absolute. Born on Brooklyn's Furman Street in April 1827, Hugh McLaughlin went to work in the Brooklyn Navy Yard, rising to the position of work boss. Active in Democratic politics, he became the city's register in 1861, and rapidly rose in the party's hierarchy, until by the late 1860's and early 1870's, he was the dominant power in the Brooklyn Democratic organization. His rise to power coincided with the Irish and German challenge to Yankee ascendancy over Brooklyn's social and political life. Moving down from New England in the decade after the War of 1812, the Yankees quickly swamped Brooklyn's original Dutch settlers, and occupying Brooklyn Heights, they dominated the city's social, economic, and political life. But their stern devotion to a public service devoid of concern for the needs of the urban masses did not answer the requirements of the Irish and German immigrants who began to pour into Brooklyn by the tens of thousands in the 1840s and '50s. The minority Democratic party, taken over by leaders of the Irish (and to a lesser extent the German) community who paid close attention to the socio-economic needs of their constituents, began to challenge and supplant the political authority wielded by the Yankees.[10] However, as Brooklyn's rapid development progressed even "Boss" McLaughlin found himself losing touch with his constituents, and Yankee and German elements within the Democratic party were waiting for the opportunity to break his power over the party.

In the Presidential campaign of 1880, a considerable body of Brooklyn's Democrats felt that General Hancock had not been properly supported by the McLaughlin machine, and their resentment at what they regarded as McLaughlin's treason to the party manifested itself in the Jefferson Hall movement of 1881. Led by *Brooklyn Eagle* editor Thomas Kinsella, the Jefferson Hall Democracy, as a reporter for the *Eagle* declared, was "The most formidable rebellion against the regular machine domination ... " up to its time.[11] In its ranks were included dissident Democrats chafing at McLaughlin's domination of the party's patronage, genuine good government reformers who wanted to democratize the party organization and end boss rule, and political opportunists seeking personal gains. Determined to smash McLaughlin's power and win control of the Brooklyn Democratic party, the Jefferson Hall leaders vowed not to support any candidate for the 1881 mayoralty who was obligated to "Boss" McLaughlin.

As the fall campaign approached, Hugh McLaughlin announced that he would support incumbent Democratic Mayor James Howell for re-election. A native of Bradford, England, who was born on October 16, 1829, Howell came to Brooklyn by way of Ohio in 1845, and established the iron foundry of Howell & Saxton. Prominent in the Brooklyn business community, Howell made a mediocre Mayor, which, considering McLaughlin's hold over the city's political life, was no mean achievement. He was fairly independent, and while the normal amount of graft and corruption went on as usual, he was not caught in any major scandal. However, being McLaughlin's candidate, Howell was unacceptable to the Jefferson Hall faction which, on October 6, 1881, named Civil War General Henry W. Slocum as its nominee for the mayoralty.[12] With the Democratic vote apparently divided between the followers of the regular organization and the insurgents under Kinsella, the chances of a Republican victory in what was a heavily Democratic city looked bright, provided the G.O.P. could secure the support of the independent citizens' groups which were as opposed to Stalwart domination as they were to "Boss" McLaughlin.

Determined to force the Republican party to nominate an acceptable and independent candidate for the mayoralty, the Brooklyn Young Republican Club had been, all summer long, booming Seth Low as a possible nominee for the office of mayor. Even though Low had resigned from the club, the Young Republicans considered him the best qualified man for the office, and their suggested choice was enthusiastically received by Brooklyn's "goo-goos," though the Republican party greeted the idea frigidly. Low had earned himself the reputation of an eccentric by requesting the Brooklyn Board of Assessment to increase its valuation on his personal property from $1,000 to $10,000. Moreover, "His appearances in Republican Party councils had been distinguished by his outspoken independence and a spirit of non-partisanship which had seldom been appreciated."[13] Seth Low did not possess the qualities which would endear him to professional politicians, besides which he was not interested in running for public office. On August 30, 1881, he released a letter to the press declaring that due to the pressure of his private business interests, he did not wish to be considered for public office, and requested that his name be omitted from the list of eligible candidates. His plea, as the Democratic but anti-McLaughlin *Eagle* stated, was "Regretted by the better elements of both parties."[14] However, his name was not dropped from consideration, and fearing that he would be called upon to stand for the mayoralty, he rejoined the Brooklyn Young Republican Club about the first of September. As he later explained to an associate, the club's constitution provided that no one holding or running for elective office was eligible for membership, and he hoped, by rejoining the club, to make it clear that he had no intention of standing for office.[15] Nevertheless, efforts to secure for him the Republican mayoral nomination continued unabated.

Towards the middle of October, the effort to nominate a suitable candidate began in earnest. On October 10, the *Eagle* lamented that "The dearth of men who are at once available and fit to be candidates for the Mayoralty on either side . . . is a matter in itself highly significant of a morbid state of public affairs."[16] It went on to assert that "Mr. Low, though a young man, has given so much time and thought to our affairs that his ability to be Mayor is conceded on all sides." It regretted that he had irrevocably declined to consider the mayoral nomination, and closed by condemning the Republican party for seeking a partisan victory rather than the good of the city. "The Republicans," it declared, "have striven to win without regard to the character of the man through whom victory was sought, and the leaders of that party have repeatedly given encouragement to the worst misrepresentations of Democracy by giving them patronage and money to prostitute themselves."

Only a day before the *Eagle's* polemic, Benjamin Franklin Tracy, Thomas Platt's law partner, who was prominently men-

tioned as a possible Republican mayoral nominee, announced
that he was "A Stalwart of the Stalwarts."[17] Tracy's nomination
would be unacceptable to the independents, and if they were
forced to name their own slate, a McLaughlin victory might
well result. The next few weeks would be of critical importance
for the cause of good government in Brooklyn.

While the Republicans were leaning toward Benjamin F.
Tracy, the Brooklyn Citizens' League and the Young Republican
Club were coming around to the support of Ripley Ropes. Born
in Salem, Massachusetts on September 30, 1820, Ropes had been
acting mayor of his native city before moving to Brooklyn in
1863 to engage in the South American trade. A fiscal conservative and champion of honest government, he served as a Republican member of the Board of Aldermen in 1872, became County
Suupervisor in 1873, and chairman of the Finance Commission
in 1876.[18] A stern, elderly patrician, he was not the type of man
to inspire the common people of Brooklyn to come to his support. The independents, though, had hopes of winning Ropes
the Republican mayoral nomination, and with the Democratic
vote split, had every prospect of electing their choice. Fearing
a deadlock in the Republican city convention, and feeling that
neither Tracy nor Ropes would be nominated, the *Brooklyn
Eagle* urged the Republicans to endorse the candidacy of General Slocum, nominee of the Jefferson Hall Democracy, and enter into a fusion alliance with Kinsella's faction in order to decisively defeat the McLaughlin machine.[19] As the *Eagle* observed, on the outcome of the Brooklyn mayoralty depended the
cause of municipal reform throughout the United States, for, if
good government failed in this city, "The conclusion will be
come to not only that the mixed populations of our great cities
are unfit for self-government, but that the poverty, the ignorance,
and the disregard of political duty on the part of the more prosperous classes require the constant operation of a steadying and
dominating influence from the rural districts."[20] The question
of whether an urban society was capable of democratic self-government would be decided in Brooklyn in the fall elections, and
to make certain that the question would be answered in the af-
firmative, the "goo-goos" continued to press for Ripley Ropes'
nomination by the G.O.P.

On October 15, 1881, it was reported that the G.O.P.'s leadership was astounded at the strength and fervor of the citizens'
movement on behalf of Ripley Ropes, and it was intimated that

the Stalwarts might have difficulty in holding the convention for Tracy.[21] The following day, the Republicans received an even greater shock when the Young Republican Club announced its formal endorsement of Ripley Ropes for mayor.[22] It was felt that if Ropes were nominated by the independents and Young Republicans before the meeting of the Republican city convention, the Grand Old Party—if it hoped to win the mayoral election—would be forced, out of political expediency, to second Ropes' candidacy. Consequently, on the evening of October 17, at the Claremont Avenue Rink, an enthusiastic citizens' gathering presided over by Abiel Abbot and Seth Low, among others, named Ripley Ropes as the independent candidate for the Brooklyn mayoralty. Commenting on the citizens' action, the *Eagle* applauded Ropes as the nominee of Brooklyn's intelligent, taxpaying, and self-respecting electorate. It was, the paper declared, "One of the most cheering spectacles to the friends of good local government that has been presented in many years," and it expressed the hope that the G.O.P. would follow the lead of the city's better element.[23] The next move was up to the Republicans.

On Friday, October 21, the Republican city convention met. Tracy was the choice of the professional politicians, but there was a strong independent element favorable to Ropes, and Seth Low, representing the Young Republican Club, made a dramatic appearance on the floor of the convention to plead for Ropes' nomination. Low's entrance touched off a spontaneous and prolonged demonstration of support in behalf of his candidacy for the mayoralty, and so fervent was the emotion generated by the rally that Ropes' delegates sought to unite with the Tracy camp in advancing Seth Low as the party's mayoral nominee. Low, as he later recalled, could have had the G.O.P. nomination on the spot, but he positively declined it, telling the convention that if it wished to compliment him, it could best do so by nominating the man on whose behalf he had come to speak.[24] With Low refusing the nomination, the Tracy delegates held firm and carried the convention for him.

It was ironic, the *Eagle* noted, that while Republican nominations for city offices usually went a-begging because no one wanted the empty honor of running without the prospect of election, now that the party had a chance for victory, it was unable to bring forth a candidate acceptable to all factions. With four tickets in the field, a McLaughlin victory loomed ominously, and for the good of the city, the *Eagle* urged a united anti-

McLaughlin slate.[25] "The next best thing," it asserted, "would be the agreement of the Republicans on a new man, whose nomination will keep alive the enthusiasm of the Young Republican Club. Seth Low is such a man."[26] For its part, the Young Republican Club was determined to end the schism in the Republican ranks and bring forth a suitable compromise candidate. To this end, it selected a committee, headed by Seth Low, to treat with the independents and the regular G.O.P. organization. A conference was scheduled for the evening of October 25, and speculation had it that Seth Low would be the compromise candidate.

With the Republican vote divided between Tracy and Ropes, the G.O.P. had little chance of victory. Moreover, with the Stalwart faction under fire throughout the state, it was imperative that the regular organization make a gesture of conciliation toward the independent Republicans if the party was to maintain its unity for future state-wide and national campaigns. Consequently, at the conference with the Young Republican Club, Tracy offered to retire from the field provided Ripley Ropes did likewise and that Seth Low stand as the Republican's compromise candidate.[27] Low was not in search of political office, and disliked the idea of running for the mayoralty, but, faced with Tracy's offer, he felt that it was his duty to Brooklyn to accept. The compromise was hailed by all factions. The *Eagle* joyously pointed out that Abiel Abbot Low was the single largest tax-payer in Brooklyn, and confidently predicted that his son could be trusted to protect the interests of the city's propertied classes.[28] And William A. Prendergast, who was then just a youth but who had a strong political bent, recalled that the Brooklyn mayoralty had made a great impression on him, and that he remembered Seth Low as "The ideal representative of the 'new look' in municipal affairs.'[29]

Upon accepting the Republican mayoral nomination, Seth Low wrote the G.O.P.'s city convention putting it on notice that he did not intend to be a partisan mayor. "If elected," he told the Republicans:

> I pledge myself to discharge the duties of my high office in the fear of God and not of man, with an eye single to the best interests alike of the poor and the rich, the high and the low, friends and foes, and to administer the affairs of the city upon strict business principles. In case of election I shall find strength and inspiration for this service in the thought

that citizens, without distinction of party, have united with
my own party friends to place me in the Mayor's chair.

The mayor of Brooklyn, he went on, "should be a man, who,
never forgetting that national issues have nothing to do with
local affairs, will yet realize that the honor of the great party
which names him as its candidate is deeply concerned in the
manner in which as Mayor, he administers his trust."[30] Aware
that Brooklyn was a heavily democratic city, Low believed that
his best hope of success lay in appealing to the people as a non-
partisan who would govern the city without regard to political
considerations. While his strategy may not have pleased G.O.P.
regulars, it electrified the "goo-goos" of both parties who saw in
Low's candidacy a chance for civic salvation. "Men of Brooklyn," one campaign flyer exclaimed, "You are to be *Redeemed—
Regenerated—Disenthralled.* SETH LOW upholds your banner.
His heart is right; his head is level; his hands are clean.... "[31]
Honest, efficient government, free of party machinations was
promised, and in that message of good hope, the "goo-goos" saw
the redemption of Brooklyn.

There was little more than two weeks between the time Low
was nominated and the scheduled election; a leisurely campaign
was out of the question, and if the candidate was to make himself and his views known, he would have to undertake a whirlwind campaign. He was, a fellow campaigner recalled, the first
candidate for mayor of Brooklyn to conduct a vigorous speaking campaign, making nightly addresses at which he answered
questions from the audience—hostile questions as well as friendly ones.[32] Taunted with being a "rich man," Low accepted the
challenge and answered, "They accuse me of being a rich man.
Well, my friends, what if I am? 'A man's a man for a' that'!"[33]
His sincerity and frankness won him the admiration and respect
of thousands of voters, and as the *Eagle* declared, gave "Proof
that a man may know a few things, although he is not a hundred years old."[34] Arguing for civil service reform, home rule,
non-partisan and businesslike government, Low conducted a typical Mugwump campaign.

According to the Mugwumps, American political life, as a result of the evils of party patronage, had suffered a marked decline since the Presidency of John Quincy Adams. The nation
had lost sight of the principles of disinterested public service
and its moral tone had degenerated. Capitalists and laborers
alike sought to use government to further their own selfish in-

terests and violate the natural laws of the economic order. It
was up to men of breeding and cultivation to set the nation right,
restore honest and disinterested public service, adhere to the
natural order of things, and raise the quality of America's moral
life.[35] Although much of Low's socio-economic views had still to
be formed, he did share much of the Mugwump's political bias.
A free trader and gold standard advocate by upbringing, he had
not yet expressed his views on labor's place in the modern industrial system or on the pressing economic questions of the day.
However, as he matured, he would break sharply with the Mugwump's faith in the efficacy of *laissez-faire* economic theory. But,
on the political issues of the age, and on his emphasis on honest, non-partisan public administration, he was every bit the
Mugwump. Unlike his fellow Mugwumps, though, he would not
become a bitter sectarian isolated from the mainstream of American life. He maintained an open, flexible mind, and bent his
preconceptions to fit the social needs of the time. Low looked
forward to becoming Brooklyn's Mayor, and his prospect of
election looked promising so long as the Democratic vote remained divided between Howell and Slocum.

On October 31, the leadership of the Jefferson Hall Democracy announced that it had reached an understanding with the
Brooklyn Democratic organization whereby General Slocum
would be withdrawn from the mayoralty race, and in return for
its support of Mayor Howell, Hugh McLaughlin would resign
from the leadership of the Democratic party.[36] With the Democrats once more united, Low's chance of victory dropped appreciably; however, a reconvened convention of the Jefferson Hall
Democracy refused to endorse the decision of its leadership, and
on November 4, just four days before the election, one thousand
breakaway Democrats, spurning Kinsella's leadership, seconded
the candidacy of Seth Low for mayor of Brooklyn.[37] The surrender of the Jefferson Hall Democrats to "Boss" McLaughlin's
machine stunned thousands of Democrats who rallied to Seth
Low's banner, and on Tuesday, November 8, 1881, Seth Low defeated James Howell for the Brooklyn mayoralty by 45,434 votes
to 40,937. As he approached his thirty-second birthday, Seth Low
prepared to take over as Brooklyn's chief executive.

Low was a firm believer in giving to the mayor absolute control over municipal affairs, and he looked forward to implement-
ing Brooklyn's new charter. While generally satisfied with the
powers granted the mayor under the terms of the charter, he

regretted that the chief executive had not been given the absolute power to remove appointed officials, and in his inaugural message, to show that he intended to administer Brooklyn's government on his own terms, he declared, "I wish to state distinctly that the acceptance of an appointment at my hands will be evidence to the community that the gentleman accepting it has personally given me his assurance that he will without delay give me his resignation whenever I ask for it."[38] Asserting that he would be mayor, and there would be no political boss giving him orders, he pledged to personally administer the government of Brooklyn in a manner which would permanently secure for the city home rule, non-partisan government, and an efficient administration responsive to the needs of the people. Shortly after embarking upon his duties as mayor, Low, while strolling the city, chanced upon the Reverend Dr. Theodore L. Cuyler and received a sage piece of advice. "Now, Mr. Low," the old gentleman declared:

> do not be afraid of making enemies. You cannot avoid it, no matter what you do. The only question is, what sort of enemies will you make? You will be surrounded by men, as every such officer is, who are striving to promote their own personal advantage. Do not be afraid of making an enemy of such an one by declining to do what he asks; but be very careful not to offend the common sense of the community at large, from whom you will seldom, if ever, hear.[39]

Unfortunately, Seth Low, in administering his office as mayor of Brooklyn, alienated both the professional politicians and large segments of the community as well.[40] Indeed, the problems which he faced while Mayor of Brooklyn would later plague him as mayor of New York, but in a much more acute form. Generally, though, Seth Low did a creditable job as Brooklyn's chief executive with, perhaps, his greatest success coming in the realm of home rule.

As American cities were the creatures of state legislatures, they were under the direct control of state governments which could, at will, alter their charters and mandate costly and intricate public works projects upon them. New York State could, for example, fix the salaries of policemen and firemen employed by the city of Brooklyn, order the construction of vast sewage systems, revise the governmental structure of the municipality, and interfere in every phase of the city's internal administration. Low and his "goo-goo" supporters regarded this state domination of municipal affairs as fundamentally unsound in that it permitted the faction or party controlling the state to exploit the cities for partisan advantage and thus fasten tightly upon the municipalities corrupt boss-ridden machine rule. Furthermore, state interference into municipal affairs was essentially undemocratic in that it deprived the urban electorate of its right to determine for itself the manner in which the city's government should be conducted. "The people of Brooklyn" Low declared, "know what is good for them quite as well as our friends of the rural counties, and out of this faith comes our desire for home rule."[41] One of his principal concerns was to prevent the Albany legislature from dictating policy to Brooklyn.

During Seth Low's four years as mayor of Brooklyn not a single bill affecting the muncipality passed the New York State Legislature if he expressed opposition to it. Personally writing the State Legislature, and asking his constituents to do likewise, Low brought to bear on all issues affecting Brooklyn the full pressure of an enlightened public opinion. By his second term, he had an unofficial veto over all "Brooklyn bills." "It will be a pleasure," Assemblyman George H. Mason wrote, "as well as a duty with me, to see your advice upon all matters in the Legislature which affect in any way the interests of Brooklyn."[42] And H. A. Barnum, Chairman of the Committee on Cities of the New York State Assembly declared:

> I need only say that no bill affecting the interests of Brooklyn shall leave the Com. of Cities of Assembly, without your having full opportunity to be heard, personally or in writing, if I can prevent, and I don't doubt that any and all such bills that do not receive your sanction will not receive mine, either in Committee or in the Assembly.[43]

In the matter of home rule, Seth Low fulfilled every expectation of the reformers, and was left free to administer Brooklyn as he saw fit. Throughout his career as a municipal reformer, Seth Low would advocate absolute home rule for cities in all matters except the issuance of bonds and the contraction of debt.

The most pressing problem Low faced during his first administration was the question of arrearage. Under the lax regime of "Boss" McLaughlin, thousands upon thousands of Brooklyn's property-owners, particularly the larger ones, had become delinquent in their payment of taxes to the city; thousands more had paid to have their property under-assessed, and there was active concealment of property improvements from the assessor's scrutiny. If Brooklyn's tangled financial affairs were ever to be put on a sound basis, the arrearage problem would have to be solved. To explain the importance of the arrears question to the people of Brooklyn, Mayor Low, in October 1882, called a mass meeting at the Rink, the cost of which he personally stood, and told the citizens' assembly:

> We are like a city set on a hill. There is not a city in all this great country that is not watching Brooklyn to see how we shall succeed at this moment. It may be that the representative of Brooklyn is held up into a little more dazzling light, but he is not on trial one whit more than every man in this audience and than every man in Brooklyn is on trial.[44]

The cause of good municipal government in the United States, Low told the people, was on trial in Brooklyn. If his administration failed, the entire nation would suffer. Reform in Brooklyn must succeed, he told his listeners, and to this end the disgraceful arrearage problem must be rectified. He announced his support of the Evarts Bill which would enable the city to sell at public auction the property of citizens who had become delinquent in their taxes. And he promised full assessment of property to insure the city a fair return of revenue.

With the passage of the Evarts Bill, the Low administration vigorously went about enforcing the new law. Arrearage was reduced from $14 million when Low became mayor, to a mere $6 million by 1884. All told, over $11 million in back taxes was collected during his two terms of office, and the city's rate of tax collection increased from 81 percent to 85 percent bringing the city additional millions in revenue. In addition, property assessments, largely as the result of new construction, were increased by $36 million under Low, for an average yearly rise of 7 percent as compared with a 2 percent per annum increase under Mayor Howell. To compound the injury, though, the tax rate went from $2.33 per $100 of assessed valuation in 1881, to $2.38 in 1882, and $2.59 in 1883.[45] Naturally, Brooklyn's property-owners protested vehemently and loudly. They had expected reform government to be cheap, anticipated that the city's budget would be drastically cut, and tax rates lowered. With Low, the reverse took place, much to the chagrin of the city's middle class. The money was, however, put to good use. Low was the first mayor of Brooklyn to reduce the city's debt, cutting it from a high of $38 million, when he took office to $31 million in four years, which resulted in a 6 percent improvement in Brooklyn's municipal credit. City services, under Low, were substantially improved with the greatest accomplishments coming in the school system.[46]

Seth Low made a practice of touring Brooklyn's schools, attending official ceremonies, sitting in on classes, and inspecting school facilities. He wanted to learn at first hand the needs of the city's school system, and he became a familiar figure at the public schools. John A. Heffernan, who was then a pupil in the Brooklyn public schools, recalled that he had been selected to deliver an oration on Martin Luther on the occasion of the latter's birthday. A Catholic, probably chosen to make the address through some error, Heffernan had prepared to "rake Martin Luther over the coals" when Silas Dutcher (president of the Board of Education) and Seth Low marched into the auditorium. Too late to do anything but deliver the original address, Heffernan proceeded to do so with some trepidation. "I could see Dutcher looking very much annoyed," he recalled, "but Low was trying very hard to suppress his mirth."[47] Amused at the spectacle of an Irish Catholic selected to eulogize Martin Luther, Low's faith in public education survived, and his school policy was perhaps the brightest aspect of his administration.

During Low's administration, textbooks were made free to all students, not just to those whose families had taken a pauper's oath. It was a reform long sought by school officials who wanted to remove social stigmas from the educational system. And, as an economy measure, Brooklyn's school system was integrated. There were about one thousand Negro children attending three all-Negro schools in the Fleet Street area. Under-attended, they were extremely costly to maintain, and to save funds for more efficient operations, Low proposed to close the Negro schools, and transfer their pupils to the nearest white school. As less than a thousand students were involved, and since it would save the city money, no important white opposition developed to the proposal, though Negro parents objected to the plan on the grounds that their children would have to travel outside their neighborhoods to attend classes. However, economy came first, and their protests were overruled. Thus did Brooklyn integrate its school system.[48]

In addition, Low took politics out of the schools by applying civil service principles to the recruitment of teachers. All teaching positions were filled by competitive examinations, with tenure being granted after a probationary period. No longer would the schools be used to pay off Democratic political debts; and to improve the quality of the teaching corps, a normal school was established by the city. Of even more importance, though, was the financial support which the Low administration gave to the city's educational system. In his first term of office $430,000 was appropriated for new school construction to accommodate ten thousand additional pupils. It was a sum exceeding the allotments of the previous six years. While the school shortage problem was not solved, Low did succeed in making considerable improvement in both the quantity and quality of Brooklyn's schools.[49]

Besides reconstructing the city's school system, Low expanded and modernized Brooklyn's police force, fire department, and sanitation services. All three departments were put on a civil service footing, with jobs and promotions awarded not on the basis of political influence but on that of meritorious service.[50] As a result, efficiency was increased and the quality of service improved. It was, however, costly. For example, in his first year in office, appropriations for the Department of Sanitation rose from $70,000 to $207,000. For the first time in its history, as Frederic W. Hinrichs testified, Brooklyn had clean streets. But the necessity of increasing taxes to pay for those clean streets could not have been popular.[51] Moreover, good Mugwump that he was, Low applied the optional civil service provisions of the state's newly-enacted Civil Service Code to all levels of Brooklyn's public service, refusing to employ patronage to build up a reform machine. He disappointed Republican machine politicians, who "rubbed their eyes and patched their trousers."[52]

"Patronage," the *New York Times* delightedly proclaimed in October 1883, "has been abolished in Brooklyn."[53] Indeed, Seth Low's administration of Brooklyn was the closest that any American city ever came to realizing the doctrine of non-partisanship. "I made up my mind at the beginning," he later told William L. Strong:

> that it would be impossible for me to cope with self-seeking politicians by underground methods; that, in the first place, I could not bring myself to adopt such methods, and, in the second place, if I could, they were expert at it where I was a tyro.... I was frank and straightforward with all applicants for office, never encouraging any man to entertain a hope where I knew, in my own mind, that there was no basis for it.[54]

Most of his appointees were Republicans; some were Democrats. All were friends drawn from well-to-do, transplanted New England families occupying the Heights. Few were professional politicians; fewer still were machine men. All conducted their offices honestly, efficiently, and without regard for partisan considerations. None of his appointees were of first-rate stature, but as Edward Morse Shepard observed, under Low, "Inferior men were made to do superior work."[55] And Low took the non-partisan doctrine literally, in its most extreme form.

"I am admonished by many signs that the fall political campaign is about to begin," he wrote James Larned, Collector of Taxes and Assessments:

> Be so good as to assure the employees of your department that their salary is intended to compensate them for faithful service to the City: that, failing in that respect, no amount of contributions for party purposes will avail them; on the other hand, that a refusal to contribute will not imperil their situations. In other words, they are in the same condition in this particular as the employees of a commercial firm.
> I look to you to protect them in this regard.[56]

Shakedowns of muncipal employees for political contributions became a thing of the past, as Brooklyn's bureaucracy was totally divorced from politics. While the Grand Old Party could not have been overjoyed, the "goo-goos" were, and Low carried the non-partisan doctrine to its logical extreme by refusing to campaign for the Republican state-wide ticket in the fall of 1882. Asked to address a rally for the re-election of Governor Alonzo B. Cornell, he declined, asserting:

> I do no propose by my example to undo what has already been done in the direction of divorcing municipal business from politics. I expect that every man employed by the city will attend faithfully to the business of the city, and neither neglect it for politics nor use his position improperly to advance factional or party ends.[57]

It was not, in any case, a sound policy to pursue, for the Brooklyn mayoralty was an elective office, and try as he might, it was impossible for Seth Low to divorce politics from the office of mayor.

To round out his first term of office, Mayor Low ordered the city's Excise Board to enforce the "rule of common sense" in the matter of Sunday closing. Under state law, saloons could not dispense liquor (beer included) on Sundays. However, Brooklyn's sizeable German-American population customarily frequented their local beer garden on the Sabbath in violation of state law. With the Democrats controlling the city's government, the excise laws simply were not enforced, but with the reformers in command, the more puritanical element of the clergy demanded the law's rigid enforcement, while the German-Americans were equally insistent upon a policy of toleration for the innocent customs of Brooklyn's cosmopolitan population. Low resolved the ticklish problem by ordering the Excise Board not to close saloons which maintained an outward appearance of calm, but only to raid those which permitted open displays of rowdyness or debauchery. The policy pleased the German-Americans, satisfied the more moderate clergymen, and ended excise as a divisive political issue. The excise question, though, would survive to plague him two decades later.[58]

Low also overhauled the city's system of granting municipal franchises. Where they had previously been awarded to the highest briber on long-term leases providing for a minimal financial return to the city, they were now given to the highest bidder on a short-term twenty or twenty-five year lease providing for adequate royalties to the municipality. The city's entire tax structure was reformed, shifting the burden of taxation from the small to the large property owner, and concealed improvements were ferreted out. On the whole, as Low's first term of office drew to a close, municipal reform had succeeded in giving Brooklyn an honest, efficient, and—as far as schools and tax reform were concerned—a socially-responsive administration. "As news of the success of the Brooklyn charter spread to other cities," Brooklyn's historian has written, "Seth Low's name became synonymous with efficient, responsible municipal administration."[59]

By September 1883, Republicans were publicly criticizing Low's patronage policy, and the Democrats were hopeful that a schism in reform's ranks would allow them to slip back into City Hall.[60] The G.O.P., however, could not very well repudiate its own standard-bearer, and swallowing their disappointment and indignation, they dutifully renominated him, declaring, "that national politics have no proper place in the consideration of municipal affairs."[61] Most newspapers and journals supported Low's reelection. The *Times* declared, "Mayor Low has given them [the people of Brooklyn] an administration pure from all taint of partisanship, absolutely faithful to the city's interests, and remarkably able, skillful, and energetic. They can get no such ad-

ministration from Mr. Hendrix [his Democratic opponent]."[62]
And the *Brooklyn Advance* editorialized:

> Mayor Low's administration has been such an advance upon
> all previous ones that many people fail to realize it. No wires
> are now being pulled to secure a renomination, no men are
> being put to work in order to vote on election day, but the
> mayor is making personal visits to the several wards in order
> to observe their sanitary condition, school accommodations,
> and the like. The question should not be, will Mayor Low be
> renominated? but, will he be willing to continue his good
> work in Brooklyn for another term?
> . . . Mayor Low has not worked in the interest of any party
> while in office, but for the interest of the whole people. . . .
> He has added to the name and fame of our city; he has set
> in motion reforms, the benefits of which will not be confined
> to his administration, but will be felt through successive years.
> He has made it easier for the next Mayor, whoever he may be,
> to rule our city righteously.[63]

There was, however, opposition. The Democratic *Brooklyn
Eagle,* the voice of the city's propertied classes, which had supported Low in 1881, roundly criticized almost every aspect of
his administration in the fall of 1883. If Low had reduced taxes,
the *Eagle* maintained, "there would be practically no opposition
to his election today."[64] But, it pointed out, "The cost of our
local government is not only absolutely greater under Mr. Low
than under his predecessor, but it is relatively more burdensome."[65] Condemning his administration for raising property assessments and the tax rate, it assailed his non-partisan claim by
asserting that too few Democrats and too many Republicans had
been appointed to office in what was a normally Democratic
city.[66] Concluding that, "His administration has been clean, but
it has not been fruitful. Nothing bad has been attempted, nothing considerable has been accomplished," it declared that it had
supported Low two years earlier only to break "Boss" McLaughlin's power, that the Democratic party was now fit to rule Brooklyn, and was to be preferred to Low's "Hamiltonian" administration.[67] Low's Democratic opponent was Joseph C. Hendrix,
an unknown but upright candidate, who had Hugh McLaughlin's backing. Generally, conceded to be the best mayor in Brooklyn's history, it was expected that Low would receive an easy re-
election, but the reformers were taking no chances.

Declaring that Mayor Low had given Brooklyn the best government it had ever had, and had won for the city home rule,

the reformers avowed that the Democratic party, under the auto-cratic leadership of Hugh McLaughlin, was incapable of giving the city a similar administration. Launching a highly moral and thoroughly Mugwumpish campaign in which they claimed that only Low's re-election could secure a businesslike administration free of partisanship, the reformers appealed to the electorate's moral sense to return a righteous government.[68] On election day, Seth Low narrowly defeated the politically unknown Joseph C. Hendrix by 49,554 votes to 48,006, a plurality of only 1,548 votes compared to a 5,000-vote majority two years earlier. It was the greatest voter turnout in Brooklyn's municipal history, and there was no doubt of a considerable falling-away of support from the reform movement. Many Democrats who had supported Low in 1881, forgetting McLaughlin's corruption and frustrated by what they regarded as insufficient City Hall patronage, returned to their traditional party allegiance; many machine Republicans who also protested the lack of patronage and who resented Low's non-partisan approach to municipal government sat the election out; and many middle class property owners deserted reform in protest against increased tax rates. Low was re-elected chiefly be-cause of the personal weakness of his Democratic opponent.

Nevertheless, he had achieved what no other candidate had in Brooklyn history. Running as a Republican, he had won two consecutive city-wide elections in an overwhelmingly Democratic city. A great many of his political admirers confidently expected Seth Low to one day become governor of New York State or, perhaps, even president of the United States.[69] Indeed, there was a movement to secure for him the Republican gubernatorial nomination in 1885. "Your name," an upstate Republican leader wrote him late in 1884:

> has been mentioned as a possible candidate for the Gover-norship on the Republican ticket for '85—I would take it as a favor if you would advise me as to whether it would be in accordance with your wish to be mentioned and worked for by the rank and file—it is now time to start the matter.[70]

Low, though, had no political ambitions beyond the munici-pal level. He had consented to stand for mayor only to heal a breach in reform's ranks. He had never sought political office, but felt that he owed Brooklyn a duty to promote its interests, and out of this Mugwump sense of civic responsibility he stood for mayor. He did nothing, however, to encourage his considera-

tion for higher offices. Besides, he was now in disgrace with the
G.O.P. regulars.

In 1884, James G. Blaine was opposing Grover Cleveland for
president of the United States. As a Republican mayor of Brooklyn, Low was expected to campaign for Blaine, and was under
extreme pressure from the Republican party to do so. However,
Low, as his nephew related, had thrown in his lot with the Mugwumps, and had resolved to vote for Cleveland. Invoking the
doctrine of non-partisanship, he stoutly refused to campaign for
Blaine, telling the Republicans, "I am not a Republican mayor,
as you say I am. I am mayor of the whole people of Brooklyn."
Blaine lost the presidency because he failed to carry New York
State by an extremely small margin. He lost the state because
the Republican vote in Brooklyn fell far below its normal level.
The G.O.P. regulars blamed Blaine's defeat on Seth Low, who
committed something very much like political suicide when he
failed to endorse the "plumed knight." Certain it was that Seth
Low never again enjoyed the wholehearted support of the regular Republican machine.[71]

During his second term, Seth Low continued the policies begun in his first term. He declined to stand for a third term, and
there was considerable doubt as to whether he would have won
a third term in any case. Alienation and resentment continued
to build against his administration, and as the fall of 1885 approached, the people of Brooklyn were thoroughly tired of Seth
Low and reform. "He fell under the delusion," the now-hostile
Eagle commented, "that the people of Brooklyn were waiting,
like the Greeks at the shrine of the Delphic oracle, for some man-
ifestation of his exalted will."[72] In 1885, Democrat Daniel D.
Whitney defeated machine Republican Isaac Catlin for the
Brooklyn mayoralty by twelve thousand votes. John R. Wood-
ward, the reform candidate who was supported by Mayor Low,
finished a poor third. Hugh McLaughlin had been returned to
power.

With the return of Democratic control, mis-government also
returned, and as time passed, Low's administration of Brooklyn
began to take on a rosy and idealized hue. "The history of Brooklyn," James Bryce wrote Seth Low in 1892, "I gather, has been
somewhat chequered since your mayoralty."[73] Indeed, it was. By
the early 1890s, the return of corruption made people look upon
Low's mayoralty as a Golden Age. As a *Brooklyn Eagle* reporter
declared:

How wisely, faithfully and successfully he fulfilled the oner-
ous duties of the office is in the city's records and the people's
memory. He was a wise, careful and economical chief executive carrying into his public life the sound business principles and strict integrity of character that had made his private career successful and respected. He redeemed every pledge
that he had given to his constituents; he improved every department in the municipal administration and did away with
many abuses.[74]

Brooklyn's charter was adjudged to have been a success, and
as other American cities copied its features, Seth Low acquired,
as Edward M. Shepard asserted, "practically without dissent, the
most distinguished personal reputation which has come to perhaps any political character of Brooklyn."[75] His policies as Mayor
and his conceptions of municipal government directly influenced
many urban reformers, including Detroit's Hazen S. Pingree and
Cambridge's William E. Russell.[76] In fact, Low's correspondence
for the late 1880s and early '90s reveals numerous requests from
municipalities and urban reformers across the country for information and advice on how best to frame city charters and
conduct municipal government. Recognized as one of the nation's
most astute observers of municipal affairs, Seth Low came away
from the Brooklyn mayoralty with his faith in businesslike, non-
partisan city government unshaken. He would again be called
upon to lead the reform hosts in the struggle for good local government.

CHAPTER III

Interlude: Seth Low as President of Columbia, 1890-1901

Then came Mr. Low, and order was evolved from chaos.
HARRY THURSTON PECK[1]

At the stroke of noon on January 1, 1886, Seth Low's term of office as mayor of Brooklyn expired. He was a private citizen again, and sixteen years would elapse before he would once more occupy an elective position. Those sixteen years were an interlude in the public career of Seth Low, but they were also among the most fruitful years of his life. For most politicians, such a prolonged absence from political life would be looked upon as so many years in the bowels of Hell, but Low was no ordinary politician—Brooklyn's mayoralty had come to him as the result of a political accident, and while an excellent administrator, he was, nevertheless, unfamiliar with the tools of the politician's craft. He had stood for election, and would stand again, only when convinced that it was his evident public duty to do so. It was during this interlude, however, that he brought grandeur to an old college and helped to turn a great city into a greater city. Indeed, it was his record at Columbia, and his performance on the Greater New York Charter Commission which again placed his name in the public arena, and brought him back into public office.

Upon leaving the Brooklyn mayor's office, Low and his wife went on a prolonged vacation, touring England and continental Europe. They did not return to Brooklyn until 1887, when Seth Low rejoined the family's countinghouse. He remained in business only long enough to liquidate the firm of A. A. Low and Brothers, which, being the last of America's great clipper ship mercantile houses, had long since become obsolete in an age of steamships. The liquidation was completed in 1888 and the New York press reported that Seth Low's share in the firm had netted him $10 million, though this figure cannot be confirmed. Now a man of leisure, living off invested capital, he had planned to devote his life to charitable work in his native Brooklyn. He was particularly interested in tenement house reform, and like Alfred T. White, he had built a row of model tenements to provide low-cost but decent housing for Brooklyn's working class. However, in 1889, a summons from his Alma Mater changed his plans, and took him from the city of his birth.

After graduating from Columbia College in 1870, Seth Low became an active worker for his school's Alumni Association. Under the guidance of Hamilton Fish, he strove tirelessly to add to the college's endowment fund; but Low quickly discovered that to the people of New York, Columbia, as John W. Burgess recalled, "was a rich old institution, much behind the times, which neither deserved nor desired any assistance from the city or the city's residents."[2] In truth, Columbia College was often hardpressed for funds, and apathetic alumni had done little to relieve their Alma Mater's distress. The general public viewed Columbia as a snobbish institution for the sons of the rich, and was quite willing that the rich should support their own "country clubs." Columbia College, in the 1870s and 1880s, was a mediocre institution, desperately struggling to bring itself abreast of the new standards being demanded by an academic community under the influence of the ideals of German university education.

Seth Low's services on the Alumni Association did little to break down the apathy of Columbia's alumni, or the hostility of the people of New York, and as one of the college's early historians proclaimed, Columbia retained its reputation as a small, parochial school well out of the mainstream of the American academic community.[3] Low's services, however, were appreciated, and in the fall of 1881, he was asked to join Columbia's Board of Trustees. Mayor-elect of Brooklyn, he did not see how he could serve both his city and his college at the same time, but he could not refuse what he regarded as the call of duty. He would accept Columbia's call, he told Gerard Beckman, but if he found that he could not do the job justice, he would resign from the board.[4] Devoting himself to Brooklyn and to Columbia with his usual intensity, Low was an ardent supporter of President Frederick A. P. Barnard, who was tirelessly battling to modernize Columbia.

Under Barnard, Columbia's rehabilitation had begun, but had

not progressed very far. In 1889, the college occupied a cramped, one-square city block area on Manhattan's 49th Street, east of Madison Avenue. Its seven schools were completely autonomous, there being no central authority capable of bringing order out of academic chaos. Throughout the 1880s, the Columbia faculty was split into two hostile factions: one, the University party, consisted of about one-third of the faculty, led by John W. Burgess, which realized that professional training rather than the traditional liberal arts curriculum was the academic wave of the future. It wanted to reorganize Columbia on a university basis, stress graduate training, patterned on the German model, and bring Columbia to the first rank among American universities. Opposed to the University party was the much larger College faction, which, content in its respectable mediocrity, felt its position endangered by a move to university status. President Barnard sided with the University party, and under his direction, Columbia was slowly but resolutely progressing to university rank.[5] However, in 1889, Frederick A. P. Barnard sickened and died, throwing the University party into the depths of despair and confusion.[6]

"It was now felt by all who comprehended the situation clearly," Professor Burgess remarked years later, "that everything hung upon the choice of the new president. On account of the sharp dissensions in the teaching body, it was not possible to take any member of either faculty for the presidency, and it was even impractical to ask the advice of any of them upon this all-important question."[7] The decision as to who would succeed Barnard was, thus, thrown entirely upon the Board of Trustees. A fifteen-man body, the trustees realized that with faculty dissension so acute, it would be most unwise to call in an outsider who was unfamiliar with the tangled complexities of the campus's politics, and since no member of the faculty could be elevated to the Presidency, one of the trustees would have to assume the burdens of the office. On October 7, 1889, Columbia's trustees met to select a new president for the college. Seth Low, who was prominently mentioned as a possible successor to Barnard, did not attend the meeting in order to avoid the embarrassment of having to vote on his own candidacy. Six trustees supported Professor Drisler for the presidency; one trustee abstained from voting, and the remaining seven urged the selection of Seth Low. With only seven of the fourteen trustees backing him, Low did not have a clean majority, but unable to agree on anyone else, the trustees tendered him the presidency of Columbia College.[8]

The decision as to whether he should accept or decline the proferred presidency of Columbia College was one of the most difficult choices Seth Low ever had to face. He was not a professional scholar, had never taught a class, and was unfamiliar with the delicate mechanics of running an educational institution. "On the academic side," he wrote his father, "I could be of small service to Columbia. The one thing I think I could do," he added, "is to bring the College into closer touch with the community; and this happens to be the one thing which especially needs to be done at this time."[9] His doubts still remained, though, and he welcomed indications of support from Columbia's faculty. John W. Burgess urged him to accept the post, and Columbia's William H. H. Beebe proclaimed that, "Columbia has honored itself, and let me say too; that the Presidency of one of our great universities is a much higher honor than the Presidency of the country, and the opportunities for good infinitely greater."[10]

"It is helping me greatly," Low intimated to Burgess, "to reach a decision to receive evidence that my election is acceptable to the Faculties."[11] Along with numerous faculty members, alumni and educators from across the nation also urged Low to accept the trustees' offer, and expressed their fath in his ability to handle the responsibilities of Columbia's presidency. Richard T. Ely declared that if Low assumed the position, "I feel that a brilliant future awaits our alma matter."[12] Andrew Dickson White proclaimed, "I must confess that I think better of human nature, and more hopefully of the future in the United States, when I see . . . yourself, President of Columbia College."[13] And Cornell's President, C. K. Adams, asserted that, "I have regarded your election as the wisest thing your trustees could possibly have done."[14]

Considering the fact that Seth Low was not especially qualified for the task of heading a major American college, the enthusiastic response to his election was cause for wonderment, and Low could do nothing else but accept the position. While he was not an academician, Columbia's choice of Seth Low was a fortunate one. "Mr. Low," Professor Burgess declared:

> was not, in the first place, a profound scholar, though not lacking in broad learning and intellectual sympathy. In this there was great advantage, an advantage which Mr. Low himself consciously appreciated. It was this very thing which enabled him to see that each professor could manage the in-

ternal affairs of his department better than the president could
do it for him. . . . On the other hand, Mr. Low was a real
man of affairs. He had been partner in a great business and
mayor of a great city. He was a man of high social standing,
of extended acquaintance and of large wealth. He knew how
to organize and administer, how to frame a budget, how to
provide ways and means, how to take advantage of all the
existing auxiliaries offered by existing institutions in the great
city, how to bring the University to the notice of the city, the
nation and the world, how to interest men of power and
wealth in it and, above all, how to secure for the chairs of
instruction men of ability and marked distinction in their
several departments. . . . A better choice could not have been
made, and the prophecy made by an eminent educator, several years before, that some day or other the right man would
be placed in the lead at Columbia and that then the old institution would find its true place in the galaxy of American
universities, had at last entered upon the course of its fulfillment.[15]

He was inaugurated as President of Columbia College, amid
the usual pomp and circumstance, on February 3, 1890. "The
date," trustee John B. Pine wrote, "will always be recognized as
the beginning of the new era in the history of the college."[16]

At the time that he took over the helm at Columbia, the American university was undergoing a rather difficult and painful period of transformation. Traditionally, American colleges had not
been dedicated to the pursuit of scholarship; rather their function had been to indoctrinate an elitist group with the orthodox
socio-political, economic and moral values of the society, and not
to challenge or question those values. However, the increasing
complexity of post-Civil War American society, and the growing
professionalization and specialization of the nation's institutions
placed new and unprecedented pressures and demands on American universities. Their reaction to these new social requirements,
as Laurence R. Veysey has pointed out, manifested itself in the
development of three distinct educational philosophies. One envisioned the university as a center for practical public service,
and emphasized the employment of applied science and social
science for the solution of the problems facing American society.
Another held that the university's basic purpose should be the
pursuit of pure scholarship and abstract research patterned on
the German model. Still another school of thought argued that
the American university should diffuse liberal culture, stress the

liberal arts, effective teaching, and the moral guidance of both students and the community.[17] Seth Low, upon his election as Columbia's president, had not yet enunciated his educational philosophy, and Columbia's future would largely be determined by his view of the university's place and function in American society.

Seth Low embarked upon his duties as Columbia's president with the single-minded purpose of continuing and fulfilling the work begun by Frederick A. P. Barnard. "I am desirous," he told alumni Erastus Wiman, "to build Columbia into a great university, worthy of New York. . . . "[18] At forty years of age, Seth Low was among the nation's youngest college presidents, and he would need all the energy and enthusiasm of his youth to realize his ambitions for Columbia. He was taking over an institution torn by dissension, severely short of funds for expansion, and squeezed into a campus it had long outgrown. Determined to build Columbia into a great university, he encouraged pure research and scholarship, but repeatedly emphasized Columbia's responsibility to use its intellectual resources to help the nation solve pressing problems and to build a better society for all.

His first act as president was to move his office out of the School of Arts and into a neutral building to show the college's warring schools that he was indeed non-partisan, and would not favor one branch or faction above another. The symbolic act apparently had good effect, for Harry Thurston Peck declared that, from the outset, President Low exhibited a sense of justice and fair-mindedness which inspired all factions with the confidence that their interests as well as Columbia's would be respected and protected. "It was felt instinctively," Peck recalled, "that the right thing would be done, that every interest would be considered and every question viewed without the slightest prejudice. . . . " It was this feeling, more than anything else, Peck felt, which made possible Columbia's smooth and orderly transition from college to university standing.[19]

As soon as he was established in his new office, Low drew up a list of questions as to how the problems and issues facing the college could best be solved, and sent the questionnaire to the professors and adjunct professors in all of the college's schools. He then summoned them to a series of evening conferences to be held at the president's house. According to Professor Munroe Smith, the conferences were held on three successive evenings, each one lasting some three or four hours, and served as a forum from which long-standing grievances and resentments could be aired. About two-thirds of the faculty, Smith recalled, were against the plans of the University party, but President Low, after carefully weighing all proposals, decided in favor of the minority plan as presented by Professor Burgess, and committed Columbia to reorganization on a university basis.[20]

A university council, composed of professors from all of Columbia's schools, was established and given administrative control over the schools of medicine, law, mines, political science, philosophy, pure science, and the School of Arts. Instituted in 1890, initially it only had control of the undergraduate colleges, but by 1892 the professional schools had also been placed within its jurisdiction. In 1900, Barnard College, the last independent unit, was brought under the guidance of the university council, and all of Columbia's branches were then subject to central authority. The university council permitted the introduction of the combined course curriculum by which students enrolled in one college could take electives in any of Columbia's other schools, and, thus, shorten the period of their post-graduate professional training. Before the establishment of the new curriculum in 1896, a student enrolled in the School of Arts, for example, could not take courses outside his college, but with the new system, if he were planning to enter Columbia's College of Physicians and Surgeons, he could take his preliminary medical courses as senior electives. Expanded graduate training was also facilitated by the creation of the university council. Back in 1880 the Faculty of Political Science was organized to coordinate graduate studies in the social sciences, and it pioneered in the introduction of the German seminar system. In 1890 and 1892, the Faculties of Philosophy and Pure Science were set up, and by 1896 Columbia was rapidly developing quality graduate education.

In addition to guiding Columbia's transition from college to university, Low actively directed the day-to-day business operations of the school, and was responsible for the introduction of many administrative innovations. A recent historian of Columbia related that until Seth Low assumed the presidency, summer mail had been dumped into a closet and not opened until the fall semester had begun. Low, however, was a full-time president, and his office functioned the year round.[21] The incident was indicative of the new spirit which pervaded the campus.

In 1891, Seth Low abolished compulsory chapel attendance,

feeling that Episcopal worship should not be forced upon the college's non-Protestant students. He believed that Columbia had no higher purpose than to faithfully serve the needs of New York City, and as New York was a cosmopolitan city so, too, should Columbia be a cosmopolitan university. In later years, it was Seth Low's proudest boast that while he was president, Columbia did not discriminate along racial or religious lines in the selection of either faculty or students, and when the infamous quota system was introduced under Nicholas Murray Butler, Low protested. "It is the glory of Columbia," he told the university's committee on education in 1911:

> that it makes no discrimination against the Jews either in its Faculty or in its student body. I hope that the time will come when the Jews will be given representation on the Board of Trustees, but I am quite content to wait for this until it comes about naturally. On the other hand, when it is suggested that Columbia enter upon some new policy that must lead to discrimination against the Jews or against any other element in our population, it must not be forgotten that much the largest part of the endowment of the University comes from the Upper Estate which was received from the State of New York. It is not too much to say that the income from this estate is fairly pledged to a use as broad and general as the State itself would make of it. The million of Jews in the City of New York have added to the increase in value of this property as much as any other million of our population. It is therefore clear that, in this indirect form, we are receiving an income from the Jews as well as from the Christians of the City of New York. Beyond that, we have received a building and many important gifts at their hands; and, if it be urged that, notwithstanding, the University is distinctly a Christian foundation, I should say, that, precisely because it is such, it ought to be a point of honor with the University not to accept gifts from people whom it proposes to discriminate against in any matter of general policy.[22]

Unfortunately, Nicholas Murray Butler was no Seth Low.

In order to attract a faculty second to none, Seth Low, in 1891, introduced the sabbatical system, and a liberal pension plan which was adopted virtually without change by many of America's major universities and by the Carnegie Foundation. He also instituted the practice of having the faculty elect academic deans which served to heighten loyalty to, and interest in, the university, and helped to satisfy faculty demands for a greater voice in the running of the college. The election of deans was discontinued by the trustees, in the interests of efficiency, when Low left the presidency of Columbia to become mayor of New York. And, in 1893, a university press was begun to make available to the academic community the fruits of scholarly research. By these means, some of the nation's finest scholars were lured to Columbia. Finally, in 1896, the University of the State of New York granted Columbia university status. In six years, Low had brought to realization the long-sought ambition of turning Columbia into an institution worthy of New York City—the world's greatest metropolis and the earth's most brilliant jewel, as he saw it, now had a university of which it could justifiably feel proud.

Seth Low had definite ideas about the role of the modern urban university in American society. The University did not exist merely to be a country club for the sons of the wealthy, but rather to serve the community and the nation by studying their problems, and by providing trained leadership and expertise in the effort to resolve them. "A university so situated," he proclaimed at the dedication of Columbia's Morningside Heights campus:

> must be blind indeed if it does not recognize its obligations reverently to study the past in order that it may faithfully serve the present, and courageously trust the future. For in the past are to be found the origins of things, of nations, of institutions, of customs, of ideas, of beliefs, and a university that traces the development of these things through the ages must needs have much to say on the living questions of every age. This university, therefore, in our day must make itself a vital part of these times and of those that are to follow, by drawing out of its treasuries things old and new. For if it be part of its mission to interpret to the present the meaning of the past, so it is equally a part of its duty to enlarge the life of the future by extending in every direction the boundaries of human knowledge.[23]

A university faculty, Low declared in his inaugural address, which acquired knowledge only to confine it to the campus was not a community of scholars but a clique of pedants. It was the prime duty of the academic man to venture out into his community and nation and use his special knowledge and talents to help raise the general standards of his society. To assist in the solution of the problems besetting urban and industrial

America were the true purposes of all scholarship, and as Columbia and her sister universities worked to make their communities better places in which to live, so, soo, would these happier communities re-enforce and uplift the humane traditions and aspirations of America's colleges. Essentially, as Low believed, knowledge was acquired and expanded by men who were a vital part of a vigorous society. Books were only the means to knowledge, its source being humanity itself; and in this sense, Columbia was the most fortunate of universities for it was situated in New York City, and New York was humanity in microcosm. By helping the city, Columbia would draw out of it, and into itself, the knowledge of all mankind. He urged Columbia's students, like its faculty, to go forth and know the city. "The simple conditions [for learning] on the student's part," he declared:

> are a recognition of inherent worth, wherever it may be found, and an open mind. The ends of the earth, then, will bring to you their contribution, and you shall come to see that this great city is full of inspiration to a man who would be noble. . . . But the real world is not to be found in books. That is peopled by men and women of living flesh and blood, and the great city can supply the human quality which the broad-minded man must not suffer himself to lack. There is a variety to life in this city, a vitality about it, and, withal, a sense of power, which, to my thought, are of inestimable value to the student whose desire it is to become a well-rounded man. . . . There is but one New York on all this continent, and . . . as there is no solitude like that of a crowd, so there is no inspiration like it.[24]

To realize his dream of bringing Columbia into closer touch with the life of New York City, Seth Low actively championed the University Settlement movement headed by James B. Reynolds which sought to improve the living conditions of the East Side. He established reciprocity agreements with three of Morningside Heights' theological seminaries, whereby the libraries and educational resources of Columbia and of the divinity schools were thrown open to each other's students. During his presidency, Columbia faculty members were encouraged to offer free public lectures at various city institutions as a means of breaking down the old image of the college as a cold, outmoded, and smug school. Under Seth Low, Columbia acquired a brighter reputation and was brought into closer touch with the community. But perhaps his greated achievement at Columbia was in his role as fund-raiser.

"I was amazed," Booker T. Washington wrote Low, "at President Butler's statement to the effect that during a period of 136 years, gifts to the University did not amount to more than $200,000 all together until you took charge...."[25] When Low assumed the leadership of Columbia in 1890, the college was hard-pressed financially, and in the eleven years that he was President he raised more money than had been raised in all of Columbia's history.[26] When Butler took over from him in 1901, Columbia was among the most well-to-do of American universities. Low was able to raise vast sums of money because he was able to convince New York's business community that Columbia was worthy of support, and his fund-raising talents were of critical importance in the college's acquisition of the Morningside Heights campus.

The 49th Street campus was intended, in 1857, to be Columbia's permanent home, but within a generation the college had outgrown its mid-town campus, and a more spacious site for the school was imperative. A number of the trustees wanted to take Columbia out of the city, and relocate it in the country—Westchester County being the favored site. Low, however, refused to entertain the idea, and insisted that Columbia remain in the great city. One of the trustees, John B. Pine, discovered that a two-square city block tract of land on Morningside Heights could be purchased for $2 million, and brought the site to Low's attention. The purchase price was considered reasonable, but it would require an additional $4 million to house the college. Columbia did not have the money. But, desiring to squelch once and for all proposals to remove Columbia from New York City, Seth Low gambled. He purchased the Morningside Heights site, and hoped that he would be able to raise a sufficient sum from the community to move the school uptown. To get the fund-raising campaign off to a good start, Low, in May of 1895, announced his intention of contributing, in honor of his father, the cost of the college's new library.[27] His princely gift and expression of confidence in Columbia's future brought forth equally generous support from the people of New York. Selling the midtown campus at an advantageous price, Low dedicated the university's new home in 1896, and to make it more secure, Columbia issued $3 million worth of interest-bearing bonds of which Seth Low subscribed for one-third of the entire issue.

By 1901, Seth Low had taken a small, dissension-ridden college and made it into a great university. He had taken a financially undernourished institution and infused it with great quantities of fresh money, and, by building Columbia a new home, he had made certain that the university would remain in the City of New York. "Low took a college," Columbia's Frank Diehl Fackenthal testified, "and made a university of it. [He] has become a forgotten man, and I think unfairly so. He did a lot for the University in putting it together, stabilizing it, getting away from the loose organization, setting up an organization that would fit a university group."[28] In short, Seth Low accomplished the greater part of what President Butler later took credit for. Butler built upon a foundation which had been constructed by Seth Low, but because Low did not boast of his achievements at Columbia, while Butler did nothing else but trumpet his own horn, Low's positive accomplishments and his place in American educational history have been largely forgotten. This is unfortunate, for as John W. Burgess asserted:

> My dear friend, I must say that I could never have accomplished much at this university except with your powerful and gracious aid. I can never forget the utter despair I felt during the year before you took up the presidency, and how that was changed to hope and then to success so soon as you assumed the leadership. Your twelve years at the helm was the great turning point in Columbia's history. You found the institution a college with some attached technical schools, and one struggling university branch and you made it a university and gave it organic wholeness. Those were years of growth and sound development and I wish I might one day write the history of them, so that the Alumni, New York City and the world might fully appreciate what you did in bringing to life and successful development what is now fast becoming the first university in the world.[29]

Besides building a great university, Seth Low also changed the character of the office of college president. He was not a bookish recluse who tended to the affairs of his college and shut off the outside world, but a dynamic member of the community who actively participated in its life and who was always amenable to the call of public duty. Low was ever ready to lend his assistance, and Columbia's, to the solution of any crisis facing his city or his nation. "By his conduct of that office [Columbia's President]," Regent Byrne declared:

> he did much to make the position of the head of a univer-

sity that which, in the minds of the people, it now is—a public office, the holder of which is not allowed to confine himself to the education of his students, but is under a duty,
when his knowledge and experience can aid in the decision of
public questions of moment, to give counsel to the people
and those in authority over them.[30]

Practicing what he preached, he never let go by an opportunity
to help his community.

CHAPTER IV

From Mugwump to Progressive:
Seth Low and the Problem of Urban Government

We have no persistent or pervasive tradition of romantic attachment
to the city in our literature or in our philosophy....

MORTON AND LUCIA WHITE[1]

The presidency of Columbia did not absorb all of Seth Low's
energies. A man of broad interests, he was continuously involved in the great issues facing American society, and in the
last quarter of the nineteenth century, perhaps the most serious
difficulty besetting the nation was the problem of municipal
government. Thomas Jefferson had declared that cities were to
the body politic what ulcers were to the human body, and to a
nation imbibing Jeffersonian agrarian values from its very birth,
to a nation accustomed to celebrating the virtues of the yeoman
farmer and declaiming that he was the backbone of American
democracy, the government of the country's great cities seemed
to be proving the validity of Jefferson's judgment. In New York,
Chicago, Philadelphia, St. Louis, and even staid Boston, vice
and gambling were not only rampant but were protected by the
municipal authorities who were sworn to enforce the law; the
rights of their citizens and the wealth and resources of the nation's cities were prostituted to unscrupulous business pirates
who were in league with the public officials charged with protecting the interests they were betraying. The cities of post-Civil
War America seemed to be hopeless sinks of corruption in which
the Yankee-Protestant moral code of agrarian America was seemingly cast aside into the mire of urban depravity.

Exposure of the villainy of urban politicians proved insufficient to alter the prevailing degeneration of municipal political life, for, while the reformers might win an isolated election,
they were seldom re-elected. It appeared that the people them-

selves sanctioned the degradation which had befallen the cities of America, and the population of the nation's urban centers was becoming ever more largely composed of southern and eastern European immigrants. The United States was fast becoming a nation of cities dominated by peoples who appeared to accept corruption as natural. The old America—a land dominated by sturdy Anglo-Saxon and northern European yeoman adhering to a stern but righteous Protestant ethic—a nation which had championed the concept of democracy, was menaced by an emergent urban society which had seemingly rejected the values which had made America great and virtuous. It was easy to blame the ills of urban America on the immigrant, and to condemn the city as evil personified. It was comforting to wish to return to a pre-industrial and pre-urban America, but that did little to solve the problems plaguing the cities.[2]

Seth Low, as a successful reform mayor of America's third largest city, was looked upon as one of the country's best-informed students of municipal government, and in the decade after stepping down as Brooklyn's chief executive, he analyzed, in a series of articles and addresses, the ills afflicting the nation's cities, and proposed a cure. Generally, Low's analysis of the American urban problem did not follow the Mugwump view in its interpretation of the causes of municipal corruption, though it did accept much of the Mugwump program as a corrective for the ills besetting urban America. This is an important distinction, for throughout the 1880s and '90s, Low's thinking on the problems of municipal government would remain remarkably optimistic and flexible. Rejecting the Mugwump temptation to blame America's ills on the immigrant or on the democratic system, he was confident that urban society in America would be made a success, and by the late 1890s had come to champion positive, socially responsive government. Accepting the tenets of Progressivism in this best sense, he discarded much of the intellectual baggage of Mugwumpery.[3]

The problems of American urban society, Low held, could not be blamed on the immigrant, or universal manhood suffrage, or on a failure of democratic institutions. The immense tide of immigration sweeping into the United States, he told the readers of Bryce's *American Commonwealth,* while tending to aggravate and magnify already existing evils, was not the cause of urban ills. The southern and eastern European immigrant was the product of a class society which sharply and rigidly differentiated between those who ruled and those who were ruled; consequently, he had no experience in the art of self-government, was ignorant of the workings of a democratic political order, and expected to be ruled. Settling in America's cities, the newly-arrived citizen looked upon the local ward-heeler in pretty much the same fashion as he had viewed the local aristocrat back in his native village. Accustomed to regarding the aristocrat as the source of all authority and bounties, it was easy to transfer this traditional deference to the ward-heeler, and when one was grateful to him for petty kindnesses and favors, it was that much easier to vote as he directed. Thus, the immigrant, not yet assimilated into a democratic culture, continually and regularly voted the machine ticket, and permitted political corruption to tighten its grip over the nation's cities. The problem confronting America, Low pointed out, was to instruct its new citizens in the art of self-government and to absorb them as an integral part of American society, not to strip them of their franchise by making the suffrage dependent upon property qualifications as some urban reformers had been urging.[4]

"Our American institutions," he told a Cornell audience, "make the man the unit and not the dollar, and I do not expect to see great cities, containing immense masses of men, made exceptions to this rule.[5] Moreover, there was a much more basic reason for retaining universal manhood suffrage. "For this is to be said in behalf of manhood suffrage," he told a Johns Hopkins gathering:

> it Americanizes our foreign-born citizens more rapidly than any other system possibly could. Hence it happens that our cities are not full of immense masses of men who have no interest in them, of any kind whatever. Their interest, under existing conditions, may be an unintelligent interest, but it is very real. As far as it goes, it is as genuine, speaking broadly, as that of the native-born. Manhood suffrage leads more rapidly than any other system to the education of the masses. It leads to this education, both by the awakening effect of participation in our political affairs, and also by the willingness to be taxed for educational purposes, which it fosters and develops in every community. It is not at all clear that the marked ability in many directions shown by American cities to provide for their own rapid growth is not largely due to the prevalence of manhood suffrage. Manhood suffrage infuses into the body politic the element that feels, as well as the element that thinks.[6]

Obviously, if the best way to teach democracy to the immigrant was to let him participate in the democratic process, restricting the suffrage to property owners would serve only to delay the immigrant's assimilation into American life, and intensify his alienation from society. A firm believer in the efficacy of the democratic process, he did not want impediments placed in its path. Besides which, the country's municipal ills were not produced by the immigrant. "The evils which our city suffers . . . .," Low declared, "are not the result either of universal suffrage or of foreign immigration. The difficulty is one that has been inherent in our system from the beginning."[7]

The government of America's cities had always been a conspicuous failure, and this was the case even when they were inhabited by native Americans of Anglo-Saxon background, and when the franchise was restricted by property qualifications. According to Low, there were a number of reasons for the failure of municipal government in America, of which one went all the way back to the country's New England heritage. America's cities, he told Philadelphia's Committee of Fifty, grew up out of villages and towns which were themselves organized as though they were miniature states. To safeguard the rights of its citizens, municipal authority was diffused among a number of agencies. The executive power lodged in the mayor was checked by a legislative body—common council or board of Aldermen—which controlled spending and approved the mayor's executive appointments. In some cases, the legislative body itself was divided into two distinct houses which further complicated the operations of municipal government. So long as the municipalities remained only villages or small towns, with few functions to perform, and a citizenry which actively participated in the political life of the community, the system worked well. But, as towns grew into cities, and as municipal functions became more highly complex and costly, it was manifestly impossible for the average citizen, himself concerned with the ever-more complex task of making a living, to actively and intelligently participate in the government of his city. Municipal government, with its systems of checks and balances, now served to mask responsibility for inefficient and corrupt administration, and when it did not actually paralyze bureaucratic efficiency, it made it possible for a small, well-entrenched body of professional politicians to control the city in their own interests, while avoiding responsibility for bad government.[8] The cause of urban mis-government, therefore, was inherent in the institutional framework of municipal administration, and not in the ethnic composition of the urban population.

Divided government was but one of the numerous difficulties in the way of honest and efficient city administration. Equally important in stifling movements looking towards municipal reform was the American political party system. "The fundamental difficulty in securing good city government thus far," Low told the American Institute of Civics, "has arisen from the fact that by the habits of our people every city is simply a pawn in the game of national politics."[9] Political parties, Low went on, were organized around national and state rather than purely municipal issues, and their *raison d'etre* was to capture control of the state and national governments. Their only interest in local government was to control municipal offices in order to further the national and state-wide interests of the party, and to enable it to win higher offices more easily. Thus, both Republican and Democratic municipal officials sacrificed the needs and interests of the city to those of their political organization. "They feel no responsibility toward the city," Low wrote, "but great responsibility toward the party. In their eyes the administration of the city should strengthen the party, whatever else it may fail to do. Few managing politicians are able to see that a man serves his party best who serves his city best."[10] Like the Mugwumps, he was suspicious and distrustful of political party organization. Moreover, where city government has been divided, politicians—seeking to enhance their larger ambitions—can put the entire civil bureaucracy to their service through the spoils system. They can also secure the support of powerful financial interests by awarding valuable public franchises at outrageously low rates.[11] And since responsibility was divided, it was difficult to fix blame for wrongdoing. No one had enough power to do much good, while every one could claim that he was not responsible for the chicanery unearthed by the reformers.[12] While the form of democracy was maintained, divided government destroyed its substance.

Moreover, a city was a corporate body whose legal existence was secured by a charter granted by the state legislature, and the legislature retained the authority to alter, amend, or revoke the city's charter at will. The powers and method of selection of the mayor, common council, and department heads could all be changed to suit the interests of the dominant party of the state legislature. Public works construction, the salaries of city officials, could all be mandated by the legislature; in short, all aspects of a city's life were subject to the direct control of the state, and this power was often used to reinforce the power of the local political machines. Defeated in a municipal election, a dominant political machine—through its influence in the state legislature— could reverse, for all practical purposes, the decision of the people.[13] Divided responsibility, the political party system with its spoils of office and franchise give-aways, together with the interference of the state legislature were responsible for the corruption and debauchery of American municipal life; and, while foreign immigration and universal manhood suffrage might well add to a city's problems, neither was the root cause of them. Limiting the franchise to native American property-owners, and the restriction of immigration, would not solve the governmental ills tormenting the cities of America.

To remedy these evils, Seth Low proposed the centralization of city government, the separation of national and state from local politics, and home rule for cities. "It is important ... to remember," Low told the readers of *The Century Magazine,* "that a city has not a single attribute of sovereignty," and moreover it should not possess those attributes.[14] A city was not so much a political commonwealth as it was a business corporation whose primary functions were to provide its inhabitants with an adequate water supply and sewer system, effective protection against fire and crime, safe and efficient transportation, and economical public utilities. The obligations of a city government were purely business ones, and the issues of national and state politics had no legitimate relevance to municipal life.[15] Because the rights of the citizens were sufficiently protected by the federal and state constitutions, a municipal system of checks and balances was not needed to safeguard civil liberties. In addition, since the city was essentially a business corporation, it should be conducted in accordance with business principles. The mayor of a city was in actuality the president of a great corporation, and should be given power adequate to the task of efficiently overseeing municipal functions. "Power without responsibility is always dangerous," Low proclaimed, "but power, with responsibility to a constituency which can readily call it to account, is not dangerous. It is the first requisite of efficient administration."[16]

The mayor should have the power to appoint, without the

consent of the common council or aldermen, all department heads and executive officers; further, these officials should serve at the mayor's pleasure rather than being appointed for a definite term. Consequently, the mayor would be personally responsible for the conduct of the departments under him, and when corruption or inefficiency was exposed, he would have both the power and the duty to remedy the abuses uncovered. The common council, or board of aldermen, should be replaced by a board of estimate, which would control the appropriation and outlay of funds. The separation of the purse strings from the mayor's office would serve to heighten financial honesty, but, except for this, absolute power and responsibility for the operation of the city government in all its phases must be turned over to the executive.[17] Such a system, which Brooklyn adopted in 1882, fixed blame, whether merited or not, for municipal wrongdoing with the mayor, and if corruption went unpunished and uncorrected, the people could vote out the incumbent and replace him with a man who possessed both the desire and the ability to clean up the city's administration.[18] Since the mayor had power, a higher grade of men would be attracted to municipal service for they would have the opportunity of accomplishing lasting good. "It appeals," Low declared, "to the best that is in a man as strongly as it exposes him to the fire of criticism if he does not do well."[19] Of course, a political boss could always hide behind a weak mayor whom he could manipulate as a puppet, but by striking at the dummy, the people could deliver the autocrat a severe blow. With the mayor all-powerful, it would be impossible to disclaim responsibility for municipal corruption.

Besides centralizing the government under the mayor, a way had to be found of removing national and state political considerations from the municipal scene. One way of realizing nonpartisan urban government, Low maintained, was to separate local from state-wide and national elections. If municipal officers were selected at the same time as state and federal positions were filled, it served to inject a maximum of partisanship into the local canvas. Party considerations took precedence over the welfare of the city and machine rule was perpetuated. However, if municipal elections were held in odd-numbered years when no national or state offices were at stake, Low believed that this would tend to reduce partisan considerations to a minimum, and the issue would turn purely on local concerns.[20] This proposal, though, was totally unrealistic, for a local election coming a year before an important state or national election would be regarded by both parties as a forecast of things to come, and they would intensify their efforts to capture the local government by claiming that it would advance their chances of victory in the more important election of the following year. Furthermore, victory in the municipality—placing as it does the spoils of office in the hands of a partisan machine—strengthens the winning party for the contests to come, and if anything, Low's plan would magnify the political importance of local contests. He probably realized that this would be the case, because he championed a number of measures designed to limit the power of the political machine—the most important being civil service and franchise reform.

"Patronage," declared Seth Low in 1882, "is the foe which has converted the machinery of Government all over our land into a formidable engine for personal or party ends."[21] With the Mugwumps, he felt that if municipal government were indeed a business, obviously its civil service should be based upon fitness, competence, and efficiency, not political favoritism. The spoils system, by making employment in the civil service dependent upon the whim of a political boss, enabled the machine to harness the full force of the municipal service to the advancement of partisan ends. Once the civil service was made independent of political influence by recruiting on the basis of competitive examinations with tenure granted during good behavior, the power of the boss would be sharply reduced and the good of the city raised above partisan considerations. "If history teaches anything," Low proclaimed, "it is perfectly clear that no nation can permanently enjoy the full blessings of liberty that permits the patronage of government to be employed systematically to sustain the powers that be. . . ."[22] While not seizing upon civil service reform as a panacea, it was nevertheless an important plank in Low's program of municipal reform. And, if civil service reform served to weaken the power of the political boss, so, too, would franchise reform.

As long as the machine was able to grant valuable long-term franchises to favored interests at low rates of remuneration to the city, the boss could count on the powerful financial backing of an important segment of the business community. Legislation, Low argued, should be enacted limiting franchise grants to short periods not to exceed twenty or thirty years, at the end of which period the franchise would have to be renegotiated. In addition, franchised corporations should be subject to strict accounting, with royalty payments to the city being based on a percentage of the company's net profits.[23] By standardizing the granting of franchises, and by mandating the royalty to be paid to the city, the tie between the boss and the businessman will be effectively cut. The separation of local from state and national elections, the extension of civil service and franchise reform all will tend to reduce the importance of partisan considerations in the selection of municipal officers and will bring local concerns to the forefront of attention.

To secure the triumph of good municipal government, the city's relationship to the state legislature must also be reformed. A long-time advocate of home rule, Low told the 1894 New York State Constitutional Convention that the State's new constitution should strictly define all areas in which the city was to be subject to the authority of the state, and all areas in which it was to enjoy home rule. A city should be restricted by the state in its use of credit and in its grants of franchises, but should be given autonomy over all other matters. Thus, "a city will then be a creature of the Constitution and free from interference by the Legislature."[24] The convention did not grant all that Low would have wished in the way of home rule, but throughout his career as a municipal reformer he clung to his faith in the efficacy of centralization of municipal government, separate city elections, civil service and franchise reform, and home rule as the surest means out of the morass of civic corruption.[25]

Through it all, Seth Low maintained his optimism that the urban problem would eventually be solved, and that democratic institutions would prove as efficacious in the cities of America as it was in the countryside. The nation's municipal difficulties were in the main occasioned by the extreme rapidity of urban growth, which in a few short years saw vast cities emerge from the fields and vacant lots of villages and small towns. The necessity of supplying these vast, growing cities with adequate housing, water supply, transportation facilities, and other utilities bred the political corruption which had thus far disgraced the nation's cities. However, this corruption was not so much attributable to the failings of the urban populace as it was to America's total inexperience with the needs and requirements of city life. All of the country's prior experience with government had been geared to serving an agrarian society, and it took considerable time to realize and meet the political demands of an urban America.[26] As the American people learned how to cope with municipal problems, city politics would be cleaned up, and its government raised to the same level as prevailed elsewhere in America. In the main, Low felt that the political life of the nation's cities was constantly improving, and that while it was not all that it should be, it could and would be further improved, until one day—hopefully a day not too distant—honest and efficient government would obtain in all of America's great cities. As he told the New York Historical Society in 1891:

> I sum up in the general conclusion, that our cities tested even by New York, are not going from bad to worse. They are doubtless worse at some time than at others, but I believe that it may be fairly claimed that the New York of 1890 was in many important respects a better governed city than the New York of 1850.[27]

The way to achieve better municipal government was not to bewail the depravity of urban life but to discover the factors making for mis-government and to educate the masses of the people to an awareness of those causes and an appreciation of their remedy. "It may justly be said," he told Lord Bryce's readers:

> that the American city, if open to serious blame, is also deserving of much praise.
> It may be claimed for American institutions even in cities, that they lend themselves with wonderfully little friction to growth and development and to the peaceful assimilation of new and strange populations. Whatever defects have marked the progress of such cities, no one acquainted with their history will deny that since this problem assumed its present aspect, progress has been made, and substantial progress, from decade to decade. The problem will never be anything but a most difficult one, but with all its difficulties there is every reason to be hopeful.[28]

Much of Low's life was dedicated to the task of improving the quality of municipal life and government, not because he wanted to lessen the tax burden on native-American property-owners like himself, but rather to employ the instruments of an honest and efficient government to uplift the condition of the poor. "If we could only have more confidence in our city governments," he told Philadelphia's Committee of Fifty:

> how much more they might do for us than now they do. Think

of what has been done in some of the best cities of Europe; bad neighborhoods have been renovated through the action of the authorities; unwholesome buildings have given way to open spaces and small parks; public baths have been erected and maintained for the public benefit. . . . Losses of this character [through lack of confidence in city government] fall almost entirely on the poor.[29]

Seth Low's analysis of American municipal problems, then, unlike that of many Mugwumps, did not hold the immigrant or the democratic political process responsible for urban misgovernment. Rather, it was the constitutional and institutional shortcomings of American political life which were at fault, and they were found wanting not as the result of any deficiency to be found in the quality of the nation's urban populace but simply because America was too inexperienced with an urban society to be able to govern it efficiently. And unlike so many of his contemporaries, Low betrayed no anti-urban bias. He did not long for the simpler virtues of an agrarian society, nor did he desire a return to "the garden," but optimistically sought to understand and resolve the problems facing urban America, confident that trained intelligence could set them right. The weakness of his analysis was that it put too much stress on institutions and constitutional forms and not enough emphasis on the social needs of an urban-industrial population. While, as mayor of Brooklyn, he had demonstrated a willingness to appropriate funds to improve social services and education, and while he was receptive to the idea of municipal ownership of public utilities, he did not as yet fully understand the importance of providing positive governmental assistance for the alleviation of social distress. Believing that the proper organizational set-up of city government would resolve all urban problems, he was largely unaware of the underlying social causes of municipal corruption. Indeed, he was not to become an active champion of the positive state until after he had left the municipal reform scene. But, as his thought matured and deepened during the years from 1897–1903, he would slowly become aware of the fundamental social discontents which made urban corruption possible, and he would take his first steps (uncertain and often ill-conceived to be sure, but nevertheless sincere) to alleviate the hardships of urban poverty. In the 1880s and '90s, Seth Low would be slowly transformed from a Mugwump into a Progressive.

Established as one of the nation's most astute observers of the municipal scene, with a record of success as a reform mayor of Brooklyn, it was to be expected that Seth Low would be looked to as the man to lead the reform forces in New York City. During the depression winter of 1893–1894, Tammany Hall—under the administration of Mayor Gilroy—had squandered a million-dollar State appropriation designed to aid the city's unemployed, and had generally made itself so obnoxious (especially in the matter of police corruption), that New York's "better" citizens had been shaken out of their normal apathy and into a spirit of rebellion against "boodle" government. Determined to redeem New York from the mis-rule of Tammany Hall, the reform element, in the spring of 1894, was searching the city's political landscape for a strong anti-Tammany candidate to lead the fall crusade for good government. Naturally, Seth Low was mentioned as a likely candidate of the reform party. On April 26, 1894, Richard Watson Gilder of *The Century* wrote Columbia trustee J. W. Harper that though it was still quite early, sentiment was tending strongly in the direction of Seth Low as the likeliest and ablest candidate of the fusion forces, and requested that Columbia give serious consideration to granting him a leave of absence from the college's presidency in order that he might undertake the mayoralty race. "Supported as he would be in office," declared Gilder, "and with his experience and prestige, he could accomplish for a republican form of government possibly as much as a president of the United States under similar circumstances."[30]

On May 4, Harper replied to Gilder, and sent a copy of both Gilder's letter and his answer to Low. While conceding that Low would make an excellent candidate, and that the vast majority of the citizens of New York wanted honest government, he expressed the fear that Low's campaign would be in vain because of the Republican machine people who had "nothing but revenge & hate & malice for such men as George William Curtis & Seth Low." They would, he went on, unite with Tammany to cheat the reform forces of their victory, "and defeat under such a man as Low," he declared, "would mean the triumph of indecency & the beginning of the end of popular government everywhere."[31] Undaunted, the reformers, early in May 1894, called upon Low, and declared that he might be the one man around whom all the forces opposed to Tammany could rally. In such an eventuality, would he, they asked, consent to make the race? Low replied that he could not make such a decision without consulting Columbia's Board of Trustees, and asked for time to deliberate with them.

It was the opinion of Columbia's trustees that with the school in a period of transition from college to university standing, and with a new campus needed for the expanding institution, an absentee president was a luxury which could not be afforded. They asserted that Low was needed at Columbia, and that they would prefer that he remain at the helm as a full-time chief executive.[32] Low informed the reformers of the feelings of the trustees, and asserted that he felt that his prime duty, under the circumstances, was to Columbia. The reformers were not satisfied. "The fact is," Edmond Kelly wrote:

> that if the trustees had any sense of their duty to the city thay [sic] would have requested you to accept the nomination, and you could then hardly have refused it.
>
> Since I have seen you indications from every side emphasize the fact that you are the only man in New York who can reconcile conflicting factions and that your inability to accept the nomination will probably result in the election of a Tammany man in November. . . .[33]

Pressure on Low and on Columbia's trustees remained strong throughout the summer and early fall of 1894. Late in July, Charles Stewart Smith told trustee Morgan Dix that if Low were given a leave of absence to accept the New York mayoralty, the people of the city would be so grateful to Columbia for their deliverance from mis-government that contributions by the millions of dollars would pour into Columbia. Moreover, Smith asserted, "Mr. Low is the only man that I can think of who is available and who will unite all the elements of opposition to Tammany."[34] A. S. Frissel, following up Smith's letter, appealed to Low, declaring that, "you are the first and only choice of the better element in the city . . . ," and called upon him to perform his civic duty.[35]

New York's Committee of Seventy was organized that September, and the search for an anti-Tammany candidate now began in earnest. Seth Low was still the first choice of many members of the Committee, and pressure mounted for him to rise to the call of the people and accept the fusion nomination. "I have," he confided to John W. Burgess:

> indeed been approached again so seriously as to compel me to take counsel with the Trustees. I confess that I have been

placed in the greatest perplexity of my life. . . . I am obliged
to say, however, if a situation arises in which it became clear
that a union against Tammany can be made around me and
not around anybody else, that I should feel obliged to make
every sacrifice to answer the call. I should deem it something
of a shame both to the College and to myself as one of the
citizens if, in that emergency, I should fail to respond. I am
also clear that it would be a permanent injury to the College
and to my ability to be of usefulness to it if the city were in
a position to say, in the presence of a realized catastrophe,
that "if Columbia and Mr. Low had been more patriotic
these things would not have happened."[36]

He did not feel justified in leaving Columbia at this crucial
time in her history, and earnestly hoped that an acceptable fusion
candidate, other than himself, could be found. When the Com-
mitee of Seventy finally settled on dry-goods merchant William
L. Strong to lead the hosts of reform, Low was relieved, and
pledged his wholehearted support to his campaign. He volun-
teered his services as a speaker on behalf of the fusion cause,
and so vigorous was his support of Strong that City College's
Alfred G. Compton proclaimed, "It is comforting to know that
the scholar has not yet retired in disgust and despair from politics, and gives us some hope for our future."[37]

Delighting in Strong's victory, he saw it as a sign that urban
America was capable of providing itself with honest and efficient
representative government. As he proudly told Washington Gladden:

> No one hereafter can say that even the population of New
> York City, living as it does in tenement houses and made up
> as it is largely of foreign-born people, cannot be trusted to
> decide moral questions aright when the issue is once made
> clear. Of course it is hard work to make such an issue plain
> to so large a jury, and when the voting population is so com-
> posed one naturally has to paint with more lurid colors than
> when appealing to a community more skilled in the art of
> self-government. In other words, the situation here had to
> become worse before it could be remedied than might have
> been necessary in a community differently constituted. But
> Tuesday settled once and for all that even here the popula-
> tion can be relied upon to decide with the right whenever
> they see it to be an issue between right and wrong.[38]

Satisfied that his world was steadily becoming the best of all
possible worlds, Seth Low hoped that he would be allowed to

return without further disturbance to the work of building Columbia into a great university. He was not to be left in peace for long, however, and soon found himself once more caught up in the maelstrom of city politics.

In the general elections of 1894, the people of New York, Brooklyn, Long Island City and a number of outlying villages voted in favor of consolidation into a Greater New York. It was then up to the State legislature to pass enabling legislation to carry into force the will of the electorate, and in the spring of 1896—under the leadership of the Platt machine—a bill was passed providing for Greater New York to come into existence on New Year's Day of 1898. A charter commission was to be created to draw up a fundamental code for the new city, but regardless of the action taken by the charter commission, Greater New York would still come into being on January 1, 1898. The legislature sent the bill to the communities affected for the approval of their mayors. In New York, Seth Low, a long-time advocate of the Greater New York, urged Mayor William L. Strong to veto the proposal on the grounds that the new city would be a dangerously unknown quantity, and that its charter might well be far worse than New York's present one. Low felt that the logical procedure would first be to frame a charter, and then submit it for the approval of the cities concerned as the instrument of the consolidation. In this fashion, unwise charter provisions could be corrected before the Greater New York came into existence. "It is rather a question," he wrote Strong, "of whether the consolidation shall be brought about in a statesmanlike fashion or whether the cities shall be thrown together with absolute disregard of foresight, to take their chances of settling down somehow into one municipality."[39] Strong, sharing Low's sentiments, vetoed the charter bill only to have the State legislature override his veto.

In May, a Greater New York Charter Commission was appointed, with Benjamin Franklin Tracy designated as president, and Seth Low—at the request of Governor Levi P. Morton—serving as Chairman of the Committee on the Draft. It was his job to supervise the various committees in the writing of their charter chapters, and to integrate the various chapters into a coherent whole. He had to familiarize himself with the details of New York's streetcleaning system, dock facilities, water supply system, and the hundreds of other tiresome details of the everyday life of a city. It was a job tedious to the point of madness, but Seth Low, having the temperament of a born administrator, relished it. The whole episode would have proved inconsequential, for Low had no direct role in the shaping of the charter, had it not been for the fact that he objected to a number of the charter's provisions, and became caught up in the political storm which whirled about the Greater New York Charter.

The work of the charter commission was completed in December 1896, and pleased few people. As John Jay Chapman's *The Nursery* put it, "We have the proposed charter. A thousand pages of chaos and complexity, through which it yet appears that the hope of non-partisan government has been abandoned, party police commissioners retained, and a double-banded legislature of great size adopted."[40] Among other features, the Greater New York Charter, as approved by the New York State Legislature, povided for a four-man police commission, on which there had to be two Democrats and two Republicans. It was felt that a bipartisan police board would eliminate the abuses within the department which the 1894 Lexow Committee had uncovered. Also, the board of elections was to be administered as a bureau within the police department. In addition, the mayor would have unrestricted authority to remove department heads only within the first six months of his term, after which period city officials could be removed only for cause. And New York City's legislature was to be a two-house body in which the upper chamber would serve as a check on the lower.

Both Low and Mayor Strong vigorously opposed these features, and filed a supplementary report with the charter commission condemning them all. They pointed out that a system of checks and balances for municipal government was superfluous, since the prime object of city administration was to provide service and not to decide issues of state. Charging that a two-house municipal legislature would produce chaos and governmental paralysis, they urged a single-chambered municipal assembly not to exceed 100 members. Condemning limitations on the removal power of the mayor, they asserted that unless department heads were absolutely responsible to the mayor for the conduct of their agencies, corruption and mis-management would be encouraged with the chief executive powerless to correct abuses, even if he were desirous of doing so. Instead, they wanted the mayor to be granted absolute power of removal. Finally, they objected to the four-man police board as providing for absentee leadership which would encourage subordinates, who would be charged with conducting the department's day-to-day activities, to use their positions for personal advantage. There should be one police commissioner, they held, who would directly run the force, and who would be accountable for any wrong-doing discovered in his department.[41]

Low was particularly disturbed by the proposal to have the board of election under the control of the police department. He felt that this would tend to corrupt the police force by giving Tammany Hall a vested interest in the control of the department, and as he told the *New York Evening Post*:

> I have urged a separate Board of Elections because I do not believe in giving to the Police Department any more power than it must have and because the presence of an election bureau in a Police Department furnishes the excuse of putting a board of four men, selected for political reasons, at the head of the Police Department, instead of one man selected simply because of his capacity to be a good Police Commissioner.[42]

Nevertheless, despite their opposition to specific features of the charter, both Low and Strong gave their support to it, because, they believed that, "as a whole its merits outweigh its defects and because they also believe that under it consolidation can safely be brought about."[43] However, the Chamber of Commerce, the Association of the Bar, the Real Estate Board, and the Medical Association, along with numerous other civic and professional organizations, went on record as being opposed to the charter, and Low was severely criticized for his support of the document. "The unctuous *aplomb*," John Jay Chapman declared, "with which Mr. Low dismisses his old beliefs, expressed in a hundred utterances and found in platforms on which he has stood, and in essays which he has published—beliefs which give him his chief title to distinction—mark this man as a wonderful specimen of the Creature of Circumstance."[44]

The *Times* pointed out that the proposed city legislature directly contradicted Low's thesis that a city was a corporation, and that for that reason alone he should have opposed the charter. "Mr. Low," the *Times* concluded, "seems disposed to use the same opportunity as an excuse for continuing a system which must inevitably keep up the party division and the rule of a partisan majority which are the source of all our civic woes."[45]

Low supported the charter as a whole, because—as he told a family friend—the benefits of consolidation would be so great for all the component parts of the Greater New York as to far outweigh the charter's defects, which could be corrected through legislative action in the future. "Good government," he asserted, "is not to be had without a struggle under any charter. The opportunity to obtain it, I think, is not less, but greater, under the Greater New York Charter than under the existing charter of either New York or Brooklyn. This being my opinion I am naturally ready to accept cheerfully all the consequences of the part I have played in framing it."[46] However, the chief determinant for his support of the charter were its franchise provisions, which, he told Governor Frank S. Black, were the best in the nation. "The rights of the city," he wrote:

> in and to its streets are declared to be inalienable, and careful provision is made for dealing with all franchises involving the use of the streets in such a way as to secure the city the privilege of periodically re-adjusting the terms on which such a franchise is enjoyed. . . . I know of no city in the Union at the present time, so fortunately equipped as to its franchises.[47]

Moreover, the features of the new charter pertaining to the police department and the mayor's power of removal were carryovers from the old charter, so that rejecting the new document for its failings in these respects would not serve to improve the existing organization of the city's government.[48]

The Greater New York Charter went into effect as scheduled, and as Low and Strong predicted, the city's legislative assembly was marked by confusion and inaction; the police department once more became thoroughly corrupt; the board of elections perverted the very democratic process it was pledged to uphold, and the city's bureaucracy was filled with knaves and buffoons. As news of Tammany's mis-government reached the Albany Legislature, the New York State Legislature appointed a commission —the Mazet Committee—to investigate abuses in the New York City government, and to recommend corrective measures. "We see incompetence and arrogance in high places," read the Committee's report. "We see an enormous and ever-increasing crowd of office-holders with ever-increasing salaries. We see the powers of government prostituted to protect criminals, to demoralize the police, to debauch the public conscience, and to turn government functions into channels for private gain."[49] The Committee recommended that the city's charter be revised so as to eliminate the causes of those abuses which disfigured the political complexion of the city, and in 1900, Governor Theodore

Roosevelt appointed a charter revision commission to carry into effect the proposals of the Mazet Committee.

The charter revision commission sought the advice of Seth Low, who, in June of 1900, recommended that the mayor's term of office be retained at four years on the grounds that a good administration grew stronger the longer it was in office, while a bad one became weaker, and would be more easily voted out of office. However, the mayor should have absolute power of removal. "I am a believer," he declared:

> under the existing political conditions in this City and State, in giving to the Mayor the right of removal at all times during his term of office, so that at all times he not only may be held responsible, but must be responsible, for the character of the city administration in all its parts. I should like to see all the appointed officers of the city appointed without term, so that they would continue to hold office from Mayor's term to Mayor's term unless removed by the Mayor. Under such a system, it is possible that heads of departments who have served the city well would be continued in office for a long period of years, to the great advantage of the city.

In addition, he urged a single-chambered municipal legislature, municipal ownership of the city's water system, and provisions for extending municipal ownership, under proper safeguards, to other utilities, a single police commissioner, a separate board of elections, and a board of estimate to control finances. All of Low's proposals were adopted with the exception of the mayor's term of office which was reduced to two years. It would later prove fatal to the fusion cause.[50]

Low's work at Columbia, his articles on municipal government, and his part in the framing of the Greater New York Charter again placed him in the forefront of the New York City reform movement, and the city's municipal reformers would shortly call upon him to once again lead them in the battle against Tammany Hall's corruption.

CHAPTER V

The Citizens' Union and the Greater New York Mayoralty Campaign of 1897

For Liberty and Union we are rising in our might,
  Shouting the battle-cry of freedom;
And we're bound to win the battle, for our cause it is the right,
  Shouting the battle-cry of freedom.

We want no Platt-and-Croker deals, we've had enough of them,
  Shouting the battle-cry of freedom.
Our city's for the people, to be ruled by honest men.
  Shouting the battle-cry of freedom.

  Union forever! Three cheers for Seth Low!
  Down with the bosses, boss rule must go!
  For we're marching to the polls boys,
  Three hundred thousand strong,
    Shouting the battle-cry of freedom.
                    BATTLE SONG OF THE CITIZENS' UNION, 1897

Seth Low's a high-born laddy,
He had "dough" left by his daddy,
Proud, as a peacock, I should say,
He hasn't grown conceited—he was born that way.
                    G.O.P. CAMPAIGN SONG, 1897

With the Greater New York scheduled to come into legal existence on New Year's Day of 1898, the 1897 mayoralty election took on an ominous significance. Greater New York would have a population of close to 3,250,000 citizens, and under the new charter the first mayor of the consolidated city would control an army of thirty-five thousand city employees, drawing an annual salary of $40 million, and would dispense a municipal budget of perhaps $100 million per year. The patronage of New York's next mayor would be second only to that of the President of the United States, and he would control expenditures far larger than that of many states. To New York's middle class reformers, it was imperative that the new city government not be turned over to the machines of either Richard Croker or Thomas C. Platt. Wanting to see the Greater New York start its municipal life under auspicious skies, the good government men of the city did not want those skies darkened by the clouds of political corruption and organized plunder. New York must be saved from the bosses. The problem was how to save it.

"The central fact of the failure of popular government in this city," *The Nation's* E. L. Godkin observed, "is that the vicious and ignorant are united solidly, while the intelligent and virtuous are split up into many sects and parties; and yet the intelligent, virtuous, and industrious are in a large majority, and must be so, or the social organizations would break up."[1] It was to organize the intelligent, virtuous, and industrious into a cohesive and effective instrument for the salvation of New York that the Citizens' Union was founded.

The Union was conceived in the fall of 1896 when the trustees of the City Club (a middle class good government organization) adopted a report vigorously recommending the establishment of an independent citizens' movement to take part in the municipal elections of 1897. Acting on the basis of this resolution, James C. Carter, who had been president of the City Club as well as of the National Municipal League, in December of 1896 sent invitations to a dozen "representative" citizens to meet at the offices of Elihu Root on December 11 to discuss the City Club's proposal. The conference, attended by such distinguished men as Abram S. Hewitt, Charles S. Fairchild, Charles Stewart Smith, James B. Reynolds, and Jacob H. Schiff, endorsed the plan of the City Club and selected a five-man committee on organization to form a large and "representative" citizens' movement which would carry its plea for good government directly to the people of New York City.[2]

Working through January and into February 1897, it was not until the twenty-second of that month that the Citizens' Union was prepared to announce its existence and request the support of New York's citizens. Signed by 165 of the city's most prominent sons, the declaration proclaimed that, "the election of 1897 will be a crisis so important:

> as to demand of every citizen the full performance of his public duty. Experience has demonstrated: First, that good city government cannot be secured through the agency of existing parties organized upon National and State issues; and,

second, that it can be secured through the united action of citizens earnestly determined that the city shall be governed solely with reference to the welfare of the city and its citizens.

The separation of municipal from State and National politics and the honest, efficient, and independent administration of the City Government are the principles of the union.[3]

At the same time, the fledgling Citizens' Union promulgated its platform—the principles for which it would stand in the upcoming election. Demanding that New York be insulated from the political wars besetting the state and nation, it called for strict enforcement of the civil service laws, better rapid transit facilities, adequate school accommodations for all the city's children, small neighborhood parks in the tenement districts to bring light and air to the residents of the city's most crowded areas, and for laws to improve the sanitary conditions of the tenements. But more importantly, the Citizens' Union's platform proclaimed that New York City should retain ownership of its franchises, leasing them to private corporations for short periods of time at adequate rates of remuneration to the municipality, and that the city government should oversee their operation to insure efficient service at reasonable cost to the public. It also left open the possibility of municipal ownership, with proper safeguards, of vital public utilities. Lastly, it called for rigid observance of the eight-hour day for all city workers, as well as for all laborers working for contractors performing work for the municipality, at the prevailing rate of wages.[4] It was in all respects a liberal charter, and though Seth Low had no hand in drafting it, it was a platform which he would have no difficulty in supporting.

From the beginning, leaders of organized labor and of newly-arrived immigrant groups played a role in the Citizens' Union and in the battle for municipal reform in New York City. Harry White and Herman Robinson of the Garment Workers' Union, William J. O'Brien of the Granite Cutters', and John T. Lawrence of the Clothing Cutters' Union, to name but a few labor leaders, were among the founding fathers of the Citizens' Union. Responsive to the needs of labor, confident that the immigrant would, after a time, reject the domination of machine politicians and accept the values of the American democratic tradition, the Citizens' Union entered upon its career determined to perfect the American democratic system by making the party machines reflect the popular will and to make the government serve the needs and to work for the greater good of the entire city. It did not, as will be shown, turn its back to the future in a futile attempt to preserve an already dead past.

The announcement of the Citizens' Union's organization was warmly greeted by the "goo-goo" press with the *New York Times* asserting that, "The organization to carry out these principles has begun none too soon, and cannot be pushed too vigorously. . . . The forces of evil never relax their discipline and never sleep. The forces of good must be equally alert and vigilant."[5] To professional reformers like John Jay Chapman, the Citizens' Union was the "altruism of the community fighting its way to the surface through the obstacles, the snares, and the oppressions of the organized world. No discouragement sets it back. No betrayal destroys it. The people come forward with ever new faith."[6] But to professional politicians like Tammany's George Washington Plunkitt, "The movement is a humbug all through. . . . They don't amount to nothin'."[7]

On March 22, 1897, at Cooper Union, the Citizens' Union held its first public meeting electing R. Fulton Cutting as chairman with Charles Stewart Smith serving as vice-chairman; J. Kennedy Tod, treasurer, and John C. Clark, secretary. The Union's platform and resolves were officially adopted; its basic premise—and what would prove to be the root of its difficulties —were enunciated: good city government cannot be obtained through the existing political parties but must be secured through a non-partisan citizens' movement seeking as its goal a businesslike administration of the city government. As the politically orthodox *New York Sun* pointed out:

> Like children at a game, her [N.Y.C.'s] citizens are to "make believe" that, for all municipal purposes, they are without politics and simply longing to vote for "the best men." One of the objects of eminent educational institutions like the Citizens' Union is to indicate, in a properly superior manner, to ordinary citizens who the "best men" are. And then the ordinary citizens, their hearts throbbing with gratitude to their kind instructors, will surge to the polls and vote for "the best men, irrespective of politics." By this means, as simple as a lamb's intellect and as miraculous as hair dye, good government is sure to be attained.[8]

Once having firmly established itself, the Citizens' Union turned its attention to the forthcoming mayoralty election. As early as February 15, Mayor William L. Strong had declared that, "under no circumstances" would he consent to stand for re-election.⁹ It was just as well that Strong took himself out of contention as a candidate, for his reform administration—while giving New York an honest and efficient government—was not popular with the voters. Police Commissioner Theodore Roosevelt's strict enforcement of the Raines Liquor Law had alienated the city's German-American population, and higher taxes on real estate did little to add to Strong's lustre. Immediately, speculation centered on the possibility that Seth Low would be asked to carry the Citizens' Union banner onto the field of battle. His tenure as mayor of Brooklyn had left him with a lasting and deep-rooted popularity with many voters in that city; his record as an arbitrator of labor disputes gave him a loyal following among large groups of the working classes throughout New York, and a series of articles published in America's leading periodicals had established him as an internationally respected authority on municipal government. Moreover, his work on the Greater New York Charter Commission seemed to indicate that he would possess a thorough knowledge of the workings of the yet-to-be established government. In addition, "his real goodness and his constitutional mediocrity have made him the idol of the shop-keeping classes in this town."¹⁰ In every respect, Seth Low was the ideal candidate—though there were a few dissenters. As a reader of the *New York World* put it, "He [Low] has not one democratic bone in his body. I may vote for him if a rascal is nominated against him, but if I do I will be under no delusion. He represents the aristocratic tradition. . . ."¹¹

The prospective candidate, however, was most reluctant to re-enter political life. As he wrote to a friend on March 23, "Nothing short of a compelling sense of public duty, however, can lead me into the field on any terms. My duty to Columbia is only less controlling than it was. The crisis in the city, as I see it, is too grave to permit me, or anyone else, to subtract himself from the situation. That is all."¹² It was not merely the coy talk of a politician wanting to be coaxed, for Low genuinely enjoyed his work at Columbia. He was wholeheartedly involved in Columbia's transition to university status and to its new Morningside Heights campus, and was reluctant to forsake this for the hard and often unrewarding life of a candidate for political office. But besides inducing Seth Low to consent to leave Columbia for the mayor's chair, a much more fundamental question faced the Citizens' Union.

The Citizens' Union, from its inception, was badly divided over the question of fusion or union with the Republican party. A formidable group, dominated by the Manhattan members of the Citizens' Union, aided and abetted by the *New York Times,* believed that as they were pledged to, "nominate no candidate unless his character and record are such as to justify public confidence in his assurance that, if elected, he will not use his office or permit it to be used, for the benefit of any political organization," and since their platform proclaimed the absolute separation of municipal from state and national politics, it was incumbent upon the Citizens' Union to eschew all thought of a union with the Platt machine.[13] The plan was for the Citizens' Union to secure a large enrollment of around fifty thousand registered voters by early summer, nominate an independent candidate in early June, cultivate his popularity, and wait for the Republican organization, out of political necessity, to endorse, without pre-conditions or "dickers," the nominee of the Citizens' Union.[14] As the *Times,* throwing political realism to the four winds, put it, "If the Citizens' Union has to fight two-party organizations, it stands a good chance of getting a vote greater than that of either."[15] While the go-it-alone faction of the Citizens' Union may have been rank amateurs, they were animated by a messianic fervor. "We are going to accomplish a great work," James C. Carter exclaimed with an almost religious rapture. "If we succeed, and have free swing in this city for a few years, we shall have a new heaven and a new earth. . . . Victory is possible, and all that is needed is the heart and the effort."[16]

Opposed to those who eschewed all "dickers" with Platt was a much smaller faction centered in the Brooklyn Committee of Fifty (the Union's Brooklyn counterpart) which, realizing that New York was a Democratic city, saw that the Citizens' Union's only hope for victory was to keep the anti-Tammany forces united. In a three-cornered race, with machine Democrats opposing machine Republicans and the Citizens' Union, only Tammany Hall would stand to gain. For this reason, the more moderate members of the Citizens' Union wanted to delay putting a candidate into the field until September when, hopefully, the nomination would be made in conjunction with the Republican party. But for the moment, the go-it-alone faction was in control, and late in May, they appealed to Seth Low to accept a

June nomination on the Citizens' Union ticket and begin a
vigorous summer campaign for the mayoralty.

On May 25, 1897, banker Jacob H. Schiff wrote to Low urging him to accept the nomination of the Citizens' Union. As
Schiff put it:

> The Citizens' Union can . . . not possibly, without endanger-
> ing the entire movement for good municipal government,
> hold out the idea or hope to the Republicans and others
> that it is ready to discuss fusion. It can only do the one thing
> —to make its nominations, and if they are such as will com-
> mand general approval, the Republicans will be compelled to
> endorse the Citizens' Union candidate. . . . Personally, I feel
> that if you see your way to accept a nomination from the Citi-
> zens' Union, all anti-Tammany forces will promptly unite
> upon you, but if you are unwilling to take the risk of a nom-
> ination, at the outset, from the Citizens' Union alone, there
> is great danger of a collapse of the movement with all the ills
> which must result as a conequence in the future government
> of our city.[17]

Two days later, Richard Watson Gilder of *The Century* made
a similar appeal, telling Low that only he could save New York
from boss rule and assuring him that hope of victory "would
not be 'forlorn' with you at the head of the movement. . . . "[18]
And Albert Shaw of the *Review of Reviews* told Low that his
campaign for municipal reform in New York City, whatever its
outcome, would inspire similar efforts for good government
throughout the United States."[19]

Under extreme pressure to lead the forces of good government against the twin evils of the Croker and Platt machines,
and told that the future of municipal reform throughout the
nation rested upon his decision, Seth Low could not refuse the
nomination. But he knew that only fusion with the Republicans
could produce victory, and accordingly, on June 7 he wrote the
Citizens' Union that:

> In view of the grave importance of the first election under
> the Greater New York Charter, I will not eliminate myself
> from the situation as I was compelled to do three years ago.
> On the other hand, I am still charged with responsibilities
> toward the University over which I have the honor to preside
> that I may not lay aside except under the compulsion of a
> public duty that cannot be gainsaid. Testing the specific
> question you have put to me, in this light, I am obliged to
> say that I do not think I am warranted in accepting the

nomination of the Citizens Union at the present time. The question of time apart, I must have more evidence than I now have of the popular desire to make it seem to me a public duty to become a candidate. If I were convinced that there was such a popular desire, and that my candidacy would prove a unifying force among the friends of good government in the City, I would not hesitate to accept your nomination; for I am heartily in sympathy with the purposes of the Citizen's Union as I understand them.[20]

The men of the Citizens' Union took Low's reply to mean that he would accept their nomination as soon as he was shown that his nomination would be favorably received by the public. They, therefore, proceeded to organize a mass petition calling upon Seth Low to undertake the mayoralty race. As the *New York News* remarked, "[the Citzens' Union] have decided to make a house-to-house canvass for signatures to a petition asking the millionaire president of Columbia College to please take over the government of the great municipality . . . , as he is the only man who is fit to rule us." "How many voters," the Tammany organ asked, "are prepared to get down on their knees and beg Seth Low to have the goodness to rule over them according to his own sweet will. . . -"[21]

A petition, however, was not what Seth Low had in mind. Feeling that the Citizens' Union had missed the point of his letter, he reiterated to former Mayor Abram S. Hewitt that he had not intended to give the Union the right to claim him exclusively as its own, and that he would consent to run only if all anti-Tammany forces—and that meant the Republican party —would rally to his candidacy.[22] He did not wish to divide Tammany's opposition, and allow Richard Croker to stroll leisurely into City Hall. The question was whether or not the Platt organization could be persuaded to make common cause with the Citizens' Union.

Thomas Collier Platt, born at Oswego, New York, in 1833, began his career as a druggist in his home town, later becoming president of the Tioga Country National Bank as well as a speculator in Michigan timber lands. Politically he had been a close associate of Senator Roscoe Conkling, leader of the New York "Stalwarts," and had been instrumental in organizing the "Southern tier" counties against Horace Greeley and Senator Reuben E. Fenton. With Levi P. Morton's election as governor of New York in 1894, Platt's power in Empire State Republican politics became irresistible. In the spring of 1897, he was at the height of his power and influence. He and he alone would determine whether the Republican party would join forces with the Citizens' Union. The Union's basic premise was that local affairs should be conducted on a non-partisan basis, but "For the doctrine of non-partisanship in local elections," Platt had only, "the sincerest and profoundest contempt."[23] For Thomas Platt, politics was not a pastime; he was not a patrician whose only ambition was to utilize public office in an effort to advance political and government standards of honesty and efficiency. To him politics was a business—influence its stock-in-trade, patronage its dividend. Under Mayor Strong, the Platt machine had not been entirely satisfied with the patronage assigned to it, and the prospects of plucking choice patronage plums in an administration headed by Seth Low were dim indeed. As an un-named Republican stated, "We know it would be easier to make a dicker with Tammany for a slice of the patronage than to get our share of it from a reform mayor whom we had helped to elect."[24] Platt was not anxious to endorse Low's candidacy, but he was under pressure from within his own organization to do just that.

Republican sentiment for Low was centered primarily in Brooklyn and in the "silk-stocking" assembly districts of Manhattan. As early as May 9, Theodore Willis was reported to have urged the Kings County Republican organization to declare in favor of Seth Low as the Republican candidate for the mayoralty. On the 11th, Jacob Worth, Chairman of the Kings County organization, defeated Willis's move to endorse Low and fuse with the Citizens' Union on the grounds that time for such action was premature. But, at a Washington, D.C. conference, held in mid-May, Worth—supported by Governor Frank S. Black —was reported to have urged Platt to throw his support to Low. Worth, in particular, was under such heavy pressure to endorse Low from within his own organization that to maintain his leadership in Kings County he had to swing behind him. The *New York Times,* on June 1, reported that Lemuel Ely Quigg, leader of the New York County Republican organization and Platt's chief deputy in the city, was in favor of joint action with the Citizens' Union, and was prepared to enter a fusion conference. But, Quigg added, the Republican party would not be dictated to; as the largest anti-Tammany organization in the city, it wanted the greater say in the selection of the mayoral nominee.[25]

In Manhattan, the anti-Platt, Brookfield-Swayne faction had

long since declared for Low and fusion with the Citizens' Union, but on June 11, the regular 27th Assembly District Republican Club formally went on record on behalf of Seth Low's nomination.[26] Clearly, in the face of a popular uprising in support of Low's candidacy, it was becoming increasingly difficult for the Platt machine to maintain an anti-Low, anti-fusion position. The Republicans had become vulnerable to fusion overtures. In the words of Lemuel Quigg, "The Republican organization sincerely desires to bring about a union against Tammany. It has not rejected the candidacy of any man, and for that reason, if for no other, there should be no attempt to force a candidacy down its throat."[27] The Citizens' Union, however, seemed to be doing everything to make fusion an impossibility.

While Willis was leading the pro-Low drive in Brooklyn, that city's Union League Club went on record to declare that it would fuse with the Citizens' Union provided that body nominated Seth Low and shunned all efforts to work out an arrangement with Thomas Platt.[28] Over the river, in Manhattan, Good Government Club C adopted an almost identical resolution, and the *New York Times* declared that the Citizens' Union should entirely ignore Platt, nominate Low and wait, until—forced by his instinct for political self-preservation—Platt, swallowing his pride, endorsed the Citizens' slate.[29] "I have seen a good many insolent attempts to usurp power and grab public benefits," Thomas Platt cried out, "but this performance of the 'best citizens,' for sheer audacity and wanton recklessness, has no counterpart within my experience of politics...."[30] To Abram S. Hewitt and his colleagues in the Citizens' Union, it appeared that Platt was "disturbed by the Citizens' Union movement; that he is afraid of its strength," and plans were made to capitalize on Platt's weakness and fear by nominating Low on the 15th of June.[31]

Seth Low vetoed the Citizens' Union's publicly announced plan to nominate him in mid-June, affirming that he would only consent to run if his nomination were a rallying point for all the anti-Tammany forces.[32] Rejecting all consideration for the wishes of the Republican party, the abortive attempt of the Citizens' Union to nominate Low was a slap in the face to the Republicans. The Republican County Committee of New York promptly condemned the dictatorship of the Citizens' Union, and Mayor Strong publicly rebuked the Union's leadership for doing all it could to guarantee the defeat of Seth Low.[33]

Late in June, Assistant Secretary of the Navy Theodore Roosevelt entered the New York political picture, even though "the President is particularly anxious I shan't mix up in our local New Yok politics." "It seems to me," Roosevelt wrote Low:

> that some of our friends who are very sincere and zealous are confounding the substance with the chaff. We want your election. As an absolute necessity, of course, we might have to be content with casting a "conscience vote," but if we possibly can we want to win, and I think we have a good show. Now it seems to me to be mere folly to throw away the chance of winning for an inadequate reason, and especially upon some point of punctillio about priority of nomination. My own view is that if the republican organization will take you on your own terms that we should soothe their pride by the trivial concession of letting them nominate you first.[34]

Roosevelt informally contacted some Citizens' Union leaders urging that they make concessions to the Republican organization for the good of the movement as a whole, but apparently he did not succeed in producing any concrete results, for one week later he asked Low, "Do you know any semi-rational leader to whom it would be worth my while writing."[35]

As July approached, positions hardened. Fearing that talks with Platt would, as "goo-goo" John DeWitt Warner sternly warned, drive independent Democrats back into the Tammany wigwam and defeat the Citizens' Union ticket, the Manhattan members of that organization continued to insist upon a go-it-alone policy. Meanwhile the Brooklyn Committee of Fifty, meeting at the Criterion Theatre, endorsed Seth Low's candidacy, but backed by the prospective candidate himself, demanded that no nomination be made until a fusion with the Republican party could be effected. In the Republican camp, Chairman Quigg initiated a purge of Citizens' Union members from the party's rolls to make sure that they would not be able to vote in the all-important Republican primaries, and eventually twenty-one thousand names were stricken from the Republican lists. Brooklyn Republicans and anti-Platt Manhattan Republicans continued to press Low on their organization, with William Brookfield predicting that the G.O.P.'s rank-and-file would vote for Low no matter what course Platt pursued.[36] Politics, however, could not compete with the pleasures of mid-summer, and the rival political armies settled down to an unquiet July truce.

In July, R. Fulton Cutting, Chairman of the Citizens' Union, left for a European vacation, and Seth Low, winding up the year's business at Columbia, went to his country home at Northeast Harbor, Maine, for the duration of the summer. "I do not hear very much from the city politically," he wrote Columbia's Nicholas Murray Butler, "but I infer from the newspapers that time is producing salutary results in bringing the various elements nearer together."[37] Indeed, his optimism appeared to be well-founded, for as Low ballots poured into the Citizens' Union headquarters at the rate of two thousand a day, a large percentage of them coming from the city's tenement house districts, Cornelius Van Cott, Platt's Manhattan Postmaster, held out an olive branch to the Citizens' Union, declaring that if only they would confer with the Republicans, the party might well settle upon Low as the mayoralty nominee.[38] Preferring to bend to the will of the Republican rank-and-file rather than risk widespread defections and revolts from the regular machine, Lemuel Quigg was willing to accept Low provided the party leadership could arrange a face-saving compromise with the Citizens' Union. Reluctantly securing the consent of Thomas Collier Platt, it was Quigg's plan to nominate Low on the understanding that the Columbia president would hold off accepting the Citizens' Union's call until endorsed by the Republican convention, and then accept both nominations simultaneously.[39] Consequently, on August 18, the Republican County Committee issued an invitation for a fusion conference of all anti-Tammany forces, but the Citizens' Union spurned the G.O.P.'s appeal on the grounds that:

> The Union having been organized for the express purpose of carrying into effect the principles embodied in the constitutional provision separating local from State and national elections, and of securing Home Rule for the citizens of New York, cannot combine with parties representing State and national issues in the nomination of candidates chosen because of their party affiliation, and necessarily under obligation to the party which they represent.[40]

Stubbornly standing four-square on an abstraction, condemning political parties as evil, in and of themselves, the Citizens' Union was foolishly throwing away its best hope for the establishment of good government in the Greater New York. However, the Committee of Fifty accepted Quigg's invitation, and immediately hope rose that the Brooklyn organization would serve as a go-between for the hostile Manhattan groups.[41] It seemed that Low's policy of waiting for a union of all anti-Tammany forces might prove successful, but a new and disturbing element had been introduced into the already-complicated New York political scene.

While R. Fulton Cutting vacationed in Europe, Charles Stewart Smith, the vice-chairman of the Citizens' Union, wrote Low at his summer home in Maine claiming that many German-Americans and Gold Democrats would vote for Low as an independent candidate, but would not vote for him if nominated by the Republicans first. He went on to say that Willim Brookfield was advised by Jacob Worth, Republican leader in Kings County that, "The Citizens' Union should certainly officially nominate Mr. Low at least three weeks before the meeting of the Republican Convention, and that the Republican Convention will then nominate him by acclamation!" The idea intrigued Low and he asked James McKeen, head of the Brooklyn Committee of Fifty, to investigate the accuracy of the report.[42] Intrigued but not altogether convinced, Low answered Smith that:

> It is clear, however, that the Citizens Union is not in a position to dominate the whole situation. It is a very valuable and influential element in it, but it cannot, in my opinion, proceed as if it could have its own way regardless of others, without losing everything. . . . The minority party everywhere is the natural ally of the independents. My nomination by the Citizens Union, unless it results in an endorsement by the Republicans, will tend to divide hopelessly the elements that must be united if Tammany is to be kept out of control. A failure to unite these elements, in my opinion, means not only success for Tammany, but success under as poor a candidate as Tammany cares to put up. . . . Unless I have the best reason to believe that my nomination by the Citizens Union would be followed by a nomination by the Republicans and by other anti-Tammany organizations, I do not think the Citizens Union will be entitled . . . to ask me to accept its nomination. . . . If the Brooklyn Republicans are prepared to advise (of course, I mean informally) that the Citizens Union should nominate three weeks in advance of the Republican Convention, that itself immediately modifies the situation.[43]

Jacob Worth had committed the cardinal political sin; he had publicly declared that his Brooklyn organization would press for Low in the Republican City Convention scheduled to convene on September 28 without consulting the wishes of Thomas C. Platt. Worth's action was a challenge to Platt's authority within the State organization which the Senator from Tioga could not allow to go unanswered. "Seldom have I seen," Worth declared to the press, "such a universal sentiment among the masses for one man," and it was his hope to capitalize on Low's popularity, force his nomination in defiance of Platt, and eclipse the Senator as the Republican party's chief luminary in the Greater City.[44] He urged the Citizens' Union to nominate Low late in August or early September at the latest and wait for public pressure to force Platt to bow to the popular will. However, Worth could not even count on the united support of his own Kings County organization. Theodore B. Willis, who had begun the Low boom back in May, joined with Lt. Governor Timothy L. Woodruff in a primary fight designed to force Worth out of the leadership of the Brooklyn Republican organization. Declaring their fealty to Seth Low, Willis and Woodruff proclaimed that their campaign was not against the Columbia president, but against a renegade Republican, Jacob Worth, who had broken party discipline.[45]

By the end of July, the enrollment in favor of Seth Low's candidacy had grown to close to eighty thousand, with thousands of ballots still coming in daily, and the Citizens' Union, determined to act upon Jacob Worth's advice, was pressing Low to declare his inttentions.[46] Richard Watson Gilder, chairman of the Citizens' Union's Press and Literature Committee, pointed out to Low that, "The liquor legislation, Black's conduct, the unpopularity of the Platt machine and "bosses" in general, make it impossible not only for a Republican ticket to succeed, but even for an independent ticket to succeed, if the people see trades or conferences in progress with the Republican machine, or with any other political machine." Of course, if the Republicans chose to endorse Low after he had been nominated by the Citizens' Union that was all well and good, but the Citizens' Union could take no action to bring about such a result. "The fact is," Gilder continued, "that this is not an ordinary campaign, but something in the nature of a revolution. The mass of the people recognize that there is a cause; and only a cause can win this time, not an old-fashioned combination."[47]

Finally, bowing to pressure, Low agreed to accept an independent nomination, but on August 23, upon the advice of the Brooklyn Committee of Fifty, he asked a week's delay in the nomination to enable his Kings County friends to make one last effort to reach an agreement with the Republicans. Deeply disappointed at Low's attitude, the Citizens' Union reluctantly granted the delay but made it clear that unless he directly refused to run, they would nominate him no later than September 14.[48] "I am inclined to think," Low confided to his aunt, that:

> when the matter comes to crisis, that I shall be obliged to heed the call of the hundred thousand men who want me to stand. I am not as sanguine as some as to the outcome of the enterprise; but I am pretty clear that, as matters now stand, the interests of the city require that I should accept the nomination of the Citizens' Union, rather than decline it. Were I to decline, Tammany would certainly succeed; for my declination, under existing circumstances, would create very bad feeling and would disappoint the great body of people who are striving earnestly for better things in the city. On the other hand, if I accept, Tammany may still win; but my influence, such as it is, will have been thrown on the side of idealism rather than on the side of machine politics.[49]

The impending nomination of Seth Low by the Citizens' Union caused consternation in Republican ranks. "It is idle to suppose," commented the *New York Sun*, "that the Republican party can be rallied to the support of a man hostile to it in his heart and by his word, and nominated by its enemies with every circumstance of insult." And quoting the *New York Tribune* of June 28, 1888, it declared that Low was "designed by nature as a first-rate Sunday school politician."[50] On September 1, the very day when Low would be nominated, Lemuel Quigg solemnly declared, "We would not accept him [Low] under any circumstances if he should be made the independent nominee of the Citizens' Union in advance of the Republican convention," and the *New York Tribune,* urging the Citizens' Union to wait, demanded that the Republican party advance a practical formula for fusion with the Citizens' Union.[51]

Ignoring pleas for delay, discounting the dire consequences promised by the Republicans if they made an independent nomination, the men of the Citizens' Union, representing all boroughs but Brooklyn, met at 32 Liberty Street on September 1, 1897, and backed by the 127,903 voters who had signed the Low nominating petition, officially designated Seth Low as their candidate for mayor of Greater New York. Low was the only candidate nominated at the meeting. Hoping that public pressure would yet force the Republican party to select him as their standard bearer, the rest of the ticket was left blank so that Thomas C. Platt could fill in the names of the remaining nominees—provided, of course, that he consented to accept the Citizens' Union's mayoralty candidate. Indeed, the Republican *New York Tribune,* while deploring the action of the Citizens' Union, declared that, "there are times when personal and party sensibilities ought to be subordinate to public duty, and this is one of them." The G.O.P., the *Tribune* implored, should make the best of an unpleasant situation, swallow its pride, and nominate the only man who could beat Tammany Hall—Seth Low.[52]

Still at his summer home in Maine when he received news of his nomination, Low continued to believe that the Republicans would fall in line behind his candidacy. "Of course," he told his secretary, William H. H. Beebe, "I shall be discreet in my utterances and shall try to word myself in such a way as to make it easy for the Republicans to join the nomination, although, naturally, I must stand unequivocally upon the platform of non-partisanship."[53] Wisely, Low requested a fortnight's delay before finally accepting the nomination in order to feel the drift of public opinion, and to give the Republicans a final chance to effect a fusion with the Citizens' Union. As he told Richard Watson Gilder, "I do not believe in the attempt to create a municipal party, as distinguished from the national parties, nor in the inference to be drawn from that attempt that the national parties have no right to make nominations for municipal offices."[54] Low would do everything possible to unite the Republican party with the Citizens' Union, for, as Theodore Roosevelt pointed out, "This is a great crisis in our history. It's not a time for kindergarten methods, and we ought not to jeopardize the future of good government in the Greater New York by taking an impossible position. Every effort should be made to combine forces."[55]

The decision was now squarely up to Senator Platt. He could accept the humiliation of seconding Low's nomination, maintain the unity of the Republican party, and be reasonably sanguine as to victory in the November canvass; or, he could stand on his pride, place a ticket in the field which would have no hope of victory, and face the prospect of large scale defections from his machine. In Washington, Theodore Roosevelt, condemning the political naivete of the "extreme goo-goo people," told Low that he would try to get President McKinley to put pressure on the New York machine, and advised Low to "make every effort to keep on good terms with them, and consult with them as far as possible about appointments."[56] A week later, up-state Republicans gave Platt a sharp warning that G.O.P. strength in the state must not be endangered by a Tammany victory in Greater New York, and denouncing the "straight ticket nonsense," they demanded that Platt unite on Low.[57] And the Kings County Republican organization, in a pre-convention caucus, voted 151 to 38 in favor of Seth Low as the Republican nominee for the mayoralty.

On September 13, Low formally accepted the nomination of the Citizens' Union, declaring:

> I am a Republican and I expect to remain one, but I am completely in sympathy with the purposes of the Citizens Union to secure a Mayor for the great city who shall be "free from all partisans obligations." Such a Mayor, if elected, I shall certainly be. In making appointments, it shall be my endeavor to fill every place with an eye single to the public good. The patronage of the city shall not be used, so far as it is in the Mayor's power to prevent it, for the purpose of either strengthening or weakening one party or another or any faction of any party.[58]

Holding out little hope of patronage for the Platt machine, Low's letter sealed Platt's decision to enter a straight party ticket in the mayoralty race. Moreover, as Lord Bryce observed, "If he [Platt] allowed his machine to adopt Mr. Low, he gave a triumph to the anti-partisan doctrine, which would encourage like revolts in other cities, and strike at the root of the whole machine system."[59] As Senator Platt himself put it:

> I did not want to see Mr. Low go into the great and powerful office of Mayor of Greater New York, with the work of consolidation before him, with no other influences about him than those of men, some of whom had impressed me as humbugs, some as cranks, and all as lacking in political experience, and as generally hostile to the Republican party, and as sure to create such a friction between the city administration and the State legislature as would weaken us in a year when we had a Governor to elect, a political off-year when we could least afford to have our strength impaired.[60]

Winning decisive victories in the Republican primaries in Manhattan and Brooklyn, Platt's forces controlled the G.O.P.

City Convention which, on September 28, designated Benjamin Franklin Tracy as the Mayoralty nominee. Like Platt, Tracy had been born in Oswego, New York; he was the law partner of Platt's son, and had served creditably as Secretary of the Navy in the Cabinet of President Benjamin Harrison. A mediocre politician, his chief qualification for the nomination was his loyalty to the Platt machine.

Returning from a self-imposed exile at his baronial estate in England, Richard Croker—the pugilist "boss" of Tammany Hall, deposing his own deputy, John C. Sheehan—took over active control of the Democratic machine and commanded Robert A. Van Wyck to undertake the mayoralty race. Judge Van Wyck was "A silent dummy. A man unknown," completely and absolutely subservient to "Boss" Croker. Throughout the campaign, Van Wyck rarely took to the stump, scarcely participated in his party's rallies, and as the *World* chided, "He has not yet opened his mouth since his nomination except for the admission of beefsteak and other forms of sustenance in which he delights."[61] To round out the field, the United (Bryan) Democracy placed Henry George in the field as its candidate for the Greater New York mayoralty.

The "goo-goos" viewed the 1897 New York City mayoralty campaign as, "the most fundamental issue presented in any election since the Civil War...."[62] The election took on the significance of a crisis whose outcome would determine the future of American democracy. City government in the United States, as Andrew Dickson White glumly observed, was among the "worst in Christendom." "If self-government finally fails in New York City," Lyman Abbott of *The Outlook* warned, "it will not finally succeed in any American city; and if it fails in the American cities, it fails in America."[63] This was not merely a local election, this was a turning point in the course of Western civilization. Of course, not everyone saw the election as a crisis. Always ready to reassure the "goo-goos," the *New York Sun* chimed, "Bless your simple little Mugwump soul, the thing isn't a crisis; it's only an inflammation. It will subside."[64]

The Republicans, for their part, had little real hope of victory. Tracy was in the race to act as a spoiler, for as Senator Platt stated, "I would rather see the Tammany ticket elected than to have Seth Low chosen as Mayor."[65] The Citizens' Union movement was not so much a crusade against the corruption of Tammany Hall, as it was a holy war against organized political machines. In refusing to take into consideration the wishes of the Republican party, the Citizens' Union was acting recklessly, and the Republican indictment of the independent movement had a good deal of merit. " 'Bossism,' " the *New York Sun* declared, "is political leadership, a necessary corollary of political organization. If 'bossism' is intrinsically an evil, so also is political organization, so also is a party, for its existence implies the others."[66] Moreover, the Citizens' Union, under the dynamic R. Fulton Cutting, itself took on the aspects of a political machine, and to many Republicans the Low enthusiasts looked like "a set of canting . . . contemptible humbugs. . . ."[67]

The Republicans almost totally ignored the Democratic candidate, and directed all their fire against Seth Low. Seeking to destroy his reputation for honesty and moral rectitude, the Republicans soon found that his record in public and private life was so impeccable that he scarcely seemed human. The *New York Sun* exclaimed in desperation, "What has Seth Low to do with humanity! Isn't he above it!"[68] The G.O.P.'s candidates had to settle for attacking Low as a renegade Republican whose Mugwumpery cost the party a presidential election. Speaking at the Brooklyn Academy of Music, Benjamin F. Tracy declared:

> Mr. Low was Mayor of this City in 1884. In that great campaign when the honored statesman, James G. Blaine, was nominated for President, Mr. Low was silent. No one knew what his position was or what it was to be until after election, when he gave it out, and I have no doubt of the truthfulness of it, that he voted for Blaine. But everybody in his departments under him, every friend of his here, supposed that he was against Mr. Blaine all through his administration. It is undoubtedly true that James G. Blaine was defeated here in the City of Brooklyn. Mr. Low was a citizen here. Nobody asked him to use his influence as Mayor, but had Mr. Low as a citizen made it known that he would cast his vote for Blaine, James G. Blaine would have been elected.[69]

Republicans, it was argued, must punish traitors, and all loyal sons of the Grand Old Party ought not to allow themselves to be seduced by the moral self-righteousness of the Citizens' Union but should rally to the support of their party.

The keynote of the Democratic campaign was candidly expressed in Asa Bird Gardiner's immortal phrase: "To hell with reform." With their opposition split three ways, Croker's forces entered the campaign confident of victory. Condemning Mayor

Strong's reform administration as a failure which had raised taxes and stringently enforced a puritanical Sunday liquor law imposed by upstate bigots, Tammany promised to give New York a more economical and more liberal government. Ignoring Tracy, the Democrats concentrated their efforts on attacking Seth Low as an aristocrat, who, never having to earn his own bread, could not understand or identify with the problems of the working classes. The Citizens' Union did not try to deny that Low had been born a merchant prince, but, citing his record of friendship to labor and his civic devotion, declared that:

> Mr. Low is in very truth the ideal citizen. Born to wealth and position, he has always used both for the public good. Not only this: Mr. Low has realized as few men have ever done the responsibilities which wealth and opportunities bring with them.
>
> The poor man knows Mr. Low to be his friend, not from what he says, but from what he does....[70]

Then, too, Richard Croker was a millionaire, but of another stripe. "We know where Low got his money," The Citizens' Union stated. "Where did the Boss get his?"[71]

Henry George centered his campaign on a crusade against "Boss" rule and in defense of the democracy of William Jennings Bryan. The most energetic and surprising campaign, however, was that undertaken by the Citizens' Union. Their campaign was not directed primarily at the middle class; it did not call merely for honest, efficient, and low-cost government respectful of property rights. It aggressively went after the labor vote, and advocated a program which frightened away many of the "best people."

Realizing that only labor support could gain a victory for good government, the Citizens' Union, from its inception, sought to bring home to the workingman the fact that "Government by corrupt bosses, in alliance with corrupting corporations, is the very negation of our free institutions...."[72] While the smiling Irishman from Tammany Hall might be a good fellow willing to do a favor for his constituents, he was also willing to serve the corporations, and in the final analysis, it was the workingman who paid for those favors. Political machines, the Citizen's Union announced, "are little else except the instruments of certain business interests of individuals, and that the chiefs of these business interests in this city are the surface railroads."[73] The Citizens' Union, however, sought to break this iniquitous system, for its demands "may be found in the platforms of the American Federation of Labor, the Order of the Knights of Labor, and in thousands of local labor organizations in every municipality of our broad land."[74]

Demanding that the city "retain the ownership of its franchises," the Citizens' Union called for "stringent supervision" of all public utilities serving the city, a municipal rapid transit system, rigid enforcement of the eight-hour day for laborers working on municipal construction projects, and tenement house codes to improve the sanitary and living conditions in the crowded workingmen's quarters of New York. A massive school construction program was promised, as well as the creation of parks and playgrounds in the tenement house districts.[75] To New York's conservative classes, the Citizens' Union's program was, "manifestly Socialistic in its make-up and avowedly Socialistic in its purposes, appealing steadily to the forces of disorder and social disturbance.... "[76]

But what of their aristocratic standard-bearer? Could workingmen be expected to rally to his side? As an arbitrator of labor disputes, Seth Low had handed down a series of decisions favorable to organized labor. A heavy contributor to the University Settlement House and to labor causes, he had a strong following among the ranks of organized labor. "Seth Low," declared Harry White of the United Garment Workers of America, "is pre-eminently a just man, and one who can appreciate the circumstances of both the worker and the employer. He has, moreover, a strong sympathy for the struggles of the workers to improve their lot."[77] Martin J. Connolly, a former grand master of the Knights of Labor, asserted that 90 percent of the members of that organization would vote for Low.[78]

As an example of his popularity with the working classes, when the Socialist Labor party held a rally at 125th Street and Lexington Avenue, one of their speakers began a vigorous attack on Low as a tool of the capitalist class. Suddenly, as an observer later wrote, a laborer in the audience interjected saying that, "New Yorkers dident want Scotch Socelists from Jersey to learn them who to vote for ... ," and that Low, "gave over a million of money to the Collage to keep hands aworking during the hard times and that you was always an Arbitrator for the Unions and was fair. He said that he might not vote for you him-self but he be d——d if he could stand to hear a Scotch Socelist [from Jersey] abuse a good American citizen."[79]

On the whole, Low ran well in the working class districts, and while he did not carry any of the tenement house areas, he ran a strong second. For example, in the 5th A. D., which ran along the East River from Grand to Stanton Streets, Van Wyck polled three thousand votes, Low twenty-seven hundred, and Tracy only eighteen hundred. With the Republicans behind him, Low would have secured a decisive victory in that working class district. What cost the Citizens' Union heavily, however, was the failure to hold the middle and upper class vote.

"I am amazed," lawyer A. R. Conkling wrote, "at the opposition of Republicans of social standing. The very men who should support you warmly, are, I regret to say, opposed to you."[80] The basis for their opposition was the franchise stand of the Citizens' Union. The demand for franchise reform struck at the pockets of New York's financial magnates. As Perry Belmont declared, it was a socialistic demand which would force the business community into supporting the Tammany candidate.[81] Pinching the profits of the franchise magnates would also have an adverse effect on the financial well-being of the Republican machine, should the G.O.P. support Low. Indeed, Jacob Worth charged that Platt's opposition to Low stemmed from his close financial involvement with New York City's franchise owners.[82] As Judge William J. Gaynor observed, the most fundamental issue of the 1897 mayoralty campaign was that of public franchise control, "the right of the people to control their own streets."[83] It was no secret that the franchised corporations, preferring to bribe Tammany Hall rather than pay the city a fair royalty, where heavy contributors to the Democratic cause.[84] "Behind Seth Low," the *Sun* declared. "stalks Henry George . . . the two are inseparable."[85] The first discovery made by the Citizens' Union, according to John Jay Chapman, was that "the worst enemy of good government is not our ignorant foreign voter, but our educated, domestic railroad president, our prominent business man, our leading lawyer."[86]

The Citizens' Union's one hope of victory was Henry George. If he could pull his usual sixty-thousand plus votes, he might be able to draw enough ballots away from Van Wyck to give the election to Seth Low. As the campaign entered its last week, the *New York World* reported that Henry George's candidacy was cutting the Democratic vote in half, and that Richard Croker, greatly alarmed at the strength George was showing, feared that it would cost Tammany the election.[87] George, however, entered the campaign against medical advice; in poor physical condition, he nevertheless conducted an energetic campaign, and as the weeks unfolded, the toll of exertion began to make itself felt. It was almost as if George knew what was going to happen, for in the last week of the race, he began to talk of Seth Low. At the Ice Palace, he declared, "Seth Low is an honorable, a high-toned, and a fit man. I have no particular quarrel with Seth Low. If no better candidate were to be had, Seth Low would command the suffrage of the men who stand with me. . . . If I thought I could not win, I could say vote for Low."[88] Two days later, weary from giving four speeches in one evening, George did not retire until 1 A.M. Stricken in his sleep, he died at 4:30 on the morning of Saturday, October 30, 1897. The election was only three days away. Without George, Van Wyck's chances of election were immeasurably improved, and all Tammany rejoiced at his death.[89]

"In view of Mr. George's death," Low declared, "I wish, therefore, to say to the people of the city that I shall give myself to this contest in their behalf with a newer and higher resolve, as though I had received it as a last charge from his dying lips."[90] It was an unfortunate statement, for it sounded to many as if he were saying, "Now that George is dead, vote for me." It wrecked Edward Morse Shepard's efforts to have the Democracy of Thomas Jefferson substitute Low's name for George's on the ballot. Instead, Henry George, Jr., was placed on the ballot. The younger George could not be expected to draw the same vote as his father, and whether the George voters swung to Low or Van Wyck would decide the election.

On Tuesday, November 2, 1897, the men of New York went to the polls to elect the first Mayor of Greater New York. Late that night, the vote stood:

Van Wyck (Democrat)	233,997
Low (Citizens' Union)	151,540
Tracy (Republican)	101,863
George, Jr. (Jeffersonian Democracy)	21,093

The result was a victory for Tammany Hall by more than eighty thousand votes. With the bulk of New York's press, clergy, and professional reformers backing Low, his defeat impressed many as a collapse of morality and as a failure of democracy. "To all right-thinking men," Walter Hines Page observed, "it seems an immeasurable misfortune that you were not elected yesterday. I confess to very severe depression, as a believer in popular government."[91]

There were many reasons for the Citizens' Union's defeat. One was the unpopularity of the Strong administration. Coming into office as a reform mayor, he was forced to raise taxes and was unable to solve the politically-explosive issue of Sunday liquor sales. Then, too, with George's death, the bulk of his supporters went back to Tammany and all hope of a Low victory vanished. Had the Henry George voters swung behind the Citizens' Union instead of returning to the wigwam, Low and Van Wyck would have finished in a virtual dead heat. In addition, the Citizens' Union's progressive platform in regard to franchises and its call for positive action to aid the working classes drove away many conservatives who would have normally rallied to a good government ticket. Also, the Citizens' Union failed to win election because Seth Low was a very poor campaigner who —viewing every problem with the detachment of a man from another planet—could not cast off his aloofness and make the average man feel that he was deeply concerned with the problems besetting the common citizen. "We learned from the rank and file," Richard W. G. Welling related, "the man in the street, that his speeches contained no spark of enthusiasm and that if anyone met him his handshake contained not a particle of warmth."[92] It was one thing to sympathize with the problems of the average man; it was one thing to help him from afar, but it was quite another thing to have to shake his hand.

The prime factor, however, in Low's defeat was the political amateurishness of the Citizens' Union. "It did seem to me," Theodore Roosevelt chided, "that a little tact would have prevented a hopeless alienation of the Republican machine people."[93] In the final analysis, it was not Thomas C. Platt but the Citizens' Union which made fusion impossible. Refusing to confer with Platt, unwilling to give him assurances of patronage, rejecting all G.O.P. overtures, the Citizens' Union was the architect of its own defeat, and vividly demonstrated the psychological impediments which prevented the good government partisans from effecting a viable political movement. Unable to compromise with those whom they regarded as politically evil men, refusing to jeopardize the sanctity of their principles by fashioning pragmatic political arrangements, clinging to the absurd proposition that municipal government could somehow be divorced from the politics of the state and nation, the amateur politicians of the Citizens' Union failed to weld together an organization capable of capturing control of New York's government. Adding the Republican vote to the Union's would have given Low a majority over Van Wyck of twenty thousand votes. The election demonstrated—as Seth Low quickly pointed out to R. Fulton Cutting—"That under our American conditions, the minority party and the independents are natural allies. They may not always succeed, even when they unite, but whatever success has been had in the past has rested upon such a union. I am inclined to think that it will be so in the future."[94] The Citizens' Union would not make the same mistake twice.

All had not been for nought, though. "I can't feel that the contest has been in vain," James Bryce wrote from England, "on the contrary it seems to me that you have rendered an immense service in fighting the battle as you have done, and that you are entitled to the heartiest gratitude of all friends of good government. No municipal event of recent years has set good and evil so sharply in contrast, nor shown better the pernicious tendency of party organizations as applied to city politics."[95] Low emerged from the election as one of America's foremost champions of honest government, and once more returning to Columbia, was not at all unhappy at the contest's outcome. "On the personal side," he confided to Admiral A. T. Mahan, "I am so happy to have escaped the burdens that would have followed my election, that I am scarcely conscious of any disappointment at all."[96] He would soon be called upon to take up those burdens again, though; for Tammany's promise that "the people will have nothing to regret during the coming administration of the faithful Democrats elected yesterday," could not have been further from the truth.[97]

CHAPTER VI

The Fusion Crusade of 1901

Sodom and Gomorrah were well enough in their time, but Tammany could have given them points.

Mark Twain[1]

If the pimp wears a blue uniform, is he any less a pimp?

New York Vigilant[2]

. . . What we are about is not electing a Mayor, but saving a city.

The Nation[3]

Shortly after the mayoralty election of 1897, Carl Schurz, dean of the Mugwumps, wrote a post-mortem of the Citizens' Union's maiden campaign for *Harper's Weekly.* Asserting that the Union made an impressive initial showing, Schurz declared that the principal element of weakness in all municipal reform movements was their lack of continuity, and he urged the Citizens' Union to remain in the political field and work for good government as assiduously as Tammany Hall worked for corruption. "The reform forces," Schurz pointed out:

> between campaigns, come more or less out of contact with the masses of the people, while the representatives and agents of Tammany Hall remained constantly among the classes of the population which furnish the most votes, doing those who were in need or trouble, or who wished to enjoy this or that advantage which the law denied them, good turns in an endless variety of ways—a systematic practice which however selfish its motives, could not fail to find response and create attachments.[4]

Like Tammany, the reformers must remain among the people, educating them to the responsibilities of citizenship in a democratic society, and where possible rendering them material assistance as well. The secret of Tammany's success, reformer Talcott Williams reminded his comrades in righteousness, lay in the fact that it provided New York's immigrant masses with charitable services on a large scale, and because it provided this service its "prodigious and colossal thefts" did not arouse popular indignation. If the Wigwam was ever to be permanently defeated, Williams declared, the reform forces would have to provide the people of New York with the services they desperately needed, but which they could only get from Tammany.[5]

Having lost the 1897 election, the Citizens' Union had to decide whether it would disband until the next mayoralty, or remain on the political scene as an independent political organization, functioning much like the established parties. The Union's Executive Committee voted to continue the organization and appointed a special committee headed by Charles S. Fairchild to prepare a plan of reorganization for the Citizens' Union. On February 16, 1898, the Fairchild Committee recommended the creation of Citizens' Union district units in each of Greater New York's Assembly Districts, with membership open to all residents signing the Union's non-partisan pledge. The Assembly District units, it held, should be locally controlled, and no overall organization should be established for the present time. When city-wide nominations were to be made, the committee recommended that the district units determine the structure to be adopted by the larger county organizations.[6] By this means, it was hoped to preserve the Citizens' Union as a truly democratic organization controlled by its constituency rather than by a clique of professional politicians intent upon perpetuating their rule, and willing to subvert the substance of democracy to do so. However, the decision of the Citizens' Union to continue as a permanent political organization in the City of New York was not taken without the vigorous opposition of many municipal reformers.

Many who supported Low's 1897 candidacy broke with the Citizens' Union when it decided to become a permanent political party, and the schism produced in the ranks of New York's reformers deepened and came to a head in the pages of *Municipal Affairs* in 1900. John Jay Chapman expressed the views of many Mugwumps when he asserted that political parties were evil *per se*. Parties, Chapman declared, were not evil because they were dominated by unscrupulous leaders, but rather because political organizations assumed a life of their own, and when the welfare of the party took precedence over the welfare of the community, as was invariably the case, corruption and municipal degradation resulted. While a citizens' party may begin as a sincere effort to reform the abuses springing from the national parties, it, too, would inevitably fall into the hands of professional politicians, who to maintain their influence and standing would compromise their ethical standards. Thus, the citizens' party would inevitably degenerate, and with time would become little better than the machine-run national parties. Consequently, the organization of a permanent reform party was both impossible and undesirable.

"Reformers," Chapman proclaimed, "have got to live at the top notch of an initial enthusiasm."[7] The true reformer sought purely moral aims; he desired to benefit the community by raising its standards of political conduct. But, to do that, he himself had to remain pure. The reformer was a gadfly, who, when corruption became blatant and ethical standards declined, stung the existing political parties by leading a revolt of the independent citizens against machine rule. Fearing defeat, the politician will mend his ways, until the next time, but hopefully as time passed the educational work of the reformers would raise the ethical standards of the public who would demand of their officials a higher state of political morality. In this fashion, the reformer made a contribution to the progress of society, but to perform his function he must remain outside the political structure, acting as the conscience of the community.[8] To Chapman, the Citizens' Union under "Boss" Cutting was only a cut above the machines of "Boss" Croker and "Boss" Platt.

Others who also sought decent government for New York opposed the Citizens' Union's decision, but they dissented from the concept of a third party for more pragmatic reasons. "I believe in parties," John W. Keller declared. "Nothing can be accomplished in politics without organization, and organization itself makes parties."[9] Political parties were both legitimate and necessary, if progress were to be realized. However, when a party became corrupt, the faithful, Keller argued, should not abandon it to form a third party, which history showed would probably never achieve its goals, but should instead stay with their party and seek to reform it from within. The Citizens' Union, like all previous third party movements, will fail, and will produce no positive benefit for the cause of good government. Moreover, the Citizens' Union was a refuge for faddists and cranks. As Keller put it:

There are individuals in the community who are so independent in their ideas, so dogmatic in their opinions, so isolated in their principles, that no party can be satisfactory to them because no large number of people can ever agree with them. These individuals are wont to flock alone and to chirp at political organizations great in number, as things of evil created against the public welfare. Such individuals can never accomplish anything in politics because they can never acknowledge that anybody else than themselves can be right even when the vast majority of their fellow citizens are of a different opinion from themselves.[10]

The case of the Citizens' Union was advanced by Union spokesman A. S. Haight, who proclaimed that between "Boss" Platt and "Boss" Croker there was no choice for an honest man save the Citizens' Union.[11] With both parties corrupt, it would not be practical to try to work within their confines; it was far better to make a clean break and reform the political machines by defeating them and discrediting their corrupt and self-seeking leaders. Seth Low endorsed Haight's position, with reservations, declaring to Arthur von Brissen in March 1898, "I am clear that it is wise, by the organization of your Committee and of district organizations, as proposed, to preserve the prestige of the Citizens' Union, accumulated last fall, so that it may be used for the advancement of good government in this city from time to time in the future, as opportunity offers."[12]

He warned the Citzens' Union, though, against undertaking independent campaigns in the future. Holding that Tammany Hall was New York's primary nemesis, he counseled the Union to seek fusion with all organizations opposed to the Wigwam, and to use its influence—holding out the threat of a third party ticket at all times—to force the Republican party, the natural ally of the forces of good government in New York City, to nominate honest and capable candidates for municipal offices. If the Citizens' Union followed this policy, Low declared, then it would successfully achieve the goals for which it had been founded. However, Low still refused to join the Citizens' Union, telling von Brissen that, "I do not believe at all in the wisdom of attempting to form a permanent city party independent of the great national parties."[13] The Union should not seek office, but rather endorse the capable candidates of the major parties.

The dominating spirit behind the Citizens' Union, however, was Robert Fulton Cutting. His family had lived continuously in New York City for 250 years, and being a man of wealth, he dedicated his life to philanthropic activity in his native city. It was Cutting who determined to transform the Citizens' Union into a permanent political party. Municipal corruption, he held, demoralized the national parties and threatened democratic institutions. If the spoilsman could be denied control of the nation's cities, if non-partisan municipal government could be made a reality, the foundation would be cut from under the spoilsman, who, having no jobs to dispense, would quickly lose his control over the national parties. It would then be possible for disinterested statesmen, devoted to the public's service, to come to the fore, much to the benefit of the nation. The Citizens' Union, then, must drive the spoilsman from the urban political scene, not to advance its own selfish ends but rather to purify and uplift the national parties so that they might provide the nation with better leadership. To accomplish these goals, the Citizens' Union must become a municipal political party and not simply an ad hoc committee of "goo-goos."

The trouble with such bodies as the City Club and the Committee of Seventy, Cutting charged, was that they drew leadership and support only from the more highly educated and wealthier segment of the population, and as a consequence did not respond to the needs or reflect the aspirations of the urban masses. While such organizations may gain occasional triumphs, they can never consolidate their victories because of their estrangement from the common people. If the Citizens' Union became a full-fledged political party, Cutting asserted, and if it sought broad-based support from all segments of the community, then it would be rooted in the people, and—drawing membership from all classes—represent the requirements of all segments of the population.[14] The reformer must go to the people, for what was needed was an "infusion into the anaemic blood of our earlier reform administrations of a few red drops of what the reactionary insists upon stigmatizing as radicalism."[15] And, once in office, the reformers must meet the social needs of the masses. As Cutting phrased it:

> There is a swelling tide of human brotherhood that seeks to express itself through Democratic institutions and the religion of the Twentieth Century is destined to employ Government as one of its principal instrumentalities for the solution of social issues. We shall have a true Democracy based upon the fundamental value of the individual....[16]

Cutting won the Citizens' Union's Executive Committee to

his philosophy, and the policies pursued by the Union in the years ahead were largely determined by him.

Having decided to keep the Citizens' Union functioning, it still remained for the leadership to digest the lessons of the 1897 campaign and to formulate more effective policies for the elections to come. In June of 1898, the Citizens' Union reaffirmed its basic proposition that municipal affairs were totally independent of national politics, and asserted, "we . . . do not admit the propriety of attempts to forward National policies by a prostitution of local concerns; and shall act upon our conviction that the success of any leadership seeking such support would curse the National party in whose behalf it pleads."[17] However, the Union's leadership now realized that a strict insistance upon the non-partisan doctrine would cost them the support of the Republican party, and without G.O.P. backing, it could never hope to overthrow Tammany. They therefore decided to adopt Seth Low's policy of seeking a fusion with the Republicans in order to defeat the common enemy. The decision for cooperation, though, was not taken without the strenuous opposition of those who believed that union with the Platt machine would compromise the integrity of the Citizens' Union. But, as R. Fulton Cutting wrote John B. Pine:

> It seems to me that while the Citizens Union *must* ignore any claim of rights made by the Republican or the National Political parties in this city, it cannot ignore the existence of those bodies and the fact that they possess election machinery more or less efficient. My proposition does not admit their right to co-operate with the Union in its campaign on terms equal or even inferior, but acknowledges their existence as organized bodies and recognizes the assistance they may render the Union in the pursuit of its ends.[18]

Cutting's views, as usual, finally prevailed within the organization, and on March 27, 1899, the Union's City Committee went on record as being in favor of fusion, in future campaigns, with all genuine anti-Tammany groups.[19] But, if fusion should fail of realization, the Citizens' Union was prepared to build its own political machine, and wrest control of New York City from the boodlers. "The Citizens' Union," its Executive Committee told the people of New York on September 10, 1900:

> has been for the past year actively preparing for the Campaign of 1901. It has secured reliable District organizations in a large majority of the Assembly Districts of the boroughs

of Manhattan and the Bronx, and it will now immediately
enlarge the powers of its Committee on Organization to enable it to complete its work in those Boroughs and extend
it to the others. In addition to its enrolled membership, the
Union believes it has secured the interest of a large number
of citizens who have been personally visited and from whom
it expects active co-operation in the campaign.
The Union also realizes the importance of promulgating a
definite and positive municipal program. Its watchword will
be "Progress" and it will demand of its candidates progressive views of municipal development as well as independence
of spirit and probity of character.[20]

The political amateurs were finally beginning to appreciate
the importance of organization, and had begun to develop a
political machine of their own.

For the election of 1901, however, the Citizens' Union was
determined not to run an independent ticket if it could possibly be averted. If it proved nothing else, the campaign of
1897 showed that Tammany could be overcome only if the independents could unite with the regular Republican organization.
To make certain that its September 10 statement did not appear
as a declaration of war against the Republicans the Union's
Executive Committee also declared in favor of a general fusion
of all anti-Tammany forces. "The Citizens' Union," the statement said, "has no desire to participate in a three-cornered contest in the Mayoralty campaign of 1901, and it hopes to find on
the part of other organizations so general a readiness to co-
operate in a bona fide good government movement as to avoid
the necessity for a third ticket."[21] The call for fusion came none
too soon, for the corruption of Tammany's Van Wyck administration was fast coming to light and rivaled that of the Tweed
ring in its excesses.

Back in 1894, a New York State Legislature investigating committee headed by Clarence Lexow uncovered broad-based corruption in New York City's police department, with graft and
blackmail extending from the common roundsman to the chief
of police. The department, the Lexow report continued, was
"thoroughly impregnated with the political influence of Tammany Hall, and that the suppression and repression of crime
depended, not so much upon the ability of the police to enforce
the law, but rather upon the will of that organization or faction
to have the law enforced."[22]
The Lexow disclosures produced a wave of popular revulsion

against the alliance between Tammany Hall and organized crime and vice which resulted in the formation of the Committee of Seventy and the election of William L. Strong as mayor of New York in the fall of 1894. The Strong administration gave New York City honest and fairly efficient government. The department of sanitation, for example, under Colonel Waring, became world-famous for the efficiency and excellence of its service. The police department, under the leadership of Theodore Roosevelt, was cleaned up, and the notorious link between the police and the gamblers and brothel-keepers was smashed. However, good government did not satisfy the people of New York.

Supported by numerous political factions, Mayor Strong was called upon to satisfy the patronge demands of every element in his coalition. He tried to distribute the city's patronage among the many political bodies in the fusion movement according to their estimated voting strength, and sought to be as fair as possible in his appointments. Unfortunately, Strong's patronage policy satisfied none of the factions which had helped to elect him, and merely alienated them all. Moreover, he had come into office pledged to enforce the law strictly and without regard to partisan considerations. Accordingly, Police Commissioner Roosevelt rigidly enforced the State's excise law which forbade saloons from conducting business on Sundays. Unable to obtain beer, and denied the social intercourse afforded at the neighborhood bar, the immigrant and working class population of the city, particularly the German-Americans, were resentful of what they deemed to be a puritanical enforcement of a law forced through the State Legislature by rural interests which disregarded the personal liberties and more liberal atmosphere of a cosmoplitan city. Strong's refusal to abide a politic disregard of an unpopular law cost him the support of much of the electorate, while the frustrated patronge damands of the professional politicians rendered impossible a continuation of the fusion alliance and helped to defeat Seth Low in the 1897 mayoralty.

On January 1, 1898, Robert A. Van Wyck became the first mayor of Greater New York. A lawyer by profession, Mr. Van Wyck proceeded to provide New York City with a brilliantly ineffectual, superbly corrupt, and downright malevolent administration. A man of weak character, he allowed himself to be dangled as a puppet on a string by Richard Croker, the semiliterate Irish street-fighter who dominated New York City's Democratic organization from his baronial estate at Wantage, England. As George Brinton McClellan, Jr., Tammany's 1903 candidate for the New York mayoralty, confided to his diary, "During the Van Wyck Mayoralty, Croker frankly and openly ruled New York as a dictator, the mayor being nothing but a rubber stamp for the boss. Van Wyck was the most pitiable object who ever held a great public office, for he entirely surrendered himself to Croker and acted exactly as though the latter held him under a hypnotic spell."[23]

Homer Folks, who was a member of Greater New York's first Board of Aldermen, declared of his colleagues that "about four fifths of them didn't pretend to understand what it was all about and followed their party leaders. . . ."[24] With a mayor like Van Wyck, and aldermen as Folks described, it was only natural to expect a return of Tammany's corruption, but its intensity surprised and disgusted tens of thousands of New York's voters.

The police department, again, was to be the chief instrument for the collection of graft for Tammany, and it was among the first agencies of the city's government to feel the tomahawk of the hungry braves from Tammany. When Theodore Roosevelt stepped down as police commissioner, he was replaced by John McCullagh, an honest and capable officer, who was still serving as chief of police when Van Wyck took office. Under the new charter, the police commissioner had to be named by the police board, a bi-partisan body consisting of two Democrats and two Republicans. McCullagh stood in the way of Tammany's "reform" of the police department, but as he could only be dismissed by the police board, and since the Republicans on the board would not sanction a police chief subservient to "Boss" Croker, the problem of how to remove McCullagh proved a difficult one. It was not until May 1898 that a scheme was hit upon for accomplishing Tammany's object. Van Wyck removed the Republican members of the police board, leaving on it only York and Sexton, the Democratic members. He then named Jake Hess, a nominal Republican who was actually an unscrupulous political opportunist, as one of the new Republican board members, and declared that he would select the second Republican member at a later date. Jake Hess compliantly voted with York and Sexton to dismiss John McCullagh as police commissioner, and picked William S. Devery as acting commissioner. Tammany now controlled the police force of New York.

Under Devery, the police department of New York was transformed into a shakedown and blackmail ring for the benefit of Tammany politicians. Pool rooms and gambling houses paid regular royalties to the wardmen (plain clothes detectives who doubled as graft collectors) to guarantee immunity from police interference. The money was divided between the wardmen and high Tammany officials. In March 1900, the *New York Times* carried a report that Tammany's share of the graft from gambling operations alone came to $3.5 million per year.[25] Gambling, however, was but one of Tammany's sources of revenue. Prostitution was equally lucrative.

Brothels, like the gambling dens, also paid for immunity from police interference, and because they could function free from the fear of arrest, the city's prostitutes and madams came out into the open. Setting up shop in the tenement districts of the lower East Side, the prostitutes would have calling cards printed, and hire small children, some as young as five or six, to distribute the cards to passers-by. It was not unusual for prostitutes, under the gaze of the police, to call down to prospective customers from the windows of their tenements, and numerous instances were recorded where men—accompanied by their wives—were stopped on the street by prostitutes, who declaring that they were more attractive than their wives, would invite the men to come with them.[26] Protests from residents of the East Side and from local clergymen produced no action from the police authorities. On those rare occasions when an honest police officer took his job seriously, and arrested the prostitutes, he would be reprimanded by his superiors, reduced in rank, or transferred to a beat on Staten Island. To guard against raids by the Reverend Charles Parkhurst's Society for the Prevention of Crime which attempted to suppress vice by raiding suspected brothels and making citizens' arrests, the brothel-keepers devised the cadet system by which children were employed as look-outs, and as part-time procurers as well.

Moving into respectable, working class tenements, the prostitutes operated under the watch of the wives and children of immigrant laborers. " 'Oh, Meester Report!' an old woman wailed one evening," wrote Lincoln Steffens:

> "Come into my house and see my childer, my little girls."
> She seized and pulled me in (me and, I think, Max) up the stairs, weeping, into her clean, dark room, one room, where her three little girls were huddled at the one rear window,

From which they—and we—could see a prostitute serving a customer. "*Da, se'en Sie,* there they are watching, always they watch." As the children rose at sight of us and ran away, the old woman told us how her children had always to see that beastly sight. "They count the men who come of a night," she said. "Ninety-three one night." (I shall never forget that number.) "My oldest girl says she will go into that business when she grows up; she says it's a good business, easy, and you can dress and eat and live."

"Why don't you pull down your curtain?" I asked.

"We have no curtain," she wept. "I hang up my dress across, but the childer when I sleep or go out, they crowd under it to see."

"Ask the woman to pull her blind."

"I have," she shrieked. "Oh, I have begged her on my knees, and she won't."[27]

All efforts to drive prostitution from the tenements failed due to the refusal of the police to enforce the law. Finally, in desperation, the Episcopal Bishop of New York, Henry C. Potter, in November 1900, addressed a public letter to Mayor Van Wyck in which he castigated the police department for protecting vice. He pleaded with him to break the alliance existing between the police and the brothel-keepers:

I know those of whom I speak [the Bishop declared]: their homes and their lives, their toil and their aspirations. Their sensibility to insult or outrage is as keen as theirs who are in your household or mine, and before God and in the face of the citizens of New York I protest, as my people have charged me to do, against the habitual insult, the persistent menace, the unutterably defiled contact to which, day by day, because of the base complicity of the police of New York with the lowest forms of vice and crime, they are subjected.

I call upon you, sir, to save these people who are in a very real way committed to your charge from a living hell, defiling, deadly, damning, to which the criminal supiness of the constituted authorities, set up for the defense of decency and good order, threaten to doom them.[28]

Embarrassed by Bishop Potter's strong letter of protest, and condemned by virtually all of the city's civic and religious organizations, the Tammany regime dared not ignore the blatant police corruption which it had fostered, but it did not wish to destroy a lucrative source of revenue. Consequently, Richard Croker announced the formation of a Committee of Five, headed by shipowner Lewis Nixon, to investigate corruption in the New York City bureaucracy. Nixon's committee frankly admitted that there was a gambling ring within the police department, and uncovered specific instances where police officials had shaken down prostitutes. The names of the offending officers were turned over to the District Attorney's office, and a few policemen were dismissed and some were jailed for blackmail.

But it was all a show. The Nixon Committee's revelations barely scratched the surface of Tammany's corruption, and after a few months of investigation, the Committee, early in 1901, announced that there were no longer any protected gambling establishments or brothels in New York and disbanded. Aware that the Nixon Committee was designed to whitewash Tammany, the reformers, late in November of 1900, set up a Committee of Fifteen whose members included Frank Moss of the *New York Vigilant,* Felix Adler, Alfred T. White, and Jacob Schiff. The Committee of Fifteen, joined by Court of Special Sessions Justice William Travers Jerome, raided gambling houses where the Nixon Committee had said that there were no gambling houses, and broke into brothels where Tammany asserted that there were no brothels; in short, it made life utterly miserable for "Boss" Croker. Evidence connecting Tammany officials and high police officers with organized crime and vice was given over to the District Attorney, but, except for isolated cases, nothing was done to smash the boodle rings.

Justice Jerome, however, by his flamboyant and quixotic raids in Tenderloin district, won the idolatrous admiration of the people of the East Side. His name became a household word, and personified integrity in the public service. Outwardly, Jerome was a crusader for decency and a tireless champion of the East Side masses, but close associates saw another side of his character. "Jerome," reformer Laurence A. Tanzer recalled, "was a man who loved publicity. He had a very active and eloquent way of campaigning and carried the people with him and they thought that he was a great man, but those who were closely associated with him, including Ephraim Jacob, used to report to me that it was a case of a man who liked to be in the limelight, always liked to have publicity."[29] With Jerome it was not what was said about him that mattered; so long as he was talked about he was happy. A demagogue in the best democratic sense of the word, William Travers Jerome would be a man to be watched. His raids garnered him publicity, but did little to eradicate the corruption which blighted the municipal life of New York.

In the winter of 1900–1901, corruption in the police department reached its zenith, and the honest members of the force had been systematically and thoroughly demoralized. Roundsmen (foot patrolmen), like wardmen, also participated in the shakedown and blackmail rackets. It was charged that police officers were shaking down beggars for a cut of their daily take, and police blackmail of pushcart peddlers was notorious throughout the city. Many officers doubled as pimps, procuring out-of-town customers for protected brothels. Demands that William S. Devery be fired as acting police commissioner fell on deaf ears, and Mayor Van Wyck had the temerity to repeatedly declare that Chief Devery was the best commissioner of police New York ever had.

The State Legislature, though, saw the matter differently, and early in 1901 it abolished the Police Board and commanded Van Wyck to name a single police commissioner. Under pressure from all sides, Tammany could not very well elevate Devery to the commissionership, so instead, on February 22, 1901, it installed the amiable and pliable Michael G. Murphy as chief of police. Murphy obligingly named William S. Devery as his first deputy commissioner, and promptly abdicated all power and responsibility to his deputy. The only aspect of police corruption which met with popular approval was the practice of saloon-keepers paying Tammany a fee to be permitted to do business on Sundays in violation of the Raines law. Part of Tammany's corruption at least had a base in the popular will. Generally, however, police corruption reached an all-time high under the Van Wyck administration. "Deveryism" became synonymous with corruption, and as the Citizens' Union proclaimed:

> Paid by the people to suppress crime and disorder, the Police Department is using its great power, under the direction and supervision of Tammany Hall leaders, to secure regular payments of money from gamblers and dive-keepers, in return for freedom from police interference. In other words, the Police Department, which is paid and maintained by the people to suppress vice, is instead licensing vice and crime and collecting large fees for the benefit of Tammany Hall.[30]

Police corruption, though, was only half the story. In 1899, the New York State Legislature appointed another committee to investigate the New York City government. The findings of the Mazet Committee were more revealing than usual because of the cooperation of Richard Croker. "So you are working for your own pocket?" Counsel Moss asked "Boss" Croker. "All the time!" was the laconic reply.[31] To Croker, politics was a business, and all businessmen were out to make a profit. Invoking the divine right of property, he frankly admitted that he used the government of the city to fatten his pocketbook, and challenged Albany to do something about it. Issuing its report in January 1900, the Mazet Committee concluded that the vast majority of New York's officials were incompetent, and held their offices only because of the favor of Tammany Hall.[32] As a case in point, John B. Sexton, the president of the city's Board of Health, when asked to comment on the contributions made to public health by the famous German bacteriologist Robert Koch replied, "Who is this man Koch?"[33] The Committee also condemned the habitual Tammany practice of selling judgeships, and of shaking down municipal employees for contributions to Tammany's political campaign chests. It was estimated that a judicial seat could be purchased for about ten thousand dollars, though all judges were expected to make periodic gifts to the Wigwams's warchests which considerably increased the total cost of the position. Every municipal employee, regardless of his rank or position, was required to kick in with weekly payments to Tammany Hall. Street cleaners, for example—to keep their jobs —had to turn over fifty cents a week to the Democratic ward-heeler.[34] In despair, the Mazet Committee urged the reduction of the mayor's term of office from four years to two, and a revision of the city's charter in an attempt to rectify the more glaring abuses. But it did little to clean up New York's government.

To win the support of the city's financial interests, especially the Whitney-Ryan traction combine, Tammany gave away valuable franchise rights on terms far below their true value, and systematically under-assessed the property of franchised corporations. Indeed, throughout the city of New York, Tammany assessors could be prevailed upon, for a reasonable fee, to undervalue real estate.

But perhaps Tammany's greatest crime was in its absolute neglect of the city's school system. Van Wyck's yearly appropriation for new school construction was well less than half the sum which would later be appropriated by the Low administration, and this neglect was reflected in the fact that in the fall of

1901, some 5,269 children were denied admission to the public schools of Manhattan for lack of accommodations. An additional 58,123 pupils were receiving only a half day's instruction. While New York's government might not have been as bad as Sodom and Gemorrah, the Citizens' Union's charge that "its city officials have come with alarming regularity from that class which bears and deserves the name criminal," was not greatly exaggerated.[35]

To the men of the Citizens' Union, Tammany Hall, more than ever before, seemed to be a towering edifice of malignancy which had to be torn out from the vitals of New York City's government before it poisoned the entire body politic. As for "Boss" Croker, he came to symbolize the nucleus of this political cancer—the man-snake who, in writhing his way through the streets of New York, polluted everything he touched. It was against this background of corruption and municipal degradation that the Citizens' Union prepared to wage its second crusade. To be successful, fusion with the Republicans must be effected, and in November 1900, Seth Low wrote the Union reminding it of its primary object. "The first duty of the hour," he declared:

> is to define clearly the object to be attained. That surely is to rescue the city from the control of Tammany Hall. No incidental object should be permitted to obscure that well-defined purpose. Tammany Hall, under its present leadership, although it makes the Democratic nominations, is not in fact a Democratic organization. Citizens of every shade of political belief ought, therefore, to be willing to unite in rescuing the city from its domination. I believe in non-partisanship in city affairs; but I also believe that in every American community, the independents and the minority party are natural allies for the purpose of disciplining the majority party.[36]

However, a crusade for good government alone would not be sufficient to win the masses away from Tammany. New York City at the turn of the century was peculiarly susceptible to municipal corruption because of the nature of its socio-political make-up. The Census of 1900 showed New York to be a city of 3.4 million people, but a million and a half of them lived in tenements and struggled for economic subsistence in an age which lacked even the rudiments of modern social welfare institutions. Almost a quarter million adult New Yorkers were illiterate, and another 175 thousand could neither read nor write English. New York's urban poor were a source of great political strength for Tammany Hall. Its workers constantly went amongst them relieving distress, aiding them out of petty legal difficulties, and helping them to find employment. Favors given so freely and unselfishly could not fail to win gratitude, and exposures of Tammany's misgovernment did not shock or dismay an electorate unschooled in democratic political institutions and ignorant of high standards of public service. If Tammany did steal, it atoned for it in the minds of the urban poor by the assistance it rendered them, assistance needed desperately and not easily available elsewhere. Moreover, New York's system of divided municipal government served to mask responsibility for mismanagement, and learning from the mistakes of the Tweed ring, the Wigwam perfected its techniques of peculation, clothing it in a mantle of legalisms which produced that curious species of political morality which George Washington Plunkitt designated as "honest graft."[37]

The reformers were not without hope, however. While Tammany fed on human misery and grew strong by alleviating economic hardship, it was not immune from the ethnic hostilities which complicated the city's political life. The backbone of the Tammany machine was New York's Irish population. Fully one-third of the city's 3.4 million residents were of Irish extraction, and with the fall of William Marcy Tweed in 1871, control of New York's Democratic organization passed into Irish hands. Their loyalty to the Wigwam was exceeded only by their loyalty to the Roman Catholic church, and while it was not exempt from the factional squabblings endemic to the Irish character, Tammany's domination of the city's Democratic party was never effectively challenged, and no large numbers could ever be persuaded to take the warpath against the Sachems of the Wigwam. In contrast, New York's Grand Old Party drew its greatest support from the city's 737 thousand Yankees, 61 thousand Negroes and from the small Scandinavian communities centered in Brooklyn. Badly outnumbered by the Irish, the Yankees would win in 1901 only if they could appeal to New York's sizeable German, Jewish, and Italian communities. The natural inclination of New York's 762 thousand German-Americans to vote Democratic was checked by their resentment at the party's Irish leadership which effectively barred non-Irish Democrats from positions of power within the party hierarchy. However, the temptation to join the Yankees in a concerted effort to dethrone the Irish from the political control of the city's gov-

ernment was tempered by the insistence of the Yankees upon
a dry Sabbath. To get and keep the German vote, the fusionists would have to pledge the widest possible latitude in the enforcement of the excise laws. Similarly, to win the allegiance of
the city's 700 thousand Jews and 145 thousand Italians, who
were also disgruntled with Irish domination of the Democratic
party, the reformers would have to promise and provide the social services which Tammany had been extending to the residents of the lower East Side and of "Little Italy."

Unless the reformers coupled their call for honest government
with a well-developed program to meet and satisfy the social
needs of the working classes, the *New York Vigilant* warned, reform government would fail. "The help now being extended to
the decent people of the East Side," the *Vigilant* lamented:

> is very tardy; few, indeed, have spoken any word of sympathy
> for the unfortunate Negroes who were clubbed for their col-
> or; and the movement for tenement-house reform lags sadly.
> If there came such a revival of brotherly kindness and of jus-
> tice and fair play as will send the cultivated and well-to-do
> with practical aid and sympathy to the dwellers in dark and
> vicious tenements, and to those who are oppressed, they will
> learn and understand, and Tammany will lose them.[38]

On the whole, though, prospects for the overthrow of Tammany Hall appeared good. The Wigwam had gone too far, become too open in its corruption and contempt of public decency,
and New York's misgovernment had become a national disgrace.
"Except Philadelphia," declared the *World's Work*, "no other
American city has suffered such degradation."[39]

During the closing weeks of 1900, the Citizens' Union began
to give serious consideration to the selection of an anti-Tammany candidate for the 1901 mayoralty. Many members of the
Union considered Seth Low to be the leader of New York's good
government forces, and fully expected to renominate him as the
Citizens' Union's standard-bearer for the coming campaign. From
Washington, Vice-President-elect Theodore Roosevelt stated, "I
do not know whether you were pleased, but I was immensely
pleased with the Sun's coming out about you for Mayor. It
showed such a wholesome change of attitude on their part."[40]
Low, however, was not pleased. As was the case in 1897, he did
not wish to undertake the race for the mayoralty, and in November 1900, wrote Jacob H. Schiff of the Citizens' Union informing him that he was upset to hear that he was being boomed

as a possible mayoral candidate. "I am much disturbed," he told Schiff:

> by the disposition, which is so evident on many sides, to use my name in connection with the contest for the Mayoralty next autumn. This is entirely contrary to my desire, for many reasons; but especially because I feel that at the University I am really rendering the public a greater service than I could render it even as Mayor of New York. Four years ago, I felt very differently. Then I felt constrained as one who had favored consolidation and had helped to draw the charter, to give to the city the opportunity to command my services if it wished them. I feel under no such constraint now. On the other hand, if I were again to accept the nomination, I should feel obliged to retire absolutely from the University, whether I were elected or not; for I could not ask the University to keep at its head a man who was constantly subordinating its interest to other   duties.[41]

Low enjoyed his work at Columbia, and was not anxious to leave the university for the uncertainties and ingratitude of political life, and he did nothing to encourage the pro-Low faction within the Citizens' Union. Writing to Lord Bryce, Low maintained that there were at least a half-dozen men in New York City who could beat Tammany, and expressed the hope that the fusion forces would be able to unite on at least one of them. He was not prepared, at this time of life, he told Bryce, to enter upon, "the very laborious duty of cleansing an Augean stable on a scale worthy of Hercules himself."[42] Bryce did not give Low any consolation, replying, "I cannot help hoping you may consent to be the Reform candidate.... "[43] However, there was a faction in the Citizens' Union which felt that having lost with Seth Low in 1897, a new candidate should be brought forth for the 1901 contest, and as New York was a heavily Democratic city, they believed that the forces opposed to the Wigwam should rally around an independent Democrat. This latter faction grew increasingly stronger as the winter wore on, and in February 1901, the *Times* reported that the majority sentiment of the Citizens' Union favored Bird S. Coler, New York City's comptroller and one of the few honest members of the Van Wyck administration, as the mayoral nominee.[44] There was yet hope that Seth Low could remain at Columbia.

Even more important than the question of who would lead the fusion movement was the necessity for effecting an alliance

with the Republican organization, the chances of which looked
extremely good as 1901 approached. Late in January, Thomas
Platt declared that the Republican party was prepared to support a non-partisan candidate for the mayoralty, and added that
he, too, favored the proposal of nominating an independent
Democrat. Asked if he had any preferences, he replied by naming John D. Crimmins. Asked if he would consider the possibility of having Seth Low lead the fusion cause, he answered,
"If Seth Low is the best and strongest candidate we can get,
then I would be in favor of Seth Low."[45] Obedient to their master's voice, the Republican County Committee of New York the
next month endorsed the idea of running a full fusion slate in
the fall campaign, and pledged cooperation with all anti-Tammany forces.[46]

The willingness of the Republicans to accept fusion was enthusiastically greeted by the Citizens' Union, and optimism was
the dominant note at its April convention held at Cooper Union.
A committee of seventy (later raised to 107 members) was elected
to select a mayoral candidate, and it was empowered to consult with other anti-Tammany groups regarding the formation
of a complete fusion ticket. Also, at its April 25 meeting, a platform was adopted which displeased many of the more conservative "goo-goos" in the Citizens' Union. Declaring that "The government of the City of New York is a disgrace, and the men
controlling it are using public office for private plunder," the
Union's platform called for police reform to end, once and for
all time, the blackmail rings feeding on protected vice, gambling, and liquor. It demanded adherence to the civil service
laws, the end of Tammany's shakedown of municipal employees,
and a stop to franchise give-aways such as the infamous Ramapo
water scheme. The Union called for municipal ownership of
the city's water supply system, and the acquisition, at just compensation, of gas and electric light utilities, provided adequate
merit system safeguards were introduced. Municipal ownership
of all public service franchises were demanded, with short term
lease to private interests at adequate compensation to the city.
Stringent supervision of all franchised corporations was asked
to insure efficient service at the lowest possible cost. As in 1897,
an expanded program of school and public library construction
was promised. More neighborhood parks, playgrounds, and public baths were pledged, and equal enforcement of the real estate
laws demanded. For labor, the Citizens' Union urged strict en-

forcement of the tenement house laws, and an effort to strengthen the city's building codes. Increased employment of labor by the city on public works projects, with an eight-hour day at no reduction in wages, was pledged.[47] The platform was not happily received uptown.

The Citizens' Union platform, declared the *New York Times,* was a triumph for the socialist and labor elements in the reform movement, it was a "tower of babel" sure to ruin the organization, and certain to defeat the anti-Tammany cause.[48] The fusion alliance, which was to be completed over the next few months, was, as John DeWitt Warner observed, an uneasy coalition of uptown conservatives who wanted honest, efficient, and low-cost government, and East Side progressives who had a broad program of social and political reform. "On questions of city progress," Warner pointed out, "it is the cultured and well-to-do classes of New York among whom ignorance and narrowness most prevail; and the wage-earning masses, largely of foreign birth, who are more enlightened and progressive in spirit."[49] Realizing what they were facing, the Citizens' Union's campaigners when they were uptown spoke of honest, efficient, and low-cost government, but, on the East Side, they spoke about franchise reform, municipal ownership, and tenement house reform. Unfortunately, too much attention has been paid to the uptown campaign, and not enough given to the downtowners.[50]

"The wage-earner of New York is not dangerous," R. Fulton Cutting declared, "but distrust may make him so. If he is suspicious, it is because he is suspected. The Citizens' Union has not distrusted him, and he has responded to our confidence."[51] The more liberal "goo-goos," such as Cutting and Low, had a genuine concern for the problems of the urban masses, and a real desire to aid them, though they did not always know how or in what ways they could best be helpful. They realized that the true test of good government was not simply honest, efficient, and low-cost administration, but rather it was how effectively government met the needs of the people. As Frank Moss observed:

> The true test of its [New York City's] progress is not in its increase of population, nor in its appropriations for governmental expenditures, nor in the size of its roll of office-holders, nor in its buildings, its lists of millionaires, nor even in its charities. It is in the condition of its common people. Are they comfortable, are they happy, are they prosperous, is

their outlook improving? If so, then we KNOW that the city is progressing on the strongest, the richest, the noblest, the most inclusive lines.

If the people are being debased by the unchecked proximity of vice and crime, if they are being diseased by bad conditions in their homes, and by lack of proper provisions by the city for health, rest, and recreation; if the education of the children is being neglected, if they are overcrowded and unfed, overworked and underclothed; if they are growing poorer and weaker and more miserable—then, in spite of the show of population and buildings and wealth and grandeur and governmental magnificence, the city is not progressing.[52]

A healthy city, they knew, could not be erected on a foundation of human misery and degradation, and despite the fulminations of the *New York Times* and the uptown conservatives, they continued to champion tenement house reform, increased employment of labor by the city, and more and better schools. The Citizens' Union's campaign book contained a chapter devoted to Tammany's "crimes" against labor, and it vigorously sought to attract labor support.

Early in May, after New York had had time to adjust to the Citizens' Union's "radical" platform, the Union selected a conference committee of twelve, headed by Willis L. Ogden, to confer with other civil and political organizations in the selection of a suitable anti-Tammany candidate for the mayoralty.[53] This was followed by a Citizens' Union invitation, on May 14, for a fusion conference of all groups opposed to Tammany in order to undertake and coordinate a concerted campaign against Crokerism.[54] However, the Citizens' Union made it clear that while it would confer with other political bodies, and that while it had no preconceived mayoral candidate in mind, it would nevertheless refuse to endorse any nominee of the fusion conference whom it considered unfit for the office, and would not tolerate the dictation of any political faction or machine. The Union made it apparent that though it would consult the wishes of many organizations, in the final analysis the mayoral nomination would be for it to make—others could accept or reject their choice as they pleased. As in 1897, the Citizens' Union still claimed infallibility and a monopoly of wisdom on municipal matters.

The appeal for a fusion conference, however, met with a favorable response from numerous groups, the most important of which was the New York County Republican Committee, which voted to confer with the Citizens' and independent groups on local nominations for the fall elections.[55] Thomas Platt's motives for endorsing fusion remain unclear, but according to the historian of the Platt machine, he had been so weakened by reform inroads into the federal patronage that he was no longer the absolute master of the New York State G.O.P.[56] Moreover, the Citizens' Union had trounced him in 1897, and a number of Republican Assembly Districts had defied his authority and endorsed Low's candidacy. If, after the disclosures of the Mazet Committee, Platt remained aloof from fusion, it would be most doubtful that he could carry the New York City Republican organization with him. Besides, with the Grand Old Party in control of the federal and state governments, Platt could afford to be magnanimous. His concern was not on what terms he would accept fusion, but rather whom would he be forced to accept as fusion's nominee—Seth Low would be too humiliating.

No action was taken by the fusion confrerees over the summer of 1901, though the chief political pastime in New York City that season was speculation on who would be chosen to lead the anti-Tammany crusade.[57] Within the Citizens' Union, the overwhelming majority of the membership, by May of 1901, was reported to favor an independent Democrat, with Bird S. Coler leading the list of those considered suitable. He was the first choice of the anti-Tammany Greater New York Democracy, but it was rumored that "Boss" McLaughlin of Brooklyn, who was feuding with the "Master of Manhattan," wanted Coler as the Democratic mayoral nominee, and this did little to help his supporters in the Citizens' Union. In any case, Coler declared that he was not interested in running for mayor on any ticket.[58] Late in July, hoping to establish a consensus as to whom it would or would not accept, the members of the Union's committee of twelve were asked to list their first three choices for the mayoral nomination. The names which appeared most frequently were those of Bird S. Coler, George Foster Peabody, and John DeWitt Warner.[59] All were independent Democrats. Seth Low's name did not appear. But, once again, the Union's confrerees were unable to agree on a single standard-bearer.

Meanwhile, the Republicans were said to favor Charles A. Schieren, former mayor of Brooklyn, who was also popular with the city's German-American voters, as the fusion nominee.[60] The Republicans, however, aware that consistency was the hobgoblin of small minds, constantly interjected new candidates for the anti-Tammany nomination. Finally, in August, the oracle spoke. Thomas Platt, asserting that no Republican could be elected in New York City in 1901, declared that for the good of the fusion movement, an independent Democrat should be named, but cautioned against premature speculation, saying that the conference room was the proper place to determine the fusion mayoralty candidate.[61] On hearing that the Citizens' Union had taken a straw poll of its committee of twelve, the Republicans, remembering the straw poll of 1897, angrily denounced the Citizens' Union for plotting to dictate the nomination of Seth Low.[62] Their charge was somewhat irrational, for Low's name was never mentioned, but as the *Times* correctly surmised, Platt's call for the nomination of an independent Democrat was made only to avoid the embarrassment of having to accept Low in 1901 after spurning him in 1897. It concluded that while Low was the logical fusion candidate, his nomination was impossible because of "Boss" Platt's vehement opposition.[63]

On August 13, Lemuel E. Quigg wrote Low at his summer home in Maine informing him that New York City's Republican A.D. leaders did not know if anyone could defeat Tammany Hall, but they felt that of all possible fusion candidates, he would run the best race. Quigg declared that the leadership's advice to nominate an independent Democrat was simply an effort to deflate the Low boom among the G.O.P.'s rank-and-file.[64] Platt's position proved to be extremely unpopular both within his own party and in the general press. The *New York Telegram,* for example, expressing its disgust at the political squabblings which threatened to wreck fusion, declared that it did not care whether the next mayor was a Democrat or a Republican, so long as he was beholden to no partisan interest.[65] Holding to his position into mid-August, Platt threw his support to Charles S. Fairchild, a former member of the Cleveland cabinet, for the mayoralty, but seeing that Fairchild's name was not greeted with enthusiasm, and under increased pressure from within his own party, he finally abandoned the idea of nominating an independent Democrat.[66] On August 23, Platt was reported to have pledged the Republican party to the support of any candidate named by the fusion conference—even Seth Low.[67] Nevertheless, he still hoped to forge a solid Republican front in favor of anyone but Low, and hoped that Brooklyn's Charles S. Schieren would be the man to stop the Low bandwagon. However, Lemuel E. Quigg reported that at a meeting of Brooklyn A.D. leaders, called by a Mr. Dady, the district chiefs voted 17 to 1 in favor of Low over Schieren, and that Lt. Governor Woodruff, on behalf of the Kings County Republican organization, would place Low's name in nomination at the September fusion conference.[68] As September approached, the Republicans of Brooklyn stood solidly for Low, while those from Manhattan and the Bronx, though committed to no one, were leaning in his direction.

Besides the Republicans, the Citizens' Union also had to take into account the wishes of the many ethnic groups and anti-Tammany Democratic splinter organizations in the fusion alliance. The powerful German-American Reform Union, led by *Staats-Zeitung* editor, Herman Ridder, united with Platt to support the candidacy of Charles A. Schieren, though the Brooklyn German-Americans, along with their Republican neighbors, spurned Schieren in favor of Seth Low.[69] The anti-McLaughlin Brooklyn Democracy was championing Col. Edward M. Knox, but the Greater New York Democracy, supported by the influential *New York World,* was still pushing Bird S. Coler. On August 23, the anti-Tammany conference committee met to set a date for the opening of the fusion convention, and the general sentiment of the conference was that a Democrat should receive the nomination for the mayoralty. But, at this point, Thomas Platt announced that under no circumstances would the Republican party accept Bird Coler, and that between the two he would much prefer Seth Low.[70] Coler was a well-known advocate of municipal ownership, and it was also known that Platt had close financial ties to the public utilities interests. This was probably at the root of his vehement opposition to the comptroller's candidacy. In retaliation, the Greater New York Democracy, much to Platt's delight, announced that it would, under no circumstances, support Seth Low, because it believed that he could not win, and declared that if he were nominated, the organization would return to the Wigwam.[71]

The situation within the Citizens' Union was no less confused. Realizing that Republican support was essential to fusion success, Willis L. Ogden, chairman of the committee of twelve, declared, the day after Platt's anti-Coler statement, "I do not believe the conference will nominate anyone in opposition to Senator Platt's wishes."[72] As for the Union's attitude toward Seth Low, the *Telegram*—on August 28—reported that the Citizens' Union was cold to his candidacy, while the *World* of the 29th asserted that he was the first choice of the Union.[73] The truth, as one might suspect, was midway between the two reports. On August 29, the Citizens' Union's committee of one hundred, voting for its first three mayoral choices, gave twenty-six votes to Charles S. Fairchild and Seth Low; George L. Rives followed with eighteen votes, while Bird S. Coler with seventeen had slipped to fourth place.[74] In the committee of twelve, however, George Foster Peabody led the pack with eight votes, followed by George L. Rives and John DeWitt Warner with seven, while Bird Coler, F. Norton Goddard, and Seth Low brought up the rear with four votes apiece.[75] The results of the voting failed to produce a strong sentiment on behalf of any candidate, although Bird Coler's strength had fallen appreciably. Part of the reason for Coler's decline was, of course, Platt's opposition, but even more important in the waning of his support were continued reports that Hugh McLaughlin was backing him for the Democratic mayoral nomination. As August ended, the Citizens' Union demanded Coler's assurance that if considered by the fusionists, he would renounce the Democratic nomination for mayor. Failing to receive any such guarantee from Coler, the Union droped his name from its list of suitable candidates.[76] As September approached, the fusion forces were as far as they ever were from agreement, and no end to their petty wrangling seemed to be in sight.

"The elements combining now in opposition to the present city administration," the *Journal of Commerce* proclaimed early in September, "are so discordant that nothing could bring them together except a profound belief in the deep-seated corruption of several branches of the city government."[77] Keeping the goal of defeating Crokerism and Deveryism uppermost in mind, the discordant forces of reform began to pull together as September progressed, and Seth Low's fortunes began to rise. The *World* reported that while Seth Low would rather not undertake another political campaign, it asserted that he would yield if he proved to be the only candidate around whom fusion could be effected.[78] Responding to Low's tacit consent to run, the committee of one hundred, meeting on September 4, conducted another preferential vote with John DeWitt Warner leading the field with forty-four votes followed by George Foster Peabody at thirty-nine, Seth Low at thirty-three, and George L. Rives at twenty-seven votes. But, more significant than this was the fact that Low received sixteen first choice ballots compared to seven for Peabody, five for Warner, and only four for Rives.[79]

Two days later, the *Times* declared that it was the consensus of professional politicians that Seth Low would be the fusion choice for Mayor.[80] The anti-Low forces prepared to make their last stand.

Charging that the independent Democrats named by the Citizens' Union as possible mayoral nominees were only figureheads, the *New York World* asserted that Thomas Platt was engineering the nomination of Seth Low by the fusion conference, and was using the Citizens' Union as a pawn in his own devious game of chess. Declaring that Low was much more of a Republican now than he was in 1897, it opposed his candidacy on the grounds that a Democrat should be named to govern this overwhelmingly Democratic city. Bird Coler, the *World* proclaimed, would have made the best candidate, but since he apparently could not be nominated, it urged the selection of George L. Rives.[81] At the same time, Herman Ridder came out in favor of John DeWitt Warner. A week later John P. Peters wrote E. P. Wheeler of the committee of twelve, declaring that while Low would make an admirable mayor, he would be a weak candidate, because "Mr. Low has not won political friends among the people at large since the last campaign."[82] He concluded by asking if Low could be relied upon to shun Platt's influence once in office. And, in Brooklyn, that borough's Citizens' Union, accusing the New York organization of dictatorship, demanded the nomination of Bird S. Coler. The following day, under pressure from its Brooklyn branch, the Union agreed to reconsider Coler, but because of Platt's vigorous opposition to him, the reconsideration was only nominal.[83] The anti-Low forces, characterizing the Columbia president as a loser, had a considerable impact, for on Friday, September 13, the *Times* reported that Low's fortunes were sinking rapidly.[84] Indeed, only four days later, on the eve of the opening of the fusion conference, a resolution mandating the Citizens' Union to nominate an independent Democrat was defeated in the Union's City Committee by a single vote.[85] The pro-Low forces, though, were by no means idle.

"What is the objection to men of the Seth Low type?" asked the *New York Vigilant*. "He is independent, fearless, not beholden to any boss political or capitalistic. His qualifications are superb."[86] And Nicholas Murray Butler also brought his influence to bear on behalf of his boss. Writing to E. P. Wheeler, Butler pointed out that Republican support would be fundamental to the success of any fusion ticket, that the Democrats could not be relied upon to vote for the fusion candidate even if he were an independent Democrat. Low, he declared, as a Republican would have the full support of the G.O.P. rank-and-file, would win the independent vote because of his stature as a municipal reformer, and would carry Brooklyn by a wide margin since he was a well-remembered son of the "City of Churches." Low, he concluded, from all points of view, would be the ideal fusion candidate.[87] Butler exerted himself beyond measure on Low's behalf, though his motives were not entirely unselfish. According to George McAneny, Low "hated to give up Columbia." But, "Mr. Butler was always anxious to have him give up Columbia."[88] So active was the Columbia faculty in the effort to secure the fusion nomination for Low that George B. McClellan later declared that, "It was an open secret that all the Columbia influence was employed to secure for Low the fusion nomination for mayor against Shepard, and that when he was elected Columbia heaved a sigh of immense relief."[89] McClellan's statement was overdrawn; Professor Butler simply wanted Columbia's presidency, and the incumbent had to be gotten rid of. In any case, the pro-Low faction was led by Timothy L. Woodruff, but as the fusion conference was about to open, the *World* reported that Woodruff could count on the support of no more than one-third of the fusion delegates.[90]

Hoping to avoid the impending stalemate, the Citizens' Union's conference committee sought an acceptable compromise candidate, and put forth the Union's chairman, R. Fulton Cutting. Cutting, however, absolutely declined to accept the mayoralty nomination, feeling that it would alienate other elements in the fusion alliance if the head of the Citizens' Union accepted the nomination of his own movement.[91] As the fusion conference opened, pro-Low forces met anti-Low factions in what promised to be a free-for-all. The opposition to Low was directed not so much at him as it was an expression of anti-Platt sentiment. Many in the Citizens' Union erroneously felt that the Republicans were pushing Low too hard, were too ready to accept him, and feared that the machinations of Thomas Platt were behind his boom.[92]

The fusion conference committee of eighteen began its deliberations on Wednesday, September 18, 1901. The confrerees represented numerous political and ethnic groups, the more important of which were the Citizens' Union, the Republican

County Committee of Manhattan, Kings, Queens, and Richmond, the Greater New York Democracy, the Brooklyn Democracy, and the German-American Reform Union.[93] It should be understood that the fusion conference was not empowered to nominate a mayoral candidate, its only purpose being to recommend a standard-bearer more or less acceptable to all factions, then each body represented in the conference, at its own city convention, would either second the recommendation of the conference or take such other action as it thought appropriate. Unfortunately, there was no record of the conference preserved, and knowledge of what occured there must be gleaned from the reminiscences of individual observers. The *New York World* described the scene as a seven-hour wrangle, and by all accounts it was a noisome, angry meeting.[94]

To begin the conference, the Citizens' Union announced that either George Foster Peabody, John DeWitt Warner, George L. Rives (all independent Democrats) or Seth Low would prove acceptable to it. The Republicans were now solid for Low, but most confrerees felt that an independent Democrat should be chosen. However, after hours of heated discussion, the Democratic organizations represented in the conference were unable to resolve their differences, and failed to unite on any Democrat. Finally, a first ballot was taken and Seth Low received eleven of the eighteen votes.[95] According to E. P. Wheeler, the strongest support for Low came from the Tenth Ward—a working class tenement district—and that this support was instrumental in turning the conference's sentiment in his favor.[96] After the first ballot had been taken, Otto Kempner of the Brooklyn Citizens' League threw his support to Low, and R. Fulton Cutting of the Citizens' Union then declared that his organization would also endorse Low. John C. Sheehan of the Greater New York Democracy also came around to his support, and on the second ballot, the vote stood seventeen to one in his favor, with only the irrascible Herman Ridder refusing to make the choice unanimous. "To nominate Seth Low," Ridder felt, "would be to invite defeat at the outset."[97]

Throughout the campaign, the Democrats would charge that Seth Low's candidacy was forced upon the Citizens' Union by a clever Republican machine seeking to promote its own partisan ends. As Edward M. Shepard was later to assert, "The Citizens' Union, as I understand, yielded to extreme pressure before it assented to Mr. Low's nomination."[98] This simply was not the case. As E. P. Wheeler, who had favored George Foster Peabody, confided to C. D. Wood, our "preference for an independent Democrat, rather than Mr. Low, was in no way overruled by the Committee of the Republican organization, but was surrendered because of [the] conclusion that it was impossible to get the various so-called Democratic organizations to agree upon any Democrat. . . . "[99] Moreover, as Wheeler told Shepard, the Citizens' Union was really the dominant body in the fusion conference, that it forced a number of candidates on the Republicans, and that no one could have been nominated without its support.[100] Nevertheless, to mollify the Democrats, the fusionists allowed them to fill the rest of the ticket as they pleased.[101] This gesture apparently pacified them, for, one by one, the Democratic forces fell into line behind Low.

Seth Low was formally notified of his selection by the fusion conference on September 21. "I suppose it is none of my business," Secretary of State John Hay wrote that same day:

> but I cannot refrain from expressing my great pleasure in learning that you are to lead the momentous fight against Tammany this Fall. It is a great sacrifice your fellow citizens are asking you to endure in making this fight, and in case of your election, for which I ardently pray, a still greater sacrifice is before you in reforming the government of that mighty and most ill-used city; but you must reflect that your success will inure to the benefit of every self-respecting American.[102]

Low, however, was not entirely sanguine about the prospect of leading another anti-Tammany campaign. "Only a week before," he told William G. Schermerhorn, when it looked certain than an independent Democrat would be nominated, "I had congratulated myself on my escape!" But, "when the city is making a fight like this it has a right to demand the services of any man it needs.

> For all that, I am genuinely sorry that the lot has fallen upon me. Acceptance of the nomination will compel me to retire from the Presidency of the University in which I am so deeply interested, and where I feel that I have been serving the public no less truly, and perhaps no less usefully, than I could serve it in the mayor's office. . . . Success, therefore, is, in effect, an invitation to cleanse Augean stables under conditions [reduction of the Mayor's term to two years] which give small prospect of permanent results. A defeat at the polls

... a second time, while it would not be dishonorable, would be, as you can readily understand, most unwelcome. And yet, given a genuine Fusion, I shall be constrained to stand; for New York cannot supinely accept such a government as it has; and circumstances beyond my control, and apparently beyond the control of anybody, have marked me for the leadership. I must therefore serve . . . happen what will, in the confidence that "no man was ever lost on a straight road."[103]

Resigning himself to his fate, he told John Hay, "I shall enter upon it vigorously and with good heart."[104]

On September 24, the Republican and Citizens' Union City Conventions endorsed the nominees of the fusion conference, and within the next few days the rest of the fusion bodies were to do likewise. To round out the ticket, William Travers Jerome, forced on the Republican managers by R. Fulton Cutting, was nominated for district attorney.[105] The idol of the East Side, he was one of the first politicians to appeal to New York's immigrant population, not as sons of their native lands, but as Americans. The issue, he declared, was "Decency against Indecency," and his whirlwind campaign did more than anything else to decide the contest in decency's favor.[106] For president of the Board of Alderman, Charles V. Fornes—a devout Catholic of German-French descent—was selected, and the comptrollership went to the hero of the Ramapo water fight, Edward M. Grout. All three were independent Democrats.

The fusion ticket was generally well-received. Publicist George Gunton proclaimed that the issue was nothing less than the universal struggle of "virtue against vice." And Seth Low, he declared "represents everything that is efficient, honest, ethical and progressive."[107] The *Journal of Commerce* asserted that if elected, Low would "take office" under every obligation to the respectable people of the city. . . . "[108] The normally Democratic *New York World,* which had opposed Low's candidacy, faced with a continuation of Crokerism, came around to his support declaring, "An honest, capable, sensible man is Seth Low . . . solid rather than brilliant."[109] And the *New York Times* asked if it were possible for sensible and respectable voters to support anyone but Seth Low.[110] As a matter of fact, about the only New York newspaper which opposed the fusion candidates was the *Tammany Times* which asserted, "Low means Boss Platt rule, hayseed legislation, and an end of good times. . . . "[111] With the bulk of the city's press, clergy, and civic groups supporting them, the fusionists were confident of victory. But, "Over such an opponent as Tammany," the *Telegram* reminded them, "victory cannot be won by sentiment, words, or even merely a good cause."[112] And, after all, the next move was Tammany's.

"By the summer of 1901," George McClellan related, "Croker at last realized that it would be almost impossible to elect a Tammany ticket in the autumn."[113] Consequently, he determined to "reform" the Democratic organization by dumping the pitiful Van Wyck, and nominated Edward Morse Shepard, a long-time foe of Tammany Hall who had an excellent reputation in reform circles, for mayor. In 1897, Shepard had been an ardent supporter of Seth Low, declaring him to be one of the nation's best-informed students of the American municipal scene, and had arraigned Tammany Hall as a corrupt cabal. He accepted the Democratic nomination in 1901, however, because he felt that he could, if elected, successfully defy the Democratic bosses and reform the party from within. Never denying Tammany's corruption, he asserted that he had made no deals to obtain the mayoral nomination, and declared that, like Abram S. Hewitt, he would be his own man. "Very few men have Mr. Hewitt's backbone"; the *Journal of Commerce* answered, "no one will suggest that, with all his other excellencies, Mr. Shepard has."[114] Shepard also pointed out that in 1897, when he supported the Citizens' Union ticket, Seth Low was running as an independent, but that now he was the nominee of "Boss" Platt, and that the fusion ticket instead of being non-partisan was, in fact, a disguised Republican slate. "The trouble with Mr. Shepard," *The Century's* Richard Watson Gilder announced, "is that he has too much brain. He has thought himself into an absolutely false and obstructive position."[115] Declaring that a Low victory would place the Democratic party in a poor position for the 1902 gubernatorial contest, he called upon all loyal Democrats to stand by their party, and resist the false allure of fusion. "His heart is still sound," *The Nation* opined. "We wish we could say as much for his head."[116] Shepard's acceptance of the Democratic nomination cost him the support of the bulk of New York's reformers. He was, as the inimitable Mark Twain put it, "the white end of a rotten banana."[117]

For their part, the fusionists conducted a vigorous campaign. Seth Low made a total of thirty-eight dull speeches. He was, as campaigner George W. Alger described him, "one of the most uninteresting-looking old burghers I ever saw, with no sex appeal whatsoever."[118] He gave the appearance of being cold, of talking down to his audience, and he did not inspire either enthusiasm or confidence. The campaign opened on Saturday, October 5, at Cooper Union. The *Times* reported that there was an overflow audience which stood waving arms, hats, and handkerchiefs, and cheering Seth Low for a solid minute.[119] But Lindsay Denison described the scene in somewhat different terms:

> A comfortable smile of complacency . . . lighted his [Low's] broad features. He spoke slowly, with great consideration for the possibly limited comprehension of some of his hearers. . . . When he stepped back to his chair and the final applause was rendered there came a great voice from under the farthest corner of the ceiling:
>
> "He's all right, but we wanter holler. Give us Jerome!"[120]

Though he entered the race reluctantly, Low told Columbia's John W. Burgess that he was looking forward to the campaign. "My personal tastes," he told him, "respond to the demands of political life; and I am so situated as to be indifferent to the interrupted service, which in our country, is characteristic of such a career."[121] It was unfortunate that his personality was not more attuned to the demands of successful campaigning, for in the final analysis, it was Jerome and the other Citizens' Union candidates who bore the brunt of campaign burdens.

To capture the German vote, which was chafing under both Irish domination of the Democratic party and the restrictions of the Raines Excise Law, the fusionists promised the broadest toleration, consistent with good order, of the innocent habits and customs of the city's cosmopolitan population. To win organized labor, they promised that there would be no clean sweep of municipal employees, no shakedowns, and strict enforcement of the eight-hour law.[122] But, their most effective issue was corruption. The Citizens' Union made Tammany stand, "before the public for what it really is—the exemplification of all that is bad in government."[123] Playing up the issue of protected vice, it appealed to New York's immigrant population to save their sons and daughters from Tammany's contamination. On October 9, Seth Low promised that if elected, his first official act as mayor would be to dismiss Police Commissioner Murphy and Deputy Devery, and challenged Shepard to make a similar promise.[124] Shepard equivocated, declaring that there was a legal question involved, and thereby showed New York that he was unworthy of its trust. "Mr. Shepard," observed George Gunton:

> As soon as he became a candidate of Tammany Hall, ceased to be the Shepard who in previous years had led the fight against Tammany. He ceased to be frank; he ceased to be open and candid; he became a quibbler.
> And so Mr. Shepard . . . convinced the people that the Tammany influence was paralyzing to manhood, destructive to honor, and utterly fatal to the moral impulses and character of all who touched it.[125]

There was little doubt that fusion would win the election. Tammany's corruption had become too brazen, and New Yorkers, with Mark Twain, would have voted for Satan if he were running on Low's ticket rather than for Croker's man.[126] The Democrats had little with which they could campaign. They could neither point with pride nor view with alarm, and confined themselves to personal attacks on Seth Low. Imitating Gilbert and Sullivan, the *Tammany Times* sang:

> Koko Low, Lord High Executioner of Tioga, Headman in General, professor of prevarication and purveyor of the policies of Pooh-Bah Platt, failing in his degree of L.L.D. of lies, will decapitate himself November 5th.[127]

"It was "Boss" Croker, though, who decapitated himself, for on November 6, proclaiming "The City is Redeemed," the *New York Times* joyously announced Seth Low's decisive victory over the forces of darkness.[128]

Seth Low received 296,813 votes to 265,177 for Shepard. However, he ran well behind his own ticket. Both William Travers Jerome and Edward M. Grout outpolled the head of the ticket, with Jerome, in Manhattan alone, running better than five thousand votes ahead of Low. Low took the mayoralty by over thirty-one thousand votes, and his election was made possible because Democrats by the tens of thousands, especially on the Jewish Lower East Side, abandoned Tammany for fusion. The *Times* estimated that over forty-three thousand Democrats voted against Tammany, and it is fair to say, as John DeWitt Warner held, that the election turned on the issue of "protected Vice."[129] The task of cleansing Augean stables lay ahead.

CHAPTER VII

"The Best Administration New York Ever Had"

New York will soon have the best municipal administration in the world, and a new era of municipal government in the United States will have successfully begun.

George Gunton[1]

Mr. Low cannot give us a perfect government, and he ought not to try. If he does try the city will be in the hands of Tammany again in two years.

William S. Rainsford[2]

> Dr. Low from Brooklyn town,
>   Came across the ferry.
> Dressed out fine in cap and gown,
>   To find New York quite merry.
> 'Tis sad to see,' said Dr. Low,
>   'The people so contented.
> In two years' time Reform will show,
>   Their smiles can be prevented.'

Father Knickerbocker Adrift[3]

The election of Seth Low as mayor of New York was hailed throughout the nation as a triumph for decency and democratic government. The nation's largest city, the municipality with one of the highest percentages of foreign-born voters, had asserted its disgust with Tammany's corruption and venality by placing Seth Low, the embodiment of American municipal reform, at the head of its government. If New York—the Sodom and Gomorrah of the modern age—still retained enough decency to elect a Seth Low, was there not hope that America's other big cities might be similarly reformed, and that representative government might yet prove itself adaptable to an urban environment? "Just think of the influence of this election"; Felix Adler told the City Club of New York, "how all through the country men have taken heart—nay, how in distant countries, among distant nations, those who believe in popular government have rejoiced."[4] The people of New York, by choosing virtue over vice, had given to "the last best hope of earth" new hope that it would yet be saved. Of course, not everyone was as hopeful as Felix Adler.

A number of "goo-goos" were not at all impressed with the result of the election. "I am rather disposed, my friends," Wheeler Peckham told the City Club audience, "to be humiliated. I am rather disposed to feel badly because the margin is so small when the issue was what it was. . . . The pitiable majority in favor of simple honesty not exceeding six or seven per cent of the whole total vote. Isn't that humiliating?"[5] In a clear-cut issue between utter depravity and sterling goodness, the forces of honesty triumphed by little more than 30 thousand votes out of a canvas of some 560 thousand ballots. With vice so strong, Peckham lamented, how could decency, subject to divisiveness under the best of circumstances, possibly hope to secure permanent results? For men like Peckham, the right, sadly but ultimately, shall fail, evil prevail, and a wicked society, with no hope for regeneration or redemption, will one day have to face its judgment. Honesty had won too close a victory to last, and as one New York newspaper put it:

> Mayor Seth Low's administrtion will be bound hand and foot during the two years of its existence by the obligations which will be bequeathed to it by the Tammany government and the restrictions placed upon it by State laws.
>
> Mr. Low will be unable to initiate any public improvement of magnitude to be paid for by the issue of bonds. When he takes office on January 1 he will find the borrowing capacity of the city exhausted, with practically no possibility of a change in the situation during his term.[6]

Between those who expected the millennium, and those who envisioned a noble but futile crusade ending in ignominious defeat, stood a third group, headed by the mayor-elect of New York City, which recognized that the cause of good government in the nation's cities would be advanced or set back by how well the reform government did or did not meet the needs of the people of the Empire City.

For Seth Low, the fusion victory was but the opening battle in what promised to be a long struggle for the redemption of America's cities, and he looked forward to scoring an initial victory in the war against partisan corruption, for home rule; against institutionalized corruption, and for honest and efficient businesslike methods of municipal administration. Viewing his election as a victory for the principles of non-partisan local government which he had been advocating for two decades, Seth Low was confident that a new era in American city government had, indeed, dawned. "It is literally true," he told a post-election celebration:

> that until very recently our cities have been treated by their own population simply as pawns in the larger game of politics. If they could carry some other point by the sacrifice of a pawn they were willing to make it. It means much, therefore, when the great City of New York, to which all other cities look, says by its example, "we decline to be any longer a pawn in the game of State or National politics."[7]

However, as Seth Low conceived himself to have been elected as a result of a revolt against partisan misuse of municipal government, the creation of a fusion or reform machine to consolidate the victory of good government through a judicious use of city patronage was, thus, precluded, and some other non-political means would have to be found to give fusion political viability. "I do not believe that that administration [reform]," Low told the City Club, "can be made successful by any use of patronage, however skillful."[8] The Mayor-elect had pledged himself to a non-partisan administration of the city's government, and having repudiated the political machine process as a legitimate tool of civic reform, Low hoped to perpetuate his administration by rooting it firmly in the needs and desires of the people of New York. If this administration is to succeed, he told the City Club:

> It must fairly represent the different races and the different creeds, the different points of view which are natural to men of different upbringing, because I take it that no government can hope to be largely successful and permanently helpful to the city that is built upon a single party. It must be catholic enough in its composition to make all of the people who have created it feel that it is their government and that they have something to do in giving it its success.[9]

As a reform government must be cosmopolitan if it would be successful in New York, so, too, must it be responsive to the real needs and problems of the urban masses. "We shall try to see," he pledged:

> that the laws which have been passed by the legislature in the interest of labor are administered just as fairly as the laws in the interest of corporations. (*Applause*). We shall

try to see that the laws that have to do with the welfare of the poor are administered, if anything, even more conscientiously than those that concern the rich. (*Applause*). For the rich can take care of themselves. If there is bad government, it is the poor that suffer. (*Applause*).[10]

Silk-stocking honesty and efficiency, he promised, would not imply disregard or callousness to the needs of the working masses, but rather, a government which, because it would be honest and efficient, would be better able to advance the general welfare of all and make New York a happier community for all its people.

Hope ran high as Low's inauguration day drew near. John Martin, assaying fusion's prospects in the pages of *Municipal Affairs,* declared that for reform to be viable in New York City, Low would have to initiate radical programs to solve the city's many problems, and that, "The supreme test of the temper and courage of the new administration will be its treatment of the franchise corporations. If it shows a timid, cringing spirit or allows class sympathies to warp its judgment in favor of the rich franchise-robbers, the voters will turn again and rend it."[11] In addition, Martin asserted, the reform administration would have to take positive steps to meet the needs of the working masses by providing neighborhood parks and open-air playgrounds, public baths open all year at nominal fees, an expansion of the kindergarten system, more trade and technical high schools, plus the guarantee of a seat for every school age child. And, municipal ownership of public utilities was demanded. Others, such as John DeWitt Warner, saw police reform as the crucial issue which would determine the fate of fusion, while men like Herman Ridder considered the excise question to be of overriding importance. Problems were many, but confidence in that season of faith following fusion's victory at the polls appeared equal to the task. On the day he was inaugurated, the *Times* proclaimed that "If anything could make us forget the abominations of Tammany Government it will be the good results to come from the direction of the business of the city by so capable a Mayor as Mr. Low."[12] The *Times'* faith was shared by many.

Low arrived at City Hall early on New Year's Day, and was cordially received by out-going Mayor Van Wyck. As the hour of the inauguration approached, hundreds gathered before City Hall to welcome in the new administration which promised so

much to a municipality abused by four years of Tammany's mis-
government. Robert A. Van Wyck, among the most mediocre in
a long line of mediocre mayors supplied by Tammany Hall, did
not remain for the ceremonies. Repudiated by the Bar Association in his bid for a judgeship, scorned by his constituents, and
discredited by his pitiable subservience to "Boss" Croker, Van
Wyck, "walked with quick step, neither looking to the right nor
the left, but with his eyes turned toward the ground. He was
alone. In his walk across City Hall Park he was not recognized
by even one of the hundreds of people hurrying to the seat of
local government to greet the new Mayor."[13] Making good his
campaign pledge, Seth Low declared his first official act as may-
or to be the removal of Police Commissioner Murphy and Deputy Devery, and promised an administration of the city which
would be honest, intelligent and progressive. For the next two
years, the well-wishers of representative government would look
to New York in hopes that Mayor Low could realize the promise of democracy in an urban environment. "I must tell you,"
President Roosevelt wrote Low:

> that Corbin informed me yesterday that while in Germany
> the Emperor told him that he was more interested in your
> success as Mayor than in anything else concerning America;
> more even than in the national administration. He knew all
> about what you were doing, about Tammany, and the dif-
> ficulties you had to contend with, and felt that strong man
> though you were the task was one which might overtax any
> powers. I thought this rather interesting; for he evidently felt
> the heartiest admiration for you. I thought it rather note-
> worthy that he should know so much about our situation
> here.[14]

The Kaiser was not alone in his interest. From London, Sidney Webb declared that, "Mrs. Webb and I have watched with
the greatest interest your work as Mayor of New York . . . :

> and I venture occasionally to say, what is as yet hardly even
> understood, that we have *some* things to learn, too, from
> American City Government, bad as that mostly is. My own ex-
> perience makes me realize the difficulties you have had to con-
> tend with; and how unjust have been many of the criticisms
> passed on your administration by the too-sanguine "Good
> Government" people, who always want better bread than can
> be made of wheat—and before the wheat has had time to
> grow![15]

Unfortunately, neither the Emperor of Germany nor Professor Webb were eligible to vote in New York City, and they were not the people whom Low had to please. After the ceremonies of inauguration came the task of realizing good government.

An administration's effectiveness cannot be accurately gauged by the zeal and efficiency of the man who heads it, but rather it is to be evaluated by the quality of the men selected to fill the subordinate positions in the government. Realizing this, and wanting to name the best available men to high city positions, Low agonized over his nominations. "Low," Charles C. Burlingham recalled, "used to worry about the appointments he made a great deal. He was a very timid man and he used to call me up a great deal and ask for my advice."[16] One suspects that Burlingham was magnifying his own importance. Seth Low could justly be accused of many faults, but timidity was not one of of them. In any event, Burlingham, who had served the Board of Education so ably in the past, at Low's plea, came out of retirement to assume the presidency of the city's school board. Colonel John N. Partridge, a Republican who had served Low well in the same capacity two decades back when the latter was mayor of Brooklyn, was named police commissioner at Senator Platt's urgings. To head the Board of Health, Low eschewed partisan considerations to name Dr. E. J. Lederle, a distinguished chemist, as commissioner. Similarly, Gustav Lindenthal, whose qualifications included the support of Herman Ridder, was selected commissioner of the Department of Bridges. Democrat George L. Rives was chosen corporation counsel, and a "professional altruist," Robert Weeks DeForest, was named to head the newly-established and highly significant Tenement House Department.

Much controversy has surrounded DeForest's appointment with a number of scholars implying that Low's refusal to name Lawrence Veiller to the post showed the essentially conservative nature of fusion's reform program. "I was informed," Veiller declared and has been cited to demonstrate's Low conservatism, "that he [Low] considered that I was too radical a person and might get his administration into trouble."[17] This simply was not the case. Low consulted Otto T. Bannard, vice-president of the Charity Organization Society, on possible appointees to head the Tenement House Department. Bannard recommended the selection of DeForest, who was the President of the C.O.S., and Lawrence Veiller if DeForest declined to serve.[18] According to

Veiller, DeForest was going to refuse, but Josephine Shaw Lowell, the *grand dame* of the social reformers, prevailed upon him to accept Low's offer. "Mr DeForest's name," Veiller conceded, "had been far more associated with the efforts for Tenement House reform than my own."[19] Veiller's radicalism had no bearing on the appointment. DeForest was simply the better man, and when he told Low that he would accept the position on the condition that he be allowed to name Veiller as the department's first deputy commissioner, the mayor made no objection.

In his appointments, Mayor Low attempted to establish links with the ethnic minorities and the progressive elements in the New York political scene. James B. Reynolds, director of the University Settlement House, was named as Low's private secretary to keep open communication with the social progressives of the East Side. He broke tradition by naming Negro George Archer as a clerk in his office, hoping that it would better enable him to answer the needs of the city's black population. Indeed, a recent student of mayoral patronage has concluded that although forty percent of Low's appointees were from the Yankee upper class, he also appointed record numbers of Jews, Italians, and Negroes seeking to effect an ethnic coalition capable of breaking Irish domination of New York's political life. Lowi, for example, found that fifteen of Low's appointments to the Board of Education were clearly made along ethnic lines. Unfortunately, the effort to effect an ethnic coalition to promote municipal reform failed for reasons which will be examined later.[20]

On the whole, Low's principal selections were well-received. Professional stature rather than political influence was the criterion, and as *The Nation* observed, "Taking the selections as a whole, it is not too much to say that a municipal government has never gone into office in this country composed of men of higher character."[21] Some, however, expressed the fear that fusion's experts might lose contact with the masses. Besides looking for quality appointees, Low sought to strike an equitable balance between the patronage claims of the various organizations supporting his fusion alliance. Back in the 1890s, in a letter to Theodore Roosevelt, Low rightly declared that Mayor Strong's difficulties stemmed from his patronage policies. "He has given appointments to almost every element which supported him," Low observed, "except to the Platt wing of the Republican party."[22] For a man who should have known better, Seth Low acted surprisingly like William L. Strong. Because the Republican party had cast eighty percent of Low's fusion vote, the Citizens' Union fifteen percent, and the Greater New York Democracy five percent, a fair distribution of patronage would have given the G.O.P. the bulk of fusion's appointments; but, of the top thirty-one offices filled by Low, fifteen went to the Republicans (however, only six of those fifteen were closely affiliated with the local Republican machine), eleven went to independent Democrats, and the remaining five to members of the Citizens' Union.[23] The independent Democrats received patronage out of all proportion to their voting strength, and whatever Low's reasons may have been for giving them so many appointments, it was extremely poor politics. Moreover, only three of his top cabinet appointees were active county or Assembly District political leaders, and the non-political character of his appointments was the fatal weakness of his patronage policy, arousing bitter partisan discontent. An angry Citizens' Union, smarting from the blow to its pride occasioned by the dearth of patronage assigned to it, introduced, at its meeting of January 6, 1902, resolutions of censure against Mayor Low's patronage policies. They were withdrawn only through the strong and persistent efforts of the Union's chairman, R. Fulton Cutting, but the Citizens' Union's resentment could not be withdrawn—even at Cutting's command.[24]

In the Republican camp, though, protest was not stifled. John S. Wise of the 29th Assembly District Republican Club angrily demanded that Low give the Grand Old Party its fair share of patronage, and two weeks later, the Republican Club of the 22nd A.D. repeated Wise's call for more jobs for deserving Republicans.[25] In April, fusion aldermen added their voice to the chorus of protest to Low's patronage distribution.[26] The Democrats, though, who did supply five percent of fusion's vote, expressed no disappointment over his appointments. Disappointed patronage hopes would plague the fusion administration throughout Low's term, and would grow in intensity. But, for now, Low's appointees entered upon their work with enthusiasm, and results were not long in coming. Just eleven days after fusion took office, William C. Lawton of Adelphi College wrote the mayor's secretary that, "we feel the steady clearing of the atmosphere, as the fighters in the pit may not, at first. Even our side street is swept, as it had not been for months." "Mr. Roosevelt, Mr. Odell, and Mr. Low," Lawton went on:

are such a trio of executives as we have not seen since Andrew Jackson came in, and offices became spoils for the unwashed. We are just turning the third corner.

Mr. Low's job is in one large respect the hardest of all, for a big Occidental city is very generally considered an *insoluble* problem, wherein even official corruption is to be accepted as a large constant factor. So he is really a lonely pioneer.

Men who can *do,* easily and naturally, can never fully realize how much mere makers of phrases, essays, and books admire their work. We all do better daily work, since pride and hope have taken the place of shame and dread.[27]

Pride and hope was the keynote of the Low administration, but problems abounded. On January 4, 1902, Seth Low startled New York City by charging that Tammany Hall was attempting to bribe enough fusion aldermen to prevent Charles V. Fornes from organizing the Aldermanic Board.[28] The fusionists had a three-man majority on the Board of Alderman, but, in order to secure independent Democratic support for Seth Low as the mayoralty nominee, the Citizens' Union and the G.O.P. allowed the Democrats to name a goodly proportion of the aldermanic candidates. As a result, many of the fusion aldermen were Democrats, and some of them had only recently left Tammany's fold. If the Wigwam could organize the Aldermen, it could considerably blunt the impact of the fusion reform program. Mayor Low hoped that his charge of attempted bribery would force the fusionists to organize the Board of Alderman along the lines laid down by Fornes, and it had the desired effect. One fusion Democrat from Brooklyn left his sick-bed to vote with his fusion colleagues, and the next day, President Fornes announced that the bribery incident was closed and that the grand jury would not hear of the matter.[29] While fusion was able to organize the aldermanic board, it proved of small comfort. Too many aldermen were of too small a stature to fill such a large roll, and the fusion Democrats. in particular, were not much above the spoilsmen who had served under Van Wyck. Often obstructive, the Board of Alderman established its mediocrity to such a degree that the Citizens' Union would be forced to admit that the aldermen were the one conspicuous failure of the fusion government. An attempt would be made, in 1903, to raise the level of quality of fusion aldermen, but by then the problem would be academic.

With the aldermen organized, Seth Low settled down to administer the affairs of New York City, but was almost immediately confronted with what would prove to be the cruelest issue of all—Sunday liquor sales. There was nothing like morality, George Gunton observed, to kill reform.[30] And the question of excise law enforcement was an essentially moral one which was not amenable to a political solution. More, perhaps, than any other single cause, the liquor question was responsible for the failure of reform government to take successful root in New York City.

The issue of Sunday liquor sales was not new. It had been complicating the New York City political scene for decades. Wanting a quiet Sunday, devoted to the worship of God, New York's Yankee-Protestant middle class, along with a sizeable proportion of the city's Protestant clergy, aided and abetted by rural legislators, secured the passage of a comprehensive set of blue laws. Among other provisions, they required that all saloons close their doors at midnight Saturday, and remain closed throughout the Sabbath. However, the law went counter to the cosmopolitan habits of the city's immigrant working class which did not share the Puritan biases of the Yankee middle class, and because of Tammany's customary toleration of human imperfections, the law usually went unobserved. Constant efforts were made to strengthen the law against Sunday liquor sales, and Seth Low's help was often sought. Low, however, was unsympathetic, for as he told John B. Pine, the question of temperance was one of moral character, and since character could not be legislated he disapproved of statutes whose primary object was to regulate morality.[31] Some years later, in declining the Reverend Dr. Parkhurst's invitation to join the Society for the Prevention of Crime, Low asserted that no law could be enforced which did not have the substantial support of the community, and that efforts to enforce an unpopular excise law only produced contempt of law and bred corruption in the police department and government of the city. The best course, he declared, would be to allow each locality to decide for itself the merits of Sunday closing, and to permit a wet Sabbath where the sense of the community demanded it.[32] While a "goo-goo," Seth Low was no Puritan, and did not believe in imposing his morality upon peoples of different cultures and backgrounds.

So long as Tammany was in power, Sunday closing was not a political issue since the Democratic administrations simply winked at violations of the law. When Strong became mayor, though, Police Commissioner Theodore Roosevelt rigorously enforced the Sunday closing law, much to the displeasure of the people of New York, who loudly demanded a revision of the law. "Personally," Low told Roosevelt, "I believe that the enforcement of the Excise Law, as it has been enforced, without fear or favor, is of the greatest possible value as a vindication of the supremacy of law."[33] But, he added. it was poor politics. Favoring the G.O.P.'s pledge to secure a revision of the law, he advocated home rule as the only solution to the Sunday closing problem. Unfortunately, the Albany legislators produced something quite different.

In 1896, desiring to ease the stringency of the existing excise law, the New York State Legislature enacted the Raines Liquor Tax Law. As under the old law, the public sale of liquor in saloons on Sundays was forbidden; however, it permitted hotels to serve liquor with meals on the Sabbath, and defined a hotel as any establishment having ten or more furnished rooms. When the Raines Act became law, many saloons rented enough rooms in the tenements above them to qualify as a Raines Law hotel, and provided that they served meals with the liquor they dispensed, they were legally entitled to do business on Sundays.

Theoretically this would preserve the semblance of a dry Sunday while allowing the people of New York to continue their normal drinking habits free of police interference; but in actuality, the Raines Law quickly became a Frankenstein's monster. Most Raines Act hotels did not serve meals as the law stipulated, but continued their customary practice of dispensing free sandwiches with the beer they sold, which was a direct violation of the Excise Law. Of far more importance, however, were the ten furnished, but unoccupied, rooms they were required to maintain. Quite obviously, the Raines Law hotels were not in the hostelry business, and unless a function could be found for those ten furnished rooms, they would be a total financial loss. Saloon-keepers, being astute entrepreneurs, soon found uses for their furnished rooms. Centers of gambling and prostitution, the Raines Act hotels only added to the city's already burdensome vice problem, and spawned corruption on a monumental scale. Roosevelt tried to curb these abuses, but succeeded only in making Strong's regime more unpopular, and at the 1897 election, the people of New York, as John G. Agar declared, "expressed its opinion at the polls that it would rather have the misgovernment of Tammany with the law not enforced than the good government of the reformers with the law enforced."[34]

With Croker in command, the Raines Law, like everything else in New York, was turned to the profit of Tammany Hall. Eighty percent of the Raines Law hotels, John DeWitt Warner estimated, were houses of prostitution and dens of gambling— all conducting their operations openly and under the gaze of the police.[35] Under Commissioner Murphy and Deputy Devery, the police department was literally a licensing agency for saloon-centered prostitution and gambling, and, according to figures supplied by Lincoln Steffens, saloon graft alone netted Devery's syndicate an average of $400,000 per month for thirty-six consecutive months.[36]

In the fall of 1901, Sunday liquor sales was a prime campaign issue, with the vast majority of the city's clergy, feeling that a liberal Sunday not only defiled the Sabbath but encouraged vice and corruption as well, demanding a return to the Roosevelt regime; and with the Germans, led by Herman Ridder, equally insistent that the blue laws violated personal freedom. Much of the difficulty in excise law enforcement resulted from a total misconception as to the social function of the saloon in working class districts. "The saloon," Felix Adler pointed out, "is the Poor Man's Club. It is a mistake to suppose that all saloons are simply hot beds of vice and bestial intoxication. [The saloon is a place] where people meet quietly, take a glass of beer without indulging to excess, and to which they go chiefly, if not wholly, for the purpose of social intercourse."[37] Particularly in the German districts, the beer garden was a wholesome center of conviviality and recreation to which entire families congregated. To close them on Sunday would be to deprive thousands of workingmen of an opportunity to satisfy their need for socialization, and in the absence of any effective alternative outlet, such a law was manifestly unjust and unworkable. This was the crux of the saloon controversy.

The question of excise enforcement proved to be an embarrassing one for fusion campaigners. The problem, as Lyman Abbott's *The Outlook* declared, was that "this law is imposed on them [the people of New York City] by legislators controlled by the rural population of the State,"

> and as thus they cannot directly repeal the law, they vote for city officials who will not enforce it; and city officials elected not to enforce the laws which it is their business to enforce are almost sure to be lawless, immoral, corrupt. If the excise question were not involved in the present election, either

directly or indirectly, it can hardly be doubted that New York would overthrow the corrupt rule of Tammany by an overwhelming majority.[38]

Needing the support of both "wets" and "drys," Seth Low was hesitant about taking a firm stand on the Sunday closing issue; consequently, he put out a statement which said nothing, antagonized no one, but did not please anyone either. "The clauses prohibiting the sale or giving away of liquor on Sunday," Low stated:

> despite the good intent of those who advocate them, lead to another class of evils, because they conflict with the habits of so large a proportion of the population, and because they interfere, as these conceive, with personal liberty in matters that do not properly come under the regulation of the law.[39]
>
> All this would be bad enough if these accomplished their object of actually preventing the sale of liquor on Sunday, but they do not even do this. It may be considered certain, after much experience, that in this community those clauses of the excise law that forbid the sale of liquor on Sunday in saloons are not competent to accomplish more than to prevent the public sale of liquor on that day; they never have stopped and they never can stop drinking on Sunday.[40]

As Low took office, the Germans expected him to adhere to a liberal enforcement policy, while the clergy was confident that the new administration would be as resolute as Strong's in the enforcement of the law. "If the present reform administration," John G. Agar warned, "enforces the law, the result will be the overthrow of reform government in this city at the fall election in 1903. . . ."[41]

Seth Low was determined to pursue in New York City the same excise policy which had proven so successful in Brooklyn. That policy was to connive at mild infractions of the law, and to allow "respectable" barrooms, which kept their front doors locked and which eschewed debauchery and drunkenness, to conduct their normal Sunday business.[42] In line with this program, Police Commissioner Partridge, on the eve of fusion's first Sunday, declared that no special orders had been issued the police force on Sunday closing, implying that the traditional Tammany policy of liberality would be continued.[43] There was no crackdown that Sunday, no Comstockian raids, and New York's saloons went about their usual Sabbath trade.[44] The people were happy, the preachers were not, and the battle was yet to come.

The Reverend Dr. Parkhurst's Society for the Prevention of Crime immediately demanded of Mayor Low and District Attorney Jerome that they enforce the law which they had sworn themselves to uphold. The issue was clearly drawn: pledged to enforce the law without fear or favor, the fusion administration could not knowingly wink at violations of the law. On January 10, 1902, William Travers Jerome warned Low that unless the Raines Law was repealed, reform would be defeated. Charging that Roosevelt caused Low's 1897 defeat, he called upon the mayor to use his influence with the Republican State administration to secure to the city home rule on Sunday closing, and lamented that until the law was changed it would have to be enforced.[45] On the next two Sundays, the number of excise arrests rose as the administration went through the motions of enforcing the law, though no concerted effort was made to make New York dry. Finally, on Sunday, January 19, Parkhurst forced the issue. Declaring in his weekly sermon that "Mayor Low has no right to choose which laws to enforce or not to enforce," he demanded that the administration close the saloons and see that they remained closed.[46] Virtually charged with dereliction of duty, Low was forced to answer Parkhurst and to clearly state his excise policy, which he did four days later.

The Sunday closing law, as regarded the saloons, Mayor Low proclaimed, was unenforceable not through any failing of the administration but rather because the people of New York did not want the law enforced.[47] That being the case, the administration would not go out of its way to close the saloons, but "It will take immediate cognizance of any complaint of breach of the law that is called to its attention. . . . "[48] Political expediency, Low realized, dictated a policy of laxity on Sunday liquor sales, and the following Monday, the *Times* reported that Sunday saloons were freely patronized.[49] Fusion could afford to alienate the ministry, but it could not survive the alienation of the populace, and as Low's first month of office drew to a close, it was decided to yield to the weaknesses of human nature. As the *Review of Reviews* summed up the new excise policy, "Since Mayor Low came into office, the saloons have kept their front doors closed on Sunday and have maintained outward quiet and order; but police have not been instructed to use espionage or to give themselves much concern over the question of whether or not side doors were unlocked."[50]

Low hoped, but failed, to secure amendment of the Raines

Law to permit saloons to open Sunday afternoons when church
services were finished. and was supported in the plan by the famous Committee of Fifteen whose exposure of police-protected
vice did so much to put fusion in office. The present law, the
committee declared, created a fertile field for blackmail and
bred vice and corruption in the city's government and police
force. Much of the ministry, however, stoutly opposed afternoon
opening, arguing that the Sabbath could not be divided between
God and Satan.[51] At this point, the unpredictable William Travers Jerome, who had warned against the dangers of rigorous enforcement and who had originally proposed afternoon opening,
declared on March 1, 1902, that he intended to enforce the
Raines Law to the letter, and pledged that not a single saloon
would be open in New York. Frightened by Jerome's threats,
the saloon-keepers remained closed that Sunday, but a week
later, confident that Jerome's attention would be absorbed in
tilting at other windmills, the saloon-keepers did Sunday business as usual. No raids forthcoming, they abandoned their cau-
tion, and once again came out into the open.[52] Jerome was quiet.
His motivations in one moment warning against the dangers of
excise enforcement, and in the next demanding the law's vigorous application are not subject to rational analysis. Only six
weeks after ordering his Raines Law crackdown, he proclaimed
that the enforcement of the excise law would doom municipal
reform in New York for generations to come.[53] Jerome was not
one who thought in terms of a cause. Extremely self-centered,
he placed himself above fusion, and only sought to keep himself in the public eye.

Between the Protestant clergy, the German-American civic
groups, and District Attorney Jerome, Low drew fire no matter
what he did on the excise question. And in April 1902, a police
revolt added to his troubles. Irked at having to sign statements
that they observed no excise violations on their beats, the police, on Saturady, April 5, vowed to enforce the law and end the
hypocrisy of having to certify a condition which was non-exist-
ent. So widespread was the police rebellion that off-duty officers
gave up their time off to help their colleagues close up the saloons. On April 6, the press reported that it was the driest Sunday in New York since Roosevelt's days, and that the small East
Side shopkeepers were especially hard hit by the crackdown.[54]
Both Low and Jerome supported the police because they were
rebelling against the powers of their precinct captains, and strik-

ing at the still widespread blackmail syndicate linking the police hierarchy and the saloon-owners.[55]

Fortunately, for Low's administration, the excise crackdown was short-lived, and by May 1902, the saloons were doing their normal Sunday business. The Raines Law did not grow in popularity, and in June, a group of detectives attempting to close a saloon were set upon and attacked by the enraged patrons.[56] For the most part, though, the excise question ceased to be a divisive issue for the remainder of the year. It was the settled policy of the Low administration to close only those saloons which openly flouted the law, or which were conducted in a disorderly manner. As long as the front doors were kept closed, and internal order maintained, the saloons were not raided. And while the clergy might clamor for strict enforcement, the working classes were grateful for official laxity. But, this happy state of affairs was not to last.

On New Year's Day 1903, the city of New York acquired a new police commissioner. Soldier, historian, and engineer, Francis Vinton Greene, who had commanded the 2nd Philippine expedition of 1898, took over the management of the department with the understanding that he would have a free hand in administering it. It was his policy to root out corruption in the police department and to enforce the laws, including the Raines Law. Announcing his intention to realize a dry Sunday, New York's saloon-keepers were careful to maintain a calm appearance, but Commissioner Greene, touring the city in plain clothes, declared that New York was not that dry after all. The next week, to show that he meant what he said about enforcing the law, he marched into Captain Michael Gorman's police precinct, informed him that there were wide open saloons in his precinct and summarily dismissed him from his post.[57] Stung by Greene's arbitrary justice, the police of New York, thereafter, made scores of excise arrests every Sunday. The enraged citizenry of New York loudly demanded relief.

Later that same month, Low prepared to once again ask Albany for liberalization of the Sunday closing law, but he received no comfort from fellow Republican Benjamin Barker Odell. Declaring that he would oppose any attempt to permit Sunday opening, Governor Odell condemned Low's vacillation on the issue of excise, asserting that strict enforcement would have gained him more political support than he would have lost.[58] Lacking Odell's backing, Low's bill stood little chance of passage, even with Jerome's testimony on behalf of the measure. The District Attorney, while endorsing the bill, derided Mayor Low's excise policy. Asserting that Low prated and juggled, he ridiculed liberal enforcement as lawlessness sanctioned by government, and stated that blackmail and corruption could never be driven from the police department so long as the existing law remained unchanged.[59]

Throughout 1903, Commissioner Greene's tough excise policy would remain in force, and thousands of harassed citizens, denied their Sunday beer, would curse fusion and vow to return to Tammany. But, to add financial injury to insulted sensibilities, Low, in March 1903, refused to receive a petition by the liquor dealers protesting Odell's highly unpopular plan to increase liquor license fees. Low opposed the measure because the state, besides raising fees, proposed to take one-half instead of one-third of the revenues raised in each locality. As he told Odell, New York City already resented the fact that it paid the state far more tax revenues than it received back from the state, and that this measure would only increase that feeling of resentment with disastrous results in the fall elections.[60] Nevertheless, he refused to receive the petition of the liquor dealers charging that they were corruptors and blackmailers not deserving of official consideration. "I suppose," the Reverend Dr. Rainsford wrote him, "many people would say it was bad politics, but I am very sure it is righteous wisdom."[61] Bad politics was more appropriate a description. New York's liquor dealers solemnly asserted that never had they suffered as much as under fusion.

Seth Low either could not or would not persuade Greene to ease his strict enforcement of the Raines Law, and ruling his department as an autocrat, Greene saw to it that there were no lapses in law enforcement. Early in May 1903, the voice of New York's German community, *Staats-Zeitung* editor Herman Ridder, denounced the idea that Mayor Low should be renominated as fusion's standard-bearer. Condemning his puritanical excise policy and his unstinting support of the unpopular Odell administration, he declared that Low could not carry the German vote, and with his typical truculence he made ready to deny him a place on the fusion ticket.[62] As the spring of that election year progressed, popular resentment at Greene's petty harrassment reached a new plateau of intensity, and astute political observers feared for fusion's safety. Greene, heedless of public indignation,

ordered the police force to redouble its efforts to close the saloons, and as protests against strict enforcement flooded the city's
press, he told the Order of Acorns that excise was no longer a
burning issue in New York City's politics.[63] All this would have
been bad enough had Greene's policy actually succeeded in dry-
ing up New York, but, while hundreds of excise arrests were
made every Sunday, little did it stay the flow of beer. "The Fusion police administration," the *Acorn* observed, "made 162 excise arrests in Greater New York last Sunday. . . . Yet what man
in New York was there who really could not get a drink?"[64] All
Greene did was to lose fusion thousands of votes.

If the excise question was that upon which the Low administration foundered, the issue of police corruption and the promise of substantive reform was that upon which the fusionists were
elected. Whatever else he did or did not do, Seth Low, if he
were to have any hope of accomplishing permanent reform in
New York, would have to make good his promise of cleaning
out the police department. His choice to head the police force,
however, was a poor one (it was, in fact, the only bad appointment he made during his term of office), for Commissioner John
N. Partridge, who had served Low admirably in the same capacity when the latter was mayor of Brooklyn, had grown weak
with age, his executive abilities had fled him, and he was unable to break the alliance existing between the criminals and
the police department. As one student of New York's police department concluded, "Partridge attempted reforms in all sincerity, but they were not drastic enough to root out the deep-seated
evils in the Department."[65]

Wishing to familiarize himself with the operational details of
the police department, Partridge's first official statement was a
declaration that no drastic measures would be instituted so long
as the police force towed the mark.[66] Many captains, interpreting
the statement to mean that no reforms would be instituted, continued to run their precincts much as they had done under Tammany's reign, and their links to the prostitutes, gamblers, and
saloon-keepers were kept open. With his military background,
Partridge prized discipline above all other virtues, and discipline meant support of the police hierarchy. It was this factor
more than any other which hindered Partridge's well-intentioned
efforts to reform the department, for except in rare instances,
whenever charges of misconduct or malfeasance were brought by
police officers against their superiors, Partridge almost invariably

sided with the hierarchy, and by defending corrupt or delinquent superior officers, the rank-and-file were further demoralized. While some inspectors and captains were transferred to new precincts or discharged from service, Partridge did little to smash the police syndicates which fattened upon the seeds of vice and blackmail. Relying for support and advice upon the very officers who were benefiting by police corruption, Partridge was forced to admit, four months after he took charge of the department, that the police force was still Tammanyized, that Deveryism was still dominant, and that much yet remained to be done.[67] Meanwhile, public disappointment with Partridge's manifest inability to reform the police was rapidly mounting.

As fusion began its sixth month in office, prostitution and gambling were as prevalent in the Tenderloin as they ever were, and violations of the excise law as flagrant as under Tammany. Numerous civic groups, spearheaded by the City Club, disenchanted with promises unfulfilled and hopes betrayed, blaming Partridge's laxity for the absence of visible improvement in the police department, prepared to demand the Commissioner's dismissal. "Commissioner Partridge's administration is a failure," the City Club informed Mayor Low preparatory to its planned public condemnation of Partridge, "and the Commissioner weak and gullible."[68] Hoping to head off a public rupture in fusion's ranks, Mayor Low immediately went into a closed door conference with representatives of the City Club. Desiring to protect the reputation of a faithful and long-time servant, Low managed to allay the criticisms of the City Club, and to secure another chance for Partridge. After the conference, the City Club asserted that it stood solidly behind Low, and the Mayor—proclaiming his entire satisfaction with Commissioner Partridge—promised that the police force would soon show substantial and visible improvement.[69] A month later, the Citizens' Union issued its own report on the police department, and while declaring that Partridge was to be congratulated on his clean-up of the department, it asserted that there was room for a great deal of improvement.[70] The Citizens' Union report, though, was far from accurate, for Partridge, in the month after Low's meeting with the City Club, "took no adequate measures either to break up the alliance between the police and crime or to get a proper understanding of the underlying conditions in the department."[71] Cries for Partridge's dismissal again rose, and pressure on Low intensified.

In August, under extreme pressure from the "goo-goos," Low demanded radical police reforms to smash the syndicates tying the police to organized crime, and proposed the creation of a Chief of Police to aid the Commissioner in the management of the police department.[72] With the aid of a Captain Piper, Partridge was able to make some progress in reforming the department, but his customary inactivity in the wake of the Rabbi Joseph riot sealed his fate as Police Commissioner. In the summer of 1902, Rabbi Jacob Joseph (leader of the East Side Jewish community) died, and as his funeral procession was moving through the streets of New York's East Side, workers in a factory overlooking the entourage rained stones, bricks, and bags of water on the heads of the mourners. Making complaint to the police officers assigned to protect the funeral procession, the mourners, instead of receiving their aid, were clubbed by the officers detailed to protect them. The Jewish community complained of the overt anti-Semitism displayed by the police, but Partridge characteristically refused to take any action, and Low was finally forced to appoint a civilian board of review to investigate the incident. After a long and thorough study, the review board found that the police were responsible for the riot, that the officers had been negligent and derelict in their duty, and called upon Partridge to institute disciplinary action against the officers involved. But Partridge, by this time, was constitutionally incapable of taking any action, and Low was forced to issue Partridge a directive to bring charges against Inspector Cross and Sergeant Brady, who commanded the police detail at the funeral, and to find out the names of the clubbers. Blaming the riot on the police, Low made it clear that he wanted an example made of the officers involved in the altercation.[73] The police department was reported to have been astounded by Low's directive—harassment of Jews, especially the shaking down of pushcart peddlers—had been regarded as one of the fringe benefits of being a police officer. Partridge, though, announced that he would follow orders, but, by now, it was obvious that a new Police Commissioner was needed.[74]

The City Vigilance League, one of fusion's staunchest allies, in October 1902, publicly condemned Low for failing to make good his promise of police reform, and asserted that unless improvement in the department was soon forthcoming, it predicted the death of reform government at the 1903 elections. Citing continued police ties to gamblers, and the department's atrocious conduct during the Rabbi Joseph riot, it called for more vigor in the Commissioner's office.[75] Low persisted in his efforts to protect Partridge, but in December, as the Citizens' Union proclaimed that the police force was impotent, and as the City Club once again demanded Partridge's head, the mayor allowed his commissioner to resign. Giving ill-health as the cause for his resignation, Partridge declared that he was tired of the incessant criticism and ingratitude heaped upon him. Most of the press, though, was glad to see him go, with the *Times* applauding his resignation and declaring that his absolute failure to effect reform was costing fusion thousands of votes.[76]

Another military man, but a much younger one, was selected to succeed Partridge. General Francis Vinton Greene proved to be a far more acceptable choice. As energetic as Partridge was lax, he vigorously set about the task of reforming the police department, and had nearly accomplished his objective when tragedy, in the form of Seth Low's 1903 electoral defeat, struck. Greene took over as police commissioner on New Year's Day, 1903, and immediately suspended an inspector and five captains for malfeasance.[77] In addition, he ordered every one of the department's 301 wardmen (detectives) back to patrol duty, and transferred them to different precincts. This simple act of remanding the wardmen to patrol duty, which Partridge was repeatedly urged to do, effectively smashed the syndicates linking the police to prostitution and gambling. The rank-and-file of the police department was, for the most part, honest; it was the captains and superior officers who were corrupt, and the wardmen, who were employed as graft collectors, were the backbone of the syndicates. Under Greene's new policy, former wardmen, after ninety days on patrol duty, could re-apply for their former positions, and if their records merited re-appointment, they would be assigned to different precincts to guard against the re-establishment of the syndicates. This, however, was but the beginning of Greene's reforms.

Realizing that the police hierarchy was responsible for the department's corruption, Greene did what Partridge refused to do: he rode roughshod over the inspectors and captains. All superior officers were made responsible for the accuracy of the reports filed by the patrolmen under them, and if discrepancies were discovered, the superior officers were held accountable. In addition, sergeants, captains, and inspectors were held responsible for the conduct of the men under their command, and in the case of wrongdoing, it was they who were disciplined. Men under charges, instead of being allowed to remain on duty pending the outcome of their cases, were immediately suspended until their cases were decided. Commissioner Greene, unlike Partridge, was given to making surprise visits at precinct houses. He personally toured the Tenderloin and the Sunday saloons, and if he felt that laxity existed, it was not unusual for him to dismiss summarily the precinct captain and to transfer the superior officers to patrol duty on Staten Island. Fearing Greene's swift and arbitrary justice, the police department visibly and rapidly improved. Hitherto immune brothels were closed down, gambling dens raided and broken up, and saloons made to stay closed on Sunday. Morale among the rank-and-file was bolstered. Knowing that their superior officers would no longer be protected in wrongdoing, police officers were now unafraid to enforce the law, and marked improvement was soon apparent. Greene's iron hand, though, was felt by the rank-and-file as well as the hierarchy. In the spring of 1903, Patrolman Peter P. Allwell was dismissed from the force for taking a candy bar from a Bowery pushcart peddler.[78]

Greene's regime met with almost universal approval. The Reverend C. H. Parkhurst, who had been a severe critic of the Low administration's excise policy, wrote Greene a letter of sterling praise in which, "in a brief way I have tried to express my appreciation of the splendid work that has been done during the last five months. . . . "[79] Editorial comment was equally generous. The *New York World,* just six weeks after Greene took over the department, declared that the commissioner had, "increased by 100 per cent his [Low's] now very faint chances of re-election in the fall."[80] The *New York Tribune* concluded that while Greene had not brought about the millennium, Low had substantially made good his promise to reform the police.[81] And the City Club asserted, "It is not too much to say that if the administration of Mayor Low had done nothing else for the city, the redemption of the police department under Commissioner Greene would entitle that administration to the gratitude of the entire community."[82] As the election of 1903 approached, New York City enjoyed what it had not had since the days of Strong—an honest and efficient police force—but not everyone was pleased.

Greene's rigorous excise enforcement did not win fusion many friends among the Germans, and while he effectively ended the iniquitous police shakedown of the East Side pushcart peddlers, he also raided their carts to make certain that they all had city peddlers' licenses. The East Side peddlers were not appreciative of Greene's even-handed justice. The fact was that Greene's stringest enforcement of the law alienated many more people than a policy of laxity would have. Greene probably hurt Low more than he helped him, but the fusion administration should not be judged solely on the excise and police questions; it could boast of numerous accomplishments.

"A public body," Seth Low wrote in 1890, "which has valuable franchises to grant, at will, is peculiarly exposed to corruption."[83] The truth of Low's statement was proven all too accurate under Tammany Hall's domination of New York City's government. Franchises were given away to the highest bribe giver without regard to the rights or best interests of the city, and as a contemporary student of American municipal government observed, "The whole question [of franchise grants] came to be settled finally by the amount of money or political influence that could be brought to bear, and the ring or company that had the largest wallet or 'pull' secured the grant."[84] A company acquiring a franchise under such conditions did so on the understanding that its assets would be under-assessed, and its stock issues not too closely watched. The Third Avenue Elevated Railroad Company, which had close ties to Tammany Hall, had its $19 million franchise assessed at a paltry $2,174,750 and paid the city an annual royalty of three percent of that assessment. The syndicate which controlled Manhattan's electric light and gas had assets of $30 million but its stock and bond issues totaled $100 million. Tammany's franchise policy did not affect the lives of the people as directly as police corruption, but it was no less disgraceful. Low pledged reform, asserting that, "The franchises of the city are a part of its common wealth. They should never be given away; neither should the city part with the control of them except for a [limited] term of years."[85]

Low's franchise policy was one of the brightest pages in the history of his administration of New York City. Every franchise which he issued required the franchised corporation to guarantee the city a minimum yearly payment, plus a royalty of three percent of its gross receipts for the first three years of the grant, and five percent for each year thereafter. All such franchises were to expire within twenty or twenty-five years, and the only exception made to this iron-clad policy was for the Pennsylvania Railroad. Proposing to erect a terminal in Manhattan which would link New York to New Jersey in the Pennsylvania Railroad system, the corporation demanded and received a perpetual franchise. It argued, and Low accepted its contention, that because of the highly expensive and complex nature of the work, it could not risk having challenges made to its sovereignty every twenty years. However, while the Pennsylvania received a perpetual franchise, its grant provided for compulsory arbitration of all labor disputes, and compensation to the city geared to rising valuation and profits, with re-assessment and renegotiation of the royalty terms every twenty-five years.

Existing franchises, which had been granted by Tammany, were re-assessed in order to force royalty payments commensurate with the value of the grant. By these means, the city's income from street railway franchises alone, under Low's administration, was sixty percent higher than it had been under Van Wyck.[86] As the *Review of Reviews* commented, "Under Mayor Low's *regime* . . . the public interest has been well guarded; and while no corporation has been prosecuted, none has received any franchise grant for which it did not have to pay on fair and business-like terms."[87] In his own way, Seth Low was taming the plutocracy, and safeguarding the public welfare from its depradations. Although the Citizens' Union's platform had called for municipal ownership of public utilities, Low made no effort to implement the proposal. Arguing that municipal ownership in a city controlled by a corrupt political machine would prove a nightmare, opening the floodgates for nepotism, he opposed municipal ownership except as a last resort. His reluctance to support municipal ownership alienated many progressives who saw him as a well-meaning but conservative defender of the status quo. The charge, however, was unfair, for when he left office, New York City—for the first time in its history—was receiving a just return from its franchise grants. Needless to say, the franchised corporations were not grateful for Low's defense of the City's interests. Corruption was far more profitable than honesty.

In fiscal matters, Low's record was as brilliant as it was in franchise reform. Finding that New York's borrowing capacity was exhausted, and that funds were desperately needed to improve and sustain vital city services, the Low administration concentrated on raising the city's revenues. Under George L. Rives, the Law Department energetically went about the business of collecting fines and back taxes, and in 1902 it brought in $553,992.99 compared to the $137,242.47 collected under Tammany in 1901. Of course, such heroics on behalf of the city of New York were not appreciated by the people, and so persistent was the Law Department in its collection of back taxes from Brooklyn that some of the mayor's old friends complained. Low, demanding to know what the complaints were about, called in Martin Saxe, who was the arrears collector for Brooklyn, for an explanation. Saxe, who later became a United States Senator, told Low that he was only enforcing the letter of the law, but that if the administration found his actions to be politically embarrassing, he would ease up. " 'Oh, of course not' "; Low replied, " 'I can't have you do anything like that.' "[88] It was good morality, but bad politics. Tammany would have let the matter rest.

The increased activity of the Law Department was, of course, inadequate to resolve the city's pressing financial difficulties, and in an effort to increase New York's borrowing capacity, Low, late in 1902, introduced his full valuation scheme. Tammany had assessed property at sixty-seven percent of its actual market value. However, wealthy property-owners, for a small honorarium, could persuade the Tammany assessors to undervalue their holdings even more than that, with the result that the small property-owner paid the bulk of the city's real estate taxes. Under the mayor's plan, property was assessed at its true market value, which increased the assessed value of the city's real estate by $1,420,885,247, thereby expanding the city's borrowing capacity by $143 million. But more importantly, since large property-owners now paid their fair share of the real estate taxes, the rate dropped from $2.31 for every $100 of assessed valuation to $2.27. This shifted the tax burden from the small to the large property-owners.[89] The Citizens' Union endorsed Low's plan as an equitable solution to the city's pressing financial needs, though Manhattan Borough President Jacob A. Cantor warned against the plan, saying that it would alienate the propertied classes.[90] The new assessment policy, however, by increasing the city's borrowing capacity reduced the annual increase in the permanent funded debt by $5 million and allowed Low to cut the 1903 city budget by $1.5 million (hundreds of Tammany office-holders were dismissed from the city's payrolls), while raising expenditures for schools, public improvements, and public welfare services to all-time highs. *The Outlook* noted approvingly that "Taxes under the Fusion administration have been decreased, and decreased most largely in the poorer sections of the city, which were as a rule the worst sufferers from the old system of assessing property according to pressure instead of according to law."[91] The *New York Tribune*, assaying Low's first year in office, proclaimed:

> A year of reform leaves the city millions of dollars better off in purse and with a far higher standard of efficiency and morality in every department than obtained twelve months ago, when the Low administration began its task.[92]

While taxes were lowered and the budget cut, Low did not neglect the improvement of city services. Under Tammany's rule, the people of New York had little to show for the tax revenues they paid to the city. The fusion administration, however, by ending graft and corruption, gave the taxpayers of New York far more value for their money than had "Boss" Croker, and demonstrated that honest officials could give the people better and more efficient services than the grafters from the Wigwam. In its two years in office, fusion appropriated $74 million for the expansion and improvement of municipal parks and buildings, which was double the amount Van Wyck had spent during his four-year term. Low allocated $14.9 million for new school construction, which, again, was twice the amount appropriated by Tammany in its four-year reign. Under Van Wyck, the school system had been starved for funds and thousands of children had been turned away from the schools for lack of room, while tens of thousands more were attending school only half a day. Low's massive construction program did much to remedy Tammany's neglect of education, but, unfortunately, by the time fusion's schools were built, Low was no longer mayor, and he was denied credit for the alleviation of the school shortage. In addition, almost $19 million was set aside for rapid transit and bridge construction, and it was under Low that planning and work began on the city's subway system and the Manhattan and Williamsburg Bridges. Over $10 million was spent to improve and expand New York's habor facilities, and—for the first time in its history—the city began to receive the benefits of an adequate water system and to enjoy well-paved streets.

Under Seth Low, New York City had an efficient and thrifty municipal government without being denied the services so vital to a modern city. The foundations of an adequate system of rapid transit had been laid, the school shortage was well on its

way to solution, and the city's streets, parks, docks, and buildings were in better conditions than they had ever been. As the
Review of Reviews early observed:

> Economy and efficiency are the watchwords in all depart-
> ments. Petty abuses are being lopped off, hundreds of super-
> numeries are being dropped from the payrolls, and high stand-
> ards of justice and intelligence, with true business-like energy,
> are ruling throughout the city as almost never before.[93]

Economy and efficiency were, indeed, Low's watchwords, and
new ways were constantly sought to increase the city's revenues.
Under Tammany, the Department of Sanitation, for example,
paid eighteen cents a cubic yard to have the horse-droppings on
the city's street dumped at sea; fusion, however, had it sacked
and sold at a profit to the Long Island Railroad at the rate of
sixteen hundred sacks per day. The Citizens' Union proudly announced that Mayor Low was effectively utilizing the natural
resources of New York City for the advancement of the public
welfare.[94]

Low's greatest achievements, though, came in the realm of social welfare. "If a city," the mayor declared in an open letter to
the public:

> is content to let its helpless ones—its children, its sick, its
> poor, its aged, and its infirm—suffer from want or neglect,
> that city is pretty sure to fall seriously short, in other respects
> also, of its best possibilities. If, on the other hand, a city in-
> sists that good care be taken of those who are not able to
> care for themselves, and strives continually to improve its
> conduct of these affairs, that city is full of a spirit that is cer-
> tain to produce good results upon the activities of the city all
> along the line.[95]

The Departments of Health, Charities, and Tenement Houses,
under fusion, did much to fulfill Low's desire of giving the city's
poor the best possible services.

The Health Department, under the auspices of Tammany
Hall, had been notorious for its inefficiency, and its chief function had been to serve as a sponge to absorb Tammany job-
holders. When Dr. Lederle took over as Commissioner, 157 Tammany employees, who performed no known function, were fired
and replaced by a corps of professional medical personnel. A
vigorous immunization program was initiated in the public
school system, and efforts to detect and control contagious dis-

eases were redoubled. The results were impressive: the death rate from tuberculosis dropped from 2.30 per 1000 in 1901 to 2.03 in 1902; fatal diphtheria decreased from 15.9 per 1000 in 1901 to 10.9 in 1902, and the number of deaths from smallpox, which was 410 in Tammany's last year in office, fell to 310 in fusion's first year and was cut to just 3 for the first six months of 1903. The general death rate declined from 20.00 per 1000 in 1901 to 18.75 in 1902, which represented 4,500 lives saved. Not only was reform government efficient and cheap; it was also healthier. Forty-five hundred New Yorkers very literally owed their lives to fusion government.

The Department of Charities, under Homer Folks, performed similar feats. To remove the sigma attached to receiving public assistance, and to restore a measure of human dignity, Folks ordered the word "pauper" be stricken from the vocabulary of city officials. It was a small thing, in retrospect, but it showed that fusion was responsive to the emotional sensibilities of the poor. A massive program was launched to modernize, humanize, and improve the city's hospitals, orphan asylums, and old-age homes. For example, under Tammany, breakfast at the city's old-age homes consisted of coffee and unbuttered bread; supper of tea and unbuttered bread. The only full meal was served at midday, and when funds were short, as they invariably were under Tammany, that meal was skimped on. Under Folks, a full-time dietician was assigned to every one of the city's charitable institutions and hospitals, and three well-balanced meals were served daily. The practice of separating married couples at the old-age homes was ended, and individual apartments were provided for them.[96] Throughout the city, better, more efficient, and more dignified services were rendered to the poor. Fusion did not economize on human needs.

The Tenement House Department came into existence with the fusion administration of Mayor Low, and was charged with enforcing the state's new tenement house code, which outlawed the dumb-bell tenement while setting certain minimum health standards which were to be enforced by the department. From January of 1902 through June of 1903, the department made 337,246 separate inspections and filed 55,055 notices of violations which resulted in 21,584 repairs being made to plumbing, the cleaning of 13,732 common water closets, the removal of 11,611 accumulations of filth from public halls and stairwells, and the cleaning of 13,732 cellars and 15,364 walls, plus the replacement of 10,000 unsafe wooden floors and the erection of 1,701 fire escapes.[97] Prostitution was effectively driven from the tenements of the East Side by the imposition on the landlord of a $1,000 fine for every prostitute found living in his buildings. Commissioner DeForest began a vigorous lecture program to bring to the attention of the people of New York the problems faced by tenement dwellers. "Commissioner DeForest exhibited pictures to an Acorn audience last week showing pigs, goats, and horses in the basements of New York tenements," the *Acorn* told its membership, "We want to point out to him that he will find bugs over in the Ninth Assembly District."[98] The *Acorn's* humor notwithstanding, DeForest and Veiller made New York's tenements slightly better places in which to live, though, landlords were not appreciative of fusion's humanitarian exertions. Tammany never did enforce the housing codes.

"It cannot be said too emphatically," Edward T. Devine of the Charity Organization Society declared, "that, so far as the social welfare of the poor is concerned, there is no doubt that reform has abundantly justified the confidence of the electorate."[99] After just a year in office, Low's administration was hailed with almost universal critical acclaim, the *Review of Reviews* proclaiming, "We have no hesitation in pronouncing Mayor Low's administration by far the best in the history of New York. . . ."[100] As the election of 1903 drew near, the critical praise continued unabated. Theodore Roosevelt asserted:

> We now have in New York the second largest city of the world, and it is no idle compliment to you and those associated with you, Mr. Mayor, for me to say that there is now no other city here or aboard of whose governing officials its people have more reason to feel proud.[101]

But, did the people of New York want a government of which they could feel proud?

CHAPTER VIII

"The Dog Has Returned to His Vomit"

Do we Americans really want good government? Do we know it when we see it? Are we capable of that sustained good citizenship which alone can make democracy a success?

The honest men are in, and this election is to decide whether they are to be kept in. . . .

Lincoln Steffens[1]

In late November 1902, the Citizens' Union, reviewing Seth Low's first ten months in office, concluded that excellent progress had been made in cleansing all city departments of corruption; that, while all problems had by no means been solved, steady progress was being made on all fronts, and that the Low administration had earned the confidence and support of the people of New York City. On the same day that the Citizens' Union issued its report, Republican "boss" Thomas Platt declared that he, too, was in favor of fusion for the coming mayoral campaign, but that he did not favor the renomination of Seth Low. The Senator from Tioga expressed anger and disappointment at not receiving his fair share of patronage, and made it clear that if the Republican party was expected to support Low for a second term of office, it would have to be awarded a good deal more political appointments than it had up to then been given.[2] The fight for the 1903 mayoralty had begun.

Seth Low ran for mayor of New York in the fall of 1901 on the promise that, if elected, he would appoint the best available men to office regardless of their political connections, would provide a businesslike administration unswayed by personal or party interests, and would be non-partisan in the conduct of his office. For the most part, Low lived up to his pledge, and because of this, he alienated the professional politicians whose wholehearted support was essential to the success of any candidate. "Mr. Low's idea," the *Review of Reviews*, noted, "is that

the people who supported him did so, not because they expected
to be rewarded with offices, but because they wanted him to
give the city the best possible government."³ Consequently, the
mayor's first consideration in all appointments was, "not the
division of the offices among the several political elements which
combined to support him, but rather the fitness of the individual
to the work of the office."⁴ It was an admirable sentiment, but
a totally unrealistic one, for the people who supported Low—
the Republicans, the independent Democrats, and even the Citizens' Union—expected jobs. Low's selection of non-political experts to fill city offices drew criticism from all the elements in
his fusion alliance, who felt that they were not receiving due
recognition for the services they rendered. The fact was, as Ervin
Wardman, political analyst of the *New York Press,* pointed out,
that Low did not lead the fusion movement, and failed to develop a political machine personally loyal to him.⁵ It was a political blunder of the first magnitude, especially in the eyes of the
Republican leaders.

In September 1902, Republican party district leaders publicly
lamented that Seth Low had given more patronage to the Greater
New York Democracy than to the Republicans, and demanded
their fair share of jobs.⁶ While Thomas Platt admitted that the
G.O.P. was faring better under Low than it had under Strong,
and that while Low made the Republicans very few promises,
he kept the ones he did make, it was known that the Platt wing
of the Republican party was disenchanted with Low's regime,
and many of the mayor's supporters feared Republican treachery
in 1903.⁷ But, fortunately for Low, the Platt wing of the Republican party was engaged in a bitter fratricidal struggle with the
Roosevelt-Odell faction for control of the State party. The
mayor's relations with both Roosevelt and Odell were excellent,
and if, as seemed probable, Platt's powers were curbed by Odell,
there would be no question of the Republicans endorsing Low.
In October 1902, Governor Odell sent the Citizens' Union a
letter warmly praising the Low administration, and the Union
was confident Odell's support would make the mayor's renomination much easier.⁸ However, Democratic support was also essential to fusion success, and in the 1902 gubernatorial campaign, Seth Low committed a grievous political blunder.

As a Republican in a heavily Democratic city, Seth Low was
dependent upon Democratic support for his election, and that
support would be forthcoming only so long as the Democrats of

New York believed him to be truly non-partisan—a mayor who had only the best interests of the city at heart. Realizing this, Seth Low consciously and deliberately eschewed taking positions on political issues which might alienate the Democrats. "The Fusion movement of last autumn," he declared in the fall of 1902, "was based frankly upon the proposition that men could differ as widely as possible upon state and national policies, and yet be at one in administering the City." However, in the gubernatorial campaign of 1902, the non-partisan mayor of New York took to the stump to urge the re-election of Benjamin Barker Odell. Knowing that if he campaigned for the Republican state ticket, the Democrats would raise the partisan cry in the mayoral election of 1903, Low felt that Odell's re-election was an issue of such vital importance as to justify the danger to his own administration which his actions would invite. "As a member of the Fusion City Government," he told the people of New York:

> [I] associate myself actively with the Republican party in this campaign. . . . The struggle for the governorship of the State of New York, which is being carried on this year, is, in a very real sense, a part of the struggle between the two parties for the control of the National government. If the President's own State slips out of the Republican column this year it will be something more than a cause for sentimental regret. It will be a source of constant weakness to the President in carrying out the policies upon which he has set his heart.[9]

The success of Roosevelt's program, Low felt, was of such overriding importance to the nation that if Odell's re-election as governor of New York would aid the president, it was his duty to work for Odell's success.

Of course, the Greater New York Democracy, under the leadership of John C. Sheehan, Jacob Cantor, and William Hepburn Russell, went all out for Bird S. Coler, the Democratic gubernatorial candidate, but Low, as the head of a non-partisan administration, had to be above partisan suspicion, and in openly supporting Odell, he forfeited his non-partisan standing. In addition to supporting Coler, Sheehan also tried, unsuccessfully, to capture control of Tammany Hall, and conducted himself in such a partisan manner that the Republicans demanded that he and his organization be read out of the fusion camp.[10] Odell won the election, but Coler carried New York City by some 120 thousand votes, and the Greater New York Democracy took a second look at Mayor Low. In January 1903, the city's press reported that fusion Democrats, feeling that Low was no longer non-partisan and too unpopular to win re-election, wanted the mayor to step down in favor of Comptroller Edward M. Grout. Coler's smashing victory in New York City was interpreted by these fusionists as a show of resentment at Low's administration of New York. Tammany Hall, it was reported, was fearful that Low would be replaced by William Travers Jerome.[11] As 1903 progressed, the belief that Seth Low could not win gained support with all political factions. It figured to be an interesting political year.

While all responsible spokesmen readily conceded that Mayor Low was providing New York City with one of the finest administrations in its history, it was far from popular, and by the spring and summer of 1903 public hostility to Low was manifest. Seth Low took office as mayor of New York already enjoying an international reputation as a municipal reformer, and too many people expected him to usher in the millennium overnight. When the city's problems did not quickly disappear, Low was blamed and the "goo-goos" felt betrayed. The persistence of abuses in the police department, the continued problems of prostitution and organized gambling, the inability immediately to eradicate the school shortage and to resolve a host of other difficulties, produced a disillusionment which soon led to apathy and defeatism. Gradually, as the Reverend Reese F. Alsop informed the mayor, "People generally are beginning to realize what an Augean stable you had to cleanse, and how extremely difficult were the conditions. They expected of you impossibilities, and they expected them of you right away. They are learning to appreciate what vast changes you have made."[12] Men were learning that Seth Low was not a God, and to appreciate the great accomplishments which he had succeeded in bringing about; but, things are never the same after the death of a God; the old fire and enthusiasm are no more. The "goo-goos" never did learn that " 'Reform' is not synonymous with perfection. A reform administration cannot in the short span of a year and a half eradicate all the evils engrafted upon the municipality during the previous four years of Tammany control."[13] Then, too, there were those who did not want good government.

Moreover, Seth Low was not a politician; he was not outgoing and warm, and people disliked his aloofness. "Politically," the *Acorn* commented, "the existing regime has not achieved the degree of popularity which is indispensable to its endorsement at the polls. There has been at times a painful lack of tact, a dearth of aggressiveness and an entire absence of leadership and team work among Fusion officials."[14] People resented Low's cold, businesslike efficiency, and politicians, above all, were antipathetic. " 'Did you ever see his smile?' said a politician who was trying to account for his instinctive dislike for the mayor. I had;" Lincoln Steffens replied:

> there is no laughter back of it, no humor, and no sense thereof. The appealing human element is lacking all through. His good abilities are self-sufficient; his dignity is smug; his courtesy seems not kind; his self-reliance is called obstinancy because, though he listens, he seems not to care; though he understands, he shows no sympathy, and when he decides, his reasoning is private. His most useful virtues—probity, intelligence, and conscientiousness—in action are often an irritation; they are so contented. Mr. Low is the bourgeois reformer type. Even where he compromises he gets no credit; his concessions make the impression of surrenders. A politician can say "no" and make a friend, where Mr. Low will lose one by saying "yes." . . . Mr. Low's is not a lovable character.[15]

The unlovable Mr. Low, however, was by all accounts a good mayor, and no one had the temerity to suggest that they could do better—not even George B. McClellan. Elected to give New York good government, he was doing that, but he did not intend to be a "hail, good fellow," and if the people wanted congenial mediocrity, they would have to find it elsewhere. "The people of the City of New York," Edward M. Grout declared, "will get just as good government as they want, and no better."[16] It was for the people to decide what kind of government they wanted.

Politically, Low seemed to be holding his ground in the spring of 1903. Lt. Gov. Timothy L. Woodruff, conceding that the G.O.P. was not entirely satisfied with its patronage, asserted that Low's was the best administration in the history of New York City, and pledged that he would support the mayor for re-election.[17] William Travers Jerome, while calling Low timid and cowardly, and holding that vigorous leadership was essential to fusion success, nevertheless declared that no better candidate than Seth Low could be found for the mayoralty, and that fusion's cause was so transcendentally good that it could not fail through the shortcomings of one man.[18] With an endorsement like that, Seth Low did not need political opponents. In mid-

April, the Citizens' Union, meeting to plan its fall campaign, warmly endorsed the Low administration, and called a fusion conference for May 11. It was reported, though, that many members of the Union were convinced that the mayor could not win re-election and favored a new standard-bearer.[19]

On May 7, 1903, Senator Platt expressed a desire that the fusion conference, scheduled for May 11, take no action relative to the selection of a mayoral candidate. He was not opposed to Low, he declared, but he wanted to avoid the tensions of a summer campaign. In accordance with Platt's wish, the Citizens' Union, the Republican party, and the independent Democratic organizations which attended the fusion conference decided to take no action until early September, but, more importantly, they also declined to endorse the Low administration. Ominously, the German-American civic groups, incensed at Greene's harsh excise enforcement, boycotted the conference.[20] Later that month, Platt, as he did two years back, asserted that the good of the fusion movement necessitated the nomination of an independent Democrat for mayor in 1903. However, Platt's efforts to force Low's removal from the ticket was promptly squelched by Cornelius Bliss who called Low's renomination an absolute prerequisite to fusion success, and threw the weight of the Odell machine behind the mayor.[21] Thereafter, while the Platt wing of the party continued to grumble about Low's shortcomings, it was no longer a threat to the mayor's renomination. "They are still talking about their patronage disappointments . . . ," the *Acorn* noted in July. "They are sulking and they are skulking and behaving generally like aggrieved coyotes."[22] But, these coyotes had long since been mastered.

Surprisingly enough, as summer approached, the most ardent fusionists were the independent Democrats, and while they might have preferred one of their own number as the mayoral nominee, they did not give voice to that preference publicly. For the most part, the anti-Tammany Democrats, unable to agree on a candidate among themselves, were satisfied with Low, especially with their share of patronage under him. Also, Jacob Cantor was borough president of Manhattan, and the Greater New York Democracy leader diligently provided jobs for thousands of his followers. As a result, "there are no stronger Fusionists than the followers of Cantor and Sheehan," the *Acorn* noted and added, "Had the others of Fusion been as good politicians as Mr. Cantor there would not be the present doubt about

Fusion victory."[23] While Cantor was a superb politician, Low was not, and disturbing rumors continued to circulate that a concerted effort would be made to force him to step down as mayor. "How could the leaders of any of the organizations that supported Mr. Low two years ago," the *Times* asked, "frame an excuse for not supporting the Reform candidate for mayor this year that would not instantly raise a public question as to their sanity or their morality?"[24] The *Times* would be astounded at the good and sufficient reasons politicians could devise for not supporting Low a second time, and their drive to deny him the nomination began in earnest in late July.

The anti-Low coalition consisted of independent Democrats, members of the Citizens' Union, pro- and anti-Platt Republicans, and last but not least, leaders of the German community. Toward the end of July, Austen G. Fox, a good government leader in the city, wrote President Roosevelt a long letter declaring that from an abstract point of view, Mayor Low should, of course, have a renomination if he so desired it, but that there was a practical reason for his declining to seek re-election. If Low again ran for mayor, Fox asserted, not only would a Republican defeat follow, but the worst element of the Democratic party would triumph, and at all costs, that calamity must be avoided. For the good of the city, Fox urged Roosevelt to use his influence with Low to secure his declination of a renomination, and to urge the G.O.P. to support the candidacy of an independent Democrat for mayor with Repulicans running for the borough presidencies. Local Republican leaders, Fox charged, desired Low's renomination only so that he would be defeated, thereby strengthening the Platt wing of the party.[25] Unable to block Low's renomination directly, the anti-Low forces hoped to bring presidential pressure to bear on the mayor. Roosevelt sent Fox's letter to Low for the latter's information, but expressed his opinion that, "your renomination is not only wise but the only wise and proper thing to do."[26]

Replying to the president's note and enclosed letter from Fox, Mayor Low told Roosevelt that Fox's estimation of the New York City political situation might well be correct, and that he would prefer not to have to stand for re-election. Citing his four years' service as mayor of Brooklyn, his unsuccessful 1897 campaign, and his two years as mayor of Greater New York, Low declared that he had served the people long enough, and merited retirement to private life. He had an interview with R. Fulton Cutting a short time ago, he told the president, and informed the Citizens' Union Chairman that fusion should not consider itself under any personal obligation to him, but should select the best available man as mayoral nominee. Realizing that his chances of re-election were slim, Low told Cutting that he would consent to run again only if the fusion conference was unable to agree on a suitable replacement. "There are some things even worse than defeat," he declared, "and one such thing is to fail to make a fight that ought to be made. When a man represents a cause worth fighting for, if this cause needs him he must stand. That, at heart, is my conception of a Citizens' duty."[27] Low was sincere in his protestations against serving another term as mayor, and opposition to his candidacy was now becoming so strong as to give Low hope that he might yet escape another campaign.

Early in August, Herman Ridder, head of the German-American Reform Union, which its allies claimed controlled forty thousand votes and its opponents forty, declared that he and his organization would under no circumstances support Low for a second term. Bitterly denouncing the administration's excise policy, Ridder charged that puritanical bigots were violating the personal liberties of thousands of German-American citizens by making the drinking of a glass of beer in pleasant surroundings, and in the company of friends, a crime against society. Holding out the hope that a Democrat would be more tolerant of the customs of others, Ridder urged fusion to dump Low in favor of an independent Democrat.[28] On August 15, William Hepburn Russell, commissioner of accounts in the Low administration, and a leader of the Greater New York Democracy, joined Ridder in demanding an independent Democrat as the mayoral nominee, but his reasons were of a different nature. "It goes without saying," Russell told Low two weeks later in tendering his resignation from office:

> that your administration has my sincere endorsement, and that to you, both personally and officially, my fullest confidence is given.
>
> I believe that your administration has resulted in great good to the City of New York, and that long after you have ceased to be Mayor, the merits of your work will be more fully appreciated than they are to-day. I gave you my unqualified and earnest support in 1897 and again in 1901, abandoning, in or-

der to do so, tempting opportunities for political preferment through local party fealty.

If, as Russell firmly believed, Low was an outstanding mayor, why did he now oppose his renomination? Because, he went on:

> The movement for your renomination is being given a decidedly political cast by Republican national leaders who are not citizens of this City, and if this unwise course continues, it may place me and other independent Democrats in a most embarrassing position.
>
> "Fusion" must not be a name for Republicanism in disguise if independent Democrats are to support the fusion movement this Fall. Fusion must mean non-partisanship in the municipal government in the fullest sense of that term, or I, for one, cannot support it.[29]

It was an open secret that President Roosevelt and Governor Odell wanted Low's re-election, and bringing their pressure to bear, the G.O.P. state committee, late in August, declared that it would attempt to force Low's renomination on the fusion conference. A day later, Senator Platt fell in line, and declared that he was for Low unreservedly, and one day after that, the Republican state committee announced that the voting strength of the fusion Democrats was so small as to make their influence in fusion councils negligible, and that consequently their wishes need not be given serious consideration. Republican votes, it held, would determine the fate of fusion.[30] It was this Republican arrogance which so alienated the independent Democrats, and the Citizens' Union, responding to the Republican declarations, condemned the G.O.P.'s demand for Low's renomination as tending to destroy the non-partisan image of the fusion movement.[31]

The Democrats were more blunt. "It is our firm conviction," Russell proclaimed, "that Mr. Roosevelt cannot carry this state in 1904 unless a Republican mayor is elected in New York City this year." If Low again became the fusion mayoral candidate, he maintained, Tammany would raise the cry of Democracy against Republicanism, "and the party lines will be drawn as closely as possible."[32] Democrats, such as Russell, argued that in 1897 Seth Low ran against both Croker and Platt, and therefore, good government advocates could endorse his candidacy in clear conscience without feeling that they had betrayed the

principles of their parties. Similarly, in 1901, the fusion movement was directed against a political ring whose corruption
ranked with, if it did not actually surpass, Tweed's. Again, all
honest partisans could back Low because the election was fought
solely on local issues, and had no State or national overtones.
However, in the fall of 1902, the Democrats charged, "Casting
aside his pretence of non-partisanship and yielding to his innate
Republicanism, Mayor Low formed an allience with the Odell
political machine."[33] Low had betrayed his non-partisan pledge,
they argued, by campaigning for Odell, and he was now an
ardent G.O.P. partisan. If he were re-elected in 1903, Low
would employ all the weight of his office on behalf of President
Roosevelt's 1904 campaign, and the national Democratic party
would be at a distinct disadvantage in New York. For these
reasons, the Greater New York Democracy wanted a Democratic
mayor in New York, and because of these partisan considerations, William Hepburn Russell resigned from the Low administration. "It is evident," the mayor replied in accepting his
resignation, "that a Commissioner who wishes to subordinate
the interests of the city of New York, in the coming election, to
some outside and indirect effect, has no longer a place in an
administration that is unwilling to subordinate the interests of
the city, at any time, to any other consideration whatever."[34]
But, it was Seth Low, who campaigning for Governor Odell in
the fall of 1902, first violated the non-partisan pledge.

Even within the Citizens' Union there was opposition to
Low's candidacy. While R. Fulton Cutting declared, "I am un-
qualifiedly for Low for Mayor," others were not so sanguine.[35]
"No one," the *Acorn* was told by one "goo-goo:"

> can truthfully deny the statement that Low has antagonized
> a large number of voters since 1901, especially among police-
> men and saloon-keepers, the latter of whom exercise an undue
> political influence, much to be deplored, yet, nevertheless,
> feared. Again, many honest, sterling, independent Democrats
> are suspicious of the repeated Roosevelt-Odell-Low confer-
> ences, and are not inclined to be made cats' paws of. The
> nomination of an independent Democrat would, in my opin-
> ion, clear the political atmosphere, and I sincerely trust
> Mayor Low will accept an appointment as Minister to Urope,
> Arope, Irope, Orope, or some other place.[36]

As the crucial month of September approached, reports found
their way into the press that the rank-and-file of the Citizens'

Union wanted District Attorney Jerome to be fusion's mayoral nominee, but that the Union would not endorse him until such time as Low publicly stated his refusal to serve another term as mayor. Jerome was alleged to be acceptable to both Platt and Roosevelt, but not to Odell who still insisted that Low run again.[37] For his part, the District Attorney continually asserted, "I am in no sense a candidate for the Mayoralty. I have no desire for the nomination under any circumstances."[38] It was obvious, though, that many fusionists favored the idea of nominating an independent Democrat for mayor in 1903, and of all the available Democrats, Jerome was the most popular. "The Fusion stable is full of good horses," the pro-Low *Acorn* declared. "The determining element will be as to whether on the eve of a presidential election, it would not be wiser to name an independent Democrat than a Republican like Mr. Low."[39] The dominant note in fusion ranks, as the time for nominating candidates drew near, was confusion.

On September 1, 1903, as the press of New York carried President Roosevelt's official declaration of neutrality in the New York mayoralty, the Citizens' Union and its allies held a pre-conference strategy meeting.[40] The minutes of the conference revealed that the Union was officially uncommitted on any mayoral nominee, but that Seth Low was favored over any other possible choice. Delegates from the Republican County Committees were strongly in favor of the mayor, as were representatives from the German-American Municipal League of Brooklyn (despite the divisive excise issue), the Order of Acorns, and the American-Italian League. No substantial support was forthcoming for any Democrat.[41] Consequently, the *New York World's* contention that William Travers Jerome was the favorite of the fusion confrerees would not appear to be substantiated by the records of the conference. Nevertheless, as the paper pointed out, the only thing that could prevent Low's renomination would be his positive refusal to stand. To deny him renomination, the *World* asserted, would be to indict the fusion government as a failure.[42]

Once again, as in 1901, the considerable anti-Low element in the fusion movement was unable to rally around an alternative candidate, and the pro-Low faction was, as usual, united in the single-minded purpose of renominating the mayor. A. S. Haight, pro-Low leader in the Citizens' Union, wrote the mayor that he was much stronger now than he was in 1901, but that aside from the question of political expediency there was a moral issue to be considered. "It were better for the cause," he declared, "that we go down with our colors flying than that we show the white feather in the face of the enemy. . . ." There could be no compromise on Low's renomination, Haight proclaimed, and he pledged his utmost efforts to secure him the nomination.[43] For these "goo-goos," the 1903 campaign was a moral not a political fight. Replying to Haight, Low asserted, "Personally, I am waiting to know what the Fusionists want. I shall have no difficulty in determining on my course when they determine on theirs."[44] He had made up his mind to do nothing to seek renomination, and hoped that fusion could agree upon another candidate, but failing that agreement, he felt it to be his duty to stand for re-election. He could not now abandon the fusion movement.

The formal fusion conference was scheduled to convene the second week of September, and in the final days before the nomination was to be made, events were to become even more confused. On the 2nd of September, the *New York World* charged that while the Republicans were openly booming Low for the mayoralty, they were prepared to drop him at the last moment in favor of District Attorney Jerome. The reasoning of Republican leaders, the paper reported, was that reform had become so unpopular in New York City that no fusionist could win the mayoralty, and therefore, since fusion was going to lose in any event, it would be better for the Republican party if a Democrat, such as Jerome, had the honor of leading the hosts of reform to defeat. With a Presidential election only a year away, Low's failure to win re-election would hurt the party's image, whereas Jerome's defeat would have no effect on the Grand Old Party.[45] This was the position of Thomas Platt, but his views were not shared by the national administration, and there was never any danger of the Republicans abandoning Low for Jerome, or for any other Democrat.

It would, indeed, have been next to impossible for the Republicans to switch away from Low, for the bulk of New York's editorial opinion was strongly in the mayor's favor, and any effort to replace him would call down scathing criticism on the party's leadership. The Republican and highly respected *New York Tribune* asserted that fusion's chances of victory were bright with Low at the head of the ticket. There was not a Democrat, it held, who could match his record of accomplishment. The Democratic *New York World* came out strongly in support of Low's renomination, and the independent *New York Times,* while conceding that Low was not perfect, declared that he was the best man available to the city.[46] In fact, the only major New York dailies hostile to Low's re-election were William Randolph Hearst's *New York American* and *New York Evening Journal.* "The attitude of the newspapers of the city," the *Advertiser* declared, "toward Mayor Low's renomination is as creditable as it is encouraging."[47] But, while the press was pro-Low, the fusion confrerees still had reservations, and on September 4, the *World* headlined that the fusion delegates had "Low on Their Lips, Jerome in Their Heart," and were desperately searching for a way to gently and courteously force Low off the ticket.[48]

By now, Low was, as Hearst's *Evening Journal* reported, utterly disgusted at the disunity in fusion's ranks. "The Mayor," an undisclosed City Hall source declared, "expected enthusiastic endorsement at Tuesday evening's conference. He was entitled to it. His pride was hurt when it developed that there was opposition to him."[49] Determined to break the deadlock, and force the fusion conference to either renominate him or unite on an independent Democrat, Seth Low, on September 7, 1903, wrote Citizens' Union Chairman R. Fulton Cutting, declaring:

> Since my return to the city I have consulted with a number of my friends as to the existing situation, and I have found in certain quarters that are entirely friendly, the opinion that the present emergency perhaps calls for the nomination of an independent democrat as the leader of the fusion forces this year. Under these circumstances, I very much prefer that the Conference should act upon that view, and, in that event, the candidate of the Conference will have my hearty support. In this situation I recognize not only the very natural feeling that turn-about is fair play, but also the natural and inevitable result of the shortening of the Mayor's term from four years to two, which brings this municipal election in the year preceding the national election. This has thrown into the coming city canvass the maximum amount of party politics, and has made it as difficult as possible for this superb city of 3,750,000 people, with business and social interests of its own far greater in importance than those of many states, to elect its city government from the point of view of its own interests only, instead [of] . . . upon state and national issues.
>
> In view of this state of facts, the Conference should face

this situation frankly, and must itself take the responsibility, if it wishes me to stand, of summoning me into the field on its own motion.

Low had virtually given the fusionists his resignation. He had freed them to nominate an independent Democrat, who would be more acceptable to New York's heavily Democratic electorate. Low did not put himself above the cause which he embodied, telling Cutting, "We should be contending for a government of Law as against a return to a government of graft; for an administration of the city's resources in the interest of the public treasury instead of for the benefit of the favored few. . . ."[50] It was of no consequence who led the fusion movement, he maintained, so long as a capable leader was found. Cutting had the letter published in all the city's papers, and it broke the back of the anti-Low coalition.

Low's letter left fusion with the choice of selecting a Democratic nominee to replace the mayor on the fusion ticket, and of course, they were unable to agree on anyone, leaving Seth Low as the lesser of the many evils facing the conference. On the night of September 9, Seth Low was renominated as mayor of New York. The conference's decision, though, was not final until ratification by the parent organizations represented in the conference. Low's renomination was not yet secured; in fact, the battle was just beginning.

When Seth Low was renamed as fusion's candidate for the mayoralty, the Greater New York Democracy, slighted that its views had been ignored, refused to endorse the mayor, and its delegates walked out of the conference. Fearing that the independent Democrats would rejoin the Wigwam, many of Low's good government supporters hoped that he would decline the nomination. It was reported that William Travers Jerome was returning to the city to persuade Low to step down, feeling that fusion must fall if the mayor ran again.[51] Editorially, the *World* scored the action of the Greater New York Democracy, asserting that, "He [Low] has made mistakes, but who would not in his difficult position?" Calling upon all true Democrats to endorse Low, it declared that he "has in the main been true to the principles and pledges upon which he was elected. He has given New York a government of a high order—the best in most respects that the city has had in half a century."[52] Pressure from Democrats of national standing in support of Low apparently had potent effect on the Greater New York Democracy, for, two days after its representatives walked out of the fusion conference, John C. Sheehan, the president of the organization, vowed loyalty to the mayor. At a stormy meeting on September 21, the Greater New York Democracy voted fifty to one in favor of Low and fusion. William Hepburn Russell was the lone dissenter, and he was forced out of the organization's executive leadership.[53] The Democrats appeared to be holding firm, but Jerome, characterized by one political reporter as a "Roundhead intolerant," was upsetting fusion's delicate peace of mind.[54]

On September 13, the District Attorney's friends charged that Jerome had the support of both Platt and Roosevelt in his bid for the mayoralty nomination when Low's public letter to R. Fulton Cutting cut the heart out of his campaign.[55] Three days later, Jerome released a public letter of his own, addressed to Charles C. Nadal of the Citizens' Union. "I have satisfied myself by careful inquiry," he declared:

> that the great mass of people to whom we must look for support in the coming campaign believe that Mr. Low cannot be re-elected and that while they may give a half-hearted support to him for the sake of the cause, they cannot overcome their dislike and disgust for him.
>
> This attitude on the part of the people—people to whom we look for support—is not due so much to what Mr. Low has done or left undone, as to the unlovable personality of the man himself.
>
> Egotism, self-complacency, and constitutional limitations are not the elements to make a leader, nor do they attract the support of an American electorate.
>
> Mr. Low is the most unpopular candidate you can select.
>
> Mr. Low should not be nominated because of his personal unpopularity, caused not by his adherence to the principles of reform, but springing from the personal character of the man.[56]

The letter shocked and dismayed New York's municipal reformers, and was received as a cowardly act of betrayal. If Jerome, they felt, had objections to Low's renomination, he should have made them known before the fusion conference, to do so afterward served only to create dissension in fusion's ranks. Greeted with repugnance, Jerome's letter only redounded to his own disadvantage. While criticizing Low, Jerome declared that he was not interested in the mayoralty, and was unable to answer the *World's* query: "If not Low, who?"[57]

Only a few months before, Jerome had asserted that fusion's cause was so worthy that no man's personal faults could defeat it. However, consistency was not one of his virtues. The District Attorney's letter, though, did rally the hosts of reform. "Jerome's attitude, so far," Low wrote President Roosevelt, "has rather helped than weakened our cause. He has made its friends fighting mad, and has scattered apathy to the four winds.[58] Roundly castigated for his unsportsmanlike conduct, Jerome, a few days after making his letter to Nadal public, revealed that he had been encouraged to write his anti-Low epistle by none other than Thomas A. Fulton, secretary of the Citizens' Union, who wanted Low off the ticket so that he could engineer the nomination of R. Fulton Cutting as fusion's candidate for the mayoralty.[59] Jerome's revelations only produced more disgust, and Thomas Fulton, who had acted without Cutting's knowledge, was dismissed as secretary. The anti-Low faction's plan to fight the mayor's renomination from the floor of the Citizens' Union convention collapsed, and with the end of September, Low had formally been renominated by all the bodies in the fusion alliance. Even Herman Ridder's German-American Reform Union fell in line behind him, though it still grumbled at Greene's excise policy. The Mayor's 1901 running mates, Edward M. Grout, Charles V. Fornes, and William Travers Jerome, who now announced that he would endorse the fusion ticket after all, were also renominated. Grout accepted fusion's call to run for comptroller a second time, in order to show that Jerome's charges against Low were unfounded. "By those who do not know Mr. Low as I do," Grout stated:

> who have not worked side by side with him for two years, and who have not seen his breadth of view and strong grasp upon municipal questions and his marked ability to get results, attack is made upon his personality, and his patience and care and conservatism are distorted into weakness.
>
> I can effectively do my part in refuting this mistaken view only by accepting renomination.[60]

But fusion had not yet heard from Charles F. Murphy. The election of Seth Low as mayor of New York in 1901 had ended "Boss" Croker's decidedly undistinguished career as the Wigwam's Sachem. For the first year of Low's regime, a triumvirate was established to administer the affairs of the Tammany Society, but gradually one Charles Francis Murphy came to dominate the triumvirs, and by 1903 he was in absolute command of Tammany Hall with powers as dictatorial, albeit more enlightened, as Croker's.[61] Born in New York City on June 20, 1858, Murphy was a product of the Gas House District, and like so many other Tammany leaders he got his first job at the shipyards. Saving some money, he opened his first saloon in 1879. Prospering, he acquired three more by 1890, and began to be a power in Tammany politics. In 1892, he was named Tammany leader of the Gas House District, and under Mayor Van Wyck, he was appointed commissioner of the Department of Docks. While serving in that capacity, his personal fortune grew considerably, and ungenerous souls suggested that he was misusing his office. A devout Catholic, known for his generosity to charity (friends said he gave away half of every dollar he stole), Murphy was a resourceful and popular leader. In 1903, he was determined to defeat the fusionists, and having won over the powerful support of William Randolph Hearst, and having crushed an insurrection in Brooklyn led by the once-formidable Hugh McLaughlin, he was in a good position to accomplish his goal. Murphy realized that in order to capture control of City Hall, he would have to win back the independent Democrats, and in the latter part of September, he systematically set about to do just that.

Exactly how Murphy enticed the independent Democrats away from fusion and back into the all-embracing fold of Tammany remains unclear to this day. But, on September 27, John C. Sheehan, accusing the Citizens' Union and the Republicans of ignoring independent Democratic sentiment, announced that the Greater New York Democracy was bolting the fusion alliance and returning to Tammany.[62] Jacob Cantor, the popular Manhattan borough president, also announced his agreement with Sheehan's position. Apparently, Murphy had convinced the independents that the national aspirations of the Democratic party were dependent upon the election of a Democratic mayor in New York, that Low was openly partisan and that support of his bid for re-election would only aid the G.O.P. Throughout the campaign, independent Democrats would declare that their opposition to Low was based on national and not local considerations.[63] That same day, it was announced that Edward M. Grout and Charles V. Fornes, fusion's nominees for comptroller and president of the Board of Alderman, would also be the Tammany candidates for those positions.

The announcement took the fusionists by surprise. "The cleverest political coup of Murphy's career," George B. McClellan remarked, "was the kidnapping of Low's running mates. . . . They were both of the brand which is known as 'independent Democrats,' a euphemism for opportunist."[64] Bewilderment, anger, despair, and disgust swept over the ranks of fusion. William Travers Jerome called it treason, and demanded the removal of Grout and Fornes from the ticket; most fusionists agreed with him. The next day, though, the influential *New York World* asserted that as fusion was a non-partisan movement, and since Grout and Fornes were admittedly capable officials, it should not object to their endorsement by Tammany. It was a compliment to fusion, the paper argued, and would guarantee the election of two honest and highly qualified public servants.[65] R. Fulton Cutting was, at first, inclined to accept the *World's* reasoning; and, though Low denied it, Grout contended that the mayor knew of and approved his intention of accepting a dual nomination for the comptrollership.[66] SenatorPlatt, however, was adamant in his insistence that the renegade fusionists be purged, and Cutting bowed to the Republican pressure.[67] Early in October, a stunned fusion conference reconvened, and removing the names of Grout and Fornes from their ticket, they replaced them with Frederic W. Hinrichs and Edward J. McGuire, who were also independent Democrats.

To head the Democratic slate, Murphy selected George Brinton McClellan, Jr., the son of the Civil War General, who had served an undistinguished stint as a congressman from New York. "Murphy," McClellan recounted, "made a personal appeal to me. He said . . . that the leaders of the organization believed me to be the only Tammany Hall Democrat who could beat Seth Low, and that they in fact demanded that I should accept the nomination as a matter of public duty. There was nothing else for me to do but accept, and very regretfully I accepted."[68] As October opened, McClellan prepared to battle Seth Low for the mayoralty, but, though, the mayor had been formally renominated by the Republicans and the Citizens' Union, he had not yet accepted the nomination.

Low had hoped to avoid another political campaign, but events again conspired to place him in the political field, and there was little doubt as to his ultimate decision to run; it was, after all, his duty to New York, though that did not make the prospect any more pleasant. Jacob Neu, a fusion confreree and ardent Low supporter, wrote the mayor in mid-September, "You have been tried in the crucible of political wire-pulling and public scrutiny, and have resisted all efforts . . . to perpetuate yourself in office." Neu had meant it as a compliment, but it was this very quality which was at the root of Low's political difficulties. As Neu also observed, there was a considerable undercurrent of Republican hostility to Low, because:

> they have been unable to make party capital out of your administration in the past, that they are aware they cannot make party capital out of it in the future, and that any unknown quantity will suit them as a candidate on the theory that they might be more successful with such an one than with you, and therefore ready to take a chance on anybody but yourself.[69]

Low's failure to employ political patronage to create a reform machine was a severe handicap, and the Platt Republicans remained sullen and lackluster. For them the campaign would not be fought with enthusiasm.

While Low may have left much to be desired from the point of view of the professional politicians, to the "goo-goo" amateurs he was more than a good mayor; he was the personification of a cause. "Mayor Low," the *Acorn* asserted, "has come to be regarded more as an institution than as a man; as something to be voted for which will insure honesty, competency and decency."[70] To abandon Low would be to destroy the symbol of the entire good government movement, and in this struggle of "civilization against barbarism," the *New York Tribune* opined:

> Something is due to principle, regardless of votes, and if there is not enough of civic virtue in New York for its citizens to continue what they know to be good government, to honor faithful officials even if they have interfered with their own pet public vices, whether of maintaining unsanitary tenement houses, or neglecting their personal taxes, or violating the excise laws, and to vote under the sway of reason rather than on the impulse of a whirlwind of excitement, it is time for New York to face its own degradation and suffer the consequences. If it has not enough of good citizenship to save itself on the plain issue of honest or dishonest government, it deserves again to suffer at the hands of criminals[71]

Righteousness, not political expediency, dominated the "goo-

goos" of the Citizens' Union, and since the Union dominated
the fusion alliance, morality again prevailed over politics. "You
are," the Reverend Alsop told the mayor, "fairly entitled to
the loyal cooperation and to the heartiest wishes . . . of the
whole best element of New York."[72]

On October 9, Seth Low, resigning himself to the performance
of his civic duty, announced his long-awaited acceptance of the
fusion nomination for the mayoralty. "The Fusion demand
now," he declared in his letter of acceptance:

> as in the last campaign, is (1) for a government of law, as dis-
> tinguished from the inequalities, the favoritism, and the cor-
> ruption due to tolerated blackmail; (2) for a government in
> the interest of the public treasury, as against a government
> dominated by 'that mercenary spirit that breeds dishonesty
> in the public service'; and (3) for a government of the city
> in the interest of its own citizens as against a government that
> is swayed this way or that by the supposed interests of national
> politics.[73]

Confidence in the desire of the people for good government,
and certitude that right would prevail again marked the fusion
campaign. At Cooper Union, William Travers Jerome, extending Low his utmost support, declared that New York's salvation
was dependent on the mayor's re-election.[74]

The election would be decided not by the votes of Republicans
or Citizens' Union members, or even by Democrats; the issue
would be settled, as Lincoln Steffens pointed out, by the independent voters—100 thousand strong. But, these "voters have
been taught to vote only once in a long while, only when
excited by picturesque leadership and sensational exposures,
only *against*."[75] Unless fusion could reach these voters, all was
lost. And while the Citizens' Union proclaimed that its platform
was the record of the best administration in the history of
New York City, this did not inspire interest.[76] Virtue is far too
dull to arouse the passion of the independent voter; only vice is
interesting, and this public apathy was conceded by Citizens'
Union Treasurer Elgin R.L. Gould who told Richard W. G.
Welling, chairman of the Union's Campaign Committee, "I fear
very much that you will have to keep your estimates as low as
possible—very much lower than the amount your committee
expended in 1901. It is exceedingly difficult I find to get
money. . . ."[77] Fusion was in trouble.

McClellan conducted a vigorous campaign, and to his credit

a clean one. He did not attempt to criticize Low's record as mayor, conceding that it was outstanding. His entire campaign was geared to a patriotic appeal to Democratic voters to stand up for their party. Asserting that the Tammany of 1903 was not the Tammany of "Boss" Croker, he promised New York a clean government serving the needs of its citizens, but, "The great issue before the people, broadly stated," he declared:

> is, shall this Democratic city be governed by a Democratic administration; shall the party to which belongs a majority of the people of New York be permitted to give the metropolis a government so efficient and honest that by the inspiration of its good deeds the State of New York will be taken from the doubtful column and its Electoral vote recorded in favor of the Democratic candidate for the Presidency; or whether the people of our city shall have two years more of Republican administration and during the Presidential campaign be misrepresented by the Republican machine, certain to misuse the functions of government in the interests of the selfish ambitions of Republican politicians?[78]

This strategy was followed by all of Tammany's campaigners, including Edward M. Grout, who only a few months earlier had ridiculed the idea that the mayoralty election would have any effect on the 1904 presidential campaign.[79]

While prominent national Democrats, such as Charles S. Fairchild, repudiated the notion that local elections had any bearing on national ones, and remained loyal to fusion, Low found the charge disturbing enough to clarify his non-partisan doctrine. "It is true," he told Richard H. Clarke:

> that I presided at a Republican meeting during the last State campaign. On the other hand, Mr. Grout spoke, not only in the city but away from the city, in behalf of the Democratic candidate for Governor. We both agreed that non-partisanship in City affairs did not mean that city officers of either party should cease to take interest in their party affairs, but only that in the administration of the City they should work for the interest of the City and not their party, and that, in so doing, they should be able to find their instruments from the membership of all parties.[80]

It is, of course, impossible to determine how many voters were swayed by the respective arguments of McClellan and Low on the connection between partisanship and city government, though a number of journals and newspapers, including the

New York Times, The Outlook, and the *Review of Reviews*
concluded that Tammany's appeal to partisanship had fallen
flat.[81]

Far more effective was Tammany's assertion that fusion
government was puritanical. Condemning Greene's excise policy
as an infringement of personal liberty, Edward M. Grout called
for Greene's dismissal, and pledged McClellan's toleration of
the city's habits and customs.[82] He was loudly cheered. Tens
of thousands of German-Americans and other immigrants deeply
resented Greene's strict excise enforcement. Charging that Low's
Health Department, Tenement House Department, and police
force were dictating the personal lives of New Yorkers, the
Democrats vowed to give the people a government tempered by
regard for individual rights. The promise found favor with
landlords angered at being forced to make their tenements liveable, with grocers forbidden to sell tainted milk and made
to clean up their stores, and with saloon-keepers irked at
Greene's perpetual raids. And, once again, Tammany's campaign
was well-financed by the franchised corporations.[83]

The fusionists, for their part, were short of funds, of speakers,
and were finding it difficult to display their campaign posters.
Eugene Blumenthal, Chairman of the C.U.'s Campaign Committee in the 19th A.D., begged Welling for speakers "that can
talk to hostile audiences. . . ."[84] And Welling, asking permission
to display Citizens' Union posters on a number of vacant buildings, was told:

> We regret very much that in behalf of the owners of the
> several properties whom we represent, we cannot consent to
> the placing of posters in the windows of stores and private
> houses which may be vacant. We know the peculiar character-
> istics of the street boys and feel quite confident that there
> would be more or less destruction of plate glass should the
> privilege be granted.
>
> We can assure you, however, that we are all doing what
> we can toward the success of the fusion ticket.[85]

Though problems were many and difficult, fusion's hopes
were high; after all, its cause was good.

"If Mayor Low had not aroused enthusiasm for his personality
and his peculiar ego," Ervin Wardman observed, "he had, by
the time this campaign opened, so ordered his official household
and so performed the work of Fusion that there was established
a compelling cause, failing a great leader, for all men of civic

ideals to follow."[86] In less than two years, fusion had driven corruption from the police department, begun the building of enough new schools to solve the school shortage, improved the health of the entire city, banished prostitution from the tenements and made them more liveable, and lowered the tax rate, while transferring its burdens to the shoulders of the large property-owners. While it had not solved all problems, and while some of its programs and policies were inept, the fusion administration had given the city, at all times, its best effort, and its failings stemmed from inexperience not from indifference. Mayor Low's government had the support of the bulk of New York's press and clergy, and of its educated citizenry. "Mr. Low," Lincoln Steffens wrote, "has learned the business of New York; he is just about competent now to become the mayor of a great city. Is there a demand for Mr. Low?"[87] Could a movement devoid of a leader win in a city accustomed to colorful leadership?

Low and his fusion colleagues considered their campaign to be part of a great effort to educate the American people to the governmental requirements of an urban society, and while victory was, of course, desirable, enlightenment was of far greater importance. Consequently, issues and principles were of larger magnitude than winning personality and inspiring leadership. If democracy was to be successful in an urban environment, the masses must be made to understand what makes for good government; picturesque leadership, though it might produce good administration for a short time, would ultimately fail to secure its permanent existence unless the people understood what was required of them. The real issue in the campaign, as *The Outlook* declared, was not between Low and McClellan; rather it was between honest, business—like government on the one hand, and paternal but corrupt government on the other. Low's personality, or lack of it, was not at issue.[88] Even a losing effort, if it helped the people to see more clearly, would be worthwhile. As Theodore Roosevelt assured Low, "It is evident that the fight will be so stiff that whatever its result, your usefullness will be increased and not impaired for the future."[89]

On the eve of election, the issues had been clearly drawn. For fusion, as the *Tribune* put it:

> This contest is part of a great movement for humanity. The problem of city government is the great unsolved problem of democratic society. Shall we, the people of the chief

city of the most progressive nation on the earth, confess that
we are tired of the higher civilization and prefer to lapse back
a few steps toward barbarism?[90]

The Democratic case was equally well-stated, if somewhat
exaggerated and oversimplified, by Hearst's *Journal*:

> Mr. Low is a Republican, who believes that a few eminently
> respectable gentlemen, divinely commissioned, are better able
> than the people themselves to govern them.
> Government of the masses by the classes . . . that is what
> Mayor Low typifies. He means well no doubt, but he is the
> reverse of a Democrat—an aristocrat.[91]

Mr. Hearst also announced that his paper would employ one
of two headlines in reporting the result of the election:

Fusion Wins—Red Lights.
Democracy Wins—Green Lights.

The men of New York City went to the polls on Tuesday,
November 3, 1903 to decide the fate of what was commonly
acknowledged to have been the finest government, up to its
time, in the history of the city. That night, Hearst's news boys
ran through the streets of Manhattan shouting: "The lid is
off! The lid is off!"[92] The lid was, indeed, off. George B.
McClellan, Jr., much to the surprise of everyone except Tammany Hall, had defeated Seth Low by 314,782 votes to 252,086—
a decisive majority of 62,696 ballots. The good ship *Fusion*,
torpedoed by considerations of national politics, sank in a mug
of beer. Progressive reform in New York City had come to a
premature end, and President Roosevelt, writing to Nicholas
Murray Butler, commented on Low's defeat, "The dog has
returned to his vomit."[93]

CHAPTER IX

The Patrician as Reformer vs. the Democrat as Villain

Tammany's democratic corruption rests upon the corruption of the people, the plain people, and there lies its great significance; its grafting system is one in which more individuals share than any I have studied. The people themselves get very little; they come cheap, but they are interested. Divided into districts, the organization subdivides them into precincts or neighborhoods, and their sovereign power, in the form of votes, is bought up by kindness and petty privileges. They are forced to surrender, when necessary, by intimidation, but the leader and his captains have their hold because they take care of their own. They speak pleasant words, smile friendly smiles, notice the baby, give picnics up the River or the Sound, or a slap on the back; find jobs, most of them at the city's expense, but they also have newsstands, peddling privileges, railroad and other business places to dispense; they permit violations of the law, and, if a man has broken the law without permission, see him through the court. Though a blow in the face is as readily given as a shake of the hand. Tammany kindness is a real kindness, and will go far, remember long, and take infinite trouble for a friend.

LINCOLN STEFFENS[1]

"I am astonished," Citizens' Union leader R. Fulton Cutting exclaimed upon learning of Seth Low's decisive defeat at the polls.

"I cannot conceive how any people," Republican chieftain M. Linn Bruce declared, "could reject such a splendid administration as Mayor Low's. . . ."

And Francis C. Huntington of the Citizens' Union—summing up the bewilderment of the city's reformers—asserted, "we cannot understand it."[2] The inconceivable had come to pass, fusion had gone down to defeat, and the next few weeks would be devoted to a *postmortem* of reform's failure.

The Democratic *New York World* argued that Low's defeat

was caused by numerous factors of which the most important
were German resentment at Commissioner Greene's excise enforcement, popular discontent with a too-strict administration
of health and building codes, the desire of Democratic voters to
give their party a head start in next year's presidential race by
electing a Democratic mayor in New York, deep-seated hostility
to Odell's tax policies, especially his increase of liquor license
fees, and finally, treachery by the Platt wing of the Republican
party. The *World* deplored the outcome, but felt that fusion had
such a burden to bear that in a short span of two years it was
impossible for it to demonstrate its advantages to the people of
New York. Even under the best of circumstances, fusion would
not have had enough time to consolidate its gains. It concluded
by declaring, "If the majority against Mayor Low were five
times what it is the fact would be unchanged that he has made
a splendid Mayor—one of the very best that the city has had in
its long history."[3]

While generally agreeing with the *World's* analysis, most of
the city's press singled out the return of the independent Democrats to Tammany Hall as the prime factor in Low's defeat.
"The artful raising of the partisan cry," *The Nation* announced,
"deluded multitudes."[4] *Harper's Weekly* echoed *The Nation's*
charge, and the *New York Times* declared:

> Republican disloyalty may account for some part of this trans-
> fer of support, but the most of it unquestionably is due to
> the fact that the Democrats deserting the Fusion cause have
> this year indulged themselves the luxury of voting for their
> regular party candidates. It is a Democratic victory brought
> about by a renewed interest in Democratic fortunes, and a
> renewed desire to see that party triumph in the State and
> Nation.[5]

But, as the *New York Tribune* pointed out, it was not simply
a case of Democratic desertion which led to fusion's repudiation.
The cause of Low's failure to win re-election was far more basic
than that. "New York voted for Tammany," the *Tribune*
asserted, "not because it disliked Mr. Low, not because it had
any sane criticism to pass upon his administration, but simply
because it preferred the Tammany ideal of government to the
fusion ideal." As the *Tribune* went on to declare:

> New York is like a dissipated man of good antecedents.
> When he gets so low that he ceases to be presentable in decent

society, he pulls himself together and resolves to walk in the straight path, but he is no sooner in good trim once more than humdrum honesty and respectability pall upon him and the temptation for his old ways is simply irresistible.

The simple fact is he [Low] gave it too good a government. New Yorkers were not in everyday life up to the moral standard of the temporarily exalted state in which they elected him.

He returns to private life the most distinguished exponent of municipal reform in the country. . . . He has served well a city that simply does not care to be well served.[6]

There was much truth in the *Tribune's* analysis, but factors were at play which it had not mentioned. Theodore Roosevelt, sharing the charging of the "goo-goos" at New York's humiliation, declared that at the heart of Low's repudiation at the polls was the baleful influence of the "anti-Low corporations" which preferred to pay blackmail instead of taxes.[7] The wealthy capitalists, he told Nicholas Murray Butler, financed Low's defeat, and they did so because Tammany's corruption served their interests better than Low's honesty.[8] And writing to Seth Low, he asserted that it was the "better element" in New York who had secured fusion's defeat, because reform, on both the local and national levels, was not to their advantage. They voted against Low, hoping it would reflect on Roosevelt's programs.[9] To a large extent, the President's interpretation was correct. Low's franchise policy and taxation reforms were not to business's liking, and much of the city's business community actively worked for Tammany's success.

Members of the mayor's administration were not only dismayed at fusion's downfall, but many were convinced that the American nation had been dealt a severe blow which would have profound effect on the vitality of its democratic political system. "The voters," Francis Vinton Greene lamented, "deliberately decided to reinstate the Tammany rule of crime and corruption. I consider this one of the most profound and significant events which have happened in this country since the Civil War. It is not alone New York that is affected, but every large city in the land."[10] The cities of America had shown, once again, that they did not want good government, and the prospect of democracy surviving long into the new century did not appear bright to men like Commissioner Greene. The people who would suffer most as a result of Tammany's triumph, Herbert Parsons wrote, will be the poor—the very ones who voted for Tammany. The Low administration, Parsons declared, had done more than any other to help the city's depressed; that they had rejected fusion was the most distressing aspect of McClellan's victory.[11]

The mayor, however, attributed his defeat to an entirely different cause—the shortening of the mayor's term of office. Early in 1901, the State Legislature had amended New York's charter to reduce from four years to two the tenure of the mayor on the assumption that more frequent elections would permit the people to more readily get rid of a bad or corrupt administration. Low had vigorously opposed the reduction, pointing out that since the popular election of New York's mayors began in 1835, Tammany had controlled City Hall continuously until 1863 when an intra-party dispute permitted the election of a Republican. In 1865, however, Tammany returned to power, holding the mayoralty until the downfall of the Tweed ring, in 1871, which brought a two-year period of reform. In 1873, Tammany, once again, was back in power and held City Hall until 1894 when scandal again drove it from office. But the reformers lost in 1897, and the Wigwam once more dominated the city. Low felt that two years was not enough time in which to consolidate reform, and the two-year term would only serve to perpetuate Tammany's rule.[12]

The reduction of the mayor's term of office, Low believed, was the prime cause of fusion's defeat, for as he wrote Assemblyman Newcomb:

> A bad administration grows weaker the longer it is in power: a good one grows stronger the longer it is in power. Under present conditions Tammany lets everything run down at the heels, so that an anti-Tammany Mayor never gets a fair start. Tammany, on the other hand, takes the city over at the end of a reform administration, with everything in apple pie order. In the latter case it takes longer than the two years for the deterioration to become very manifest, and in the former case the necessity of making radical changes all along the line increases the dis-affection growing out of such changes which it takes time to overcome. I think this is the most fundamental lesson of the last election. . . .[13]

He urged Newcomb to support legislation restoring the mayor's term to four years, and to allow the city home rule in regard to Sunday closing so as to remove excise as a divisive issue in the city's political life.

As Low also explained to Governor Odell, vital city services had been so neglected by Tammany that fusion was forced to appropriate vast sums of money in a short period of time to try to overcome the decay fostered by the Wigwam. This naturally led to public criticism of what appeared to be a spendthrift administration, and since the reformers were inexperienced with city government to begin with, the mistakes which they made while learning their trade—plus intense public criticism—only added to the political difficulties of reform government. In addition, two years was too short a time for the benefits of reform administration to become apparent, or for new or improved programs to adequately take hold. Citing school construction, Low told Odell that the schools which he had ordered built would not be finished until after McClellan took office, and consequently, the Democrats would reap the benefits of fusion's schools. Indeed, all along the line, Tammany would inherit the dividends of fusion's programs and innovations. It took two years, Low argued, to conquer the problems left over from a corrupt regime, and while it struggled with those problems, it made enemies. It was only in the last two years of a four-year term that reform could show positive results; only then did its programs start to take hold and did it win friends.[14] Fusion, he declared, was doomed even before it took office.

Professional party politicians like Thomas Platt saw Low's problems as stemming from a somewhat different source. "Elected as a political hybrid," Platt recounted in his memoirs:

> with the well-to-do, easy going, thoughtless aristocrats, organized in some independent guise, pulling in one direction, with such bodies as the City Club pulling in still another, and such fag-ends as the Jimmy O'Briens, the Stecklers and the Sheehans, with their demands and distractions to plague and pursue him; selected for his social position or his standing as a banker or merchant, with little or no experience of public administration no man alive could justify the expectation that secured for him the office of Mayor of New York City, and the prompt return of Tammany to its own is a foregone conclusion from the day he takes office.

"He came and went," Platt concluded, "and New York City is still the same old town. . . ."[15] The trouble with Seth Low, in Platt's opinion, was that he was not a politician, and had no conception of how the political order functioned. Instead of building up a powerful machine rooted in the Republican party, which supplied eighty percent of his vote, he wasted his patronage on non-political experts who carried with them no political following, or gave appointments to independent Democrats in a futile attempt to win the political allegiance of men who despised everything he stood for. As a result, there were no substantial political bonds holding the fusion alliance together, and it easily fell apart at the first partisan conflict. There was a good deal of merit in Platt's argument. Low never did appreciate the importance of patronage in holding political movements together.

Contemporary observers, then, explained the fall of the Low administration in terms of a Democratic desire to strengthen their party for the 1904 Presidential campaign, Republican disloyalty, anger at Low's excise policy, Odell's taxes, business disaffection with reform, fusion's own political ineptitude, and weariness of the heroics demanded by the fusionists. "After two years of Mayor Low," John DeWitt Warner concluded in an effort to explain why fusion failed, "our City voters could think of nothing further they wanted done that they thought him a specially good man to do."[16] Lincoln Steffens, however—that astute observer of the American municipal scene—discerned a much more basic reason for fusion's collapse. "Tammany," he explained, "is honestly dishonest. . . . Tammany is corruption with consent; it is bad government founded on the suffrages of the people."[17] The American people, Steffens reminded his readers, were above all else a people devoted to business, and all businessmen are more or less corrupt; more or less on the make. Always looking for that easy profit, that fast "buck," Americans saw no evil in graft if it helped them accomplish some desired end. They regarded corruption as a necessary—if somewhat tainted—part of a man's world; they associated honesty—devotion to the public service, and a desire to uplift society—with effeminate idealists. Low's government, it was felt, was soft; it was, like religion—fine for women and children, but with no place in a man's world.[18]

Tammany, however, was a business organization: its business was politics, and as with all business concerns, it was working for its own profit all the time. Corruption was something a business-oriented people could understand. Tammany was corrupt and, therefore, congenial; in a democratic society, where mediocrity was the standard aspired to, Tammany—provided it did not become outrageously corrupt—was always to be preferred

to reform. Moreover, reform government, Steffens pointed out,
obstructed the populace in the conduct of its normal business
by insisting upon adherence to the letter of the law, and by
the even-handedness of its administration of justice. As he
observed:

> Trinity Church, the old and rich establishment that faces
> Wall Street, had no good words for the good administration;
> Trinity owns acres of tenements and is governed by high
> financiers and other leading laymen. The police courts were
> just. The reporters said so, and the people who had to go to
> them, either to make or to answer complaints, did not deny
> it. Mr. Low had appointed as magistrates upright gentlemen
> and lawyers, who read the law to the people and did not often
> yield to "pull," like the Tammany heelers whom they dis-
> placed. But apparently, the poor, like the rich, preferred a
> human element in their judges. It was precisely the righteous-
> ness of the reform magistrates that was unpopular. In the
> tenements the tenants felt about the new and really good
> tenement house laws and regulations as Trinity and the other
> landlords felt. The two parties complained of different evils,
> but the new laws hit them both, and—it was the even justice
> that was so detestable. So with the real estate and the tax-
> payers. And so with business men generally and with the
> reformers.[19]

The American people had corrupt government, Steffens concluded, because that was the kind of government they wanted.

Analyzing Low's overwhelming repudiation at the polls, an
anonymous reporter for *The Independent* saw the cause of
Tammany's triumph in terms very much different from Steffens'.
Reform failed in New York City, this caustic critic asserted,
"Because it was neither radical nor democratic. Its watchwords
were the hackneyed ones of 'a business administration, honesty,
efficiency and economy' ";

> New York Reform has failed to 'make good' its promise of
> reform "for the people", because it is not of the people. Un-
> democratic in its origin, it has been permeated with a fear
> of democracy and has tried every means to restrict it.[20]

Conceived and nurtured by "goo-goos," aristocrats who knew
nothing of the desires or the needs of the people, selecting its
candidates behind closed doors in conferences which represented
no one but the men attending them, the fusion movement
presented the people of New York with a slate of nominees who

were as far-removed from the masses as were the men who picked them. Seth Low was not of the people. He was given to them as a Saviour by an omniscient Citizens' Union. New York accepted him because it had no suitable alternative, but Low, our unknown critic argued, neither knew nor understood the people of New York. In office, he gave New York a middle class government; responsive to his bourgeois constituency, he was honest, efficient, and economical. But his honesty knew not of pity, his efficiency was ruthless and unfeeling in its application, and his economy bordered on parsimony.

Declaring that Low feared municipal ownership, which *The Independent's* analyst held to be a needed democratic reform, he charged that his franchise policy, while commendable, did not result in lower fares or better service. Similarly, the strictness of the Tenement House Department discouraged the building of new tenements, and made those which were built so costly as to be beyond the reach of all except the aristocrats of the working class. In short, fusion did not meet the needs of the people because it did not know what those needs were, and it was too aristocratic and smug to take the trouble of finding out what the people wanted. Seth Low gave the appearance of being an enlightened despot holding court, magnanimously dispensing righteousness and justice. He smiled not, nor did he laugh; his concern appeared to be only condescension, his interest as smug self-conceit, his devotion to duty as a cold disregard of people's feelings. "Seth Low," George B. McClellan, Jr., confided in his diary:

> was entirely devoid of any sense of humor. Had he been a man of extraordinary ability, he might have overcome this terrible handicap, but unfortunately for him he was a dull, obstinate man with an excellent opinion of himself. He never could see a joke, especially at his own expense.
>
> Low made a respectable, honest, industrious, and incompetent mayor. With all his good intentions he never won the public who by the end of his term was thoroughly tired of him.[21]

"People," Sydney Brooks concluded, "felt that he would rather not be slapped on the back."[22]

Modern scholarship, building upon the contemporary view that fusion was a middle class reform movement led by "The unlovable but impeccable Mr. Low. . . . ," has concluded that Low's administration was essentially conservative, and that

Tammany was returned to power because the Wigwam was better able to meet the needs of a largely immigrant and working class population. "Eager, humorless reform," Carl Carmer called it, and declared, "Pompous righteousness, no matter how honest and well-meaning, has never found favor among New York voters."[23] Steven C. Swett, one of the few scholars to have studied Low's administration at any length, concluded that Seth Low was, ideologically, a product of the early nineteenth century, who was unable to comprehend the demands of the people, and who—constrained by the conservative, middle class reform organizations which backed him— could not, in any case, have instituted any radical and thorough-going reforms. "The fascination of his political career," said Swett, "lies in the fact that a man of such frigid austerity could have enjoyed even one success in a city whose dominant political social and economic mores bore so little resemblance to his own."[24]

Perhaps the most articulate exposition of the view that fusion was a conservative movement came not from a professional historian, but from a participant in the fusion crusade. Robert S. Binkerd recalled that on most social and economic issues, the men who made up the Citizens' Union were generally supporters of the *status quo*. They championed municipal reform not to uplift the masses, but because they were outraged at graft, inefficiency, and the subversion to private ends of the true functions of government. Once having captured control of City Hall, these "structural reformers"—as a later historian would call them—were content to simply eliminate corruption without instituting any basic reforms in the city's social and economic structure. There were, however, within fusion's ranks a small group of progressive "social reformers" who wanted to institute substantive reforms to help the immigrant and the working classes. Blocked by the conservatives controlling fusion, the progressives were unable to achieve their goals, and dis-illusioned, they returned to less doctrinaire political organizations in the hope of finding in them more favor. As Binkerd viewed it, fusion was torn apart by a conservative/liberal split on social and economic questions.[25]

With Binkered, many historians, most notably Oscar Handlin and Richard Hofstadter, ascribed the inability of the "goo-goos" to appeal to the urban masses to their innate conserva-tism, and argue that despite their faults, political machines like Tammany Hall, devoid of philosophical and moral rigidities, were able to provide the people with many of the vital services which they craved and which the reformers were either unable or unwilling to offer. According to this view, Tammany workers met immigrants at the docks, helped them find apartments, assisted them in locating jobs, and brought them baskets of food and coal to tide them over hard times. Aiding them out of legal difficulties, obtaining special privileges for them, Tammany—through its seemingly unselfish friendship—quickly won the loyalty of the urban masses who, having come from an autocratic and highly-structured European society, were unfamiliar with the workings of a democratic political system. Grateful for Tammany's favors and services, these new citizens gladly and willingly voted the straight party ticket, and saw the machine's corruption—provided that it did not become too blatant—as an unpleasant, though natural, part of life.

Tammany Hall, it was also argued, functioned in an age without social welfare agencies as an unofficial department of welfare, providing the immigrants with essential aid which could be obtained nowhere else. Unless the "goo-goos" could compete with Tammany Hall in satisfying the needs of the lower classes, they could never hope to permanently end the machine's domination of the city's government. As Hofstadter and others pointed out, the "goo-goos," with their emphasis on honest, efficient, and low-cost government, were constitutionally unequipped to provide the types of services which would win the urban masses away from the political machines. This view of Tammany Hall, though, is somewhat idealized, and the contention that the reformers did not understand the needs of the immigrants or the reason for their attachment to the Wigwam is not entirely accurate.

The "goo-goos" were aware of the ties that bound the masses to Tammany, but they interpreted the relationship in a somewhat different light. As Albert Shaw's *Review of Reviews* declared:

> Tammany controls the annual collection and expenditures of a municipal income now amounting to about $100,000,000. Besides its direct authority over a great army of voters who hold office subject to its pleasure, Tammy has close relations with contractors and large private corporations, so that it can provide "jobs" for other thousands of men willing to vote the Tammany ticket. Again, it has in its power thousands of

saloons, each of which controls several votes. Thus Tammany Hall binds together, not by ties of disinterested and patriotic political conviction, but rather of private interest, something like half of all the voters who live in New York City. . . .[26]

Tammany appealed to the worst instincts of the electorate. It connived at saloons which violated the blue laws and won their support; it protected gamblers and brothel-keepers, winning their backing as well as that of their clients; it gave away valuable city franchises thereby earning the gratitude of the public service corporations which repaid Tammany's kindness by using it as an employment agency. By ignoring the city's building codes, it gained the friendship of New York's developers; neglecting health standards in the tenements, it was rewarded with the political support of the landlords. Allowing unscrupulous businessmen to fleece both the public and the city, it won over powerful business support.

While Tammany helped a man find a job, or aided his family in time of distress, it permitted him to be exploited by *padrones,* his children to be neglected in schools starved for funds, and his family to be abused in city hospitals and institutions whose conditions rivaled those described in the novels of Dickens. Tammany, Lincoln Steffens concluded, "not only ruin fathers and sons and cause the troubles they relieve; they sacrifice the children in the schools; let the Health Department neglect the tenements, and, worst of all, plant vice in the neighborhood and in the homes of the poor."[27] There was a song in the Broadway show, *Fiorello,* which declared that "Tammany spelled tyranny, like R A T spelled rat." To advance any other interpretation of Tammany's social role is to distort reality to fit a sentimental conception which seeks to humanize political scoundrels and rationalize petty selfishness and corruption into something approaching nobility. The "goo-goos" did not intend to compete with Tammany on those terms, but this is not to say that they neglected the welfare or interests of the working masses.

The Citizens' Union was aware that to be successful it had to have broad-based popular support, and to obtain this, and to educate the immigrant masses in the workings of political democracy, it established branches in every one of the city's Assembly Districts. Its greatest success, of course, came in middle class areas of the city, but the Union actively sought lower class membership, as well as the support of New York's organized labor movement. It also attempted to render practical aid to New York's working class. R. Fulton Cutting, in 1902, sent a circular letter to all major employers of labor announcing that the Citizens' Union had formed a committee to help the "intelligent, ambitious and decent citizens" of the East Side to find jobs. "We ask employers of labor who wish to aid us," he declared:

> to notify our headquarters whenever they need men to fill vacancies in their establishments.
> This is not an attempt to use you for paying off political obligations. Should you call upon us to help fill any vacancies in your business, we will send you only competent men. They must stand upon their merits and we will see that you are not annoyed by inefficient applicants.[28]

The Citizens' Union employment bureau was not as effective as Tammany's in providing jobs—the "goo-goos" were, after all, tyros—but it did show that the Union recognized the cause of Tammany's hold over the masses and made an effort to compete with the Wigwam on its own terms. And its positive accomplishments were by no means insignificant.

"At other times," the English journalist Sydney Brooks told his readers, "it has been possible to find excuses [for the defeat of reform]; it is impossible to find a single one now. . . . He [Low] furthered a really extraordinary number of projects for the improvement of the health and convenience of the people, for the development of the city's resources, and especially for the redemption of the festering East Side."[29] Under fusion, for the first time since it had been enacted into law, the eight-hour statute was enforced. In October 1902, Mayor Low issued a directive ordering the city's transit board, which had been a notorious violator under Tammany, to observe the eight-hour law for all its employees, and as a result of fusion's insistence that the law be honored in the building trades, it sharply increased wages in the construction industry. The *Review of Reviews* estimated that the average New York City laborer working in construction received $24–30 per week for a forty-eight-hour week. On the whole, the *Review* concluded that the conditions of labor in New York City were more prosperous than they had been in years.[30]

Under Mayor Low's administration, the people of the East Side were provided with public baths, neighborhood parks, and playgrounds for their children. The creation of a kindergarten system (among the first in any large American city), and a greatly expanded high school program with an adult education curriculum were among Low's proudest achievements. Abuses in city hospitals and institutions were rectified and their services modernized and expanded, the tenements were made more liveable, and health conditions were materially improved (for the first time in its history, New York was assured of pure water and wholesome milk). There was also toleration shown for the customs of minorities. Low issued orders to the police department that it ignore the Sunday closing laws on the East Side prior to major Jewish holidays.[31] And the shakedown of pushcart peddlers was ended. Where Tammany gave the immigrant a basket of food, fusion gave him an improved school for the education of his children; where Tammany gave the worker a bushel of coal, fusion ordered a clean-up of the tenement in which he lived; where Tammany gave picnics up the Hudson River, fusion modernized the city's hospitals. It was not the "goo-goos" who neglected the masses, but Tammany Hall. That the people did not realize this was the tragedy of fusion's defeat. Low was rejected not because he did not meet the needs of the urban masses, but rather because Seth Low was a Mugwump with the personality failings so common to political mavericks. Organized labor and ethnic groups, it should be noted, had no criticism of his administration, only of his personality.

Low was nominally a Republican, but found it impossible to support the party when it adopted positions he did not agree with or nominated candidates of whom he did not approve. As mayor of Brooklyn, he found it intellectually dishonest to campaign for James G. Blaine in the 1884 Presidential election, and he remained silent throughout the fall canvass. Blaine lost the Presidency because he lost New York State, and he lost New York because his vote in Brooklyn fell far short of the party's normal strength in the "City of Churches." Low could not support Blaine, for the "plumed knight" stood for the spoils system whereas Cleveland championed civil service reform and official integrity. Republican party bosses blamed Low for Blaine's defeat, and he never again enjoyed the full endorsement of the G.O.P. Some years after stepping down as mayor of Brooklyn, he resigned his membership in the Republican party in protest against its extremely high tariff policy. "I often wonder," he confided to James Bryce, "whether there is any political career possible, in this country, for a man who can move with his party only when he thinks it right."[32] His correspondence showed that he voted for Cleveland in 1888 and 1892, with some reluctance to be sure, but out of conviction that the "Burbon leader" represented the better element in American political life.[33]

An ardent civil service reform advocate, Seth Low saw patronage as the root of all political evil, and had no conception of how a modern political party was held together. He assumed that all men were as selflessly devoted to duty as he was. Professional politicians scorned him, and the G.O.P. endorsed him in 1901 only because of the pressure exerted by Theodore Roosevelt. Close personal friends, Low energetically campaigned for Roosevelt in the 1898 Gubernatorial election. Relying heavily on Low, the "Rough Rider" entreated him to attend the opening meeting of the campaign, declaring, "I very earnestly want *you* to be with me when I make my first speech."[34] The election over, Governor Roosevelt sought out Low, Elihu Root and Joseph Choate as his principal advisors.[35] Low was closely consulted by Roosevelt on numerous pieces of major legislation, including the Ford Franchise Tax bill.[36] Over the years, the friendship and confidence between Low and Roosevelt grew. When running for vice-president in 1900, Roosevelt wrote Low:

> I am so glad you are to open the campaign next Tuesday. I was not entirely satisfied with Depew's speech in reference to me. He spoke of me as a cowboy and the like as undignified. In your hands I am entirely safe. You are able to put in touches of humor and yet both be dignified yourself and treat the subject with dignity.[37]

It was only because of Theodore Roosevelt that Seth Low enjoyed Republican support after his betrayal of James G. Blaine.

Holding office, Seth Low had all the virtues and failings of the Mugwump. Whatever else was said about him, no one ever questioned his absolute honesty and integrity, or his devotion to the public duty. On becoming mayor of New York, he sold all the stock which he owned in corporations which did business with the city to insure that no temptation would be placed in his path. He rejected every gratuity, even those which he had previously accepted while president of Columbia. "I have received, as for many years past," he told John H. Starin:

> a pass for myself and family on your New Haven line. I appreciate the compliment, and thank you heartily for the kindness of the courtesy.
>
> I think, however, that you will appreciate why I prefer, while I am Mayor, not to avail of such privileges. Under the circumstances, therefore, I hope you will allow me to return, herewith, the pass which you have been so kind as to send me.[38]

As he insisted upon personal integrity while in office, so, too, he conceived that it was his duty to strictly and precisely execute his official functions without regard for personal feelings or considerations. His adherence to what he conceived to be his duty cost him a good deal of public support; he gave the appearance of being stern and unfeeling. His nephew related the case of a young New York fireman who lost his life in the line of duty before his family was entitled to collect the life insurance provided by the city—a year's service being necessary for eligibility. Friends of the dead fireman became interested in the case, and secured a special act of the legislature giving the mayor discretionary power to waive the one-year service requirement. Armed with the statute, the fireman's friends descended on the mayor. "He met them," his nephew recounted:

> cool and aloof, as they came crowding into his office. When they had stated their case, he turned to his legal adviser and said: "Aside from this special discretion vested in me by act of the legislature, what is the law?" "I am compelled to advise your Honor," the latter replied, "that a full year's service is a prerequisite." Turning to the petitioners, Mayor Low said: "You hear the law, gentlemen. I can do nothing for you." They went out, boiling mad. Whereupon Seth Low, the private citizen, sat down at his desk; wrote his personal check for the entire amount of the insurance, and sent it to the bereaved family. "I begged him," adds the teller of the story, "to make it public. But he never would."[39]

It was such acts which established Low's reputation for coldness and austerity, and political opponents added that his private life was every bit as frigid as his public life. "Cabot Lodge told me," George B. McClellan noted in his diary, "that after Low's father died he met the then mayor and offered appropriate condolences. 'Yes,' replied Low, 'it was very sad. I was eating my breakfast when the nurse came into the dining room and told me that Father had passed away. I remember that I had buckwheat cakes for breakfast that morning. I finished my cakes and folding my napkin, I went upstairs to Father.' 'Just think of it,' added Lodge, ' "I finished my cakes and folding my napkin I went upstairs to Father." My God!' "[40] The story was not quite accurate, for shortly after his father's death, Seth Low wrote a cousin that, "The end was very sudden, and came with an especial shock because we had become quite sanguine as to his recovery."[41] As a matter of fact, those who came to know him, found him quite warm.

"I revered the old gentleman," Frederick Tanner recalled, "and I found that he had a very sweet and patient nature."[42] Tanner was not alone in his liking for Low. Democrat George McAneny declared that he was a "dear old soul," and nephew Benjamin Robbins Curtis Low remembered that:

> He had a keen sense of humor and a way of throwing back his head and laughing, almost silently, but evidently with immense relish, which was the richest reward a story teller could ask. One of his nephews still cherishes the recollection of an entirely satisfactory and realistic bear which used to growl its way, on all fours, out from behind the portieres for his delectation, and at a later age, of a stoutish figure in a bathing suit, which good naturedly consented to attempt various methods of entering a swimming pool, some of which bordered upon the ignominious.[43]

Seth Low was neither cold nor austere; he just appeared that way to outsiders. He could not communicate his genuine warmth and concern to the general public. His nephew called it "New England reserve," but Lawson Purdy, a Henry George supporter, saw the true cause of Low's public frigidity. "I knew Seth Low quite well," he remarked, "I liked him, and I didn't find him cold at all. It's true that some people did find him cold, but I think that is because he didn't mix well with people who were not of his own upbringing."[44]

Before large crowds, Seth Low became stiff and reserved. Meeting the common people, he froze and withdrew behind a cold exterior. He was not the type of man a New York City electorate could warm up to, and his stubborness in his adherence to his duty, stoutly resisting all pressure to change his course once he had decided upon it, did not enhance his popular appeal. "The newspapers," he told Charles A. Schieren:

> do not always appreciate how hard they sometimes make it for public officials to do what they think is right; aen [*sic*] if they happen to agree with the newspaper. I have always felt that a public officer ought never to permit himself to be influenced by such writing. Certainly he ought not to be deterred, by misunderstanding, from doing what he thinks is right.[45]

He was not a consensus mayor.

Frigidity and stubborness marked fusion's leadership as well as its standard-bearer. R. Fulton Cutting was formed from the same material as Seth Low. To preserve and solidify a reform machine, he created a fusion alliance which he dominated through the force of his indomitable will and ran, as reporter James Creelman declared, like an "enlightened despot." Authority flowed from the top down, and the professional politicians in the fusion camp soon became disenchanted with Cutting's variety of political righteousness. Again, like the mayor, while he had a social conscience, he did not want it to show. "He [Cutting]," Creelman noted, "fights for the poor and ignorant, even though he does not unite with them socially."[46] Fusion's human side left little to recommend it to the people of New York. The idea, however, that fusion went down to defeat solely because the working class returned to Tammany Hall is an over-simplification; the middle and upper classes also abandoned Seth Low.

From the very beginning, the fusion alliance was formed of ephemeral material. Its core was the Citizens' Union, which was dedicated to the non-partisan administration of municipal government, but the minority and dissident elements which formed the alliance had more specific goals in view. The Republican party saw a chance to dominate the government of New York City, and expected to control fusion's patronage. When it failed to do so, its enthusiasm for fusion cooled. The dissident Democrats, organized into the Greater New York Democracy and the Kings County Democracy, saw in fusion an opportunity to break Tammany's grip over the party machinery and to control the Democracy for their own ends. To the extent that fusion enabled these Democrats to achieve their intra-party ambitions, they supported it. But, given a chance to return to positions of influence within a Tammany-dominated party, they were quick to desert fusion, and they took tens of thousands of voters with them. The ethnic groups, especially the German-American organizations, entered fusion because Irish domination of the Democratic party allowed them no access to positions of leadership, and because they hoped in an alliance in which they were the balance of power to be able to alter the obnoxious Sunday closing laws. They found, however, that Irish domination had been replaced by that of the Yankee Protestants, and the Raines Law remained unchanged. Uptown aristocrats looked to fusion to provide honest, efficient and low-cost government which would eschew all attempts to impose radical features in the city's administration. Downtown progressives trusted that Tammany's neglect of the East Side would be replaced by a genuine effort to improve the areas' living conditions, and most of them were satisfied with fusion, though the more radical progressives condemned Low for failing to institute municipal ownership, and called for faster and more basic reforms. "The cause of reform," John DeWitt Warner stated, "was constantly imperiled by the necessity of keeping together the Conservatives upon whom it was dependent for journalistic and financial support, and the Progressives without whose votes a reform campaign would be futile."[47] Low, pledged to non-partisan administration, neither desired nor tried to wield this loose coalition into a political machine loyal to himself. Fusion was pre-ordained to failure by its very platform, for as Roswell P. Flower had long since observed:

> There would be more to commend in non-partisanship in local affairs if the sentiment for it were more generally and absolutely honest. The fact is, however, that sincerity in the cause is confined to a comparative few, unable of themselves to exert much influence; so that the main support, under present conditions, must come from disaffected political factions and minorities who seek by such alliances to gain power.[48]

The mayoralty was a political office, and politics could not be divorced from it.

Moreover, fusion was hampered, from the start, by an inability to subordinate private ambition to the good of the larger movement, and this did not stem solely from political considerations but rather from the personality failings of the fusionists themselves. "The typical reformer," Alfred Hodder observed, "is a 'star,' and a typical reform administration is basically a company of 'stars.' Mr. Low is a 'star,' Mr. Grout is a 'star,' two-thirds of the professional reformers who voted for them are 'stars'; each one is too excellent in his own kind to subordinate himself to team play."[49] Grout, Fornes, and Jerome, as well as others, all had their own political ambitions, and all subordinated fusion to their own ends. Grout's and Fornes' desertion of fusion was a severe blow, but Jerome's intemperate and irrational attacks, holding up Low to derision and contempt, did little to help the cause. Seth Low, to his credit, never responded to these attacks, and never allowed them to interfere with his duties as mayor. He remained magnanimous, and openly received Jerome back into the fold for the 1903 campaign. "Will you pardon me," Josephine Shaw Lowell wrote the mayor shortly after the election, "for congratulating you on the dignity with which you have, during all these two years, treated that foolish, spoiled baby, Jerome?"[50] "Baby" Jerome and his like-minded colleagues, though, did little to help Low implement his programs for reform, and the mayor was doubly handicapped by civil service laws which made it impossible for him to weed out incompetent office-holders appointed by Tammany officials in contravention of those same civil service laws which now protected them.[51] Considering the difficulties under which he had to work, Seth Low's accomplishments were astounding.

In 1901, Seth Low carried Manhattan by a rather slim 5,667 votes. He drew 128,048 votes on the Republican line, 25,021 from the Citizens' Union, and 9,775 from the Greater New York Democracy. It was the Democratic vote which gave him his majority over Shepard. His 1901 plurality in Brooklyn was a respectable 25, 767, but this included considerable support from the Kings County Democracy. In 1903, the Democrats returned to Tammany, and Low's vote on the Republican line fell by 25,100 votes, and 4,786 ballots on the Citizens' Union ticket. His vote in the East Side Assembly Districts fell sharply from his 1901 totals, but it is seldom pointed out that his vote was greatly reduced in every A.D. in Manhattan and Brooklyn (with the exception of Brooklyn's 18th A.D.), including the high-income Yankee-Protestant Assembly Districts. The falling away of support from fusion was not confined to any single socio-economic or ethnic group, but was general throughout the voting population of the city. Undoubtedly, the defection of the Democratic splinter groups was an important factor in Low's defeat. As *The Outlook* declared, "the regular Democracy was aided by the support of all those classes—saloons, tenement house landlords, and public service corporations—whose material interests had been injured by the reforms of the Fusion administration.'[52]

New Yorkers, forgetting Tammany's recent abominations, simply did not take the trouble of voting in an off-year election. New York rejected Seth Low because it preferred not to have good government. "I know that every administration makes enemies," he told Theodore Roosevelt shortly after the election, "and mine has been no exception. The time may come, however, when it will be valued, if not loved, for the enemies it has made."[53]

Low's administration did have one beneficent effect; it made impossible a return to Crokerism. "The signs of the times," "goo-goo" John J. Bealin wrote, "point in the direction that we are not going to have a red-hot Tammany administration; that the influence of your administration is such that the administration which is to take effect the first of January will have, in a great measure, to conform to the lines you have laid down. This in itself is somewhat of a recognition of the services rendered."[54] McClellan was a competent mayor, and was independent of Tammany dictation. And, fearing another Seth Low, Tammany was forced to nominate men of the quality of a Gaynor and a Hylan. Seth Low's personal qualities were not such as to endear him to the people of New York, but as *The Nation* put it, "Mayor Low's Administration will be good in its future effects. It has given us an example from which succeeding Mayors will fall away at their peril."[55]

Seth Low's political career was at an end; never again would he run for elective office. But his usefulness to America was just beginning. Defeated in his attempt to win re-election, he left public life one of the most respected men in the ranks of American reform. As a co-worker phrased it:

> In this hour—you have nevertheless the satisfaction of knowing that your duty was well performed, and while not properly recognized at this present, your Administration has left its impress so strongly upon the conscience of the people that in future years your name will be the synonym of decent, honest, progressive administration of City Government.[56]

While he was a respected reform mayor, Seth Low's political career never reached the heights which many of his admirers had expected it to. The reason for this was that Seth Low was essentially a one-issue man. His overriding concern was the achievement of good municipal government, and to realize better city administration he stood for elective office. Yet on the great issues confronting the nation, he was rather silent. A lifelong advocate of the gold standard, he, at the request of the G.O.P., made a number of speeches in the Midwest on behalf of McKinley and gold during the 1896 campaign. However, the defense of the gold standard never became a major issue with Low, and while he opposed silver coinage, his opposition was subdued and low-keyed.

Likewise, he supported the Spanish-American War—regarding it as a humanitarian crusade to free a small but noble people—and was an advocate of retaining the Philippines and Puerto Rico, feeling that America had a moral obligation to uplift the "benighted" races of the world and advance the progress of civilization. But, again, Seth Low was never considered to be a major proponent of imperialism. His imperialistic sentiments were, at most, but a minor strain in his thought.[57]

Similarly, in 1899, Low accepted President McKinley's appointment as one of the American delegates on the United States Commission to the Hague Arbitration Conference. The records of the Conference indicated that Low did not participate in the Conference debates, and his role at the Hague was very minor. Indeed, he had never demonstrated any great interest in foreign affairs, and went to the Hague only because the President requested him to do so. Returning to America, he wrote an account of the Conference proceedings for the *North American Review,* but otherwise made no reference to the issues raised at the Hague.[58]

Obviously, Low's refusal to speak out decisively on national issues limited his political effectiveness. But his unwillingness to publicly commit himself on the issues of the day was entirely consistent with his non-partisan conception of municipal administration. If city government was to be conducted on a non-partisan basis, its officials should ignore questions of state and national politics and pay strict attention to the business of the city. This was Low's view as to the duty of municipal office-holders, and he never deviated from it.

However, in the period after 1903, for reasons which are unclear, Seth Low abandoned his earlier interest in urban reform, and concerned himself exclusively with the problem of reconciling labor and capital. Devoting his energies completely to the quest for a labor-capital entente, he did not wish to have larger political issues obscure his efforts on behalf of industrial justice and he maintained his silence on the great political issues confronting American society.

The Patrician as Social Architect

Foreword to The Patrician as Social Architect

Plutocrats to the right of them, socialists to the left of them, the indifferent and uncaring in front of them—into the valley of despair wandered the patrician reformers. Isolating themselves from American life, the patricians harassed their country's philistine culture from behind the bastion of self-pity which they had erected to protect their Yankee sensibilities against the unpleasant realities of modern life in industrial America. Eventually, polite sneering at the follies of money-grubbing businessmen, the rascality of pocket-lining politicians, and the degeneracy of newly-arrived immigrant groups proved unrewarding; and ending their self-imposed exile from the life of America, they abandoned Olympus. Descending into the lower depths of political life, the patrician reformers—armed only with family pride, education, and moderate wealth—entered into the contest for what they felt was the possession of America's soul. Thus, in the infancy of the twentieth century, a socio-economic and political movement which came to be called Progressivism was born, led by the patrician reformers and followed by the American middle class.

The patrician reformers, scions of old families accustomed to providing social leadership and receiving the respect of a grateful and indebted populace, came of age in an America which had seemingly rejected the values by which they had been raised. In those halcyon days of ante-bellum America, the patricians (Anglo-Saxon Protestant lawyers, clergymen, merchants, and professionals) had been looked to for models upon which the lesser men of the nation could pattern themselves.

However, in the half-century after the Civil War, a new class of men—ill-bred, ill-mannered, and ill-educated—had come to dominate American life and had fastened tight upon the nation their brand of utilitarian morality and practical culture; and the plain people, following the lead of their new idols, had made American society as coarse and as corruptible as the "robber barons" themselves. Seeking to regain their lost status, the patricians resolved once again to enthrone the Yankee-Protestant moral code, upon which they had been reared, at the helm of American life. To do this, they would have to purge the nation's body politic of the cancerous influence exerted by the plutocrats in conjunction with the corrupt, immigrant supported, political machine; and once more the master of America's political destiny, they would bring the plutocracy to heel and force the country's political and economic order to obey the commandments of the Yankee Protestant morality. As one of our leading Progressive scholars has proclaimed, "Its [Progressivism's] general theme was the effort to restore a type of economic individualism and political democracy that was widely believed to have existed earlier in America and to have been destroyed by the great corporation and the corrupt political machine; and with that restoration to bring back a kind of morality and civic purity that was also believed to have been lost."[1] So runs the standard interpretation of the Progressive, or at least the Eastern Progressive, movement.

It is generally believed that the Progressive movement in the Eastern United States was a conservative one, seeking to return America to the tried and true ways of her past—a past marked by small-scale industry, loosely-structured political institutions, and a negatively-oriented government, existing primarily on the local level, and dominated by the "best people"—a past in which the good was triumphant and in which justice reigned supreme, showering its blessings upon the entire land. It shall be the aim of this work, however, to try to show that a large and important segment of the Eastern Progressive movement was not, by any definition of the word, conservative. And further, the author will endeavor to demonstrate that not all Eastern Progressives were motivated by a desire to return to the socio-economic conditions obtaining

---

1. Richard Hofstadter, *The Age of Reform: From Bryan to F.D.R.* (New York: Vintage Books, 1955), pp. 5–6.

in pre-Civil War America, in order to regain their lost prestige. It will be the thesis of this study that many Progressives in the Eastern states sought to solve twentieth century problems by invoking the techniques and knowledge not of the nineteenth—but of the twentieth-century.

The central focus of this study will be the National Civic Federation under the presidency of Seth Low, a group whose members included some of the most prominent businessmen, labor leaders, and political Progressives in the Northeastern United States, an organization which advocated an essentially liberal program designed to solve pressing socio-economic problems, and a body which, unfortunately, has never been adequately studied by historians. The author's prime object will be to analyze the manner in which the men of the National Civic Federation viewed the social and economic difficulties besetting early twentieth century America, and to consider how they proposed to resolve those problems. Finally, the author shall try to place the Civic Federation within the liberal context of American history. As this is primarily a study in intellectual history, the author has felt it best to allow the participants to speak for themselves whenever possible, and has refrained from excessively paraphrasing the ideas of the Federation's leadership.

CHAPTER X

The National Civic Federation to 1905

> The real ideal of a democracy must be to level up, not to level down. . . .
>
> E.R.A. SELIGMAN[1]

While the Progressive impulse and Seth Low's public career both began in the nation's urban centers, the socio-economic problems confronting America forced both to expand their original focus of interest and fight for reform on a larger scale. Indeed, to many observers it appeared that the United States, in the decade of the 1890s, was faced with imminent peril; it seemed to be a time of dread, of unrest, and of irrational fear. Beneath the public facade of faith in the nation's future lurked the nagging thought that America would soon be called to account for its arrogance. The direful projection of America's future which Brooks and Henry Adams were to advance in the coming decades was already in the air during the "Gay Nineties." For a large segment of the country's propertied classes, for much of its aspiring middle class—indeed, for many who possessed a stake in American society—the closing decade of the nineteenth century was one of foreboding.

The nation's business, for the decade of the 1890s, was, for the most part, in a prosperous condition. The decade was witness to a great advance in heavy industry, and the efficiency of the mass-production system plus the skill of American labor led to a gradual drop in price levels and a corresponding rise in real wages. The United States could justly lay claim to being one of the richest nations on earth, and yet there were severe urban poverty and acute rural distress. Also, one important element was lacking in the country's industrial life—commercial stability. The financial collapse of the Philadelphia and Reading Railroad, early in 1893, ushered in a depression which resulted in the failure of 491 banks and over 15,000 business establishments before the year was out. By the close of 1896, 33.5 percent of all railroad mileage in the United States was in receivership. Though business improved substantially after 1897, industrial America was hit by commerical panics in 1903, 1907, and 1910–1911. In the last quarter of the nineteenth and the first quarter of the twentieth century, America was a land where fortunes could be made and lost overnight. The entrepreneur who prospered mightily in one year might find himself bankrupt the next. Many who lacked the instincts of the gambler saw the American economy as chaotic and anarchic.

If the nation's industrial life was uncertain, its social and political structures apeared equally insecure. On the wheat-choked prairies of the Middle West, and on the cotton lands of the South's rural backwash, Populist orators, whose radicalism could be measured by the rise and fall of commodity price quotations, railed against the depradations of the plutocrats and bankers of New York and London who, they believed, bled rural America to the point of financial exhaustion in order to fatten their pocketbooks. When the Populist fever, with its demand for the nationalization of railroads and utilities, infected the Democratic party in 1896, many Eastern business interests literally quaked with fear.

Rural America was not the only section of the nation that was alive with the spirit of radicalism. In the industrial cities of the Northeast, numerous respectable, property-loving, old-stock Americans looked askance at the hordes of new, racially distinct immigrants who threatened to topple America's middle class citadel. Crowding into the slums of America's cities, the immigrants lived in squalor, susceptible to the preachments of the socialists and anarchists who attempted to persuade them that American life held no promise for its new subjects. The immigrants, though, found that they could do better by the corrupt political machine which clung, like so many boils, to urban America's body politic than they could with the dreams of the socialist visionaries. All the socialists succeeded in doing was to alarm the respectable gentry.

On the eve of the twentieth century, large segments of America's business and professional classes were thoroughly frightened. Alarmed at the disorder plaguing American industry, fearing the radicalism which had swept over the farmlands of the country, and dreading the prospect of a violent social upheaval in the nation's cities, it seemed to many propertied, old-stock Americans that the United States was precariously poised on the precipice of social and industrial anarchy. But there was also another America, an America of which Seth Low was a part.

If the 1890s was an era of fear and unrest in American life, it was also a period of optimism when the idea of Man's infinite capacity for progress and perfectability had almost achieved an apotheosis in the American mind. There were many people who believed in America, and while recognizing the existence of numerous acute problems, they held to a confident faith that somehow the democratic institutions of American society would resolve those difficulties. For these people, imbibing the spirit of American democracy from their infancy, this was a unique nation which existed not to raise up a privileged industrial aristocracy feeding off a degraded and despoiled mass of laborers, but rather it was a country whose reason for being was to offer all men dignity and material abundance. They had a deep and sincere belief in the basic goodness of American institutions, and the basic problem, as they saw it, was not to effect radical alterations in the fabric of American society but to improve and perfect the nation's existing institutions which, while flawed, were worth saving. Holding dear to the vision of a better America, these men of good hope were, in the 1890s, looking for a vehicle—political, social, or economic —with which they could proceed to implement their vision of an American society fulfilling its democratic promise. This heady optimism, in the early years of the twentieth century, expressed itself in movements to improve the quality of American political life, to aid the urban poor, to ease the hardships of the industrial system, and generally to raise the well-being of the entire society. One such organization which sought to realize a nobler America was the National Civic Federation. While Low did not actively participate in the organization's activities until 1905, a consideration of the Federation's work during its first five years of existence is necesary in order to make intelligible the policies pursued by the N.C.F. under the leadership of Seth Low.

The National Civic Federation evolved out of the Civic Federation of Chicago which itself was a by-product of the optimism engendered by the 1893 World's Fair.[2] Depression had struck America in 1893, but the great Columbian Exposi-

tion had shielded Chicago from its effects. In November, however, the fair having ended its run, jobless men wandered
Chicago's streets. Stalking the soup kitchens by day, they
sought out doorways, abandoned buildings, and flop-houses by
night—any place which would protect them against the freezing
winds blowing in from Lake Michigan. Social action was
needed to meet the critical situation besetting the city. To
help alleviate the problems of unemployment, Chicago's trade
unions called a mass meeting for Sunday, November 12, 1893
to be held at the Central Music Hall. It was well-attended,
and an observer reported that:

> Side by side sat leading businessmen and labor leaders, repre-
> sentatives of the city government and of its exclusive clubs,
> preachers and saloon-keepers, gamblers and theological pro-
> fessors, matrons of distinguished families and notorious "ma-
> dames" from houses of ill fame, judges of the courts and one
> of the men convicted in the Haymarket Riot trial who had
> been recently pardoned. . . .[3]

They had all come to hear the dynamic London editor,
William T. (*If Christ Came to Chicago*) Stead, who had just
helped to organize his native city's Civic Church. A forceful ora-
tor, Stead had the ability to whip his audience into a frenzy of
righteous emotion—a frenzy which did not soon die away and
which manifested itself in a resolve to perform good works. As
the astute Graham Taylor observed:

> To me, when he was at white heat denouncing preventable
> evils, he seemed to rise to the stature of one of the Hebrew
> prophets. At his best he was the Christian apostle tenderly en-
> treating us, by the sufferings of Christ, "to take home some
> of the sorrows of the men, women and children living in our
> midst and try to help them so as to understand something of
> the sorrow and agony of Christ. . . ."[4]

If Mr. Stead's admonition to "take home some sorrow" fell
on skeptical or cynical ears, veteran socialist Thomas Morgan
gave the audience a much more practical reason to help their
less fortunate fellows. As Mr. Morgan phrased it, "If the plead-
ings of editor Stead, in the name of Christ and for justice,
cannot shake you out, may someone blow you out with
dynamite."[5]

The meeting at the Central Music Hall resulted in the
establishment of the Civic Federation of Chicago which, in

addition to meeting the pressing need of aiding the jobless, was designed to promote a multitude of civic reforms—social and political as well as economic. The Federation was governed by a Central Council of 134 members representing all elements of Chicago's population—business, labor, religious, cultural, and ethnic leaders were all present on the council. Lyman J. Gage, of the First National Bank, was the Federation's president, and Mrs. Potter Palmer, the acknowledged leader of Chicago high society, was first vice-president. The council was divided into six departments—political, municipal, philanthropic, industrial, educational, and morals—each one charged with the performance of a specific function. In order to obtain grass roots participation in the Civic Federation, a council—patterned after the Central Council—was established in each of Chicago's thirty-four wards so that local problems and needs would not be overlooked.

In the winter of 1893–1894, the Civic Federation raised $135,000 for its Central Relief Association and succored the homeless. The next year, it organized and met the expenses of the permanent Bureau of Associated Charities. In June 1894, a committee of the Civic Federation which included Jane Addams, investigated the Pullman dispute. It recommended that substantially all of the American Railway Union's demands be granted and repeatedly, but without success, called upon the Pullman Company to submit to arbitration. The Civic Federation, in 1895, declared war on Chicago's gambling houses, and much to the chagrin of the city's complacent and compliant administration, drove the gamblers out of town. Emboldened by their success against the gamblers, they extended their crusade to the brothels, and as Ray S. Baker assured the readers of *The Outlook,* the campaign against the prostitutes gave every promise of being successful.[6] Having improved Chicago's morals, the men of the Civic Federation set about to improve its political life. Smashing the boodlers, and the gas and traction trusts to which they were subservient, the Civic Federation drafted, forced through the legislature, and had ratified by the voters of Chicago the city's first effective civil service law with a vigorous Civil Service Commission to see that the law was faithfully enforced. In the realm of social welfare, it established vacation schools to provide recreation and outings for the city's underprivileged children, and it helped to subsidize the activities of Chicago's settlement house movement.

Finally, and perhaps most importantly, in June 1902 the Civic Federation established a Board of Arbitration consisting of the heads of seven unions and seven employer's associations, the purpose of which was to offer its good offices in labor disputes in order to provide arbitration, mediation, or conciliation for the settlement of industrial disputes. Entering labor disputes only when it was agreeable to both parties, it offered a variety of services designed to effect a quick and mutually satisfactory solution of strikes and lockouts. Between June 1902 and April 1903, the Board arbitrated, mediated, or conciliated thirty-three serious labor disputes to the apparent satisfaction of all parties.[7]

After a decade of existence, the Chicago Civic Federation could point to a number of positive accomplishments. It had broken the power of the boodlers, reduced vice, aided thousands of jobless men during the depression, and had helped to settle numerous industrial disputes to the satisfaction of organized labor. The Federation included in its membership Chicago's wealthiest and most prominent citizens, many of whom had never manifested any social consciousness and had never taken part in movements looking toward civic reform. What was it that impelled these people—some having been quite callous toward the less fortunate in the past—to suddenly acquire a social conscience, to suddenly wish to aid and uplift the underprivileged? To some extent, a genuine religious impulse to perform good works was at play, and there was also a sincere humanitarian desire to help alleviate suffering and to lighten the burdens of poverty, but above all else the well-to-do members of the Chicago Civic Federation, "realized that there is a prudential reason . . . for placing some of the strength of the strong at the disposal of the weak."[8] Unless something positive were done to alleviate human misery and to offer hope of improvement to the poor, social upheaval—which threatened property—loomed as a distinct possibility. If only to preserve their stake in society, the well-to-do had to aid their less fortunate brethren.

While some might call this conservative reform, its motivations were humanitarian, idealistic, optimistic and essentially liberal. The prime policy of the Chicago Civic Federation, Ray Ginger tells us, was the protection of collective bargaining, and its major goal was to facilitate the entry of the working class into the great American middle class—to bring more and more people within the middle class umbrella. While the motivation, in some instances, may have been selfish, the end which sought a more equitable distribution of the wealth created by modern industry was in the best traditions of American democracy.[9] As Albion W. Small so aptly observed, "The dynamic of social reorganization is the economy of enlightened selfishness. It is only our stupidity which imagines that altruism and egoism are antithetical."[10]

The secretary and guiding spirit behind the Chicago Civic Federation was Ralph Montgomery Easley. Born February 25, 1856 in Frederick, Illinois, Easley moved to Hutchinson, Kansas, where he was variously a school teacher, postmaster, and newspaperman. Returning to his native Illinois, he became a political reporter for the *Chicago Inter-Ocean,* and was one of the organizers of the Civic Federation. Appalled by the violence of the Pullman Strike, he determined that there must be a better way of settling labor disputes than through naked force. The next two decades of his life would be dedicated to the search for that better way. With the Chicago Civic Federation well established, Easley, by 1899, was looking to broader fields for the exercise of his considerable publicity talents. The question of the trusts had begun to disturb the placidity of American life, and realizing the enormous publicity which could be garnered from such a gathering, Ralph Easley, in September 1899, organized the Chicago Conference on Trusts and Combinations. "It should be distinctly understood," he told Chicago businessman, L. L. Loeb:

> that the conference is not called in any spirit of antagonism toward such combinations, nor is it called in behalf of them. There is no assumption that the organization of great combinations, whether of labor or capital, is advantageous to the country, nor any assumption to the contrary. What we all need on the subject just now—what the country needs—is knowledge. The object of the meeting is not to give countenence or support to any class of opinion, but only, if possible, to make some progress toward furnishing the American people with data on which an intelligent opinion may be based.[11]

The conference, true to Easley's intentions, passed no resolutions and adopted no stand in regard to the trust question, but it did offer a forum, well covered by the nation's press, for the expression of all shades of opinion, from those favoring the trust as an integral part of the modern industrial system, to those like Hazen Pingree, who—seeing the trust as the precursor of industrial serfdom—wanted them annihilated but "with due regard for property rights, of course."[12] Samuel Gompers, though, made the prescient point that the trusts, if confronted by an equal power, posed no threat to American democratic institutions, and that the most effective force with which to check the trust was not the government but the labor union.[13]

The favorable reception accorded the Conference on Trusts and Combinations encouraged Easley to organize the Civic Federation on a national basis. However, unlike its parent organization in Chicago, the National Civic Federation concerned itself only with efforts to solve the labor-capital problem. By 1900, the year the National Civic Federation was launched, the question of labor's proper role in the modern industrial system had taken on a somber aspect. All too many employers, refusing to recognize labor's claim to the right of collective bargaining and to a voice in policy-making decisions, had forced their employees into long, costly, bitter, and often violent strikes. It seemed to many observers that American industry had become a battleground, and something had to be done to resolve what was becoming a grave threat to the security of American society. As Oscar S. Straus, an early member of the Civic Federation, put it:

> The rapid growth of our industries and the impersonal relations between employer and employed made it apparent that social justice required that reciprocal rights be recognized in order to bring about a better understanding of a relationship which had already become increasingly strained and often embittered, resulting in serious strikes and lock-outs.
> Industrial justice, to be permanent, cannot rest upon force, but must rest upon justice. . . .[14]

Moving on to New York City early in 1901, Ralph Easley began the quest for industrial justice by organizing the National Civic Federation as a tripartite body representing—in equal numbers—capital, labor, and the general public, the latter being a supposedly neutral third force standing between the often-hostile forces of capital and labor. A large general membership was not sought, and at no time did the N.C.F. have more than five thousand members. Easley, from the outset, sought a small membership of strategically-placed and prominent leaders of business and organized labor, with a leavening of eminent politicians, clergymen, and publicists to add lustre to the Federation's membership roll. These business, labor, and public leaders formed the executive committee of the federation, which—meeting once a year (usually in December)—was theoretically the highest governing authority within the organization. The N.C.F.'s first executive committee, organized in 1901, listed such eminent public figures as Grover Cleveland, Cornelius N. Bliss, Oscar S. Straus, Archbishop John Ireland, Bishop Henry C. Potter, and Harvard's President Charles W. Eliot. Low also joined the N.C.F. at this time but was not an active member. Labor members included Samuel Gompers, John Mitchell, Daniel J. Keefe of the Longshoreman's Union, Martin Fox of the Iron Moulders', Harry White of the Garment Workers', and Edgar E. Clark of the Railroad Conductors'. The capitalists were represented by Marcus Alonzo Hanna, Marcus M. Marks, Charles M. Schwab, William H. Pfahler, S. R. Callaway, and Lewis Nixon.

How Ralph Easley persuaded men like Hanna, Cleveland, and Bliss to join an organization run by a relative unknown, and with a rather ill-defined program, must remain one of the great unsolved mysteries of the time, but suffice it to say that Easley was an excellent salesman and publicist, and since the N.C.F. had noble aims, it attracted men of reputation who wanted to enjoy the feeling of performing good works without expending any great amount of time or energy, and more importantly, without antagonizing large interest groups. In any case, the executive committee was tightly controlled by the president, secretary (Ralph Easley), department heads, and certain other key officers of the organization. It was this executive council which conducted the day-to-day business of the Federation and which formulated policy.

Established to help in the settlement of labor disputes, the fledgling N.C.F. soon found itself involved in two of the era's major strikes. In the spring of 1901, T. J. Shaffer, minister-turned-labor-leader, determined to unionize the newly-created United States Steel Corporation. In June, his Amalgamated Association of Iron, Steel and Tin Workers struck U.S. Steel demanding the closed shop (*i.e.* one in which all employees are union members with such membership being a prerequisite to employment), and recognition of the union's wage scale throughout the U.S. Steel empire. Shaffer's insistence upon the closed shop was taken against the advice of Samuel Gompers, who felt that it was unrealistic to expect U.S. Steel to recognize a closed shop when only ten thousand out of a total of one hundred and sixty thousand Steel workers were unionized.[15] Moreover, Shaffer demanded that Gompers and John Mitchell call sympathy strikes on the railroads and in the coal fields in order to increase the pressure on U.S. Steel. It was widely believed in labor circles that Shaffer was seeking to create a new labor council, employing the sympathy strike on a wide-spread scale, which would supplant the more reserved American Federation of Labor. Aside from the potential threat posed to the A.F.L. by Shaffer, his call for a sympathy strike was contrary to a long-standing policy of the American Federation of Labor against such strikes.

Gompers and Mitchell, in July 1901, called upon Marcus A. Hanna, a member of the N.C.F.'s Executive Committee, to arrange a conference between officials of U.S. Steel and the union in the hope of obtaining a mediated settlement. On July 27, Hanna arranged a meeting at U.S. Steel headquarters between Gompers, Mitchell, Morgan, Schwab and some others. At the conference, Morgan declared that he was not hostile to organized labor, agreed to recognize the Amalgamated as the bargaining agent for the union men employed by U.S. Steel, and offered to meet the union's wage scale, but he refused to recognize the closed shop until after the organization of the Steel Corporation had been completed. He promised, however, to sign a general agreement with the union after two years covering all plants.[16] Morgan's offer proved satisfactory to Gompers and he urged the Amalgamated to accept it, but Shaffer—still insisting upon the closed shop—scuttled the agreement. The strike went on. Gompers and Mitchell refused to call a sympathy strike, and Shaffer was eventually forced to settle for much less than Morgan had originally offered. The National Civic Federation—through Hanna—had brought both sides together, and an agreement promising to labor's cause had been hammered out at the Morgan-Gompers conference. It was defeated through the obstinacy and short-sightedness of T. J. Shaffer, and the strike ended in a severe defeat for labor. The Civic Federation's first effort on behalf of industrial peace had not been too successful.

Marcus Hanna had been instrumental in the efforts to mediate the Steel Strike; he had become deeply committed to the Federation's philosophy of seeking peaceful adjustments of labor disputes, and, in December 1901, he consented to become the Civic Federation's first president. It was common to think of Hanna as "Dollar Mark," the bloated personification of the plutocrat, who—without regard for the needs of the masses—ran the United States government in the interest of American business. But yet, Samuel Gompers could declare that, "Mark Hanna [was] an outstanding employer of that day who stood for the principle of collective bargaining before others were ready to accept it."[17] "He was," Gompers went on, "a friend to organized labor, because he was convinced that through its agencies it would be the means of accomplishing better conditions and be helpful in bringing about more rightful relations between employer and employees. . . ."[18]

Hanna was, indeed, regarded by leaders of organized labor as a fair employer, always ready to correct abuses once they were brought to his attention, and as holding liberal views toward unions. As early as 1874, he had pioneered in the establishment of a trade agreement between the Ohio coal operators and the mine worker's union. Gompers, in his *Autobiography,* related that when workers in Hanna's Buffalo blast furnace went out on strike, Hanna indignantly demanded to know the cause of the strike. Gompers told him that the employees at his plant were required to pay plant superintendants and foremen kickbacks in order to secure jobs and promotions. Hanna at first refused to believe the allegation, but he investigated it, nevertheless, and finding it to be true, he fired all the foremen and superintendants involved in the shakedown system which automatically ended the strike. Hanna was reportedly very apologetic about the incident, declaring that he had no idea such conditions existed in his plants.[19]

In his later years, Mark Hanna came to the realization that, "there ought to be a better way to settle disputes between employer and employee than by strikes and lockouts."[20] He resolved to use his considerable influence to adjust the differences between capital and labor, for, as he declared upon becoming president of the National Civic Federation:

> I would rather have the credit of making successful the movement to bring labor and capital into closer relations of confidence and reliance than to be the President of the United

States. If by resigning my seat in the United States Senate I could bring to fruition the plans that we are now fostering to make strikes and lockouts and great labor disputes impossible, I would gladly do so. I think it is the grandest thing that could be accomplished in this country. I would want no greater monument than to have the world remember that I did something to end wars between American labor and American capital.[21]

Hanna's, and the Civic Federation's, chosen instrument for the realization of this goal was the trade agreement whereby capital recognized the trade union as the bargaining agent for its employees, and both sides then sat down and worked out a detailed written agreement specifying conditions and degree of labor, and remuneration. The underlying assumption of the trade agreement was the recognition of organized labor as an integral part of the modern industrial system and its right to a voice in determining working conditions and wage rates. What Hanna was urging was nothing less than universal recognition of labor's right to collective bargaining. As he conceived it, the labor union, and the Federation's trade agreement program sought, "to improve the condition of the classes who need help in this country, to elevate them in every way, to obtain for them a wider scope of education and welfare and through that to make them better citizens of a happier land." It was, Hanna concluded, "a feeling of humanity [which] underlies this movement..."[22]

Hanna's good intentions were soon put to a severe test. Back in July 1900, the United Mine Workers had begun to organize the anthracite coal fields. By September of that year, with less than eight thousand members, the Union called its first strike, and since working conditions were so abominable in the mines, the strikers were joined by eighty to one hundred thousand non-union miners. The strike lasted into October, when Mark Hanna—fearing its effect on the up-coming presidential election—intervened and forced the operators to grant the miners a general ten percent pay boost.[23] In April 1901, Hanna helped to arrange a trade agreement between the operators and the United Mine Workers which would extend until March 31, 1902. On February 14, 1902, the U.M.W. requested a conference with the operators in order to renegotiate the soon-to-expire trade agreement, and indicated that it would press for a twenty percent pay raise and the implementation of the eight-hour workday. The operators emphatically refused to negotiate, and on March 17, U.M.W. President, John Mitchell, requested Ralph Easley, the N.C.F.'s secretary, to help arrange a conference with the operators. Hanna sought such a conference, but with George F. Baer, the operator's spokesman, invoking the divine right of property and asserting that, "The rights and interest of the laboring men will be protected and cared for, not by the agitators, but by the Christian men to whom God in his infinite wisdom has given the control of the property interests of the country," his efforts were fruitless.

The National Civic Federation, on March 26, asked Mitchell for a month's delay in strike action in order to give it time to effect a conference with the operators. Mitchell agreed to the delay, and as he later testified, "During this month, the National Civic Federation made every possible effort to bring about a satisfactory adjustment and urged upon the operators the necessity of making some concessions."[24] A conference was arranged, but the operators were unwilling to grant any of the union's demands. In April, still hoping to avoid a strike, Mitchell reduced the union's demands to a ten percent pay increase and a nine-hour day instead of the eight hours originally requested. Mitchell also informed Hanna that to avert a strike he would settle for a five percent pay hike, but the operators—taking this as a sign of weakness—remained adamant in their refusal to negotiate. In desperation, and confident of the justice of his case, Mitchell, on May 8, offered to submit labor's demands to a five-man arbitration panel, whose members would be selected by the Civic Federation. Again, though, the operators refused the proposal. On May 15, 1902, the miners went out on strike, and John R. Commons, dispatched to the coal fields by the N.C.F. to observe conditions there, reported that the miners, contrary to the operator's expectations, were capable of holding out until well into winter.

Once the strike began, all efforts at conciliation proved futile, but Hanna, nevertheless, continued to urge the operators to treat with the miner's union. "The National Civic Federation," John Mitchell declared, "made noble efforts to avert the threatened calamity, but no word came from the operators and no concessions were made by them."[25] Finally, in the fall of 1902, fearing a shortage of coal for the winter months, President Roosevelt secured the operator's consent to arbitration, but as reporter Walter Wellman pointed out, Morgan accepted Roosevelt's proposal only because of the incessant pressure exerted by Mark Hanna.[26] The arbitration panel subsequently awarded the United Mine Workers substantially all that it asked, including a ten percent pay raise.

The Federation's efforts on behalf of organized labor in the steel and the anthracite strikes were not overwhelmingly successful, but this should not be regarded as typical of the Civic Federation's conciliation work. When capital was willing to deal with organized labor on a basis of equality, the National Civic Federation was able to achieve positive results. For example, a trade agreement between the Iron Moulders Association and the Iron Moulders' Union provided that in shops having fifty percent or more union members, union rules would obtain for all, but that non-union employees would not be coerced into joining the union. However, as vacancies developed in the shop, only union men would be hired to fill the places once held by non-union workers. It also provided that all misunderstandings or disputes, arising during the life of the agreement, would be settled by arbitration.[27] A similar agreement was reached between the New York, New Haven and Hartford Railroad and the Order of Railway Conductors, and between the American Newspaper Publishers' Association and the Typographical Union.[28] For obvious reasons, the Federation did not publicize its conciliation work, secrecy being essential to success, so that it is difficult to ascertain just how successful its mediation efforts were. By 1905, however, the Civic Federation claimed to have handled 156 cases of which 82 were referred to it by capital, and 74 by labor. It declared that in over 100 of these cases its efforts were successful in securing a mutually satisfactory trade agreement.[29] On the whole, the industrial conciliation department of the National Civic Federation was more often successful than not.

The National Civic Federation has often been accused of being an employer's association whose only purpose was to maintain industrial peace and commercial prosperity by making labor acquiesce in its depressed conditions of life. According to the Socialist *Appeal to Reason,* "The Civic Federation, [was] the organization whose object is to make the slaves satisfied with their lot...."[30] This simply was not the case. As the men of the Civic Federation viewed it, the American economy had, with the dawn of the new century, assumed a radically different structure from that of the last quarter of the nineteenth century. As George Gunton remarked, "It is what the laborers consume in their general daily standard of living that furnishes the only reliable foundation for the success of the most highly developed methods and undertakings in modern industry. As consumers, therefore, the masses have become the very foundation of the modern market."[31] The American economy, in the view of men like Gunton, had become, or at any rate was rapidly becoming, consumer-oriented rather than being dominated by capital goods production. This being the case, widespread prosperity within the working class was essential to the health of the American economy and to the well-being of the general society as well.

Besides becoming consumer-oriented, American industry was fast approaching a state of oligopoly. Small producers were being absorbed or driven out of business by great combinations having large capital reserves and producing vast quantities of goods. The age of the trust had arrived, and the new turn of events disturbed many Americans. The National Civic Federation, though, welcomed the advent of the trust as being in the best interests of the general society. Declaring that, "excessive competition is an evil," the Civic Federation went on to proclaim that, 'When excessive competition occurs in the field of capital it shows its havoc by depression of trade, long and risky credits, bankruptcy and 'demoralization.' "[32] The tendancy toward combination, then, "is the highest form and the culmination of the movement on the side of capital to do away with destructive competition."[33] It was an attempt to rationalize the operations of the American economy, to try to eliminate that "boom and bust" cycle which did so much to unsettle the smooth, steady ascent of the economic order. Trustification, in and of itself, was not to be feared; but, the trust wielded great economic power, and unless checked by a strong countervailing force, it could bode ill for the democratic institutions of American society. This new and enormous economic power came to rest first, and most heavily, upon labor, and it was here that the Civic Federation made its chief contribution to the new economic order arising in the United States.

As business sought to escape excessive competition, so, too, did labor. When excessive competition existed in the field of labor, "its consequences are the sweating system, long hours, low wages, the 'exploitation' of labor, unsanitary and dangerous work places, miserable homes and other phases of poverty."[34] As capitalist John Hays Hammond observed, "organized labor was needed to protect the workingman against organized capitalism."[35] As the trust was not to be feared, neither was the organized labor movement. The labor union, like the industrial combination, was a reaction to a new set of economic circumstances, its existence was not to be bemoaned, but understood, its growing power not dreaded, but employed to advance the common welfare of the whole nation. Asserting that, "the betterment of labor is the betterment of the entire social structure...,"[36] the National Civic Federation welcomed the labor union as a wholesome movement which was, "striving to improve the condition of the working masses." "It deserved," Ralph Easley declared, "the friendly cooperation of . . . all."[37] But aside from improving the lot of the worker, the union, by demanding its fair share of the proceeds of modern industrial production, was acting as a brake upon the great corporation, reducing its potential for harm, and safeguarding equal economic opportunity for all classes. In the words of Oscar S. Straus, "The stronger each side grows, and the stronger the leaders they have, the fewer will be the occasions for conflict."[38] "We want," he went on, "labor [to] get its full share, we know that capital will take care of itself."[39]

Few employers in the first decade of the twentieth century were willing to accept the labor union on anything approaching a basis of equality. Viewing the union as a conspiracy in restraint of trade, whose demands were an infringement on the managerial prerogatives of capital, many employers, such as the immortal George F. Baer, forced their workers into long, and often violent, strikes. "There confront each other in the United States," the Civic Federation warned in 1905, "two titanic forces, whose power waxes daily with the growth of their organization and the improvement of their discipline. These are the forces of employer and employed."[40] Hostility between them threatened to rend the fabric of American society. "To prevent the industrial revolution threatened by extremists and to promote industrial peace, are [the organization declared] the reasons for the existence of the National Civic Federation."[41] To prevent industrial chaos, the Federation advocated nothing less than full recognition of labor's right to collective bargaining. "It is not revolutions and strikes that we want," John Rogers Commons, an early member of the Civic Federation declared, "but collective bargaining on something like an organized equilibrium of equality," and this could only be realized in the trade agreement.[42]

The trade agreement was, first and foremost, a recognition on the part of capital that, as John Mitchell emphatically stated, "The time has passed when wages and conditions of employment can be fixed satisfactorily at the door of the factory or at the mouth of the mine. . . ."[43] The union was acknowledged to be the legitimate bargaining agent for the workers employed by the corporation, and, moreover, by negotiating with the union, the company was granting labor the right to determine, in part at least, working conditions and pay scales—the managerial prerogatives which capital had so jealously guarded. A trade agreement specified, in precise language, the duties expected of each type of worker within a factory; it contained detailed provisions and standards respecting the conditions under which the work was to be performed, and an iron-clad wage scale which could not be cut during the life of the trade agreement. Most trade agreements also provided for small, but periodic, wage increases geared to rising productivity and efficiency of operations.

For organized labor, the trade agreement conferred union recognition, stable wage rates, the promise of regular pay raises, and to John Mitchell it was, "Unmistakable recognition of the mutual dependence of capital and labor. It is the essence of trade unionism."[44] The more reserved Samuel Gompers pointed out that in the trade agreement, "There is no attempt to confuse the situation by proclaiming that the interests of the workers and employers are identical," but he added, "there is a natural desire for peace with the hope for industrial improvement and economic, social, and human progress."[45] For capital, on the other hand, the trade agreement meant stability of labor conditions without the unsettling outbreaks of strikes, walk-outs, and work stoppages. Chauncey H. Castle of the National Stove Manufacturers' Association declared that the results of trade agreements, "have been satisfactory beyond all former expectations of possibilities. Failures, in general, come through lack of discipline of the membership, or of misunderstanding of the meaning and intention of certain classes of agreements. It is with regret that I feel obliged to say that in some cases failures are through faults of the employer."[46] And Francis L. Robbins, president of the Pittsburgh Coal Company, added his mead of praise proclaiming that, "Nothing, in my judgment, is so important for the future of the country as the trade agreement as a method of reaching harmonious relations between capital and labor."[47]

After the anthracite strike of 1902, the incidence and severity of labor disputes dropped sharply, and according to John T. Wilson of the International Brotherhood of Maintenance of Way Employees, "A potent factor in the partial elimination of strikes and lockouts during the past few years has been the National Civic Federation, which is endeavoring to substitute conciliation and arbitration in lieu of the wasteful and barbarous strike and lockout so frequently resorted to in the recent past.... "[48]

The period from 1902 to 1905 was the zenith of the Civic Federation's trade agreement program, and these agreements— all providing for some form of conciliation, mediation, or arbitration—greatly helped to reduce labor disputes and strikes. Unfortunately, the trade agreement was an extra-legal device which could not be enforced in the courts, and it was entirely possible that if challenged, the courts might find the trade agreement to be a restraint of trade in violation of the 1890 Sherman Anti-Trust Act. Consequently, the efficacy of the trade agreement was dependent upon the honor of capital and labor, and their mutual desire to faithfully adhere to their commitments.

On the whole, the agreements were successful. Capital, priding itself on its adherence to contractual obligations and constantly invoking the sanctity of contracts, had little reason to violate its trade agreements. Labor, for its part, had long argued that the unions were responsible bodies which, once recognized by capital, would not disappoint their trust and would scrupulously live up to its bargains. A trade agreement broken by the union would discredit the entire organized labor movement, and the unions were determined not to allow this to happen. For example, in 1901, Daniel J. Keefe, head of the Longshoreman's Union, sent strike-breakers to Buffalo to smash a Longshoreman's strike which had been called before the conciliation apparatus provided for in their trade agreement had been exhausted in the effort to resolve the dispute with the dock managers. Labor's attitude was summed up by James Duncan of the Granite Cutters' Union, who declared, "No contract should be more sacred than the trade agreement of organized labor. It is a matter of honor between the contracting parties that is neither circumscribed by surety companies' bonds nor by compulsory edicts which enslave the body or dwarf the mind."[49]

The National Association of Manufacturers, and those employers in accord with their philosophy, however, regarded labor unions as "a danger to the state and a menace to civilization." The National Civic Federation—with its union recognizing trade agreement—was the N.A.M.'s chief target, next—of course—to the American Federation of Labor itself, and the N.A.M. kept up a constant legal battle against the trade agreement. In the spring of 1904, the Illinois Appellate Court struck down a trade agreement which had provided for a closed shop as a conspiracy in restraint of trade and a violation of freedom of contract. The *N.C.F. Review* indignantly declared, "We believe that the decision is sound neither in law, nor in common sense, nor in policy. It declares that the specified agreement to employ only union workmen strikes at the right of contract. It appeares to us that the decision itself strikes at that right."[50]

By 1905, such court decisions had seriously undermined the efficacy of the Civic Federation's trade agreement program, and the organization was forced to re-evaluate its techniques. To this point, the federation had not stressed governmental intervention into the economy as a means of achieving a more just economic order; rather it had relied primarily upon fostering a recognition of organized labor's place in a modern industrial system, confident that the unions could best promote their own interests while —at the same time—curbing the trusts, and that they could do this without the intervention of the government. But with the courts striking down trade agreements, the need for a legislative program—more fully-developed in later years under the leadership of Seth Low—was apparent. Fortunately, the Civic Federation had a sympathetic friend in Washington, for with a number of his cabinet officers and advisors active in the Federation, President Roosevelt had had a thorough exposure to the philosophy and program of the N.C.F. "I assure you," he wrote Samuel Gompers in December 1904, "that I am in hearty accord and sympathy with the purposes of the National Civic Federation in its efforts for the establishment of 'more rightful relations between employers and employees.' It is a movement so praiseworthy and so thoroughly American in conception that it should, as a matter of course, receive the earnest support of all good citizens who are awake to the vital needs of our nation."[51]

Proclaiming that, "Organized labor cannot be destroyed without the debasement of the masses," the Civic Federation, by 1905, through its trade agreement program, its defense of collective bargaining, and its efforts to conciliate, mediate, or arbitrate labor disputes, had established itself as a friend of labor.[52] "I believe the Civic Federation," John Mitchell stated, "is doing more to establish confidence, to bring into closer and more rightful relations the interests of capital and labor, than any other institution in this country."[53] And Samuel Gompers asserted, "It [the N.C.F.] helped to establish the practice of accepting labor unions as an integral social element. . . ."[54]

While it can be argued that the N.C.F.'s trade agreement program was merely a clever attempt to lock labor into a capitalist system dominated by the great corporations, there was a much deeper motivation guiding the Federation's work. Underlying the entire movement was a feeling of optimism and of confidence in America's universal mission to advance human happiness and welfare. "I have grown more and more hopeful," Oscar S. Straus exclaimed, "that, as this country was the first to organize religious and political equality, it will lead the way to a peaceful co-ordination of the economic forces by equalizing the opportunities for advancement, which is the nearest practical approach to economic equality."[55] Also, there was a sincere desire to uplift the working classes. Midwest industrialist, Col. John J. McCook, stated that he supported labor unions, "because they make better men, better mechanics, better citizens, better Americans."[56] And conditions were improving. "We are glad to admit," John Mitchell remarked, "that the conditions of our lives and of our labor were never better; but we also propose to say, and to insist, that they are not too good yet."[57] With labor constantly advancing, strikes, disorders and revolutions were not what was needed—or wanted—by labor. But the program proposed by the National Civic Federation was. Accept the trust as a necessary part of modern industrialism, recognize the principle of collective bargaining, and use the labor union to check the power of the trust. Accept the newly-emergent economic order as inevitable and desirable: this was the Civic Federation's program. "In the dawn of a new century," Mark Hanna urged:

> looking back over our history, we are almost bewildered by the great and wonderful progress of the country; and no matter how we may demoan [*sic*] against the changes that are thrust-

ing themselves upon us, we must, sooner or later, grapple with the question—the serious problem—of the adjustment of these matters, instead of trying to turn back to conditions that have passed. Is it not better courageously and manfully to face the proposition of the future, and make a united effort to settle it?[58]

In 1905, Seth Low joined the National Civic Federation.

CHAPTER XI

The Industrial Philosophy of Seth Low

I feel, with you, that the heart of the nation is as far as possible from being corrupt, and that what is really going on is the effort of democracy to realize itself under entirely new and very trying conditions. . . . Society is learning to move as to personal property along lines which it has long pursued as to real estate, when real estate was the only form of property that counted. In other words . . . all our legislation so far has aimed to facilitate production and very little consideration has been given, comparatively, to the question of distribution or control. To-day these last two questions are fairly above the horizon; and I am confident that democracy will justify itself in this field as it has done in so many others.[1]

"This century," James Bryce wrote Seth Low in July 1900, "is coming to its end here among such clamor, bloodshed, hatred of nations, and a general lessening of the ideals which you and I were brought up forty years ago to cherish."[2] The view was shared by many members of the "natural aristocracy" in England and America, but Seth Low never subscribed to the doctrine that the western world's "Golden Age" had passed. Always an optimist, he was confident that better things were awaiting mankind in the new century. The battle for political democracy, for equality before the law, seemed to be fairly won by the new century's dawn, but the problem of industrial democracy seemed to many to be an insoluble one. What was to become of the entrepreneur in an age of trusts, what was to become of the workingman in a factory owned by an impersonal financial institution, what would become of society when the labor trust and the industrial trust fought it out? These were but a few of the fears which cast a shadow of dread over the new century, and these were the very problems which the National Civic Federation hoped to resolve.

In January 1901, the newly organized National Civic Federation invited Seth Low to become a member of its Committee on Conciliation and Arbitration. The idea behind the Civic Federation appealed to Low. A firm believer in conciliation and arbitration as a means of settling international disputes, he saw no reason why the same method should not be applied to domestic labor disputes. However, his position at Columbia University and his deepening involvement in New York City politics were a heavy drain on his time and he had little to spare for other causes, no matter how worthy. "I am always a little shy," he told Bishop Henry C. Potter, "of national movements in which I am too busy to take personally an active part. On the other hand, I have the feeling that everything that can be done to advance the cause of conciliation and arbitration ought to be done. I am inclined, therefore, to give a favorable response to this invitation."[3] The Federation was particularly anxious to obtain Low's support since he was a well-known friend of organized labor, but as long as he was engaged in New York City politics, he could not give the Civic Federation anything more than the benefit of his name. Nevertheless, Low remained a firm believer in the purposes of the National Civic Federation. While mayor of New York City, Seth Low officially welcomed to the city the Federation's 1902 industrial conference declaring, "there is no problem affecting the people of the United States more important than the industrial problem. . . . " And the way to resolve this, he went on, "is to prevent trouble by bringing about a just relationship between capital and labor, and that justice is most likely to prevail when each side recognizes that there are rights on the other side that must be considered."[4] Upon leaving political life on New Year's Day 1904, Low shortly became an active member of the Civic Federation, but his basic industrial philosophy, and his reputation as a friend of labor, had been established a decade earlier.

Unlike his father, who was a well-known opponent of organized labor, Seth Low, from the outset of his career, showed no fear or apprehension at the prospect of large and powerful labor unions competing against equally imposing industrial combinations. "These are certainly times full of new problems," he wrote his father back in 1886, "I suppose the labor world is undergoing a revolution as complete as the commercial world experienced in making the old-fashioned merchant a thing of the past."[5] But this revolution, Low felt, was no more to be dreaded than was the rise of the corporation, for as the corporate form made possible a more efficient method of doing business and resulted in a higher standard of living, so, too, would the rise of organized labor prove beneficial to society as a whole. By the late 1880s, Seth Low had developed a progressive and socially-advanced conception of the modern industrial system, and in a revealing essay published in 1888, he cogently enunciated his view of this new, and often frightening, society which was still in the process of becoming.

As Low saw it, every society was a complex of special interest groups; many, though not all, of these groups were rooted in opposing economic interests—worker versus employer, manu-facturer against importer, retail merchant opposing whole-saler and others. These conflicting economic groups were, in turn, divided into "ins" and "outs." The "ins" dominated the political system of their society, enjoyed social prestige, and received a heavy share of the benefits of the prevailing economic order; they were in command and wished to remain so. The "ins" were the natural conservatives in every society. The "outs," on the other hand, were a minority interest within the political order; generally they did not enjoy as much social prestige as the "ins," and received a smaller share of the fruits of the economic system. The "outs" wished to secure all the rights and privileges possessed by the "ins" and, therefore, in all societies, the "outs" were the forces making for change— the people who demanded reform, the liberals, if you will. Of course, the "outs" wanted change so that they could become the "ins," and the "ins"—wanting to preserve their position—resisted change. Hence, there was a constant struggle for power within every society, between those forces which held power and those which sought it. Conservatism had always to do battle with the forces of liberalism.

However, this continual social friction was beneficial to society as a whole, for, "Were it not for conservatism among men, progress would always be revolutionary; were it not for liberal-ism conservatism would make society stagnant. By the opposi-tion of these two forces, wherever the equilibrium is maintained, social progress is both steady and orderly."[6] In Low's dialectic, the conflict between the forces of conservatism and liberalism was the dynamo which propelled society up the road of progress. The incessant struggle for power was not to be feared as a force tending to destroy society, but should be understood for what it, in fact, was—an instrument for social progress.

However, the dynamo of social progress needed a governor to keep the opposing forces in equilibrium lest violent social upheaval and revolution result. One could argue that upheaval and revolution were as good a vehicle for progress as any other, but violence took a heavy toll of lives and property, and if progress could be achieved by other, even if somewhat slower, means it was to be preferred. The governor was society itself, which to preserve its stability and well-being, sought to keep the forces of conservatism and liberalism within reasonable bounds and not at each other's throats.

In America, the opposing forces within society were, respectively, organized capital and organized labor. The former, enjoying political, social, and economic power, represented the force of conservatism; the latter, politically, socially, and economically deprived, was the force of liberalism, demanding change and a larger share of power for itself within the society. This natural process of social conflict in American society was, however, complicated by the nation's traditional and almost religious devotion to the values and ideals of individualism. But, the new economic forces—besides tearing American society apart—appeared to be destroying individualism itself. "On the one hand," Low declared, "there never has been a time when the individual has counted for so much; on the other, there never has been a time when the individual has counted for so little."[7] Here in America, he pointed out, the individual enjoyed more freedom than anywhere else in the world; yet, here in America, the independent merchant, a pillar of civic virtue within his community, was fast disappearing into the coldly impersonal corporation, and the corporation itself was being absorbed by the trust whose vast economic power threatened to crush out individual initiative everywhere. Also, the sturdy, capable workman of old, who took pride in his craft, was rapidly being changed into an automaton, who turned a bolt on an assembly line, and who had no more individuality than a sardine in a can. The American workingman was no more than a cog in the industrial machine, who could be replaced as easily as one of Mr. Whitney's interchangeable parts, and what individuality he still possessed was being further diluted in the trade union, which increasingly made his decisions for him.

Many Americans, proud of their nation's individualistic heritage, bemoaned the apparent loss of individuality in a society becoming ever more highly structured. Low, though, did not see it that way. In the United States, he argued, the individual was the freest. The humblest citizen enjoyed the same political and civil rights as the mightiest. Because of this freedom, America was one of the most tightly organized and highly structured societies in the world.[8] The individual, be he capitalist or workingman, realized that only by combining with his fellows could be achieve the full promise of his individuality. The worker advanced only by concerted action with his co-workers; the capitalist prospered only by pooling his resources with other entrepreneurs. Hence, the labor union and the corporation, rather than being a denial of individuality, was actually the fulfillment of individualism.

Granted that the corporation and the labor union were not hostile to the values of individualism, what of the conflict between the two forces which threatened to turn America into a battleground? Unlike some optimists, Seth Low did not argue that the interests of capital and labor were identical. He did hold that the long-run interests of the two were identical, for as all of society was interdependent, neither side could prosper without the cooperation of the other. Also, both capital and labor had a vital interest in the stability and well-being of their common society. However, most men, he realized, lived in the short-run, and the short-run interests of capital and labor were not identical. Labor demanded higher pay, shorter hours, better working conditions and assorted fringe benefits; capital wanted maximum profits and minimum production costs. It was labor's insistence upon a greater share of the profits of economic production which was causing industrial strife in American society, for as Roger Williams once declared, "What are all the strifes and contentions about except for more and larger bowls of porridge?" Again, though, this industrial strife was to be welcomed as the engine of progress.

"The present relation between labor and capital in this country," Low wrote, "seems to me simply to reflect the fact that we have not yet perfectly learned the laws which control these new forces that are expressing themselves in combinations of labor and capital alike."[9] According to his analysis, the industrial combination and the labor union were both outgrowths of capitalist society, responses to changing economic conditions which were inevitable, irrevocable, and beneficial. But, because the trust and the union were new phenomenon, arising from a changed economic environment, neither the new environment nor its phenomenon were as yet clearly understood. What the nation needed, Low maintained, was not breast-beating, nor a futile effort to turn back the clock of human progress hoping to return to a pre-industrial society; but rather, a scientific study of the new economic order in an attempt to discover the laws governing that system, and, thereby, learn how to control the economic processes in the interests of the general society. "If my premise be correct," he went on, "it becomes us, then, first of all, not to be alarmed by the apparent difficulties which confront us, owing to the presence in our midst of these two antagonistic tendencies. What we are to do is to find their equilibrium."[10] Once the equilibrium between capital and labor was discovered, America could proceed along the path of infinite progress; and the government, being democratically elected and representative of the entire people, would act as the governor, keeping the two forces perfectly aligned by employing its legislative power on behalf of one side and then the other, whenever the pull of one threatened to overwhelm the other. The state, in Low's conception, must exercise a positive influence in the economy to preserve the vital interests of society.

Seth Low's analysis of industrial society was rather idealistic, and the problem still remained of how to translate this intellectual analysis into a practical and workable reform program. With capital dominating all phases of American society, the forces of labor, *i.e.* of liberalism, had to be strenghtened in order to bring labor into equilibrium with capital, and to achieve this end the power of the state should be exerted on behalf of labor and of legislation to promote the welfare of the workingman. He was, for instance, an early advocate of reducing through law, the length of the working day, and was an exponent of the eight-hour day. "I am in sympathy with the desire of the working people for an 8-hour day," he told American Federation of Labor President Samuel Gompers:

> My reasons, however, are sociological rather than directly economic. I am not confident, for instance, that an 8 hour day would result in work for more men, unless the 8 hour standard were of world wide adoption. But, I think the shortening of the hours of labor is a direction in which the use of machinery may reasonably be expected to benefit the wage worker quite as genuinely and quite as valuably as in cheap-

ening the prices of commodities. "The life is more than meat and the body than raiment", and to develop the best there is in manhood, I conceive requires some command of time other than that which is given for wages. Probably the most useful men whom the world has known always have worked more than 8 hours a day, and men will do so in the future as in the past, but there is a wide gulf of difference between giving all the working hours of a long day for simple wages, and commanding a portion of those hours for one's self.

In the desire of the working people, then, for an 8 hour day, I see the desire of humanity for something more than mere subsistence, the hunger and thirst of men for a life which shall have some leisure in it for family, and for the opportunities which leisure brings. How near we may be to such a consummation I cannot tell. The nations of the world are in such close touch to-day that it is hard for any one of them to stand alone. I cannot even imagine what the effect of the 8 hour day would be on the economic, industrial, and commercial condition of this country, were we alone to adopt it. But I am not afraid of movements towards that end. They seem to me in the line of progress, and some day they should succeed.[11]

His sympathy for the cause of labor was deep, genuine, and constant. Born to wealth, and never having had any anxiety for his economic well-being, Low, nevertheless, possessed a quick social conscience and an active sympathy for the deprived. This feeling was rooted in a sincere religious faith which manifested itself in a desire to aid his fellow man. In an address delivered in 1900, Seth Low candidly admitted that, "It is hard to maintain an active living sympathy with those who are struggling for bare support, when one is himself exempt from the necessities and terrors of such a struggle." But, he added, "There must be room in a man's life for pity. There must be time and thought given for the help of the helpless."[12]

During the depression winter of 1893–1894, Low urged upon the city of New York an extensive park improvement and public works program to be financed by grants from the State Legislature and bond issues, as a means of providing work and sustenance for the city's unemployed. The state awarded New York City a sizeable grant for that very purpose, but the Tammany administration squandered the funds in short order. As president of the city's University Settlement House, though, Low strived to alleviate the hardships of the unemployed by mobilizing New York's many private charities in a concerted drive to improve conditions in the tenement house areas. And, throughout the depression, his optimism never dimmed. This was just one more obstacle which American society had to overcome in order to prove its worth. As he told a Madison Square Garden audience, gathered to aid the unemployed:

> It is by overcoming difficulties that men become strong; it is by being brave when it is hard to be brave that men become noble. Just so it is with a nation. Its greatness is born in trial. We may be sure, men of New York, as we meet here in the midst of these hard and distressful times, that we can, if we will, from this 'nettle, Danger, pluck the flower, Safety."[13]

In April 1896, Seth Low was called upon to arbitrate his first labor dispute. On April 24, typographers at J. J. Little & Company went out on strike demanding extra pay for certain technical operations involving the composition of type, and also called upon the company to recognize the closed shop in its printing offices. On April 30, both sides agreed to submit all points in dispute to a ten-man arbitration committee, five of whose members would be from the union, and five from the Typothetae, the employers' association. The strikers returned to work pending the outcome of the arbitration, and the committee decided that all points which it was unable to resolve would be referred to an outside arbiter, whose decision would be binding. By unanimous consent, Seth Low was selected arbiter.

On most of the technical points in dispute, Low decided in favor of the typographers, but there remained the delicate question of the closed shop. He had declared that, "from my point of view the Trade Union . . . is of value to society as well as a benefit to its own members."[14] Moreover, on numerous occasions, he had stated that he, "always felt that if I were a workingman, earning my living by my hands, I would certainly join a union. . . . "[15] The closed shop, however, was a volatile subject, and he disliked having to take a stand on it. On the one hand, the typographer's union argued that J. J. Little had, thirty years earlier, been a member of their union and had sworn that if ever he became an employer he would hire only fellow union members. Moreover, the union maintained that since most Little employees were union men, in any case, the closed shop existed *de facto* and should be formally recognized by the company. The union also held that non-union typographers at Little's were enjoying the benefits of a union shop without having to bear the burdens of union membership which was an inequity. The company, on the other hand, declared that it did not discriminate between union and non-union members in its employment policies, fitness being the only test required, and that to impose a closed shop upon it would be to violate its right to obtain the best-qualified men regardless of their union affiliation. Low's decision declared that since no evidence could be cited to show that Little had ever discriminated between union and non-union labor, he was justified in maintaining his current employment policy. While asserting that the union's demand for a closed shop was unreasonable, he, nevertheless, condemned J. J. Little & Company for refusing to recognize and to treat with the typographer's union as the bargaining agent for the union men in its employ. Low called upon the company to negotiate with the union as the legitimate representative of its members in all matters affecting their duties as Little employees. And since J. J. Little was largely a unionized company, all agreements entered into by the parties would also apply to the non-union typographers employed by the company.[16]

The decision apparently proved satisfactory to both the typographers and the Typothetae. Theodore L. DeVinne of the employers' association stated that, "All the members I have met so far fully agree with me in expressing the heartiest thanks for the able manner in which you have managed this difficult question. . . . I am sure that you have paved the way for peace."[17] The union was also pleased, for Low's correspondence during this period revealed numerous requests, by labor and capital alike, that he arbitrate labor disputes. Due to the pressure of his duties as president of Columbia, he was forced to deny most of these requests. However, in the New York printing industry, his one decision, as the typographer's union declared, had, "served as a precedent in every similar case that has arisen. . . . "[18]

In late March of 1897, plumbers and steamfitters halted work at Columbia's new Morningside Heights campus over a dispute as to which union was entitled to perform the thermostatic work in the college's buildings. The jurisdictional dispute threatened to be prolonged, and to expedite a settlement both unions agreed to let Seth Low resolve the quarrel. Pondering the merits of each side's case over the April 2nd weekend, he decided in favor of the plumbers, and work promptly resumed the following Monday.[19] And, a year later, he arbitrated another dispute between the Typothetae and the Feeders' union. In this case, only technical issues were in dispute and Low, this time, found in favor of the Typothetae.[20] The point of these various arbitration cases was that organized labor trusted Seth Low sufficiently, believed in his basic honesty and fairness to such an extent, that it was willing to freely place its fate within his hands. Generally, labor opposed arbitration as a limitation upon its freedom of action and prejudicial to its vital interests. But, with Seth Low, labor felt secure, and it never had cause to regret the trust it placed in him.

By 1900, Low's basic philosophy as to the role of organized capital and organized labor in modern industrial society had been formed. In the decade and a half to come, this conception would be refined, elaborated upon, and broadened, but substantially nothing was to be added. With the turn of the century, however, the question as to the proper role and function of the industrial combination and the labor union within American society, which Low had been concerned with for more than ten years, began to occupy a position of primacy as a political issue. William Jennings Bryan was seeking the Presidency upon a platform which appeared to many to be one of open hostility to trusts and monopolies, and appeared to be seeking nothing less than a return to a pre-industrial America of small producers. Low considered Bryan's economic program to be pregnant with disaster, a defense of a social order which no longer existed, and which could not be resurrected even by an evangelist of the "Great Commoner's" stature. Campaiging vigorously for William McKinley, Low declared in a June address that, "The internal problems of the country to-day are largely those that spring from its abounding prosperity."[21] And because it gave America prosperity, Bryan's efforts to abolish the existing economic order were unsound. They were a rejection of the fundamental law of industrial society: the efficiency of combination. This was not meant to imply that there was not a severe capital-labor problem in America, but the way to solve this puzzle was to learn from experience and rule out those solutions which experience had proven fallacious. "A man," he told the Brooklyn Young Republican Club:

or a party, or a combination of parties, that either will not or
cannot learn from experience, would be a most unsafe guide
for a progressive people.[22]
   All ought to realize that the subject ought to be to control
the use of this new power in the interest of society as regards
both capital and labor, and not to prevent its use.[23]

The trust—the monopoly—Low maintained, provided cheaper
goods of higher quality and lower cost than did the smaller,
independent producer, and if properly regulated, these new
combinations were of benefit to society.[24] America's efforts
should not be to smash, but rather to learn how to control the
trusts.

Once more active in political life, Seth Low's interest in
labor-capital relations had to take second place to more pressing
demands, but, leaving political office for the last time in 1904,
he again turned to a consideration of the economic problem.
He began an intensive reading program, absorbing such works
as Washington Gladden's *Tools and the Man,* Lyman Abbott's
Christianity and Social Problems, John Graham Brooks' *The
Social Unrest,* John Mitchell's *The Organization of Labor,* and
the report of the Anthracite Coal Commission among other
works. And, for a light change of pace, he read Platner's
Topography and Monuments of Ancient Rome.[25] The more he
studied the question, the more convinced he became that
nothing need be feared from the rise of the combination, and
he came to the conclusion that they were actually of positive
benefit. "Except for great combinations, the laboring man would
be at the mercy of combined capital much more than he is
now."[26] In 1905, he joined the New York branch of the National
Civic Federation. He felt that in the Federation he could make
a positive contribution to the settlement of what he regarded
as the nation's foremost problem. Upon joining the N.C.F., he
declared, "No one should be surprised, therefore, and no one
need lose heart, if progress in learning the limits of safety in
the use of the power of combination, on the part of both
capital and labor, is slow, and if, in the process of learning,
much injury is done."[27]

Low was to remain with the New York Civic Federation for
only a brief period. In November 1905, it was proposed to
name him as chairman of the National Civic Federation's
Department of Conciliation and Arbitration. As Ralph Easley
told Samuel Gompers:

As you are aware, Mr. Low is identified with all practical
methods of conciliation and arbitration; is a member of the
Hague Court of Arbitration [Low was a member of the American delegation to the 1899 Hague Conference, but was not
thereafter associated with the Court of Arbitration]; is not engaged in active business and therefore has the time to give to
the work. While Mr. Low is not an employer of labor, he is in
touch with all the big forces, and we all feel that his appointment would be an ideal one.[28]

But, Easley added, Low will not give his consent to serve
until assured that his appointment would be satisfactory to
organized labor, and the Civic Federation's secretary requested
the N.C.F.'s labor members to write Low telling him that
he was wanted as chairman of the Conciliation Department.
Gompers and Mitchell did so, with Mitchell stating that, "I
think no better man could be secured."[29] Informed of labor's
support, Low accepted the chairmanship and was formally
installed at the Federation's December meeting.

Until Low took over the department, the Civic Federation
had never intervened in a potential or actual labor dispute
until requested to do so by one or both of the parties involved.
However, when the possibility of another strike loomed in the
bituminous and anthracite coal fields in 1906, Seth Low decided
to take preventive action in the hope of averting the threatened
stoppage. As he wrote August Belmont, the president of the
Civic Federation, since both John Mitchell of the United Mine
Workers' Union and Francis Robbins, spokesman for the
bituminous operators, were members of the Federation, the
N.C.F. could not afford to sit idly by while its own members—
forgetting the purposes for which the organization had been
formed—drifted into industrial warfare.[30] Consequently, Low
sent identical letters to John Mitchell and Francis Robbins
telling them of his concern over the progress of their negotiations. He reminded them that the National Civic Federation
viewed the trade agreement as the surest and most equitable
method yet devised for the establishment of just and harmonious
relations between capital and labor, and that their failure to
produce a new trade agreement would discredit the efficacy of
the Federation's program throughout the nation. Expressing
his hope that they would be able to iron out their difference,
he urged them to submit points in dispute to arbitration and
to employ all possible means to avert a strike.[31]

Low, however, did not confine his efforts merely to the parties involved, but sought to bring to bear all available pressure. Writing his old friend Theodore Roosevelt, he declared, "The time seems to be close at hand when outside sentiment may have to be brought to bear to compel arbitration if the parties in interest will not agree." He requested the President to hold himself ready to throw his influence in favor of arbitration when the time became ripe.[32] "I think you are entirely right in your position," Roosevelt replied:

> both about the bituminous and anthracite situations. I am delighted that you wrote as you did both to Robbins and Mitchell. I can suggest nothing more at present. Do keep your eyes open and act precisely along the lines you indicate. If in any discreet way I can render you help, of course, I will.[33]

On March 16, John Mitchell responded to Low's appeal, saying that both he and Mr. Robbins "are bending our every effort . . . ," to reach an amicable settlement, and he assured Low that his union would be willing to arbitrate issues which he and Robbins could not resolve. He also asked that the Civic Federation help arrange a conference between the U.M.W. and Mr. Baer so that an agreement could be worked out for the anthracite fields as well as the bituminous.[34] Encouraged by the replies from both sides, Low told Roosevelt, "The inference I drew from what I learned is, that there is very good hope of an amicable settlement in both fields, despite all appearances to the contrary."[35] However, when it came to offering concrete concessions, the operators, again, proved stubborn. They demanded that the wage scales established in 1903 be continued, a demand which Mitchell, supported by Low, refused to consider. "I doubt," Low again wrote the President, "a great deal whether any of the operators would sell their coal stocks to-day at the prices which were obtainable in 1903; and, if they would not, it is not clear to me why labor should be foreclosed from asking a still further share in the prosperity of the country."[36]

Asking Roosevelt to apply pressure on the operators, Low suggested that a presidential plea for arbitration, at this time, might prove effective in achieving an agreement. Roosevelt replied that public opinion was only aroused after a strike occurred and not when it only threatened, and that if his call for arbitration failed because of lack of public support, it would damage the prestige of his office. He felt the time had not yet arrived for overt action on his part, but he promised to do all he could in an unofficial way to aid in a settlement.[37] Persisting in his application of pressure, Seth Low finally saw a trade agreement worked out and a strike averted. Of course, it is difficult to ascertain exactly how much effect Low's pressure had in bringing about the settlement of the threatened strike, but Low was not afraid to "butt in" in labor negotiations, and his constant appeals for a settlement, along with his invocation of the President's name and influence, at least induced both sides to do some serious thinking about their positions and to sound out the other side.

During his tenure as chairman of the Conciliation Department, Seth Low was able to assist in the settlement of many disputes before the strike stage was reached, and he was also able to aid in the resolution of many strikes before the passage of time could engender intransigence and bitterness. He was fond of telling how one day, while at his farm in Westchester, he received a phone call from a Philadelphia banker whose firm had a controlling interest in a street railway company in a city in the Mississippi Valley. He asked Low to use his influence to obtain from the union a delay in strike action, saying that his firm would accept the Civic Federation's conciliation services if this delay were granted. Low wired the union's president, who was in Detroit, and secured his consent to a mediated settlement. A week later, a mutually satisfactory trade agreement was negotiated and the impending strike averted. With a few phone calls and telegrams, and by using his good offices to bring both sides together, what promised to be a major strike had been amicably settled.[38] Needless to say, work of this nature went unpublicized.

Low's experience in the conciliation department convinced him that, "American men, whether employer or workingman, want to do the fair thing."[39] The only problem was to bring them together on terms of equality and fairness. In order to put an end to the warfare between American capital and American labor, however, the employer must recognize the union and be prepared to enter into collective bargaining. "I look forward to the time," he wrote Otto M. Eidlitz of the New York Building Trades Association, "when every shop that employs union men, even if it be an open shop, will allow the union men to be represented by their union, and will deal with the union as the representative of their men."[40]

When the employer was unwilling to recognize and to confer with the union, the Civic Federation's efforts were futile. In 1907, the United States experienced only one national strike, that of the Telegraphers' union against Western Union; and Seth Low, in an effort to bring about conciliation, wrote Jacob Schiff, requesting the aid of the Kuhn-Loeb partner. Condemning Western Union's refusal to meet the representative of the union, he declared, "I think the day has gone by when the great corporations can decline to confer with the representatives of unions except at the hazard of forfeiting the support of public opinion at the outset; and in this particular case, where an increase of rates has been made, the corporations are especially liable to unfriendly interpretation."[41]

Schiff, reflecting the prejudices of many businessmen, angrily replied, "My sympathies are ever with labor. I fully recognize its right to organize, but the individual employer or a corporation should not be expected to turn over the management of their affairs to an outside body which chooses to dictate the terms and conditions on which they shall deal with their employees."[42] Jacob Schiff was zealous in the defense of what he regarded as management's prerogatives, and he was not about to surrender them to a union.

Low, though, felt that Schiff was missing the whole point of unionism. "If labor has the right [to organize]," he wrote back:

> as is now almost universally conceded, it has all the rights which this right implies; and one of these is the right to be represented in any labor controversy by its own chosen representatives. One might as well ignore the officers of the Western Union and claim the right to deal direct with the stock-holders of that Company, as to deny to Union employees the right which the stock-holders enjoy of being represented by their chosen officials.[43]

"You do not," Schiff indignantly answered, "have an open mind on at least some of the phases of the subject in regard to which you desire to act as conciliator."[44] The company remained stubborn, the Civic Federation failed to bring about conciliation, and the strike dragged on through the summer of 1907.

As chairman of the Federation's Conciliation Department,

Seth Low quickly came to realize that industrial combinations
had to be controlled, and since the unions were too weak to
effectively exercise restraint, it was up to the government to
impose this control. He did not fully develop his ideas on
government regulation of industry until after he assumed the
presidency of the Civic Federation. But, even in this early
period, one can discern the genesis of an industrial philosophy
emphasizing the positive intervention of the national government in the economic order. Late in 1904, he wrote Commissioner of Corporations, James R. Garfield, that it was
patently impossible to effectively regulate industry so long as
each state was permitted to charter corporations. Only the
national government, he argued, could restrain national industries, and to perform its regulatory functions properly a
system of federal licensing or incorporation was desirable. Once
the national government incorporated businesses, it could set
regulations and standards as the price of incorporation.[45] Seth
Low was calling for an increase in the positive powers of the
federal government—a most unconservative demand.

Ardently supporting President Roosevelt's efforts to regulate
the railroads, he told him in February 1905:

> I believe that the defective legislation which has permitted
> all sorts of favoritism in rates, both as regards individuals and
> as regards places, and which has made it possible to pile up
> abnormal fortunes, even by methods that will not stand criti-
> cism, is due to the effort to deal with a subject that is National
> in scope, by forty-five different legislatures. If this be true, we
> do not escape danger by avoiding National control. We are
> pledged, in effect, to make our choice between two dangers,
> and of the two, I would rather run the rick [sic] of having
> the Government control the Rail Roads than of having the
> Rail Roads and a small group of abnormally rich men control
> the country.[46]

Low was beginning to formulate what would later become
known as the "New Nationalism," and for the next few years
he would urge these policies upon Roosevelt, who was moving
in that direction in any case.[47] In response to Low's letter, the
President replied, "It seems to me you have stated the case
exactly. We do not escape danger by the plan I propose, but
we incur still greater danger by failing to take action." But,
he added, "when we try to make too-drastic legislation, it simply
acts in favor of the very corporations aimed at."[48]

The thought of the men of the National Civic Federation and of the President were moving in similar channels, and with many of his cabinet members closely associated with the Civic Federation, Roosevelt was amenable to its philosophy; moreover, he and Low were old friends from the days when both were fighting for political reform in New York. They found one another compatible, and Low had great hope that his administration would be able to solve America's pressing industrial problem. As he wrote Eugene A. Rowland of the Rome, New York Republican Club:

> The Republican party, with its magnificent tradition, under the wise leadership of President Roosevelt ought to exercise a profound influence in bringing about progress without throwing all conservatism to the winds. The danger always is in times of change that conservative men will resist all change so bitterly and so long that, when change becomes inevitable, it sweeps everything before it. President Roosevelt fully recognizes that danger and is endeavoring to make the Republican party itself the instrument to bring about necessary chages [*sic*], so that the country shall not fall into the hands of men of extreme views and radical opinions.[49]

Low's prime objective was to preserve basic American values and institutions while placing the American economy on a more equitable basis. A part of the difficulty in controlling the nation's new economic forces was the federal system of government, which, Low felt, had largely outlived its original usefulness and was now creating difficulties. "It is interesting to observe," Low wrote Roosevelt:

> how irresistibly time is strengthening the national government. Our division of powers between the States and the nation has certainly many advantages, but the lawlessness of the great corporations has been favored by the situation more than by any other circumstance. Indeed, except for this, I doubt whether any such condition would have prevailed as has grown up almost unconsciously. It was certainly high time that the people, through their Government, should show not only the desire, but the capacity to exert the control.[50]

Roosevelt, already under "New Nationalist" influence, told Low, "I quite agree with what you say in your last paragraph. The powers of the National Government are being steadily strengthened, and must be steadily strengthened, and the chief cause in bringing this about is the lawlessness of the great corporations, their lawlessness being itself a chief and entirely unexpected product of the division of power between the States and the Union."[51]

For the last two years of his administration, Theodore Roosevelt was in close touch with the economic philosophy of the National Civic Federation. He supported and championed much of its legislative program, and so enthusiastic was he as to the merits of the Civic Federation that he sought to graft his Nobel Peace Prize endowment onto the federation. The idea originated with Oscar S. Straus and John Mitchell, and would have provided for the establishment of a foundation, supported by the prize funds, to which the Civic Federation would be grafted as chief beneficiary. As the President explained to Seth Low:

> It would not be possible, in my judgment, to take a gift of this kind, which is made by me in a semi-official character, and graft it on a private enterprise. The graft must be made the other way. You understand that neither my name nor Nobel's will be used in connection with the gifts; but I do not feel that I ought to let it be swallowed up in any private-movement.[52]

Ralph Easley, however, insisted that the integrity of his organization be retained and the proposal never got beyond the planning stage.

In any event, late in 1907, August Belmont tendered his resignation as president of the Civic Federation. It was proposed to name Andrew Carnegie as his successor, but Carnegie declined the offer on the ground that he was too old to take on the many burdens of the Federation's presidency. John Mitchell thereupon proposed the nomination of Seth Low as the N.C.F.'s new president, and the nomination committee seconded the proposal.[53] As New Year's Day 1908 approached, Seth Low prepared to take on the responsibilities of guiding the work of the National Civic Federation. He hoped to find a means of wisely and justly regulating the new economic forces spawned by modern industrialism. "The effort to destroy the trade union, on the one hand, and the trust on the other," he once declared and now sought to implement, "will give place to the wiser effort to regulate both so as to do away with the abuses of which each side is capable."[54]

On January 1, 1908, Seth Low took over leadership of the

Civic Federation. "I am glad that you have accepted the Presidency of the National Civic Federation," the University of California's Benjamin Ide Wheeler wrote. "I feel more confidence in it, and I feel certain that the position the Federation has already acquired in the country will be enhanced by your Presidency. I think people will have confidence and feel safe and inclined to co-operate."[55] Indeed, the Federation's most important work lay ahead.

CHAPTER XII

The Effort to Regulate the American Economy, 1908-1911

Mr. Seth Low . . . has been giving his entire time to the work of carrying on this conspiracy against the people of this country.

THE SQUARE DEAL[1]

In 1890, the Sherman Anti-Trust Act became a part of America's federal law. Declaring that, "Every contract, combination in the form of trust or otherwise, or conspiracy, in restraint of trade or commerce among the several States, or with foreign nations, is hereby declared to be illegal," it was a classic example of the sociological concept of cultural lag. At a time when the American economy was moving, seemingly irresistibly, in the direction of consolidation, the law appeared to many businessmen, lawyers, and economists as an attempt to undo history, an effort to repeal the economic growth of a generation. Moreover, the Sherman Act was disturbingly imprecise in its definition of what was and what was not a combination in restraint of trade, or what specific business practices tended to lessen competition. By the first decade of the new century, it was apparent that if the Sherman Act were to be rigorously enforced, the current conduct of the nation's business would have to be drastically altered. And a haphazard enforcement of the law would work havoc with the country's business. Since the economic system could not very well be undone, it appeared to many far simpler to change the Sherman Act to reflect the new realities of the American economic order.

In 1906, the National Civic Federation became interested in securing a revision of the anti-trust laws in order to bring federal statutes in line with economic developments. As one midwestern lawyer wrote Ralph M. Easley:

> I agree with you that if the Sherman Act is to remain upon the statute books it should be amended, if it is to be a bene-

ficent act, and not one hostile and injurious to the industries and prosperity of the country. It should be made specific and definite, so that the men who are conducting the commerce of the country may know from the act itself, or at least have some means of learning with certainty, what acts or conduct is forbidden by the law and made criminal, and what is not. The present law lacks this definiteness. It does not discriminate, in its terms, between that which is good and that which is evil. It furnishes no rule for the guidance of merchants in the conduct of their business.[2]

Seeking to formulate a definite position with respect to the Sherman Act, the Civic Federation called a national conference on trusts and combinations which met in October 1907. Largely ignored by historians of American economic thought, the conference offered rich materials for an analysis of the thinking of much of the American business community.

Attended by prominent business leaders, lawyers, intellectuals, and labor union officials, the National Civic Federation's 1907 conference was unique for its rejection of *laissez-faire* economic theory, and for its call for positive regulation of business by the national government. There was general agreement that, as Judge Peter S. Grosscup observed:

Somewhere in that life [American economic life], something is wrong; for though in the midst of material prosperity, the country is without contentment; and there must be something wrong in a prosperity that does not bring contentment—something that, in the nature of things, in some way pinches and wounds some deep-seated human instincts.[3]

To remedy the pervading discontent with American institutions felt by many people, Grosscup called for the democratization of the country's industry, declaring that the ownership of the nation's business must be widely diffused among the common people.[4] While Judge Grosscup spoke in generalities, others were more specific. All, however, agreed that America's industrial problems could not be solved by the tired formulae of the classical economists, for as Hamilton Holt, editor of *The Independent,* put it, "under modern methods of production and distribution the *laissez-faire* policy carried out to its logical conclusion means economic monopoly, business corruption, swollen fortunes, and social discontent."[5]

The primary requirement was to realize that large-scale industry was here to stay. "We cannot, if we would," commented

Samuel Gompers, "turn back to the primitive conditions of industry which marked the early part of the last century. It is therefore idle chatter to talk of annihilating trusts."[6] What was so frightening about the trusts was not so much what they did, but rather the enormity of their size. The vast amounts of capital which they controlled, their tremendous power, and their potential for harm were disconcerting to many Americans. But, as Columbia's Nicholas Murray Butler reminded the conference, "nothing is necessarily to be feared from a corporation because of its size." The problem, as he saw it, was that, "We are face-to-face with economic conditions that are new, and with economic abuses that, though manifold, have grown up slowly and in the dark. There is ample power in our institutions, in our constitution and our laws to check and to remedy them all."[7]

There was a general consensus that industrial combinations must, in some fashion, be regulated, and that the separate states were not adequate to the task. "In regard to the management of these great national trusts," Indiana's William Dudley Foulke remarked:

> born, perhaps, of national necessities, certainly of national exigencies, exercising their power throughout the length and breadth of this land, if they are ever to be shorn of that power, if that power is ever to be regulated by anything mightier than themselves, it will not be by the individual States, which for the last fifteen years, have tried in vain to curb the trusts, but it will be done through the supreme power of the National Government, the only power that is fully capable of dealing with this great question.[8]

It was obvious that as American businesses crossed state boundaries and became regional and even national, the states could no longer be expected to exercise a restraining influence over them, even if they had the will to do so. Only the national government, as Ohio's Attorney General Wade H. Ellis declared, could control an institution as broad as its own domain.[9] According to such speakers as Minnesota lawyer A. T. Ankeny, the Founding Fathers expected the national government, not the states, to regulate commerce, and that it was high time that the federal authority met its obligations.[10]

Granting that national supervision of the trusts was desirable and necessary, what form was this regulation to assume? William Dudley Foulke called for large-scale industries to be required to supply the national government with full data regarding their purchases, sales, and prices and to submit to federal control over their price-fixing policies and their general conduct.[11] Attorney Bartlett Tripp asked for federal incorporation of all businesses engaged in interstate commerce, with governmental supervision and regulation written into their charters of incorporation.[12] Asserting that lower federal courts were creating industrial chaos by sustaining acts of Congress in one jurisdiction only to strike them down in another, A. T. Ankeny asked that only the Supreme Court be permitted to pass on the constitutionality of federal statutes.[13] All agreed that existing law, especially the Sherman Act, was inadequate for the proper regulation of the industrial order. "Our corporate law," Herbert Knox Smith stated, "is in an unfinished and ill-balanced state, and as a piece of machinery for the direction of our great industrial forces it is in a highly unsatisfactory condition."[14] What was needed, Smith added, was administrative rather than judicial regulation of industry. A specialized commission, not a court of law, must oversee the day-to-day conduct of the great industries.[15]

The businessmen, corporation lawyers, and publicists who attended the Civic Federation's trust conference were asking for an increase in the positive regulatory authority of the national government—an increase of federal power at the expense of the state governments. And they were asking that their businesses be regulated by the national government. It was a demand not usually made by conservative businessmen. We need, Charles F. Ziebold, president of the West End Business Men's Association of St. Louis, said:

> a radical change in the relation now obtaining between the United States and the several States; a change that would substantially establish the same legislative and constitutional relations between the United States and the several States as now obtain between these States and their respective counties and cities.[16]

With the nation's business centralized, it was imperative that the government become centralized in order to meet the problems imposed by the new economic order. And, as Ziebold added, "Nor need there be fear of a centralized monarchy, because there is nothing to fear even from a monarchy, when the people themselves are the monarch."[17] The old fear of an overpowering government was giving place to a new fear of the power of unregulated business. "Both communities and individuals," William Dudley Foulke conceded, "may be at the mercy of the government, but it is better to be at the mercy of a representative government than of an irresponsible corporation, whose chief aim is to acquire profits for the officials and stockholders."[18] Even New York banker Isaac N. Seligman sang the praises of the national government. Holding that federal regulation was essential to the smooth functioning of American industry, he expressed his confidence in the equity of democratic government, adding, "Let us remember that our business interests have become national interests, and let us have confidence in the integrity, wisdom and equity of our government. It appears to me, gentlemen, that we can safely trust the present Administration and that it is our duty to strengthen its hands.... "[19]

As the trust was to be accepted as an integral part of the industrial system, so, too, was the labor union. Realizing that only a prosperous working class could keep American industry healthy, the Civic Federation's confrerees were aware that only the union could effectively advance the interests of the laborer. "More unions is what our country needs," J. A. Everitt proclaimed. "When everything and everybody are organized, unionized and co-operating, then there will be no weak to be preyed upon by the strong.... "[20] Besides seeking to rationalize the conduct of America's business, the men attending the trust conference sought to improve the quality of American life, not merely for the benefit of business, but for the good of the general society. "The labor unions," Indiana's Robert Taylor told his compatriots:

> are essential to the happiness, prosperity and perpetuity of this country. That we may be a happy and prosperous people, the laboring men, the working men of the country must make enough to live comfortably—comfortably according to the standard of to-day, and the higher standard of tomorrow, and the still higher standard of years to come.[21]

America, the Civic Federation's conference agreed, was moving into an era where big business would be confronted and challenged by big labor and big government. This was inevitable, a natural outcome of the capitalistic mode of production, and the nation must learn to master the difficulties born of the new times. "In an age like this," Seth Low declared:

> when the large unit is demonstrating its economy in every-

thing . . . it is not only idle to suppose that the industries and transportation system of the country can be successfully conducted in small units, but it is also manifestly to the disadvantage of the public to try to have them so conducted. The large corporation has demonstrated its efficiency, and its economy, too strongly to leave any room for doubt that in a country like ours, if the people are to be well served, there must be large combinations in the transportation services as elsewhere.[22]

No one knew precisely how to govern the newly-risen industrial order, but all were aware that the old verities were no longer applicable. "The so-called law of supply and demand," businessman J. E. Defebaugh declared, "has been set up as a fetish by many theorists, who have sacrificed to it life and the means of life. . . . Its unrestricted operation regulates by destroying."[23] The conference passed resolutions condemning the Sherman Law as unrealistic and called upon the national government to permit trusts and combinations which were not unreasonable in their conduct and which were manifestly in the public interest. Finally, it asked the federal government to face up to its responsibility to regulate the economy, and delegated a committee to present their resolutions to the administration and congressional leaders.

Seth Low, on October 26, 1907, wrote Theodore Roosevelt informing him of the resolutions adopted by the conference on trusts and combinations, and told the president that there was a strong sentiment in favor of federal incorporation of businesses engaged in interstate commerce, but that the subject needed a good deal more study before any definite legislation could be proposed. He went on to say that he had read the speeches which Roosevelt had delivered on his recent western tour, and that, "They seem to me . . . to constitute the best body of addresses which you have ever made. I delighted in the national, and constructive, and patriotic note that rang through every one of them.[24] Roosevelt had enunciated his "rule of reason" doctrine in regard to industrial combinations, for, as he told Seth Low:

> I believe that there should be a modification of the Sherman Law permitting combinations when the combination is not hostile to the interests of the people; and I do not see how such permission can be given unless there is some supervision by the national government along the lines of, say, the national banks. . . .[25]

When the recently-elected president of the National Civic Federation went to Washington early in 1908 to present the resolutions of the conference on trusts and combinations, he found an administration receptive to the ideas embodied in them. Delivering the resolutions to Roosevelt, his Cabinet, and the leaders of Congress, Low was told that the petition was not in a form upon which legislative action could be taken, and he was invited to draw up bills incorporating the conference's ideas in specific legislative language. Since the conference had given him no authority for the preparation of detailed legislation, Low requested instructions from the Federation's executive council which promptly empowered him to select a committee for the preparation of such a bill.[26]

At virtually the same time Seth Low was in Washington conferring with congressional leaders, the United States Supreme Court, early in February 1908, handed down its decision in the Danbury Hatters' Case. Declaring that the labor union boycott was a combination in restraint of trade within the terms of the Sherman Anti-Trust Law, it awarded the Manufacturer's Association triple damages. The decision, which made little or no distinction between a labor union and an industrial combination, appeared to many labor leaders to threaten the very existence of the organized labor movement by endangering its right to strike without incurring the penalty of the law. Samuel Gompers, viewing the Supreme Court's edict as a mortal blow at labor unions, was determined to have the decision nullified through legislation specifically exempting labor from the provisions of the Sherman Act. "We expect that the present Congress," the *American Federationist* declared, "will take prompt action to so amend or modify the Sherman law that there can be no question as to its application."[27] Gompers called upon all friends of labor to rally to its cause, and if Congress failed to act, declared that labor was prepared to launch a vigorous political campaign to reward its friends and punish its enemies. The Court's anti-boycott ruling in *Loewe v. Lawlor* added urgency and importance to the Civic Federation's effort to amend the Sherman Anti-Trust Act.

Seth Low appointed himself chairman of the Federation's committee to revise the anti-trust laws, and named Samuel Gompers and John Mitchell to represent the interests of labor, while Isaac N. Seligman and Elbert H. Gary were to represent the views of the business community, and Professors Nicholas

Murray Butler, Talcott Williams, Jeremiah W. Jenks, and Dr. Albert Shaw of the *Review of Reviews* were to safeguard the interests of the general public. Corporation lawyers Francis Lynde Stetson and Victor Morawetz were to supply the technical knowledge needed for the drafting of legislation. George W. Perkins of the House of Morgan was closely consulted regarding the bill's contents, but contrary to popular opinion, he did not have a direct hand in the drafting of the measure.[28]

Formed in February, the committee worked into early March in its attempt to devise an effective alternative to the Sherman Anti-Trust Act. The problem of securing relief for the unions proved to be the most difficult proposition facing the committee. A method had to be devised whereby the business community would benefit to such an extent from the proposed revision of the Sherman Law that it would accept the clauses exempting labor from the law's operation. As Ralph Easley wrote President Gompers:

> I had heard of a sentiment alleged to have existed in certain localities that now that the Sherman Act had knocked out the unions, it had better be let alone, and that employers would rather be inconvenienced by that Act than to get the unions "out of the hole" they are now in. I put the matter squarely up to Mr. Beck and Mr. Smith [of the Illinois Manufacturers' Association] and they did not feel that way; they both said they were of course opposed to a proposition which would enable the unions to get legislation exempting them alone. I told them both just what your position is in that matter and they are in thorough accord. I said that you did not expect the railroads and industrial corporations to propose measures for them, and, likewise, those interests should hardly expect labor to propose legislation for the other interests. They acquiesced with that view.[29]

Samuel Gompers demanded labor's total exemption from the provisions of the Sherman Act and this made it incumbent upon the Civic Federation's committee to grant the railroads and industrial combinations enough relief from the threat of anti-trust prosecution to persuade them to accede to labor's demands. Late in February, all difficulties were apparently overcome as Easley informed Gompers that, "I had a long talk with Mr. Perkins this morning and he is not at all averse to meet your contention.... I feel sure that we can get our people to stand back of the proposition to exempt the Unions from the operation of the Sherman Act." He went on to declare that Secretary of War Taft was in agreement with the effort to take the unions and the railroads out from under the jurisdiction of the Sherman Law, saying that it was never intended to apply to them.[30]

In the first week of March, the Civic Federation's draft bill was ready to be introduced into Congress. Writing Seth Low, Samuel Gompers again reiterated labor's demand that it specifically be exempted from the anti-trust laws, and warned that the American Federation of Labor would support the N.C.F.'s bill only so long as its labor clauses were not weakened by legislative amendments or revisions.[31] The following day, Low requested a conference with President Roosevelt in order to present the Civic Federation's draft proposal, and described the bill's provisions and their importance. Asserting that business was depressed largely through a lack of confidence in the government's policy toward industrial combinations, Low maintained that business was entitled to have, "what is reasonable and fair and not contrary to the public interest [made] lawful." But the Federation's greatest contribution to the anti-trust laws, Low declared, was in the bill's labor clauses which would alleviate the trade union fear that the Supreme Court had struck unionism a deadly blow. "I also learned that the labor men generally," he told the President:

> have reached the conclusion that, under the Sherman law, as now interpreted by the Supreme Court, even a strike that may affect inter-State commerce is probably unlawful, (under the Sherman law,) as a conspiracy in restraint of trade. This being so, I think you will realize that I did not use too strong a term when I said that the men identified with organized labor were, to a great extent, terrified.
>
> I can imagine no greater misfortune to our country than to prolong a situation which may undermine the trade unions. . . .[32]

To place labor's right to strike on a firm legal footing was, Low held, the primary purpose of the Federation's proposed legislation. Gompers, he told Roosevelt, was fighting to hold the radicals in the American Federation of Labor behind the bill.

A few days later, Seth Low again went to Washington, this time to present the administration with the final draft of the Civic Federation's bill. He had lunch with Roosevelt and the members of his cabinet several times that week, and had numerous conferences with congressional leaders. Finally, the President had been won over to the support of the measure when, at the last White House conference, Attorney General Bonaparte raised objections as to the constitutionality of certain of the bill's clauses which necessitated a redrafting of the entire proposal.[33] "Have met obstacles," Low wired George W. Perkins, "hope to overcome them."[34] And overcome them he did. On Thursday, March 12, Low, Gompers, and Victor Morawetz conferred with Roosevelt and his cabinet at the White House until one o'clock the following morning, and resolved all outstanding differences. Roosevelt had kept an open mind on all phases of the bill, Samuel Gompers recalled, and accepted the concept embodied in the measure that when the law went contrary to economic realities, it was the law and not the economy which had to be altered.[35] After the meeting, the President gave his official blessings to the bill and asserted that he would fight for it as his "irreducible minimum legislative demands." However, as the *New York Times* reported the next day, there were mutterings of discontent in the Congress over Roosevelt's bulldozing legislative tactics, and that the bill might well expect heavy going.[36]

Introduced into the House of Representatives by A. Barton Hepburn (Senate version was the Warner bill), the Federation's proposed law would have enabled corporations planning mergers to register with the Bureau of Corporations (in the case of railroads, with the Interstate Commerce Commission) their intentions and plans. If the bureau viewed the announced combination as an unreasonable restraint of trade, it would have thirty days in which to file its objections with the courts. If, on the other hand, no action were taken within the thirty-day period, the proposed combination could then be completed and the government would institute no anti-trust proceedings against the corporations involved. However, to retain immunity from future prosecution, the combination would be required to supply the government with such information concerning its purchases, production, sales, and general policies as might, from time to time, be demanded. So long as such data was freely and truthfully given, the government would refrain from anti-trust prosecution. The Hepburn Bill would have made possible advisory opinions as to what the government would or would not allow; it would also have permitted businessmen to submit their plans to the government and receive its blessing or disapproval before the proposed merger became a reality. Security would have been given to the business community, and the national government, by calling for detailed information concerning the operations of the great industries, would have been strengthened in its efforts to regulate the American economy. As for labor, the bill declared:

> Nothing in said act approved July second, eighteen hundred and ninety, or in this act is intended, nor shall any provision hereafter be enforced, so as to interfere with or restrict any right of employees to strike for any cause or to combine or to contract with each other or with employers, for the purpose of peaceably obtaining from employers satisfactory terms for their labor or satisfactory conditions of employment. . . .[37]

The measure would have enacted into law the "rule of reason" doctrine which the Supreme Court later applied to the trust question, and it would have granted organized labor the exemption from the Sherman Law which it finally received in the Clayton Act.

From the outset, the Hepburn-Warner bill faced difficulties. Many labor leaders, wanting explicit legalization of the secondary boycott (*i.e.* a strike against the suppliers and distributors of a struck corporation), objected to the labor clause as insufficient protection of their interests. Gompers was under extreme pressure from within the American Federation of Labor to demand a more stringent wording respecting the boycott, with specific protection of the secondary boycott, and it was feared that, in order to maintain his position in the labor movement, he would have to withhold labor's approval of the bill. Indeed, the *Times* reported that while the Senate had capitulated to Roosevelt's pressure, the unions would not push for the bill's passage because it did not legalize the secondary boycott.[38] The *Times* account, however, was not entirely accurate. "Labor," Seth Low wired George W. Perkins, "not hostile to our bill but fels [*sic*] like it must ask for more brotherhoods favor bill. . . ."[39] Three days later, Ralph Easley explained labor's position to Attorney E. A. Bancroft at some length:

> They [A.F.L. leadership] have not broken with us in any way, excepting at this time they feel they must ask for more than what our Bill grants them. The leaders understand perfectly well that it would avail them nothing to secure the

Amendment they have asked for two reasons; First, that it is likely to be declared unconstitutional; Second, that it would leave them under the common law which would not very materially improve matters for them. They also are sure that the President would not sign a Bill to which there was any doubt as to its constitutionality, should such a Bill get that far. They further understand that Congress would not likely pass any bill of that character, but there are political reasons why it is important for them to stand on that proposition at this time.

Mr. Gompers will strongly take the grounds that the business of the country is entitled to the relief that it asks in these Bills and he will heartily approve all of the provisions in our Amendment excepting the ones relating to labor, and in that matter will submit some suggested changes. In the end, however, [he] will support our Bill as the best that they can secure at this time.[40]

This was precisely what happened. The exigencies of union politics necessitated a hard-line approach on this subject, but Gompers and the A.F.L. leadership were pragmatic enough to realize that in a presidential election year, the Hepburn Bill was the best they could hope for, and in any event, the measure appeared to concede their basic demand: the right of labor to employ the primary boycott free from the fear of anti-trust prosecution.

There was, however, a far more formidable opposition to the Hepburn Bill. The anti-labor *New York Times,* on March 20, took the National Civic Federation to task for sponsoring a measure which would legitimize the boycott as a tool which labor could freely use in its contests against capital. Continuing its attacks upon the Hepburn Bill, it asserted six days later that the measure would hand President Roosevelt too much power, and give impetus to the "cowboy" President's overweaning ambition.[41] The nation's anti-union employers also took up arms in the effort to kill the Civic Federation's revision of the anti-trust laws. *American Industries,* the official organ of the National Association of Manufacturers, declared that, "A close examination [of the Hepburn bill] inspires the suspicion that under its fair-sounding provisions lurks a crafty attempt to legalize the boycott.... It concedes the chief demand of Mr. Gompers, that labor . . . should be made a privileged class...."[42] The Citizens' Industrial Alliance's *The Square Deal* labeled the Hepburn Bill a conspiracy against the American people, and writing in its pages, James A. Emery condemned the proposal as "The most dangerous measure yet proposed to Congress . . . ," and a grave threat to the validity of the Supreme Court's ruling in the *Loewe* case.[43] Corporation lawyer Morefield Storey wrote Low that he was disappointed in the Civic Federation, saying, "I do not approve either the attempt to relieve labor organizations from the provisions of the Sherman Act."[44] And from Chicago, E. A. Bancroft informed George W. Perkins:

> The truth of the matter is, that the controlling people in this organization are hostile to that measure—are very suspicious of it—and are more influenced by the packers than by anybody else. The real ground of their opposition—though they discuss the laborer phase of it always—is in the publicity and registration features.[45]

"How long it does take some people to learn!" was Perkins's laconic reply.[46] Opposition to the Hepburn Bill was centered in the anti-union employer associations and in such industries as meat packing which preferred not to have the public become aware of the conditions existing in their plants. Their effort to kill the bill was vigorous and unrelenting.

As it turned out, the only support for the Hepburn Bill from within the business community came from the financial interests, chiefly the House of Morgan, and from a few individual capitalists such as Andrew Carnegie who proclaimed that "No objection can be taken to the provision safeguarding rights of labor. It is only fair and fully meets their case. I hope the bill will be promptly passed."[47] Two days later, Easley confided to Samuel Gompers, "Evidently, we have quite a fight on our hands, which will add interest to the occasion. I think we can afford, however, to be lined up with the President as against the Van Cleavites, the Parry- and Post-ites, and their non-union editorial and legal allies."[48]

Almost simultaneously, President Roosevelt sent off a message to Congress asking it to promptly pass the Hepburn Bill, and expressed his enthusiasm over the bill's labor clause.[49] An effort had been made in Congress to substitute judicial for administrative enforcement of the bill's registration and publicity clauses, but the White House stoutly resisted the move, for, as Roosevelt told Low:

> My desire is to strengthen the hand of the executive in deal-

ing with these matters, and not to turn them over to what I regard as the chaos and inefficiency necessarily produced by an effort to use the courts as the prime instrument for administering such a law. Whatever they may say, I think we have what is in substance a very good bill. You have done admirable work for the public, my dear fellow—as usual.[50]

Armed with the administration's full support, the National Civic Federation prepared for its crucial test—the defense of the Hepburn Bill before the House Committee on the Judiciary, chaired by Maine's notorious foe of labor, Congressman Littlefield. "I have no hesitancy in believing," Samuel Gompers wrote Ralph Easley, "that when you say Mr. Van Cleave unguardedly said that 'it'—referring to the bill—would never get out of committee, he had Mr. Littlefield in mind. . . ."[51]

The bill was defended by Seth Low, Samuel Gompers, and Cornell Professor Jeremiah W. Jenks, none of whom had any legal training. As a result, they all proved incapable of answering the legal points raised by the bill's opponents. Samuel Gompers testified that he did not favor the submission of trade agreements to the Commissioner of Corporations for approval, and that he wanted recognition of the secondary boycott and labor's complete and total exemption from the anti-trust laws. "The conceptions of the rights of men," he declared, "will be broader as time goes on."[52] He expressed his faith that one day labor would be accorded all the rights to which it was entitled, but he realized that for the present the Hepburn Bill was the best that labor could get and emphatically stated, "We are in favor of the bill."[53] Professor Jenks remarked that Seth Low had been the chief architect of the Hepburn Bill, and he strongly supported the bill's protection of the primary boycott.[54] Seth Low, the measure's chief spokesman, argued that the Hepburn amendment would enable businessmen to learn whether or not their present conduct was legal, and would, therefore, do much to restore confidence in the business community.[55] On the labor provision, he held that:

> Organized labor is built up upon the recognized right to combine, to strike, and to make trade agreements. A law that raises doubt as to these rights for which labor has successfully contended in other countries, when it was a hanging offense to do so, strikes a blow not only at organized labor, but at the whole structure of modern democratic society.[56]

Under close examination, Low declared that the bill would

legalize the primary boycott, which labor was entitled to have placed beyond question, but that it would not sanction the secondary boycott which he, and the Civic Federation, regarded as an unjustifiable restraint of trade. The committee, however, declared that the proposed law did not make that distinction clear.[57] The measure was vigorously opposed by the National Association of Manufacturers, the Citizens' Industrial Alliance, and the Anti-Boycott Association, and no substantial support developed in favor of the mill. To many observers the Hepburn Bill appeared to be an underhanded attempt by the great corporations to remove the Sherman Law from the statute books.[58] With Congress hostile to the measure, President Roosevelt—not wanting to risk a major political defeat and a possible schism in the Republican party in a presidential election year—allowed the bill to lapse and it died in committee.[59]

The failure of the Hepburn Bill was a severe disappointment to the men of the Civic Federation. The Federation realized, Low declared at the organization's December conference, that with a presidential election approaching, it was not possible to change the substantive law embodied in the Sherman Act; the best it could hope for would have been a clarification of the law's provisions. However, the Hepburn Bill itself seemed to many people to be as imprecise and as vague as the Sherman Law, and the chief difficulty with the proposed amendment, as Ralph Easley told Arthur T. Hadley, was that, "It is a very easy thing to say that we should draft a bill that would permit reasonable combinations and prohibit unreasonable ones as President Roosevelt said in his message but when we undertook to crystallize that sentiment into a statute we found it a difficult proposition."[60]

The simple fact of the matter was that America was too inexperienced with the mechanics of the industrial system to devise an effective means of regulating it. Both government and law, with respect to the economic sphere of American life, were in an extremely primitive state. Nevertheless, the Civic Federation was resolved to continue the search for a method of regulating the country's business, and was reinforced in its determination to promote the interests of labor. "The fact that the Van Cleave-Post-Parry crowd is making such a vigorous fight on labor organizations," Easley wrote railroad and utility executive Melville E. Ingalls, "makes it necessary for us to proceed cautiously, but strongly, in defense of the right of men to organize for the purpose of bettering their condition."[61] That December, it was proposed to form a committee to study the feasibility of drawing up a bill embodying a Charter of the Rights of Labor.[62] The effort to amend the Sherman Law, however, gave way to movements for national incorporation and uniform state legislation.

The battle to modify the Sherman Act had brought the administrative and the Civic Federation into close contact, and over the next few years this relationship would deepen and broaden. As Theodore Roosevelt prepared to close out his tenure as President of the United States, he came to rely heavily on Low and the Federation. "As soon as the election is over," the President asked Low, "I wish you would come on here so that I may discuss with you what I shall say in my message about labor and corporations."[63] Close intellectual contact continued long after Roosevelt left the White House, and a number of the reforms which he was later to urge in his subsequent "New Nationalism" strongly resembled the philosophy and programs of the National Civic Federation. According to Seth Low, the primary achievement of Roosevelt's presidency was the interest it awakened in the economic problems confronting the American people. "But when all the specific things have been catalogued which make for the country's welfare with which you have identified yourself during your presidency," he wrote Roosevelt as the latter left office:

> I am inclined to believe that the intangible results are the most important of all, which you have brought about in touching the conscience of the American people and in elevating their business standards; and, on the other hand, in awakening the mind of the people to a sense of some of the great dangers which confront the country by reason of the great accumulation of the power of wealth in the hands of a few, unless we somehow learn to regulate its use so as to get the benefit of such accumulations without at the same time losing national qualities of initiative and destroying the uniformity of opportunity which has enabled our country in the past to profit more generally than any other by the God-given talents and abilities that are to be found among the poor, even more generally than among those whom the world calls more fortunate.[64]

To preserve economic opportunity in an age of monopoly, Low refined his conception of the role of industry in modern society, and proposed specific remedies to safeguard democratic values and institutions.

While accepting the trust as inevitable, Low was cognizant of the dangers inherent in great concentrations of wealth. The states, in many instances under the control of the corporate interests, competed with one another to pass corporation laws favorable to business but hostile to the welfare of society; and the holding company, which permitted a small group of financiers to control whole industries, made for a dangerous concentration of economic power. Moreover, the trusts often sold below cost in order to drive out competition, and once more dominating the market, they charged all that the traffic would bear; to expand capitalization they issued watered stock and rode roughshod over minority stockholders; and by controlling the source of raw materials and wholesale distribution, they totally dominated the market for their products.[65] All these practices were prejudicial to the interests and well-being of American democratic society.

But to say this did not mean to imply that the trusts should be abolished. The Sherman Anti-Trust Act, which ostensibly sought to prevent monopolization, was quite obviously a failure, and was unsuited to the exigencies of the economic order because:

> It disregards the demonstrated economical advantage of large capitalization in bringing about economy in production, in permitting the payment of high wages, in availing of the highest results of science, however costly, and in making the best possible provision for the prevention of industrial accidents.
>
> The problem before the country, therefore, would appear to be to secure the benefits of industrial combination, as far as this can be done, without subjecting ourselves to the evils, most of them wholly unnecessary, which have marked the business era just coming to a close.[66]

In short, the American economy was in a state of anarchy as a direct result of the federal system of government.[67] The United States, Seth Low pointed out, possessed the oldest federal system of government in the world, but it was framed at a time when the industrial revolution was just beginning to develop. The problem facing the Founding Fathers was how to form a national government able effectively to meet the political needs of American society without giving it so much power that it would become a tyrant. In the federal form, which divided power between the states and the nation, the framers found a means of providing capable, but limited, government. The system worked because eighteenth-century American society was decentralized. Economic production was on the local level, carried on by small producers, and government itself was largely a local concern, conducted by men of station who usually knew many of their constituents personally. The legitimate functions of government in a society such as this were few, and except for the necessity of paying taxes, seldom touched the life of the average man. If the states had few governmental responsibilities, the national government had still fewer, and since the states were considered to be the best guardians of the people's liberties, the federal government had best be kept feeble.

The industrial revolution, however, changed all this. The corporate form of business permitted greater efficiency, economy, and production than the older individually-owned or partnership enterprise. As long as the corporation was fairly small, so long as the bulk of its business was conducted within the boundaries of a given state, there was little reason for the national government to interfere in the economy. However, with the creation of national transportation networks, with the rise of the factory system, and the development of mass production techniques, industrial corporations soon spread across state lines, becoming regional and even national institutions. The state governments, assuming they had the will to do so, could regulate the corporate form, but they could not in any way control the business done by the corporations which they had chartered once this business became interstate in nature. On the other hand, the national government could control interstate commerce, but it had absolutely no means of regulating the corporate form. While it had authority to govern the movement of goods, it could not control stock issuances, holding companies, or any other device bearing on the internal structure of the corporation. There was no single governmental authority, Low pointed out, which could regulate both the corporation and the business which that corporation conducted. "This situation," he declared, "results in what may fairly be called industrial anarchy."[68]

With the twentieth century, the United States had developed a national economy. A corporation like United States Steel obtained its raw materials from many regions of the country, and operated factories in numerous states, selling its finished products from one end of the land to the other. For all practical purposes, state boundaries no longer had any viable function, at least as far as economic activity was concerned. A highly-centralized economic structure was erasing state lines, destroying older regionalisms, and transforming America from a sectional empire into a unified nation whose people were increasingly sharing the same ideals and struggling to achieve a common mode of life—middle class and consumer-oriented. While the midwestern farmer purchased his clothes from a Montgomery-Ward or Sears-Roebuck catalog, the American system of government was oriented to an eighteenth century social order, and was incapable of governing the newly-risen national economy. In order to effectively regulate a centralized economy serving the entire nation, the federal government—at least as far as the economic sphere was concerned—must take on new powers, and itself become a highly-centralized organ. The regulatory power of the states, with regard to economic institutions, must be transferred to the national government, and, hence, national authority must be increased at the expense of state's rights, and the nation's political system must be altered to meet new economic conditions. Only the federal government could manage an economic system which had become national in scope, and it could not much longer refuse its obvious responsibilities.

Almost all corporations, Low argued, were engaged in interstate commerce; consequently, such corporations—if their capitalization exceeded one million dollars—should be required to incorporate under federal law, and if their capitalization was less than one million dollars, they should be obligated to operate under federal license. Federal incorporation should prohibit corporations from owning stock in other corporations, thus outlawing the holding company, and should require full publicity regarding stock issuances, production, sales, and general conduct. No attempt should be made to control the size of corporations functioning under federal charter, but provisions should be made to protect both investors and consumers from exploitation. Federal licenses should require the same general type of information, but since the corporations involved were small, enforcement need not be so rigid. Any corporation found in violation of the terms of its charter or license would have its charter or license revoked or suspended, and would be forbidden to engage in interstate commerce. Such charters and licenses would provide for supervision of the corporation's general conduct by an appropriate government administrative agency with revocation of charter being the penalty for failure to heed administrative decrees. The system would have provided effective governmental regulation of the economy, and would have solved the trust problem by placing them under democratic control instead of trying to annihilate them.

It was one thing to advocate national incorporation; it was another to achieve it. Having failed to amend the Sherman Act in 1908, the Civic Federation spent the next two years studying alternatives to the existing anti-trust laws, and settled upon national incorporation as the best solution to the problem of trust control. After first trying to educate the business community and the general public to an acceptance of the idea, it sought legislative enactment of its program. Unfortunately, many businessmen were wary of the idea, and only the national administration was completely won over to the concept. "I believe," William Howard Taft wrote Seth Low, "you are leading a movement that will ultimately gain strength because of its usefulness. . . ."[69] And Attorney General George W. Wickersham observed, "It seems to me you put the case very succinctly and very clearly. I see no escape myself from the adoption of [national incorporation], and I believe that the country will come to it befor a great while."[70]

Many businessmen, though, argued that it would be suicidal for a corporation to put itself under the control of Congress on the grounds that—subject to a fickle popular passion—it might, after revelation of a particularly nasty corporate abuse, be led to pass laws prejudicial to the interests of all business, honest as well as dishonest. If, on the other hand, corporate control was left to the states, it was most unlikely that all forty-six of them would be carried away by the popular frenzy, and even if some were, businesses could always incorporate in those states which had kept their legislative heads. Therefore, to protect the interests of business from the passions of the people, incorporation had best be left to the states.[71]

Then, too, there was another factor to be considered. "I have read your very interesting article on National Incorporation," businessman R. D. Silliman wrote, "and cannot see how anyone can deny the soundness of your reasoning. I presume the public is a little slow in responding simply because people hate to yield up any portion of their local control in favor of a more general authority no matter how much more effective it may be. But it is coming as surely as it is coming slowly."[72] State's rights sentiment was still quite strong; many people genuinely feared the expansion of the powers of the national government as a possible threat to the liberty of the individual, and seeking to preserve what they considered to be a basically sound political system, opposed all efforts at national incorporation. According to John W. H. Crim, United States Attorney of the Southern District of New York, there was much popular sentiment in favor of federal incorporation:

> During the past few days it has been my privilege to come in contact with a number of prominent Western business men and their attitude upon the various phases of "New Nationalism" demonstrates beyond doubt the fact that a great many of our best thinkers look with favor upon what may be called an enlarged control over corporations by the Federal Government.[73]

Yet when the time came to push legislation looking toward national incorporation, this business support was not forthcoming.

Early in 1911, legislation was introduced into Congress calling for federal incorporation of businesses doing interstate commerce. Introduced at the behest of the business interests represented in the National Civic Federation, the proposal never got beyond the planning stage. As President Taft pointed out:

> I expect to have prepared a Federal incorporation bill and have it introduced in Congress before its adjournment. I do not expect, however, that it will pass Congress; indeed, it will be impossible to secure its consideration. But I shall have something on record to show where we stand. As a matter of fact, the Democrats would never pass a Federal incorporation bill, and all we can do is to educate the public on the subject. A Federal incorporation bill is not a matter of one Congress, but of several.[74]

As predicted, nothing came of the bill and all subsequent efforts to secure its passage failed. Even though a poll of the business community taken by the Civic Federation revealed that eighty-four percent of the sixteen thousand persons responding to its questionnaire favored federal regulation of interstate commerce, agreement could not be reached as to the form such regulation should assume.[75] By late 1913, the Federation admitted defeat. "However desirable it may be," Low conceded, "to substitute National Incorporation for State Incorporation, the public opinion of the country has not yet grown to a point where it would be willing to do so."[76] His efforts on behalf of federal incorporation of interstate commerce was indicative of the gropings of many Progressives to find some means by which the nation's business could be subjected to the rule of a demo-cratic society.

Simultaneous with the movement for national incorporation was the effort to secure uniform state legislation. In the absence of federal laws governing economic activity, the only means of realizing some uniformity in the laws relating to the business world was to make state laws as nearly uniform as possible. The Civic Federation held a conference on the subject in Washing-ton, D.C., in 1910, and as an outgrowth of that conference, state and regional branches of the Federation lobbied for the passage of model, and therefore uniform, laws respecting child labor re-striction, workman's compensation, factory safety, stock issuances, and a variety of other industrial subjects. The movement had uneven results. In the more progressive states, the Federation was successful in having enacted its legislation concerning workman's compensation, factory safety, and other industrial matters, but nothing approaching uniformity was ever achieved. In any event, it was an inefficient and ineffective way to regulate a national economy. The Federation's efforts in these areas often dupli-cated those of the American Association for Labor Legislation. But it should be clearly understood that the two organizations worked independently of each other. In fact, Low refused to join the A.A.L.L. on the grounds that membership in that organiza-tion would only duplicate the work he was already performing in the N.C.F.

The efforts of the National Civic Federation to regulate the economy, in the years from 1908–1911, were a failure. The men of the Federation accepted the trust as a fact of modern economic life, and realized that if American democratic institutions were to be preserved, the trusts would have to be regulated. The only instrument capable of exerting this control was the national government. The N.C.F. wanted the trusts controlled not to permit their owners to more effectively and securely exploit the American people, but to protect individual liberty against con-centrated economic power, the operation of which was yet to be clearly understood. And since the national government was democratically elected and responsible to the whole people, the power it exercised was not to be feared, and it was best suited to guard individual liberty in an era of big business. As William Dudley Foulke told the Federation's 1911 annual meeting:

> The transformation of our industrial system from the regime of competition to the regime of cooperation and monopoly is the most radical change which has occurred in the constitution of human society since the proclamation of equal political rights for all mankind. And the question now is whether these political rights against the privileges of an individual or a class shall now yield to an industrial oligarchy or find a remedy by which the industrial rights of the people shall be protected against the favored few, and by which equal industrial opportunity . . . shall be given to every individual. The longer the control of the Trusts is delayed the more difficult and dangerous it becomes.
>
> Free institutions are in greater ultimate danger from the corrupt and unscrupulous use of accumulated wealth than from domestic dissensions or the sword of the stranger.[77]

CHAPTER XIII

The National Civic Federation
between Scylla and Charybdis

It is now proven beyond the last shadow of a doubt that it is the particular and especial function of the National Civic Federation to knife labor, to strangle it and to prevent it from getting any good thing.

In the Civic Federation are allied the principal chiefs in the army of big business, and the Civic Federation is used by them as a disarming mask behind which they may plot and knife, while the guileless hosts of labor walk unsuspectingly to the slaughter.

NEW YORK CALL[1]

My opposition to it [the National Civic Federation] has been relentless, however, and will be relentless, because of its close alignment with the dominating influences of labor unionism. . . . The American Federation of Labor is engaged in an open warfare against Jesus Christ and his cause.

JOHN KIRBY, JR.[2]

The National Civic Federation had failed in its efforts to exempt organized labor from the anti-trust provisions of the Sherman Act, and in the years from 1908–1911, its energies were increasingly directed toward the attempt to effectively regulate the nation's great industries, but labor was never forgotten. In addition to continuing its activities on behalf of labor, the Civic Federation, after 1908, branched out to a consideration of uniform state legislation, industrial welfare work, immigration reform, municipal ownership of public utilities, and primary election law reform, among other topics. If anything, the Civic Federation over-extended itself, and sought to undertake many more activities than it could adequately finance. It was forced to abandon many of its projects for lack of funds. However, it was in this period that the Federation and organized labor entered into their most productive partnership, and consequently, it became the subject of severe verbal onslaughts by the socialists within labor's ranks and by the reactionaries amongst the employers. Also, in this era, Seth Low came to a clearer conception of the role of labor in the modern industrial system, a conception which alienated many businessmen who still adhered to the older economic theories.

For the presidential campaign of 1908, organized labor, seeking relief from the implications of the Danbury Hatter's Decision, formally announced its endorsement of the Democratic nominee, William Jennings Bryan, who was undertaking the last of his quixotic crusades in quest of the White House. The business-oriented members of the Civic Federation, on the other hand—including Seth Low—remained firm in their loyalty to the Grand Old Party. However, both the labor and business members of the Federation had a vital stake in safeguarding the legal standing of the trade agreement, "The best method yet devised, in this age of universal organization, for promoting alike industrial peace, industrial well-being, and industrial progress."[3] Many lawyers were convinced that the Supreme Court's decision in *Loewe v. Lawlor* had, besides casting doubt as to labor's right to strike, also placed the trade agreement under the ban of the Sherman Law's prohibition against conspiracies in restraint of trade. This belief persisted for many years, during which the Civic Federation unsuccessfully sought to establish the legal validity of the trade agreement, for as Ralph Easley wrote W. G. Lee of the Railroad Brotherhoods, "Lawyers tell me that there is not a national trade agreement in the United States which is not in violation of the Sherman Anti-Trust Act."[4]

The instrument chiefly employed to deny labor its right to strike was the writ of injunction, an odious device whereby an employer could go into court and charge that the threatened or actual strike at his plant menaced his business with irreparable damage, which could not be compensated by means of ordinary judicial recourse. On the basis of this *ex parte* testimony, the court would issue an injunction forbidding the strike, and its violation would place the union's leaders in contempt of court. The weapon was potent and kept labor weak. In an important article in the October 1908 issue of *The Century Magazine*, Seth Low compared the injunction planks of the Democratic and Republican platforms, and stated his position in regard to the rights of labor. The American Federation of Labor had endorsed the Democratic party, feeling that its platform was far more favorable to the interests of labor than the Republican. But, the Democratic injunction plank, which stated that "Injunctions should not be issued in any cases in which injunctions would not issue if no industrial dispute were involved," struck Low as an absurdity.[5] Injunctions were not, he pointed out, issued in the first place to break labor strikes, but rather on the allegation that irreparable harm (the cause of that harm being irrelevant) would ensue if the injunction were not issued. Hence, the Democratic plank was devoid of any practical meaning and would in no ways alter the then current practice of dispensing injunctions. Moreover, Low did not consider the Democratic party, under the leadership of the "evangelist" from Nebraska, as a fit instrument to safeguard the rights of labor, since the party was basically hostile to modern industrialism and unwilling or unable to deal with its problems in realistic terms.

The Republican platform, on the other hand, while it did not pretend to call for an abolition of the injunction in labor disputes, did ask that legislation be passed strictly governing the conditions under which they could legitimately be requested. Low assumed that the Republicans would define the terms under which injunctions could be issued, and that they would be barred, at least for the primary boycott, except in cases of imminent danger to property. He also called for amendments to the Sherman Act which would guarantee labor's right to strike and to make trade agreements, for, as Low emphatically declared:

> It is intolerable that there should be any doubt cast upon the right of labor to strike; for that is a necessary incident of freedom of contract. A man cannot be made to work unless he is a slave or under some sort of temporary control. It is equally intolerable that employer and workmen should not be at liberty to enter into trade agreements, provided such trade agreements, on their merits, do not contravene any public interest. As the Sherman Anti-Trust Law now stands, in view of this recent decision of the Supreme Court in the Danbury Hat Case, I have maintained and firmly believe that the right of labor to organize, to make trade agreements and to strike should be explicitly recognized by the laws of the United States. . . .[6]

Needless to say, no substantive change was made in the injunction procedure until the Norris-LaGuardia Act. But the working alliance between the Democratic labor leaders and Republican businessmen of the National Civic Federation survived the 1908 election, and late in that year, John Mitchell became chairman of the Federation's Trade Agreement Department. To enable him to accept the post, the Federation gave Mitchell a salary of $8,000 (later raised to $10,000) per year. Ralph Easley, the N.C.F.'s executive secretary, had been the only salaried member of the Civic Federation, all other officers and department heads giving their services without compensation. But as Mitchell had no outside income, he would have to draw a salary if he were to become a full-time officer of the Federation. A special fund was established to pay Mitchell's salary, financed by contributions from Andrew Carnegie, George W. Perkins, Isaac N. Seligman and some other prominent business figures. Formally installed in December 1908, Mitchell entered upon his new duties with enthusiasm.

Unlike the socialists, the leaders of the American Federation of Labor did not feel that the interests of capital and labor must forever be antagonistic and border on open warfare, or that labor could advance only by tearing down the capitalist system. John Mitchell, Samuel Gompers, and the other leaders of the A.F.L. were believers in the efficacy of the American democratic system, and rather than replace it with a socialist order of society, they preferred to advance by working within the capitalist social structure. "After all," John Mitchell exclaimed at the Civic Federation's 1908 gathering, "this is a pretty good country in which to live. . . . I have an abiding faith in the humanity and in the business sagacity of the American workman and the American employer, and I am confident that a basis of harmonious cooperation will be established between them."[7] The basis for that harmony was the trade agreement, for the essential problem as labor's leaders saw it, was that the worker was not getting his fair share of the production of modern industry. Instead of trying to reform society, the organized labor movement should concentrate on winning a larger share of the proceeds of industry for the working man. This process of winning more for labor was not an easy one; it could not be realized by the incantations of slogans, but rather by steady, organized pressure applied year after year. As Mitchell told his fellow miners, "For ten years I was president [of the United Mine Workers] but I did not revolutionize the industrial world. I did not solve the labor problem. It will never be solved. We only hope to gain little by little more and more of our proper share of what we produce."[8] In the Civic Federation, Mitchell hoped to make a positive contribution to labor's cause.

The trade agreement was a collective bargain by which the union set the terms for its labor, and by which it hoped to secure an ever larger share of the rewards of industrial production. But, more importantly, it was an acknowledgment by capital that the conditions of labor were not all that they should be. As Louis B. Schram of the National Brewer's Association pointed out, "The law of supply and demand does not furnish a satisfactory guide. Might does not make right. No answer has yet been found to the question: In what ratio shall the profits of a plant be divided between capital invested and labor employed?"[9]

The Civic Federation was groping for a solution to the problem of the distribution of economic wealth. It never solved the problem, but it was hopeful that one day it would be solved. As Andrew Carnegie declared, "There will be capitalists and laborers [in America's future] but every laborer will have a minimum wage, and he will be a stockholder and a participator in the profits."[10] The trade agreement would help bring this utopia into being. "I believe in it," Samuel Gompers testified, "I think it is wise; it is economic; it has its foundation in a sound philosophy, and it is a wise policy in governing the relations of workmen and employers. . . ."[11]

It is not known how many trade agreements were negotiated as a direct result of the Federation's work, but it is probable that its efforts to conciliate labor disputes and effect trade agreements lessened in importance over the years. Many states had established conciliation departments within their labor bureaus, and as more employers came to recognize the unions and negotiated with them on their own initiative, the need for the Federation's mediation services decreased appreciably. This situation was reflected in the organization of the Civic Federation, which prior to 1905 was exclusively designed to mediate labor disputes. After 1908, however, it concentrated on persuading employers to institute welfare programs in their factories—profit-sharing, recreation centers, restrooms, dining facilities, and paid annual vacations were but a few of the innovations championed by the Federation. Profit-sharing, though, was vigorously opposed by the Civic Federation whenever it was used as a device to smash unionization. As Seth Low told a fellow reformer, profit-sharing was desirable as an incentive for efficient and productive labor, but it should be instituted only after the right of labor to organize had been recognized and solely as an adjunct to a trade agreement.[12] The Federation also acted as a lobby, pushing for state legislation bearing on workman's compensation, factory safety, and women and child labor restrictions. The Civic Federation also attempted to persuade United States Steel to alter its policy of total hostility toward organized labor.

Deploring U. S. Steel's refusal to recognize organized labor, Seth Low wrote Judge Elbert H. Gary in April 1911, asking him to improve labor conditions in the industry. Declaring that U. S. Steel represented to the people of America the personification of capitalism, he called upon the corporation—in its own self-interest, if for no other reason—to abolish its twelve-hour labor shift in favor of the eight-hour shift, to reduce the number of work days per week in its plants, and to improve its accident-prevention program. He closed by expressing the hope that, "some day it [U. S. Steel] will frankly recognize that the men have the same right to combine and to make collective bargains as the stockholders have. . . ."[13] "With most of the sentiments expressed," Gary replied, "I heartily concur. I hope we can work out conditions for employees which will increase their benefits and decrease their burdens." But as for the unions, Gary declared, "I formerly entertained an opinion something like your own, but have been forced to modify it by the action of the men themselves."[14] U. S. Steel did not reform, and it remained an embarrassment to all who believed in the capitalist system but who sought to give labor its due.

The close alliance between the American Federation of Labor and the National Civic Federation proved profoundly disturbing to the socialists, and they undertook a vigorous campaign to drive organized labor out of the Civic Federation. Indeed, the labor leaders who entered the Federation did so not without second thoughts and a nagging conscience. "I entered the organization," Samuel Gompers recounted in his autobiography, "with many reservations and with a distinct attitude of alertness if not suspicion."[15] From the beginning, there was opposition to Gompers' joining the Civic Federation, and he never quite suppressed the feeling that he was entering Satan's snare. Never fully at home at Federation dinners, he recalled that he always left his food untouched, unable to bring himself around to eating with the "buccaneers of industry." He would not break his self-imposed fast until he was no longer in the company of the business leaders. But no matter how distasteful membership in the Civic Federation might have been to Gompers' nature, he entered the organization at an early stage in its career, hopeful that it would prove beneficial to labor's cause. "I would," he declared, "appeal to the devil and his mother-in-law to help labor if labor could be aided in that way."[16]

The leaders of the American Federation of Labor entered the Civic Federation in the hope of avoiding and/or reducing the number and severity of strikes. To the socialists, a strike was a splendid sign of labor's class consciousness and solidarity—an indication of labor's militancy—holding the promise that the iniquitous capitalist system would soon be overthrown. It was also a splendid opportunity for the socialist ideologues to make themselves heard; but, for labor, a strike was something very different. In January 1908, the *American Federationist* pointed out that from 1881–1900, strikes had cost labor $258 million in lost wages and had cost employers $123 million in lost production. Lockouts cost the workers an additional $49 million and employers $19 million.[17] Obviously, strikes hurt labor far more severely than it did capital. A strike meant that a worker's family might have to skip meals, sleep in unheated flats, and be deprived of many of the necessities of life. If the strike was won, it resulted in higher wages, but lost wages—like lost business—were never made up. If, as was far more likely in those days of weak unions and hungry immigrant laborers, the strike failed, it promised even greater hardship and misery for the working men, and might well result in the collapse of the union itself. A strike was therefore not to be called lightly, but should be postponed until all other methods of improving labor's lot had been tried and been found wanting. It was an act of desperation against grievous and unbearable wrongs. The A.F.L.'s attitude toward strikes was best summed up by Daniel J. Keefe of the Longshoreman's: "Personally, I am opposed to strikes, under any circumstances, except as a last resort. If, however, there is no alternative and men *must* strike, then I say, strike with all your might."[18]

Samuel Gompers and John Mitchell never deceived themselves into the belief that all the businessmen represented in the Civic Federation were labor's friends. They realized as well as the socialists that many business members of the Federation were simply seeking industrial peace by granting cheap reforms, while refusing to satisfy labor's substantive demands. Consequently, many labor men viewed membership in the Civic Federation as a sellout of labor's cause. In May 1902, the Western Labor Union, a socialist-dominated rival to the A.F.L., condemned the National Civic Federation as a tool of Mark Hanna, designed to advance his presidential ambitions and to further the fortunes of the business-controlled Republican party. Under the leadership of Eugene Victor Debs, the Western Labor Union anathematized the leaders of the American Federation of Labor as traitors to their class who had sold out to Mark Hanna's Civic Federation.[19] In 1905, the ultra-radical Syndicalist Industrial Workers of the World was organized. It rejected all efforts to advance labor by working within the confines of the capitalist economic system, and openly called for the violent overthrow of capitalism. As the socialists gained strength within the ranks of organized labor, Gompers and the rest of the A.F.L. leadership were often called upon to defend their relationship with the N.C.F. In February 1905, Gompers, writing in the *American Federationist,* declared that the Civic Federation did not require that labor leaders surrender their convictions or independence, and that the Federation's decisions were not binding upon anyone. Furthermore, the organization took no stand on any issue unless it had the approval of its labor members. "Concede," he went on, "that there are enemies of labor who attend the meetings . . . of the Civic Federation; how," he asked the socialists, "is it possible for trade unionists to contravene their position unless by meeting them face to face."[20]

The American Federation of Labor had an abiding faith in the justice of its cause, and believed that if only it could present its case to employers on a basis of equality and honesty, its demands would prove irresistible. As the *Shoe Workers' Journal* put it, "Where the cause of labor is given every opportunity to be heard it never suffers, and it has been ably defended and advanced by its representatives in the National Civic Federation and at its meetings."[21] "There are good men of all classes," Timothy Healy told the International Brotherhood of Stationary Firemen, "there are good men and women in high society as well as there are in the most lowly; and I want to say, as a trades unionist, that any man or any woman who is willing to sit down with me and discuss the questions that affect my organization is looked upon by me as a friend to labor and not an enemy."[22] Businessmen, the A.F.L. leaders believed, had souls and were amenable to righteousness. If they but knew of labor's problems, they would take steps to alleviate them. "The class-conscious comrades," Gompers recalled, "in horror declaimed that we were being blinded and chloroformed." But, as Gompers tells it, "I never failed to point out the sophistry of some 'nice' proposal and was insistant in presenting labor rights and in making conspicuous injustice for which even well-intentioned employers were responsible. Often, after I finished such a speech, one of the labor men would inquire with a grin: 'Chloroformed again, Sam?' "[23]

The socialist tirade against the Civic Federation pleased Ralph Easley. "If," he wrote industrialist J. Borden Harriman, "by bringing Capital and Labor together and making it possible for us to get on, I have interfered with the Socialists' promotion of class hatred I am proud."[24] Above all else, Easley dreaded socialism. It was a foreign doctrine, he argued, which was totally unsuited to the needs of the nation, and which threatened to destroy free American institutions. It must be opposed at all costs, and one suspects that much of Easley's zeal in defense of labor was simply an effort to help destroy the socialist movement. "Could there be any better tribute paid to the efficiency of our conciliation work," he wrote Seth Low, "then the charge that we are destroying the militancy of the unions by persuading them that capital and labor have interests in common. . . ."[25] With World War I, Easley would become rabid in his hatred of socialism. Low, while opposing socialism on philosophical grounds, never feared it, and never advocated a holy crusade against it. "It is not just," he told Easley, "in my opinion, to say that the Socialists, as a body, do not work for reasonable reforms. . . . They are working for objects which are entirely legitimate, whether one can agree to every point they make or not. The truth is that the Socialist Party is not all made up of extremists any more than the Republican or the Democratic party. . . ."[26]

However, besides having a more reasonable attitude toward the socialists than did Easley, Low also acted as a brake on the Federation's secretary, keeping his often-repeated desire for a nationwide campaign against socialism under a tight rein. For example, in 1912, frightened by Debs' growing popularity and the socialists' increasing strength, Easley once more requested that the National Civic Federation launch a vigorous educational campaign to alert America to the dangers of socialism. Preparing a long and detailed indictment of socialism, he sought to have it circulated by the Federation as the opening round in its fight for "Americanism." Low, however, decisively scuttled the plan, telling Easley:

> I feel sure that I am right in believing that the Federation should not be involved directly in a controversy with the Socialists. It is true that they attack us, and we do not hesitate to criticize them; but that is more or less incidental. If we enter upon a campaign of open antagonism, it will, in my judgment, interfere very greatly with what I conceive to be the proper work of the Federation, and it would be apt to be, in the end, just as fatal as if we were to enter into politics. These are the reasons, in brief, why I want to keep the Federation clear of the whole movement.[27]

Moreover, Low took exception to the factual basis of Easley's anti-socialist polemic. Asserting that the socialists believed that society was retrogressing, Easley attacked them for failing to see that progress was being made in improving America's industrial system. Low pointed out to Easley that the socialists did not deny that improvements were being made, but argued that the capitalist system was so radically wrong that isolated reforms were useless, and that the logical procedure was to reform the entire system from the foundations up. He also condemned Easley's castigation of the Christian socialist movement as treasonous, declaring that while they might be wrong, the men who advocated Christian socialism were as fine a group of citizens as any other class of Americans. In conclusion, he politely suggested that Easley learn more about the subject he was excoriating. While Low was battling to check Easley's irrational hatred of socialism, the socialists delivered the Civic Federation a blow which nearly succeeded in driving organized labor out of its ranks.

At the January 1911 convention of the United Mine Workers' Union, socialists and anti-Mitchell officers of the national union joined forces to amend the U.M.W.'s constitution, effective April 1, 1911, to read, "persons engaged in the sale of intoxicating liquors and members of the Civic Federation shall not be eligible to membership."[28] The only U.M.W. member who was active in the Federation was John Mitchell, and the constitutional amendment was designed to force him to choose between the two organizations. Quite obviously, if he resigned from the United Mine Workers his usefulness to the National Civic Federation would be ended, but if he quit the Civic Federation he might yet bring the U.M.W. back to reason. On February 15, 1911, Mitchell wrote Low asking to be released from his contract with the Federation. "It is needless to say," he declared, "that I regret the action of the miners' convention, not so much because it requires me to choose between the two organizations, as because of the unjust and gratuitous attack upon the National Civic Federation, which . . . has stood consistently as an advocate of righteous industrial peace."[29]

The Civic Federation granted Mitchell's request with Seth Low asserting, "I feel personally under special obligations to you for enabling me to understand better than ever before the workingmen's point of view. . . ."[30] Emboldened by their success against the N.C.F. thus far, the socialists prepared to force through a similar constitutional amendment at the next convention of the American Federation of Labor.

The A.F.L.'s leadership made ready for the impending battle. Determined to stop and to counter the socialist offensive, they undertook a vigorous defense of the Civic Federation. "When a man like President Seth Low of the National Civic Federation," Gompers exclaimed in an *American Federationist* editorial:

> who for a quarter of a century has systematically given his time to that work, comes forward and lends his influence, his honored name, his experience, his judgment, his character, to this purpose, the act to our mind should command the respectful attention of the entire American public, and when the history of the last decade shows that the National Civic Federation has, time and again, by bringing together the representatives of the employing class and of the employed class, prevented losses amounting to millions that can not be calculated—and when any such conference has been held due to the efforts of the Civic Federation the results have ever been to the advantage of labor—it seems to us that this fact should further arrest the attention of the public and insure commendation of the movement.[31]

Gompers challenged the socialists to cite one concrete example of where the National Civic Federation had injured or betrayed labor, and maintained that it was the socialists who were betraying labor by breeding prejudice and hatred. Repeatedly, he scorned the socialists, ridiculing their programs and castigating them as hopeless visionaries. "Economically," he thundered, "you are unsound; socially, you are wrong; industrially, you are an impossibility."[32] In the Civic Federation, he told his constituents, both capital and labor, "are acting according to the dictates of common sense and a common social obligation instead of indulging in blind prejudice, class rancor, and individual antipathies, and yet always having in mind the rights and interest of labor."[33]

The member unions of the A.F.L. also came to the Civic Federation's defense. Daniel J. Tobin lumped the socialists with the Van Cleave-Post-Parry-Kirby crowd of the N.A.M. as enemies of labor, holding that the Civic Federation was under attack because, "it is trying to do some good." "The Socialists," he declared, "may be right in some things, but, in our opinion, they are absolutely wrong in this case."[34] And in April 1911, John Mitchell defended his actions and the Civic Federation in the pages of the *United Mine Workers' Journal,* proclaiming that, "the formation of the National Civic Federation and its declarations in favor of the trade agreement, was of great assistance to the labor movement in carrying forward its work and in promoting its policies."[35]

In June, Ralph Easley became embroiled in a debate with Morris Hillquit over the respective aims of the socialists and the National Civic Federation. Hillquit offered a classic socialist indictment of Progressive reform. The conflict between capital and labor, he held, was inherent in the capitalist system of production. Capital wanted maximum profits and to obtain that it oppressed labor, seeking to drive wages down to the subsistence level. Labor, however, constantly struggled to raise its wage scales, and thus the conflict between the two great forces spawned by industrial society "is a fight to the finish. . . ." Labor and capital had no interests in common. The ultimate goals of one were antagonistic to those of the other, and efforts to bring about a community of interests between the two were absurd. No good could come to labor through attempts to work within the capitalist economic system; the reforms championed by the Civic Federation were shallow and did nothing to satisfy the substantive needs of labor. The laboring masses must be awakened to the truth that capitalism had to be overthrown for, "The final victory of capital would mean universal enslavement and national decadence, [while] the triumph of labor would mean social harmony and progress."[36] Labor's militancy must be increased, and the worker must seize control of his government and shape his own destiny in a society forever freed from the oppression and injustice of the capitalist system. On the other hand:

> The National Civic Federation . . . regards the struggles between the workers and their employers as purely accidental, as results of deplorable misunderstandings. Its social philosophy is based upon an assumed harmony of interests between the exploiting capitalists and the exploited workers, and its policy is to bring the two classes together, to patch up their differences, to gloss over their struggles.
>
> The game played by the Civic Federation is the shrewdest yet devised by the employers of any country. It takes nothing from capital, it gives nothing to labor, and does it all with such an appearance of boundless generosity, that some of the more guileless diplomats in the labor movements are actually overwhelmed by it.[37]

The Federation's reforms were trivial, Hillquit thundered. Designed to avert the threatened revolt of the workers, it threw labor the crumbs of its economic production, hoping that it would acquiesce in the present iniquitous system. It robbed labor of its independence, stripped it of its virility, destroyed its self-respect, corrupted its leaders, and emasculated its program of social reform. "To the organized labor movement the policy of the Civic Federation is the most subtle and insidious poison," and therefore, the Federation must be the socialists' prime target. It impeded the revolution.

Easley's reply fell far short of being inspired. He sought to prove that the Civic Federation was a friend of organized labor by citing the National Association of Manufacturers' constant condemnation of his organization. Recounting the many labor reforms championed by the Federation, and the friendship shown the N.C.F. by the leaders of the American Federation of Labor, he asked Hillquit if he thought that men like Gompers, Mitchell, Keefe, and Daniel Tobin were fools who could be hoodwinked by employers. Easley argued that the Civic Federation sought to ease labor's path into the middle class, and to facilitate its acquisition of more of the material benefits of modern American society. Expressing his faith in American institutions, he proclaimed his conviction that labor not only could but was steadily advancing by working within the confines of the capitalist economic system. However, he did not address himself to Hillquit's argument that labor and capital, because of the very nature of the existing economic order, must forever be in a state of hostility.

The Civic Federation's attitude toward the socialist contention that labor and capital must ever be at war was best summed up by Seth Low at the Federation's March 1912 convention:

Least of all does it [N.C.F.] imply that either the employers or the representatives of organized labor look upon the interests of capital and labor as identical. It does, however, imply that those who belong to The National Civic Federation believe that the interest of capital and labor are, for the most part, if not always, reconcilable. The interest of the two are not identical, because capital naturally strives to obtain the largest return in labor for the least pay, while labor just as naturally strives to obtain the greatest possible pay for a given amount of labor. . . . It is entirely consistent with the recognition of this difference of interest, however, that labor should strive continually to improve its working conditions; to shorten its hours of labor; to increase its pay; to better the sanitary conditions under which it is called upon to work; and generally to increase the share which labor obtains from the operation of the industries of the nation.[39]

While labor should contend for its own advancement, it need not abandon the amenities of civilized society. Granting that labor and capital had opposing interests, those interests could be advanced through the instruments of peace far better than through the instruments of war. This was what the National Civic Federation was all about. "It is in the power of the democratic spirit," Seth Low declared, "that the great economic questions of our time and country are to be met and settled; for that spirit, if I interpret it aright, recognizes freely the essential brotherhood of men, and it also believes with all its heart that nothing is ever settled until it is settled right, and that in every just settlement the interests of the weak as well as of the strong . . . must be considered."[40]

The thirty-first annual convention of the American Federation of Labor met in Atlanta in November 1911. Duncan McDonald, socialist delegate of the United Mine Workers, introduced a resolution which would have required all members of the A.F.L., in view of the "conflict between the two economic forces in society," to sever all connections with the National Civic Federation.[41] The resolution sparked a heated debate which lasted for several days. The socialists employed the standard arguments against cooperation with the Civic Federation, and the A.F.L. leadership had to throw its full weight into the debate to stem the socialist tide. Vice-president Hayes reminded the delegates that "the mission and the object of organized labor is to make for brotherhood, more love for one another, more charity towards all people. To talk of more democracy and more liberal conditions of employment, and at the same time foment feeling between classes seems to me like a contradiction."[42] Finally, the resolutions committee reported to the convention that, "Your committee has had no evidence presented to it which would indicate that the influence of the National Civic Federation has ever been unfriendly to organized labor. . . ."[43] McDonald's resolution was voted down by 11,851 proxies to 4,924. The socialist offensive had been blunted, the A.F.L. had preserved its ties with the National Civic Federation, and the alliance was not again to be threatened.

The most useful service rendered labor by the National Civic Federation was in shielding and defending the unions from the sustained and vicious attacks of the anti-union employer associations and their allies. Robert Underwood Johnson of *The Century Magazine* was among those who regarded "Gompers as one of the most dangerous elements in this country," because of his rebellion against the Courts in the Buck's Stove and Range contempt citation.

Replying to Johnson's characterization as a "caricature," Seth Low declared that "This country owes more to Mr. Gompers than to any other dozen men," and defended his stand in the contempt case as a defense of free speech against an arbitrary and illegal usurpation of judicial authority. Gompers, Low told Johnson, is "contending for the right that concerns us all, that a citizen is not bound to obey an illegal order of the Court."[44] To the editor of another periodical, Low declared that while labor was certainly guilty of abuses, it was not labor alone which was at fault. "It seems to me worthwhile to point out, at this juncture [Re: the McNamaras' bombing of the *Los Angeles Times* building], that organized labor may sometimes be found sinned against, as well as sinning."[45] All, however, was not sweetness and light, for Seth Low, along with many another patrician friend of labor, would not abide labor violence.

When the McNamaras were arrested for bombing the *Los Angeles Times* building, Low sent off a letter to Samuel

Gompers expressing his disappointment that he had not condemned violence on behalf of organized labor. He demanded that Gompers speak out against labor violence, and pledge the A.F.L. to help run down the perpetrators of industrial crimes.[46] It was a letter written in the heat of the moment, and was as inaccurate as it was unwise. More than a month passed before Gompers responded to Low's letter, then in an eleven-page polemic, he cited chapter and verse from addresses in which he had condemned all labor violence. He charged the nation's press with conducting a conspiracy of silence in regard to labor matters, and accused it of deliberately failing to report his remarks accurately. He told Low that he was, first and foremost, a workingman, that the labor movement took precedence over all personal considerations, and declared that for Low he "entertained and still entertain a great respect and regard.

> I know of the great services you have performed. I am not unmindful of the splendid work you are doing, and I have in the past and am willing now to co-operate to the best of whatever ability I may possess, but I have no desire to place you in an embarrassing or uncomfortable situation. If you do not think that you can longer work with me as I am, and as I propose to be, a consistent, persistent defender of the rights and the cause of labor, if there be anything in the course I have pursued which meets with your disapproval, I shall be glad at any moment it is intimated to me to sever my relation with the National Civic Federation. . . .[47]

Realizing he had made a mistake, Low apologized to Gompers for having written him on the basis of faulty and insufficient information.[48] The friendship between Low and Gompers survived the McNamara incident, and they continued to work for the improvement of labor's status.

While Seth Low had always been a warm supporter of organized labor, it was in 1911–1912 that he articulated a radically new conception of labor's place in modern industrial society. As long as business was under individual management, Low maintained in a 1912 article in the *Annals of the American Academy of Political and Social Science,* as long as the men who invested money in a business actually took personal charge of the enterprise, they were the sole and undisputed owners of their businesses. The typical employer, Low went on, therefore felt that modern industry belonged to those who invested capital in it, that the man who worked in a plant was simply an employee who was not entitled to any say in the management of the enterprise. However, he pointed out that the old industrial order in which a man invested both his capital and his labor in his own business was gone forever. Nowadays, tens of thousands of people owned stock in America's great industrial complexes, and the vast majority of those stockholders devoted neither time, energy, nor thought to the industries in which their capital was invested. Most industrial concerns were run by a corps of professional managers who were themselves employees of the corporation. Thus, in Low's conception, capital's claim to an absolute control of modern industry was not as valid as it once was under the older conditions of small, individually operated enterprise.[49]

On the other hand, the socialists went to the other extreme. Claiming that all industrial wealth was the product of labor, they called for the common ownership of the means of production. They neglected entirely the contribution made by invested capital to the production of economic wealth, and proposed a solution which was not only unjust but impractical. Both the extreme employers and the socialists were wrong, Low argued, and neither were capable of solving the problems facing industrial America. While both sets of extremists sought to convince the world that they were right, "the average employer and the average workman are trying somehow to better conditions day by day, in the hope that some day the ideal relationship of every workingman to the enterprise to which he gives his time and labor which are his life will yet be developed."[50]

"Can a property right," Low asked, "be created only by money; or can it also be created by the labor of those whose labor helps to make an industry wealth-producing?"[51] In America today, he held, there are essentially two types of employment. One rendered a personal service to an individual —for example, gardeners, maids, physicians, and others—and were paid out of the personal income of the individual benefited by the service. Such employment, Low argued, created no wealth and was basically non-productive. However, those who worked in industrial plants were engaged in wealth-producing labor, and consequently:

> There has grown up very widely among employees the feeling that the men who put labor into a railroad system, or into any

other vast industrial plant, help to create that system just as truly as the men who put their money into it; and out of this belief there has grown, and is growing, a constantly strengthening conviction that those who work for such an enterprise acquire a property right in it just as real as the property right of those who embark capital in it. The problem of modern industry, so far as it relates to the relation of the employer and the employee, seems to me to be to discover the just and equitable and practicable way of reconciling these two claims to property right in modern industry.[52]

Once the claims of labor and capital to its fair share of the dividends of wealth-producing industry were resolved on an equitable basis, a new industrial era of peace and justice would dawn.[53] Low was, quite frankly, in search of utopia, and of course he never found it. While recognizing labor's property right in modern industry, he was unable to formulate an effective method of gauging and rewarding this property interest.

In a letter to a colleague, written in June 1912, Low suggested that labor's property claim in the great industries might best be recognized by giving the workingmen a dividend identical to that received by the stockholders. If, for example, a ten percent dividend were declared, labor should be awarded a bonus of ten percent of its salary.[54] But again, unless the worker's basic wage was just, the added dividend would be meaningless. Low believed that the conflict between the rival property claims of capital and labor could best be resolved by allowing each party to work for its own betterment through the agency of the trade agreement. By a continuing process of collective bargaining, labor eventually would secure for itself a more just share of the proceeds of industrial production, until one day, in the far distant future, the machinery of collective bargaining would produce industrial harmony and justice. Labor must shape its own destiny, win its own victories, create its own utopia; but to make it possible for labor to advance under its own power, the state must guarantee its right to collective bargaining. "My belief," he told the Civic Federation's 1912 convention:

is that unless the corporations, generally, concede this right [to collective bargaining] of their own accord, it will not be many years before the States and the Congress, by legislation, will compel all who wish to avail of the corporate form for the purpose of doing business, to recognize in their workmen the same right to collective bargaining, through leaders of their own choice, as they themselves exercise.[55]

Quite naturally, Low's ardent support of labor, and the National Civic Federation's efforts to promote the cause of organized labor, earned the enmity of the anti-union employers associations. Many otherwise rational businessmen were convinced that the Civic Federation, especially during the presidency of Seth Low, was one-sided in its advocacy of organized labor. Jacob H. Schiff, for instance, declared that, "the Civic Federation, while no doubt it did some good, was after all under the sway of the labor leaders, who in turn seldom considered the interests of the public.... "[56] In many business circles, there was—as lawyer Arthur T. Lyman reported—"a feeling of distrust about the position of the Civic Federation in connection with the American Federation of Labor."[57] These businessmen sincerely and honestly believed in the efficacy of the *laissez-faire* economic order, and regarded the Civic Federation's championship of labor's cause as a disservice to the common good of the nation. For the most part, these men—while disagreeing with the intellectual premises of unionism—were realistic enough to deal with organized labor as a fact of modern industrial life, and to keep peace within their industries. They were not about to journey out of their way, however, in an effort to help labor, and hence their antipathy to the N.C.F. which, in their eyes, was helping to destroy the old and natural order of economic relationships. Generally, they were apathetic, if not hostile, to the Federation's industrial program, and their indifference was a severe handicap to the Federation's work. Within the business community, though, there was a lunatic fringe of employers who stoutly refused to have any dealings with labor organizations, and who condemned the Civic Federation as a positive danger to American institutions. This viewpoint was expressed by printer William Green, who told the N.C.F.'s John Hays Hammond that, "feeling as I do, I am unwilling to belong to any organization using a Union label on its literature."[58]

"We can take care of the labor question," John Kirby, Jr. of the National Association of Manufacturers proclaimed, "without any of this philanthropic aid which these people [of the N.C.F.] think they are giving for the benefit of humanity."[59] Mr. Kirby devoutly believed that:

> The American Federation of Labor is engaged in an open warfare against Jesus Christ and his cause. Analyze it as you may,

you can make nothing else out of it, and those who profess Christ, yet *hobnob with the leaders of that wicked conspiracy and give them encouragement by eating and drinking and smoking and holding social relations with them, cannot segregate themselves from the responsibility that attaches to such affiliation.*[60]

Worshipping a *laissez-faire* economy which did not exist in his day, and which never obtained in American economic history, Kirby personified those businessmen who could not accommodate their sacrosanct nineteenth century ideals to the realities of a twentieth century industrial order. Celebrating the virtues of an economic system in which every office boy could grow up to be the company's president, in which honest, hard-working, and thrifty young men went from the depths of grinding poverty to the exalted heights of material well-being, the National Association of Manufacturers, the Citizens' Industrial Alliance, and the Anti-Boycott Association could not face the reality of an America in which these feats were the accomplishments of a dead economic order. The huge industrial combine, the tightly-organized trades union were the frightening features of a newly-emergent industrial society which shattered the comfortable and secure world of the self-made small businessman. The Civic Federation—in urging America to come to terms with a twentieth century economy—was leading a frontal assault on the sacred and hallowed beliefs of all the John Kirbys. Their resistance was loud and vitriolic, and the Federation had to waste much time in the effort to counter their oposition. "If," Ralph Easley commented, "the papers would only publish what he [Kirby] says, he would be a complete answer to himself."[61] Unfortunately, the newspapers rarely reported Kirby's speeches uncensored.

The Civic Federation let no opportunity slip by to make peace overtures to the National Association of Manufacturers. Low invited Kirby to participate in the Federation's 1910 conference on uniform state legislation only to be told, "I will express the hope that the day is not far distant when the National Civic Federation will clear its literature of the union label and will stand squarely before the public committed absolutely to the interests of *all the people,* and freed forever from any alliance with the labor trust and from any affiliation with labor union demagogues."[62]

"Mr. Kirby," Low wrote the Reverend Peters, "no doubt

understands the difficulties which manufacturers suffer at the hands of unions better than I do; but he seems to me to be a perfect child in his appreciation of any other aspect of the problem!"[63] While the breach between capital and labor might well have been reconciliable, as Low fervently believed, the breach between the N.A.M. and the N.C.F. was not, and by 1911, Kirby's organization had anathematized the Civic Federation as "a menace to free American industrialism."[64] Ignoring the N.A.M.'s attacks, as they did the socialists', the Federation and its president continued to champion labor's cause. Low's stand forced such employers as Marcus M. Marks to condemn him as "a class advocate."[65]

The National Civic Federation, in the period from 1908–1911, vigorously defended labor's right to organize, to strike, and to engage in collective bargaining with the employers of labor. It helped convince organized labor that advancement was possible within the confines of American capitalism, and helped to blunt the growing strength of the socialists. For its pains, the Civic Federation earned the strong condemnation of both the socialists and the anti-union employer associations, the latter because it saw in the Civic Federation a threat to the traditional *laissez-faire* order to which it clung religiously. The Federation's chief contribution, however, was in showing organized labor that there are, as businessman Harris Weinstock declared, "many in the ranks of the capitalists who appreciate the wisdom and justice on the part of labor to organize for the purpose of bettering its condition by collective bargaining, and who stand ready to recognize and deal with organized labor."[66]

CHAPTER XIV

From the New Nationalism to the New Freedom

We need more men in this country who can be public men without holding public office.

SENATOR MOSES E. CLAPP to SETH LOW[1]

The National Civic Federation, from its inception, had been advocating a program which, by 1910, would closely resemble the New Nationalism of Theodore Roosevelt—a recognition that the trust was an irrevocable fact of modern industrial conditions, and the acknowledgment that only the national government could effectively regulate a national economy. The philosophy which the Civic Federation had been urging for more than a decade was embodied in the program enunciated by Theodore Roosevelt and the Progressive party. That philosophy, however, failed to win the American electorate and the destiny of America was given over to the Democratic party; largely controlled by southern agrarians, it was a party which stood for state's rights—*laissez-faire*—and which was essentially hostile to the new order of large-scale industrial production. Yet it was during the Democratic administration of Woodrow Wilson that the National Civic Federation reached the zenith of its influence, and performed its most useful services to the nation. While the New Nationalism was defeated in 1912, its spirit, which was the spirit of the age, proved irresistible. Even President Wilson was forced to adopt many of its features.

In 1910, Roosevelt took to the stump to advocate a broad range of reforms lumped together as the New Nationalism. Low was an early supporter of Roosevelt's reform program. "I have read your speeches with great interest," he told Roosevelt prior to the 1910 elections, "and, in the main, I am in complete accord with your ideas. I do not know that I am prepared to go quite as far as you have done in the matter of a National Inheritance Tax, and perhaps not as to some other details; but on the main question, and in the general trend, I am heartily with you."[2] Yet by 1912, he had broken with the colonel and remained a Taft Republican.

While sympathetic with the progressive wing of the Grand Old Party, Low firmly believed that Progressivism could best be promoted by a united Republican party; schism would only work to the advantage of the Democrats, who, under their current leadership, were not fit to lead a progressive people. When the results of the 1910 elections proved disappointing to both the old-line and progressive Republicans, Low felt that the party's defeat was due to the obvious division between Roosevelt and Taft, and in November 1910 he pleaded with Roosevelt to patch up his differences with the incumbent President for the sake of the progressive program which he hoped to advance. "I hope very much," he implored Roosevelt:

> that such an understanding may be reached between the President and yourself, if it does not already exist, as will enable you in the future to put yourself squarely behind him; for, unless this is done, I apprehend that the present division in our party is likely to be as long continued as the split in the Democratic party which was caused by Mr. Bryan. It is possible, of course, that out of such conditions a new party may grow; but I am sanguine enough to believe that at heart the rank and file of the Republican party are loyal to Progressive policies, and that it will be much easier to keep the Republican party in line with such policies than to secure their acceptance through a new party.[3]

A few days later, Roosevelt replied—more in despair than in anger—that he was largely the prisoner of circumstances and could not, if he would, repair the rupture in the party. "I greatly fear," he told Low, "we are up against an impossible situation for 1912 also.

> I need not tell you that after events have reached a certain point, it is not possible to work a complete cure. I have power over my followers only within certain narrow limits. . . . When I came back to this country, I found some of my followers devoted to Taft, and accepting him as the regular Republican leader, and demanding that I should so accept him; but I also found that most of them were strongly and in many cases bitterly against him, and sore with me for having, as they felt, misled them into supporting him; and these men I could not influence for him in any way, save exactly as I have done in

that campaign. If I had come out more strongly for Taft, or less strongly, the disaster would have been even greater.[4]

Instead of moving closer together, however, the differences between Roosevelt and Taft, much to Low's chagrin, became irreparable. Roosevelt openly challenged Taft's bid for re-nomination, and the bitter rivalry between the two men threatened to split the Republican party. In New York, the *Tammany Times,* relishing the intra-party squabble, suggested that the best way to heal the Roosevelt-Taft breach would be to nominate Seth Low as the party's compromise candidate for 1912. "Why not?" the paper wanted to know:

> Seth Low is a New York man, born and bred. He has a bully good name to juggle with. His name would win the Republicans North, East, South and West.
> Seth Low would have the necessary rhythm and jingle for campaign literature and song. For instance:
>
> > Seth Low
> > Is all aglow
> > To strike the
> > Presidential blow

Besides, the *Tammany Times* pontificated, this was going to be a Democratic year and what the G.O.P. needed was a good born loser, like Seth Low.[5] For Low, though, the Republican schism was a threat to America's best agency for reform.

One aspect of Roosevelt's program—the recall, and especially the recall of judicial decisions—greatly disturbed Low. "I can think of no better way," he declared in a 1911 letter to Roosevelt, "to make men time servers than to subject them to the Recall."[6] Seth Low was a political independent all his life, who—when in office—acted as he saw fit, irrespective of party or popular pressure. Like Edmund Burke, he felt that while public officials must be responsible to the electorate, they should have enough backbone to act in accordance with their own conscience while in office. The recall of elected officials would serve only to turn them into cringing puppets swayed this way and that by the popular whim of the moment. All independence would be lost, and the quality of elected officials—rather than being uplifted—would actually be degraded with the facile crowd-pleaser at a distinct advantage over the sturdy, upright official whose sense of duty might often force him to take unpopular stands. As for the recall of judicial decisions, it threatened the very basis of civilized society. "My present feeling," Roosevelt replied, "is against the Recall save with very careful safeguards."[7] Roosevelt's conservative state of mind, however, was shortlived and by 1912 he was favoring the recall of all judicial decisions affecting the police powers of the state or national governments. Low began to have severe misgivings about Roosevelt's brand of Progressivism, and early in 1912 he declared in a letter to President Taft, "I also think that you are doing the Country a great service in opposing that action [judicial recall] to the utmost."[8]

Throughout 1912, Low was torn between his affection for Roosevelt and affinity for the colonel's industrial program, and his horror of judicial recall. "Like all other Republicans," he wrote *The Outlook's* Lyman Abbott, "I am turning the matter over in my mind to determine where my duty lies. At the moment I am inclined to favor the renomination of Mr. Taft."[9] However, he told Abbott that the only thing preventing his endorsement of Roosevelt was his conviction that the recall was a grave error. Many of Low's colleagues and associates, though, were ardent Progressives who sought to allay Low's fears about Roosevelt's radicalism. "Has it surprised you," lawyer Lawrence Abbott asked, "to find that some men, and good men too, look upon you as a dangerous enemy of society because you advocate justice to the labor organizations and especially to Samuel Gompers?"[10] Asserting that on all social and industrial issues Low's views were identical to Roosevelt's, Abbott assured Low that the recall, like universal manhood suffrage, was not the end of democratic government but rather an extension and refinement of the democratic spirit.

The urgings of Roosevelt's supporters apparently had an effect, for by mid-summer of 1912, Low was leaning heavily in favor of the Progressive party. "I find myself very much perplexed by the present political situation," he wrote Columbia's John W. Burgess:

> So long as it was a matter of choice of candidates by the Republican party, I was in favor of Taft as against Roosevelt. Now, however, the choice is very different, and there is much in the platform of the Progressive party with which I am greatly in sympathy. In particular I think its pronouncement in favor of the exclusive federal control of interstate commerce is much sounder than that of either of the other platforms.[11]

He went on to declare that while objecting to the recall of judicial decisions on general principles, he recognized that the courts were often an obstacle to the enactment of social legislation. He cited a decision of the New York Court of Appeals which struck down as unconstitutional a state law abolishing manufacturing in tenement houses as a case in point, and asserted that a sense of justice demanded that some means be found to reverse such reactionary edicts of the courts. Regarding Burgess as the nation's leading authority on constitutional law, he asked him if the Progressive platform's limitation of judicial recall to questions involving the police powers of a state was a check sufficient to rule out the many abuses to which, he felt, the doctrine could give rise, and if it was not, he asked Burgess if some other way could not be found to accomplish the same end without the draw-backs of recall. Burgess replied that Roosevelt was leading America down the road to Caeserism, and that all patriotic Americans should shun him and his program.[12] "I am not quite sure," Low wrote back, "that I take the same view of the political outlook as yourself; but I am free to say that I am increasingly reluctant to let go my anchorage in the Republican party."[13]

A nephew, who was also an attorney, wrote Low that judicial recall was simply a method of returning to the people a power usurped by the courts in order to annul legislative acts concerning public policy rather than points of law.[14] Nevertheless, Low was unconvinced, and on September 16, 1912, he wrote Charles D. Hilles, Chairman of the Republican National Committee, offering to campaign on behalf of Taft.[15] His offer was accepted, and in October he delivered a number of speeches in support of Taft's candidacy in which he defined his concept of Progressivism.

The chief problem facing America, in Low's estimation, was the trust and the question of how it should be controlled. He ridiculed the Democratic contention that the tariff was the mother of trusts as arrant nonsense which proved the Democrats' unfitness adequately to grapple with America's most pressing difficulties. He, too, objected to high tariffs, but realized that the tariff had no bearing upon the trust question. The rise of the trust as an uncontrolled agent of business was the direct outgrowth of the federal system of government which provided no authority capable of regulating interstate commerce. Generally, he favored the Progressive stand on the trust question, but warned that only a system of federal licensing or federal incorporation could adequately deal with the problem. Expressing his hope that the Republican party would adopt his position, he declared that "Until Congress does one or the other of these things [incorporation or licensing], we shall be playing with the surface of our commercial troubles, instead of striking at the root of them."[16] On all social and economic matters, Low sympathized with the Progressive party, but he disapproved of third party movements unless both major parties had proven themselves incapable of solving the difficulties facing the nation, and in the case of the Republican party, he did not feel that such incapacity had been demonstrated. "Mr. Roosevelt is denouncing, in unmeasured terms," he told the readers of *The Outlook:*

> the Republican party, which has been, for the last two generations, in my view, the principal agent of progressive legislation in the Country as a whole, and in all parts of the Union. . . . It [the Chicago Convention] did not at all demonstrate that the party had ceased to be capable of progressive action. On the contrary, I believe that it still has more capacity for bringing about desirable legislation in the Country, and throughout the States, than the Progressive party now has or is ever likely to have unless the unexpected happens.[17]

Third parties, he contended, usually proved to be failures which often hindered reform more than they helped it. The Republican party had shown itself aware of, and willing to face the problems of an industrial America, and therefore, Low argued, it should not be cast off because of one disgruntled man's whim. Then, too, there was the question of methodology. "There is in the platform of the Progressive party," he told Lyman Abbott's *Outlook:*

> a human note to which I respond, and I am, moreover, deeply sensible of the indebtedness of the Country to Mr. Roosevelt for awakening its idealism. . . . In this campaign Mr. Roosevelt seems to me to be playing the part of Wendell Phillips, rather than of Abraham Lincoln. Wendell Phillips denounced the Constitution of the United States as "a league with death, and a covenant with Hell" because it recognized slavery; but Abraham Lincoln realized that the Constitution of the United States must be maintained if the Union were to be preserved and slavery itself abolished. Wendell Phillips, by his denunciation of slavery, awakened the public conscience; but the cure

of the evil of which he complained was brought about by other
agencies. So now, Mr. Roosevelt, with less occasion I think,
thunders against constitutional restraints in the name of social justice. Greater social justice will come year by year, I
doubt not, but it is more likely to come by maintaining fundamental Constitutional restraints than by overthrowing them![18]

Reform was obviously needed; the status of the workingman
had to be raised, the trust controlled, and oppression eradicated
wherever it was found. However, the humanitarian reformer
could be as much of a tyrant as the demagogue; one man's
heaven could easily be another man's hell and if democracy were
to be sustained, the people must not be allowed to become a
law unto themselves. Low realized that in the name of
democracy, the people could be turned into despots, and society
must be protected against the excesses of which democracy
was capable. While desiring to uplift America, Seth Low was
aware of man's basic irrationality, and civilization could be
preserved only by the supremacy of law which, while it might
impede the establishment of social justice, was still society's
best safeguard against despotism, able to check the majority as
well as the minority. For these reasons, he had only contempt
for the initiative, the referendum, and the recall.

The bulk of the American electorate, Low sadly reminded
his audience, was notoriously complacent, and only bestirred
themselves to political action when their vital interests were
immediately affected. Consequently, more often than not, the
initiative—rather than permitting the people to directly control
legislation—would simply allow a well-organized minority to
better control legislative enactments. And in states where well-
oiled political machines were able to produce votes on demand,
the initiative would only serve to re-enforce the power and
influence of the bosses. The same objection could be made to
the referendum, though Low favored it, with safeguards, as a
means of sounding out public opinion.[19] While opposing the
initiative and referendum, Low did support direct primary
legislation as an effective means of curbing the political bosses.
Since state nominating conventions were often under the thumb
of some party boss, the sole chance of breaking his power was
to have the people at large select their party's nominees. Though
the machine would probably win most primary elections due
to voter apathy, reformers stood little chance of influencing
conventions, and their only hope of capturing their party was

at the polling booth in a direct primary.[20] As for judicial recall, he did not believe that the general public was competent to decide points of law, and the device would be used by an overbearing majority to sweep away protection of minority interests. Recognizing that some method should be adopted to strip the courts of their power to negate social legislation which were largely matters of public policy rather than of law, he preferred a constitutional amendment instead of popular recall as providing more safeguards for minority rights.[21]

With the election over, Low expressed the hope that the breach between the Republicans and the Progressives would speedily be closed, for basically he saw them as of one mind. "The Republican and Progressive parties," he told the editor of the *New York World:*

> are not likely to differ in regard to definite humanitarian proposals that come within the scope of practicality.
>
> In my judgment, the division of republicans in this campaign was more the result of conflicting personalities than of irreconcilable differences in policy. . . [T]he Republican party . . . will survive as long as the American people are true to the great principles upon which our Republic is founded. Loss of power is often a refining experience. I, therefore, look for the gradual elimination of the influences that have made the present breach in the Republican party. I look for the ultimate re-union of its broken parts; and I look for many more victories to be won under its banner.[22]

One suspects that Low had a higher opinion of the Grand Old Party than was merited, but, in any event, he declared to President Taft that, "history will do both you and your administration more justice than your contemporaries have done, and that you can face the future with a conscience void of offense."[23] The consciousness of having done my best," Taft replied, "will serve me until history has rendered its verdict, and I am content to abide that time."[24] As a result of Republican disunity, the Democrats had elected their first president since Grover Cleveland; the party of the nineteenth century had been given charge of a twentieth century America. Would Woodrow Wilson prove adequate to the task before him? "Just now," Low told J. B. Bishop, "we are watching President Wilson with interest, and, I may add, with great hope."[25] The National Civic Federation would soon have occasion to test that hope.

Under the terms of the Erdman Act, labor disputes involving the nation's railroads could be submitted to a government board of mediation and arbitration, provided both employers and employees were willing to accept such conciliation services. The Erdman arbitration panel was a three-man board, having one representative from the unions, one from the railroads, and one appointed by the government to represent the general public. Between 1906 and 1913, sixty-one controversies were settled without a strike, much of this success being attributable to Martin A. Knapp of the Interstate Commerce Commission and Charles P. Neill of the Bureau of Labor Statistics, who had served as the government's mediators. The act was originally intended to handle disputes between a single road and a single union, and functioned to the mutual satisfaction of both management and labor. However, by 1912, labor disputes on the railroads came to involve entire railroad systems spanning vast sections of the country, and the Erdman arbitration panel, which essentially rested upon the decision of a single man, proved unacceptable to the railroads.

Early in 1912, a strike threatened between the Brotherhood of Locomotive Engineers and the Eastern railroads. There were, all told, fifty-four separate points in dispute and both sides were willing to accept suitable arbitration. The railroads argued that it was not fair to submit fifty-four complex demands to the decision of one man (a proposition to which the Brotherhood readily acceded), and proposed instead to have all points in contention arbitrated by a seven-man panel, five of whose members would represent the public. The Locomotive Engineers agreed to the plan, which proved disastrous. Under the Erdman Act, the arbiters could only consider those points which had been submitted to them in advance of the arbitration, and were not permitted to go beyond the questions submitted for their deliberation. Also, the panel had the power to compel testimony, and those giving false evidence could be prosecuted for perjury. The arbitration was conducted under the sanction of law and was, therefore, binding. In this case, however, the seven-man arbitration panel was an extra-legal body which could not compel testimony, and which went far beyond the bounds of the questions submitted to arbitration. The award proved unfavorable to the Engineers, and the Brotherhoods resolved never again to arbitrate outside the Erdman Law.[26]

Later that same year, another railroad strike threatened, this time between the Brotherhood of Firemen and Enginemen and the Eastern roads. The union was willing to arbitrate, but only under the terms of the Erdman Act, while the railroads again insisted that it was not fair to ask them to submit all disputed points to the decision of one man. An impasse developed and a strike seemed certain when Seth Low stepped into the controversy. He pleaded with the railroad presidents to accept arbitration under the Erdman Act, imploring them to consider the public's interest, and not to work needless hardship on the people. Finally, the railroads agreed to accept Erdman Act arbitration provided that the National Civic Federation and the Brotherhoods assist them in securing an amendment to the Erdman Law which would meet their objections by enlarging the arbitration panel. The unions agreed to the proposition and the strike was averted.[27]

Late in January 1913, Seth Low, Martin A. Knapp, and Charles P. Neill as representatives of the public and of the government met with Samuel Rea, William C. Brown, R.S. Lovett, Daniel Willard, Frank Trumbell, and Charles A. Wickersham of the railroads, and with A.B. Garretson, W.S. Carter and H.E. Wills of the Brotherhoods at the Hotel Astor in New York City to consider revision of the Erdman Act. It was agreed, from the outset, that arbitration must not be made compulsory, but should remain—as it was under Erdman— voluntary. "Arbitration that is voluntary," Seth Low declared, "is highly useful, because, when it is voluntary, both parties agree to abide by the result; but compulsory arbitration is impossible, because not [even] the community itself can compel men to work unless they are willing to work."[28] It was further agreed that in disputes involving a single road, the original Erdman panel of three men should be kept, but that for larger disputes the panel should consist of six men, two each from the railroads, the unions, and the general public. A seven-man panel was specifically ruled out in order to avoid 4 to 3 decisions. With six men, at least two-thirds would have to agree to carry any point.[29] In addition, the confrerees urged that an independent board of mediation and conciliation be established to administer the new law—a commission not under the control of any existing federal department. It was felt that this would enhance the conciliation department's stature and influence. Also, it was decided to allow the proposed arbitration commission to intervene into labor controversies on its own initiative, without having to wait to be called in by the parties to the dispute. However, this did not smack of compulsory arbitration since both parties were at liberty to refuse the department's services.

Low declared that railroad employees were entitled to good wages, and urged that the Interstate Commerce Commission be prevailed upon to grant railroads rate increases in order that they might be able to afford the higher wage scales. "I think the American people," he told the confrerees, "are not only willing that railroad employees should be paid good wages. I think the people are desirous that such wages should be paid. I also believe that the people are entirely willing that higher freight rates and higher passenger rates should be allowed . . . to allow good wages to be paid to railroad employees."[30] He was ever the optimist. Low also called for the creation of an Interstate Trade Commission to have the same powers over the large corporations as the I.C.C. had over the railroads.[31] Both the Brotherhoods and the railroads were unanimous in their support of the amendments to the Erdman Act enumerated above, and all that remained was to have the measure enacted into law.

In mid-March 1913, the Civic Federation's bill was ready to be presented to Congress, and Seth Low, on the 19th wrote President Wilson requesting an interview at the White House in order to explain its features, and solicit administration support for the measure. He declared that the proposed amendments to the Erdman Act would obviate the threat of railroad strikes for years to come, and urged upon Wilson the necessity for prompt action.[32] Five days later, Low received a curt reply from J.P. Tumulty, President Wilson's secretary, advising him that the president was far too busy to grant his request for an interview at any date in the foreseeable future, and suggested that he write Wilson in detail about the proposed amendments to the Erdman Law.[33] Low persisted in his efforts to see the President, but was unable to get beyond Tumulty. Late in May, he determined to go to Washington and help line up Congressional support for the Civic Federation's bill, and he again requested an interview with Wilson.[34] A week later, Tumulty again gave Low his by-now usual reply that Wilson could not spare the time to see him, and suggested that he write the president in detail.[35] This time Low followed Tumulty's advice.

On June 7th, Low informed President Wilson of the details

of the Civic Federation's proposed modification of the Erdman Act, and finally succeeded in obtaining a personal reply from Wilson, though it was small improvement over Tumulty's cold responses.[36] The President assured Low that he would give the matter "my most earnest consideration," but made no firm commitment to support the measure.[37] While Wilson was too busy to see Low, the Brotherhood of Conductors and Trainmen were threatening to strike the Eastern railroads, and it was hoped that the Erdman Act amendments could be enacted into law in time to avert the walk-out. This gave added impetus to the Federation's efforts to secure congressional approval of its bill, but Wilson and his White House staff seemed totally oblivious to the impending railroad tie-up and were ice-cold toward Low's efforts to amend the Erdman Act. Meanwhile, Low, in mid-June, was in Washington seeking support for the Federation's measure, and secured the backing of Senator Francis G. Newlands, who introduced the bill into the Senate. Hearings would commence later that month, and Seth Low continued his efforts to secure the administration's approval of the proposal. While the White House remained cool, a number of Wilson's cabinet officers—notably Franklin K. Lane of Interior and William C. Redfield of the Commerce Department—gave the bill their earnest support. "Not only I," Secretary Redfield declared, "but the resources of this Department are at any time at your service." "Furthermore," he continued, "let me add a word of personal appreciation of the great service you are rendering the country in such work as you were doing here. I earnestly hope for its full success. Nothing is more important now than to bring the human factors in management and in industry into mutual accord. Those who can bring this about will put the crown upon the great work America is doing in the world."[38]

Hearings on the Newlands bill were to begin on June 20th, but even before the measure came before the Senate's Interstate Commerce Committee, a snag developed. William B. Wilson, secretary of the newly created Department of Labor, backed by Samuel Gompers, insisted that any commission established to conciliate, mediate, or arbitrate labor disputes affecting the railroads should constitute a bureau within the Department of Labor. The act creating the Labor Department had stipulated that the Secretary of Labor should appoint and control all boards or commissions engaged in industrial conciliation work, and Secretary Wilson claimed that the proposed United States Board of Mediation and Conciliation envisioned by the Newlands bill properly belonged within the confines of his department. However, both the railroads and the Brotherhoods had agreed to the creation of an independent agency to administer the amended Erdman Act, and as Low told Franklin K. Lane, if the new commission were placed within the Department of Labor it would have the appearance, whether justified or not, of being one-sided in favor of labor. If placed anywhere, Low told Lane, it should constitute a bureau within the Interstate Commerce Commission.[39] Unfortunately, Secretary Wilson had control of Henry Clayton's House Committee on the Judiciary, and unless Wilson's demands could be satisfied, the Newlands bill had little chance of securing Clayton's approval.

On June 20th, the Newlands bill was defended before the Interstate Commerce Committee by the heads of the railroad Brotherhoods and the presidents of the Eastern roads. In his testimony, Low re-affirmed the voluntary nature of the arbitration proposed by the Newlands bill, and impressed upon the committee the urgency of quick enactment. "If we can have this law," he told the senators, "I think you can look forward to industrial peace, so far as the railroads are concerned, in the near future without doubt. If you do not have it, I can not say what both sides will do; but there are two strike votes being taken now, and unless we can have this law in force in the very near future we may be confronted with railroad disturbances on a scale which this country has seldom seen. . . . "[40]

The initial hearings went well and both sides were confident of favorable Senate action. "I think," Daniel Willard of the Baltimore and Ohio Railroad wrote Low:

> I properly appreciate the amount of work which you have personally done in this connection, and while it has been for the best interests of *all* the people, I suppose at the outside not more than *fifty* individuals will appreciate *your* efforts, or give you the credit which you so justly deserve. I want you to feel, however, that I at least realize the personal work that you have done for the benefit of all of us, and furthermore I do not know of any other man who could have accomplished what you did in that direction, nor do I know of anyone who could have handled the matter so tactfully and at the same time have presented it so clearly and forcefully as you did at yesterdeay's conference.[41]

Low's work, however, was just beginning, for there remained the obstacle of Henry Clayton's House Committee.

In order to secure favorable House action, Low, on the 22nd, telegraphed Secretary Wilson that he would not object to a House amendment of the Newlands bill placing the board of mediation and conciliation in the Department of Labor. He simultaneously sent a telegram to Henry Clayton advising him of his communication to William B. Wilson, and added, "Favorable action in some form by your Committee tomorrow and by caucus on Wednesday absolutely essential. Shall do everything in my power to harmonize views of Secretary Wilson and of those who must work under bill; but time presses, and consent of caucus of Wednesday to action by the House must be had if railroad disturbances are certainly to be avoided."[42] The Senate version of the bill proposed an independent mediation board, and this was the plan Low favored, but realizing that quick House approval of the Newlands measure was essential to its success, he was willing to accept the House amendment in order to secure its support of the act. He felt that it would be far easier to smooth out differences at a conference committee than to try to force House approval of the unamended Senate version of the Civic Federation's proposed legislation. On June 26th, Low wired Francis G. Newlands informing him that the House had reported favorably on the amended version of the Federation's bill, and asked Newlands to pass the Senate version unchanged, expressing his hope that he could arrange a suitable compromise in the conference committee.[43]

The railroads objected to putting the mediation board under the control of the Department of Labor, and were supported in their stand by the Brotherhoods who—as Seth Low wrote Secretary Wilson—"have taken the position that, after agreeing to act together with the Railroads for the amendment of the Erdman Act, they will not be parties to changes in the bill as presented to the Congress without the concurrence of the Railroads."[44] Wilson, though, remained adamant, and Low —hoping to break the deadlock—on June 27 proposed a compromise. Instead of insisting upon having the mediation commission controlled by the Department of Labor, would he consent, Low asked, to a compromise making the board independent but requiring that one of the two representatives of the government on the arbitration panel be the Commissioner of Labor Statistics?[45] "I do not want to see the Department of Labor crippled," Wilson replied, "nor the interests of the wage workers generally neglected, while trying to meet that emergency. The amendment which you suggest would not meet my objection."[46]

Stalemate ensued, and the legislative process on the Newlands bill had ground to a halt. Only White House intervention could save the measure, so at Easley's suggestion, A.B. Garretson of the Brotherhoods confided to Mrs. J. Borden Harriman that unless the Newlands bill was promptly passed a nationwide railroad strike was imminent. Mrs. Harriman, who had been a heavy contributor and active campaign worker for the Democratic party in the 1912 election, had entry to the White House. On July 1, she telephoned J. P. Tumulty to relay the information she had received from Garretson, and Tumulty, who feared the effect of a national railroad stoppage on the fortunes of the Wilson administration, promptly threw White House support behind the measure.[47] Meanwhile, A.B. Garretson, W.S. Stone, and W.G. Lee of the Brotherhoods were in conference with Secretary Wilson in an attempt to persuade him to drop his insistence upon administering the arbitration panel. Their efforts failed, but on July 10, the White House decided to call the parties concerned to a conference on the bill in the hope of obtaining legislative agreement. The Brotherhoods and the railroads selected Seth Low as their joint spokesman, and at the July 14 conference, his arguments proved so forceful that Secretary Wilson withdrew his demand that the arbitration commission be within his department. The bill was made an administration emergency measure, and passed both Houses of Congress forty-eight hours later. "Twice today," the N.C.F.'s Gertrude Beeks told Low, "the tears came into Mr. Easley's eyes when commenting upon your remarkably fine address at the White House. He said even the tone of your voice gave evidence of the kindly attitude you took and of the fair spirit shown. It is truly wonderful and we are proud of *our* President."[48]

There still remained problems, though. As soon as the Newlands bill cleared Congress, the railroads demanded that the arbitration panel consider certain questions regarding the rate-making structure which they desired to bring forth. The Brotherhoods quickly objected on the grounds that only those points raised at the original conference which formulated the

Erdman amendments ought to be considered at the initial arbitration. The disagreement threatened to wreck the New-lands Act's arbitration machinery; and Low, not willing to see the labor of months go for nought, intervened on behalf of the Brotherhoods. "Mr. Garretson had told me," he wrote the railroad presidents:

> that the introducion of new questions at this time without notice seemed to him and to Mr. Lee to involve bad faith. From my letter you will perceive that I myself think that any questions which were not at issue when the Newlands Act was passed ought to rank as new quesions and be brought up in the regular way after due notice. I feel confident that the railroads cannot sustain themselves in insisting upon a con-sideration of these proposals at this time. It is, of course, entirely within their right to bring them up later in a new proceeding, and after proper notice to the other side.[49]

The railroads capitulated to Low, and the final obstacle in the path of arbitration had been cleared.

After President Wilson signed the Newlands bill into law, he asked Seth Low to advise him as to whom he should name as chief mediator. After canvassing the Brotherhoods and the railroads, Low informed Wilson that the most acceptable Com-missioner of Mediation would be Judge W.L. Chambers, and the president promptly appointed him to head the board.[50] At long last, the machinery to avert the threatened railroad tie-up was ready to operate. "Your own action," Wilson declared in a letter of thanks to Low, "in this matter has throughout been admirable."[51]

The passage of the Newlands bill was regarded by Seth Low as his proudest achievement, and the Civic Federation's most spectacular victory. "I think you will agree with me," he wrote Andrew Carnegie, the Federation's chief financial con-tributor, "that if the National Civic Federation had done nothing else this single achievement would have justified its right to be...."[52] Low was now at the height of his popular prestige; showered by praise from congressmen, labor leaders, businessmen, and newspaper editorial writers, he was looked upon as one of the nation's most successful labor mediators. Sereno E. Payne of the House Ways and Means Committee —after congratulating Low on being the author of the New-lands Act—declared, "I sincerely believe that most of the credit [for its passage] is due to your own individual efforts."[53] W.G.

Lee of the Brotherhood of Railroad Trainmen, thanking Low for his efforts on behalf of organized labor, asserted that, "while the Newlands Act can hardly be expected to meet the unquestioned approval of all concerned at all times, I am firmly convinced that it will be the means of bringing about more satisfactory and harmonious relations between our organizations and the railways of the United States for many years to come."[54] "You have placed," Percy S. Grant informed Low:

> the Civic Federation . . . in a position of great strength with the working classes. Whatever the difficulties may be of such a working fellowship as exists between employers and employees in the Civic Federation, whatever the suspicious and criticisms levelled against the officers of the Association, here at your hands is a conspicuous example of services the Federation can perform. The courage, promptness and judicial clarity of your action will stand monumentally [before] whatever may befall the demand of the trainmen at the hands of the new Board. . . .

Fittingly, Low was requested by both the railroads and the Brotherhoods to serve on the Newlands Act's first arbitration panel, and while it was against the Civic Federation's policy to permit its officers to directly serve as mediators in labor disputes, Low did not feel at liberty to refuse the request. On November 10, 1913, the arbitration panel made its award, granting the Brotherhoods a seven percent pay increase (eighteen percent had been asked), but refusing to grant parity between the wage scales on the eastern and western roads on the ground that the two systems were not yet sufficiently integrated to permit such standardization. "Our board," Low told Judge Chambers, "has made its Award, and I have taken to the woods!"[56] This was not necessary, however, for while not completely happy with the award, the Brotherhood was generally satisfied with its gains.[57] During its first year, the United States Board of Mediation and Conciliation handled ten cases of which seven were settled by mediation, and three by arbitration. Initially, at any rate, the conciliation machinery of the Newlands Act was a success.

The National Civic Federation never abandoned its efforts to amend the Sherman Anti-Trust Law to exempt labor unions from its operation, and it continued to work for federal control of the American economy. "I am a Hamiltonian in my political philosophy," Seth Low declared to Columbia's Talcott

Williams.[58] And flushed with a feeling of victory after success-fully aiding in the enactment of the Newlands Act, he sought to have established his long-called-for Interstate Trade Commission. In February 1913, the Civic Federation sounded out its membership on a proposal to create an Interstate Trade Commission having jurisdiction over all corporations whose gross income exceeded $10 million or more per year (an estimated 200 corporations would be affected), and which would rule on the legality of all trade agreements affecting competition.[59] The response to the proposition was favorable. As A. Leo Weil asserted, "This bill, together with other similar legislative proposals, is in my opinion the logical sequence of the present progressive movement which seeks direct control of government by the people, and through the government, direct control of industry, and, by direct control of industry, the control of the social status of the people."[60]

This was, perhaps, the best expression ever penned of the economic goals of the National Civic Federation. It did not seek economic reform in the interests of big business, but rather it aimed to democratize the American industrial order and uplift the entire people. By requiring the great corporations to operate under federal license, the people—through the proposed Interstate Trade Commission—could control business in their interest and end the abuses which threatened to undermine equality of opportunity for all.

The movement to enact the Newlands bill had diverted the Federation's attention from the effort to foster national regula-tion of industry, but in January 1914, Low wrote Wilson of the Civic Federation's desire for an I.T.C. and urged his considera-tion of legislation to promote that end.[61] The administration, which was rapidly abandoning the principles of the New Freedom for those of the more practical New Nationalism, was preparing its own trust legislation which—while it did not go nearly as far as the Federation would have wished—appeared to Low as a step in the right direction, at the very least. The Federation supported Wilson's call for a Federal Trade Com-mission, for as Low wrote the president:

> I am thoroughly in sympathy with your proposal gradually to put an end to interlocking directorates, and to separate the business of transportation completely from the business of production. I am also greatly pleased by your suggestion to do away with the holding company, which seems to me to have

been the most unfortunate device ever hit upon by business
men in this country, because the direct effect of it has been
to multiply, for purposes of industrial control, the value of
a dollar; and a dollar carries weight enough without any
artificial increase of its power.[62]

He went on to urge Wilson to define a trust in such a manner
as to exclude from the operation of the law farm cooperatives
and labor unions. In the Clayton Act, the Wilson administration
did exempt farm cooperatives and labor unions from the
penalties of the Sherman Anti-Trust Act. However, though it
brought legislative realization to a reform which the N.C.F.
had long been advocating, and which it unsuccessfully tried
to achieve in the ill-fated Hepburn-Warner bill of 1908, the
measure was an administration bill and the Federation had no
role in its framing or passage, although Low and other officers
of the Civic Federation did support it.

Wilson's Federal Trade Commission, though, was not radical
enough for the men of the Civic Federation. Low wanted the
F.T.C. to include a requirement that all large interstate
businesses operate under federal license, which would subject
the corporations to governmental regulation of their stock
issuances, pricing structures, and trade agreements with other
corporations, as well as certain other practices and policies.
Only under proper public control could modern industry be
made a servant rather than an exploiter of mankind; and to
enforce public regulation of industry, Low would have had the
licenses of offending corporations forfeited and the corporations
debarred from interstate commerce. "The vital thing," he
declared:

is that Congress shall, once for all, assume all necessary
control of the agents that do interstate business, as well as
of the business that they do. Any less radical treatment of
the situation, whatever else may be said of it, cannot be
permanent. The need for a more perfect unity in the interest
of trade and commerce is as great today as it was when the
Federal Union was formed. A Federal license would mean
unity of law, unity of control, and unity of opportunity.[63]

Too radical for an America which still regarded government
regulation of business as intrinsically wrong, Low and the
National Civic Federation had to settle for what they regarded
as half-measures. Nevertheless, even the Federal Trade Com-

mission as envisioned by Wilson was an improvement over the Sherman Anti-Trust Act.

It was during the era of the New Freedom that the National Civic Federation performed its most useful services to the nation. In framing the Newlands Act, the Federation prevented a major railroad strike and kept peace in the industry until the national government—to meet the needs of a wartime economy—took over the operation of the nation's railroads. By advocating an increased federal responsibility for the regulation of the economy, the N.C.F. helped prepare the ground for the Federal Trade Commission, and for restrictions of private enterprise in the interest of social justice. On the eve of World War I, America was gradually coming to an acceptance of the Federation's basic proposition: to achieve a just social order, the government had to limit the freedom of action of big business. It was also in this period that Seth Low's identification with the cause of organized labor deepened.

Low had always championed labor's right to organize and to strike as a counterpart to capital's right to combine and to cooperate for mutual advantage through the corporate form; thus, the rights of labor were essentially economic privileges arising as an outgrowth of the modern industrial system. However, by 1914, he had come to look upon the workingman's desire for a union not as an economic but as a human right. Freedom to join a union, to engage in collective bargaining with management, and to strike were as much the rights of American citizenship and manhood as were the rights to trial by jury, *habeas corpus,* or religious liberty. Moreover, since the rights of labor were among the natural rights to which every free citizen was entitled as a member of society, it was proper that the state take measures to secure those rights under law. For example, an eight-hour day should be established not for reasons of economy, but because after it was established in the cigar industry the percentage of deaths among cigar workers from tuberculosis decreased from forty-nine percent to twenty percent and longevity increased from thirty-seven years and six months to fifty years and one month. Labor's right to organize, therefore, was tantamount to labor's right to life, and it was justified in seeking legal recognition for it.[64] At hearings before the Interstate Commerce Committee and the House Judiciary Committee, Low declared, "in my judgment, labor [is] justified in asking for some legislation that would place beyond dispute its right to collective bargaining within the domain of wages, hours of labor, and condition of employment...."[65]

Low had never advocated the closed shop, preferring a true open shop in which a man could join a union or not as his conscience dictated, but in which union men would not be discriminated against and would be granted the right to collective bargaining through representatives of their own choosing. However, by 1915, he came to realize that, "in the open shops the men do not enjoy the privileges of collective bargaining.... As long as these conditions prevail, it seems to me that industrial warfare is inevitable."[66] Industrial America, he argued, could prosper only when elemental justice had been accorded to labor, and only when the national government curbed the power of business in the interest of preserving democratic institutions. "I note," Easley informed him, "that you are classed by Mr. Lennon [of the House Ways and Means Committee] as one of the labor men! You know I always suspected you had leanings that way but I did not know before that you were a 'card man.' How murder will out in unexpected places!"[67]

Low's conception of labor's place in industrial society was not realized in his lifetime, and had to await the New Deal before it was achieved. Seth Low was a man of noble vision who dreamed of a happier America; he did not pretend to know all the answers to the problems besetting the United States, but as he told Oswald Garrison Villard, "in a transition period like this, when industry the world over is trying to adjust itself to new conditions, the only thing to do is to do the best we can, and to learn, from mistakes, what should thereafter be avoided."[68]

CHAPTER XV

The Measure of a Man and a Movement

The genius of Seth Low was not that of the prophet. He assumed no esoteric wisdom, he claimed no insight denied to his fellows, he acknowledged no guidance inaccessable to others. Nor did he spend time or substance on lamentation. The world might be out of joint, but he rejoiced in the opportunity to do his part in setting it right.

JAMES E. RUSSELL[1]

In Mr. Low the "smaller peoples" of Europe, the ostracized and boycotted Asiatic immigrant, and the Negro freedman had a champion, constant and valiant, whenever injustice was done them, or whenever they were in pecuniary need.

CHRISTIAN SCIENCE MONITOR[2]

In the name of Abraham Lincoln, let us all dedicate ourselves anew to the effort to make this Country a land in which every man, whatever his race, his color, or his creed, may enjoy the opportunity to become everything that is in his power to be.

SETH LOW to BOOKER T. WASHINGTON.[3]

Industrial problems were not the only matters which concerned Seth Low. In 1905, when he joined the National Civic Federation he also became a member of the Board of Trustees of Tuskegee Institute, and in 1907 he assumed the chairmanship of Tuskegee's Board of Trustees. He was convinced that unless America could solve the labor problem and the race question, the nation would never achieve the full measure of the greatness its founders had envisioned for it. In Tuskegee Institute, he saw the means of enabling the American Negro to realize his own salvation and to shape his own destiny. Until Seth Low became chairman of Tuskegee's Board of Trustees, the school's trustees had been men too busy with their own business to devote any considerable amount of time to Tuskegee's affairs; however, when Low took over leadership of the Board, "it was definitely understood between him and Dr. Washington that he was not to be a 'figurehead' but was to have full latitude in bringing his 'effective help' into the work."[4]

He took his duties seriously, and in the Seth Low Papers at Columbia University are some half-dozen bulging file boxes devoted to Tuskegee's affairs. They are replete with lengthy letters from Low to Booker T. Washington giving detailed advice on new methods of increasing milk production, egg output, and of increasing per acre yields of corn, peas and other vegetables. A gentleman farmer with a dairy farm in Westchester County, Low was an inveterate innovator and when one of his experiments proved successful, he would immediately write Washington urging him to adopt the new procedure. He made yearly visits to Tuskegee, which were not connected with his duties on the Board of Trustees for it normally met in New York City, and inspected every foot of the school's buildings and grounds seeking ways to improve the institution. When new buildings were constructed, or improvements made in old ones, Low—having a detailed knowledge of the campus—gave close instructions from far-off New York as to precisely where the new buildings should be located and exactly what improvements should be made. What is important, however, for our purposes was not so much Low's activities on Tuskegee's Board of Trustees, but his conception of the Negro's place in American society.

Slavery, Seth Low declared in a 1906 address, made work the badge of servitude; labor was the symbol of the Negro's degradation and emasculation. Consequently, many slaves, upon obtaining their freedom, equated work with slavery and refused to look upon physical labor as a suitable method of achieving economic and social advancement. The significance of Tuskegee, then, lay in the fact that Booker T. Washington—through personal example—was teaching his fellow Negroes that work was honorable, and that in a free society it was the best means of promoting economic and social progress.[5] But even more important than this new attitude toward labor was the fact that Tuskegee was an institution founded, maintained, and run by Negroes. "I am sure," Low wrote engineer Frederick A. Goetze:

> you will enjoy the visit to Tuskegee as illustrating what the negro is capable of doing. . . . When you remember that every building upon the grounds has been designed by a negro, and that in most cases the bricks have been made, the trees felled

for lumber, the boards cut, and all the work of erection done
by the students of the Institute, you will acquire a still deeper
sense of respect, I am sure, for Mr. Washington, and the great
work that he has accomplished. I do not believe it would have
been possible, through the teaching of whites alone, to have
broken down, in the negro race, the notion that work was
the badge of slavery.[6]

Through institutions like Tuskegee, the Negro could gain
confidence in his own abilities and acquire pride and self-
respect, and these qualities, Low felt, were prerequisites to the
success of any group of people, white or black. Armed with the
confidence born of acquired skill, the self-respect gained from
a good education, and the pride of individual fulfillment, Low
was hopeful that the Negro could enter the mainstream of
American life. But, in the final analysis, he realized that confidence, pride, and self-respect could only be achieved by the
Negroes themselves; all white America could do was to lend
encouragement and understanding, and help them to acquire
the educaton needed to achieve those qualities. Education must
not be denied the Negro because of the South's peculiar social
institutions, and if the South was not willing to provide proper
training for its colored citizens, it must be made to do so.
"Many of us at the North," Low wrote Bishop Charles P.
Galloway of Jackson, Mississippi:

appreciate in a way the difficulties connected with the problem
by which the South is confronted. We are quite prepared
to be patient and lenient in all our judgments, and yet
there are some fundamentals as to which we cannot waver
without being false to everything that we believe. When, for
example, it is proposed that the Negro should be left in
ignorance because to educate him will make him more
dangerous, those who believe that this involves not only a
great wrong to the Negro, but perhaps an even greater wrong
to the whole South, cannot be silent, even though we do look
at the question in a sense from the outside.[7]

The South needed more Tuskegees, for here the Negro was
raising himself by his own boot-straps, and it was this which
appealed to Seth Low.

Low had a genuine sympathy for the underdog, whoever he
might be, and it was this quality of compassion which motivated
his interest in the welfare of the Negro. He came to exert a

strong influence over Booker T. Washington, and in a 1907 letter, Washington declared:

> I used many of the points which you suggested, and I am glad to say that without exception they were loudly applauded by the whole audience. When I used the suggestion which you gave me to the effect that each white man should try to put himself in the Negro's place and then ask how he would like to be treated under similar circumstances, there was tremendous applause.[8]

Low had a positive genius for putting himself in the other fellow's place, and was a firm believer in the fundamental equality of the races. He stoutly maintained that in matters of civil and political rights there should be perfect equality between the races, and he vigorously combatted the growing spirit of "Jim Crow." In 1907, for example, the Episcopal Church, on whose governing board he was a member, proposed to appoint Negro bishops over exclusively Negro dioceses. The plan appeared to Low to smack of segregation, and yet it also promised to extend the Negro a status which he had not previously enjoyed. Unable to make up his mind to support or oppose the plan, he wrote Washington asking for advice:

> As a matter of theory, I confess that a racial separation seems to me out of place in a religion that claims that in Christ there is "neither barbarian, Scythian, bond, nor free" I confess, also, that I do not pretend to know how two races are to continue to live together on terms of individual and political amity who will not mingle socially even in their churches.
>
> On the other hand, dealing with the question as a condition and not a theory, is not this proposal in line with the general educational policy which seems to so many of us not only inevitable at the present time, but on the whole advantageous, for the negro as well as for the whites. In other words, how is the negro to develop leadership without opportunity? And how is he to get opportunity if not among his own people?[9]

In the case of the Episcopal proposal to create Negro bishops there was a measure of merit to the plan, even though it would result in segregation; but President Wilson's introduction of segregation into the federal civil service was totally without merit, and Low—along with three associates—condemned the president's course of action as a threat to the "spirit of unity and mutual respect which we all so earnestly desire to see prevail."[10] The appeal, however, fell on deaf Southern ears.

His desire to aid the Negro was not motivated solely by an altruistic desire to uplift the underdog. Low understood that helping the Negro was an excellent way of aiding the upward progress of the white man as well. "No man," he declared, "can keep another in the ditch without remaining in the ditch with him to keep him there."[11] Injustice and oppression impeded the advancement of the human race, and while it might produce heroism, nobility, and self-sacrifice amongst the oppressed, it only demeaned and degraded the oppressors. He, of course, was somewhat paternalistic in his concern for the Negro, and failed to realize that Washington's program of training Negroes for primarily agricultural pursuits was totally unrealistic in a society becoming ever more dependent on industrial skills. Nor did he feel that the Negro should push for immediate social equality, preferring that they concentrate on basic economic advancement. Yet, considered within the context of his time and place, Low's attitude toward the Negro was both liberal and optimistic. Andrew Carnegie, after visiting Tuskegee and being told by Booker T. Washington of Low's services to the Institute, declared, "I would be inclined to giv [sic] you first prize in any competition for him who is performing the best service to his fellow men."[12]

As he sought to uplift the Negro, so too did Seth Low seek to help the immigrant. Addressing the Naval Officers of the German Squadron upon their visit to New York City, he told them of their countrymen who came to America by the shipload in search of a better life. Taking any job that presented itself, these sturdy German immigrants spent their lives as laborers in their new land; but, he pointed out, the children of these laborers did not follow in their father's footsteps as was done in Europe; rather, they surpassed their fathers. In art, science, business, politics, and law, the sons of immigrants found the door to advancement open, and because America granted equality of opportunity to all, they were able to capitalize on their natural talents and abilities to achieve positions of influence, wealth, and power in American society. For them, as for Seth Low, "America spelled opportunity."[13]

The United States found it easy to absorb Anglo-Saxon Protestant and German immigrants for they blended well with those who were already here. In the 1890s and early 1900s, however, non-Anglo-Saxon, non-Protestant, ethnically distinct eastern and southern Europeans began pouring into the country, and many Americans found it impossible to accept these new immigrants. The illiterate newcomers from Italy or Poland, Russia or Rumania—unable to speak English, clinging to an unyielding, ofttimes slavish, and narrow religious orthodoxy, and crowding into the filthy tenements of America's industrial cities—appeared to many old-stock Americans to be an ingredient too strange, too foreign to ever be digested into the nation's body politic. Indeed, these new immigrants threatened to swamp traditional American values of individualism, and republicanism with their insistence upon maintaining their old world social patterns which were rooted in authoritarian cultural traits. Seth Low, though, never gave credence to these fears.

Speaking at Columbia, South Carolina in April 1905, Low declared that he had always considered it New York City's special function, "To interpret Europe to America and America to Europe. . . . "[14] In New York, the European immigrant met America, and adopted those values of his new country which were worthwhile for him; at the same time, America met the culture of Europe and took from it those features which had relevance for its needs. Out of this cultural interchange emerged a new, richer and better culture for both the immigrant and the native American, and it also helped to make one from the two. New York, he asserted, was America writ small, and what was good for the city was good for the nation. The free interchange of cultures must not be stopped because the people who now sought America's shores were different from those who had come before them. Admittedly, they were "People that are strange to our civilization; and they come in hordes that sometimes make us wonder what is to happen. We sometimes wonder if even the City of New York can carry such a burden. . . . " But:

> I personally glory in it, because I know that the City of New York would perish of fatty degeneration of the heart if it did not have a mighty burden for humanity placed upon it. . . . So I glory in the fact that New York City, rolling in its millions, as it sees these poor people coming from Europe, degraded people, degraded by their treatment for centuries, has had given to it the proud privilege of being the first American community to say, in the name and in the spirit of the people of America: "Rise up, stand on your feet and be men."[15]

Believing in the open door, Seth Low welcomed all to America's shores—Occidental and Oriental, gentile and Jew.

He championed the right of every people to breathe free, and to develop their native capacities to their fullest extent. This held true for unpopular peoples as well. Though an observer as sensitive and humane as Jacob A. Riis could declare of New York's Jews, "Money is their God," Low's perspective was somewhat different.[16] "The approaching Two Hundred and Fiftieth Anniversary of the Landing of the first Jews on the American Continent," he wrote Marlen E. Pew:

> is a fitting occasion on which to testify to the value of this element in our citizenship. As a race, they are industrious orderly and law-abiding. Many individuals among them have shown themselves possessed of public spirit of a very high order. They have illustrated here, as everywhere, the strong intellectual traits which make them influential in every country in the world. In the care of their poor and in the small percentage of crime traceable to members of their race they set an example worthy of admiration and imitation. Altogether they make a contribution to our citizenship that could ill be spared.[17]

Since every people had a contribution to make to American civilization, Low strongly opposed all efforts to close the open door. "I do not believe," he told J.H. Patten in 1905, "in the restriction of immigration, except as against individuals evidently unfitted to be admitted, such as criminals and the like."[18]

If, however, the nation did choose to limit immigration, Low wanted to see it regulated on a basis of equity which would not discriminate against any people on account of race, color, or creed. The literacy test, therefore, was totally unacceptable to him, for it favored the privileged over the downtrodden, and was unjustly arbitrary. The literacy test, he remarked, "Could not fail to work great injustice both to many persons to whom this country is the land of promise and also to our country itself, which has no prouder title to the affection and respect of mankind than that which belongs to it because of the welcome that it has given to the millions of immigrants who has [sic] sought its shores."[19] He did not feel that it was necessary, at that time, to restrict immigration in any way; but if restrictions should become necessary in the future, he felt that it should be limited by assigning national quotas based on the proportion of that nationality already in the country. Any such system, must be fairly established, and must apply equally to the Oriental peoples, for as he remarked to Huntington Wilson, "We shall have great troubles in the future . . . unless we can find some way of avoiding discrimination such as now exists between East and West."[20]

Discrimination against the Chinese and the Japanese on the West Coast, like prejudice against the Negro and the southern and eastern European immigrant, stirred Low's innate sympathy for the underprivileged. For many years, he served as president of the American Asiatic Association, and worked to increase cultural contacts between the two great civilizations of the East and the West. With other Americans, Low believed that as the world's center of gravity had once shifted from the Mediterranean Sea to the Atlantic Ocean, so now—in the early years of the twentieth century—it was shifting again, this time from the Atlantic to the Pacific Ocean. The western world would soon be facing an eastern world awakened from centuries of stagnation, and how the West treated the people of the Far East would determine whether the Pacific would be as its name implied or the scene of frequent and bitter strife between East and West. To bring about a better understanding between the two cultures, Low advocated a vigorous educational and commercial interchange. "If we want to have influence in the awakened China that is surely coming into being," he wrote Theodore Roosevelt in 1905, "we must encourage Chinese and Chinese merchants to know us at first hand, as the Japanese have done."[21]

For this reason, if for no other, discrimination against Orientals must be halted. Speaking at San Francisco's Panama-Pacific Exposition in 1915, Low told his audience that their city had the opportunity of playing the same sole as New York played, only instead of interpreting Europe to America, the Bay City could interpret Asia to America. "It is a noble function, this of interpreting unlike peoples to one another," he declared:

> and it can be done only by a community which sees what is noble and fine in foreigners rather than what is simply unlike and strange. San Francisco, I am confident, can play a like part among American cities as between the United States and the Orient. It is an infinitely harder part to play, because the element of unlikeness is greater; but it is an infinitely more important part to play, because the destiny of mankind in the future will be largely determined by the

creation and development of a good understanding between the United States and the nations of the Far East.[22]

"Somehow," he went on, "I hope that California will work out a relationship to the East, which will involve no discrimination based upon race or nationality...."

In Seth Low there was not the slightest trace of racial prejudice, nor was there manifested any feeling of racial superiority. He urged that the Negro be incorporated into the mainstream of American society, and that discrimination against Orientals be ended because he felt that it was just to do so. The immigrant from southern and eastern Europe was also to be welcomed with open arms for what he could contribute to America, and because it was America's mission in the world to help the oppressed of every land realize human dignity. They came to this nation, Low knew, in search of material and spiritual fulfillment, wanting what America had to offer, and willingly adopting the values of their new country. Nothing was to be feared from them. Low did not live in dread of lower class revolution. The idea was so preposterous that he probably never bothered to even consider its possibility. Regardless of a man's race, color, or religion, he wanted but one thing—the opportunity to become part of the American middle class. This aspiration, he profoundly believed, was both just and proper, and he—born to wealth and privilege—dedicated his life to helping the underprivileged of all nations realize their ambitions in America.

The motivations for Seth Low's espousal of social justice can be traced to his Puritan heritage with its emphasis on the doctrine of stewardship; his own family background which evidenced a concern for the unfortunate with an effort to help them to help themselves, and to his own personal experience. He was, for example, a strong advocate of state-run workman's compensation systems, and he came to a realization of the need for overhauling the liability laws as a result of an accident at his own Broad Brook farm.

In 1906, having purchased a tract of land in Westchester County, forty miles north of New York City, Low began the construction of buildings to house his dairy operations. Aware that if a serious accident befell one of his employees, he would be liable for a considerable damage claim, he took out an employer's liability policy. Early in September of that year, a carpenter in his employ lost a finger on his left hand. Low paid all the hospital and medical expenses involved, and was permitted to keep the carpenter on his payroll until the completion of the construction work the following November, all expenses including the carpenter's salary being paid by the insurance company. Low wanted to keep the carpenter on his payroll until the end of the year, by which time he would be able to return to work without embarrassment to his working capacity. The company, however, refused to allow this, but Low was going to keep him on his payroll anyway, when he was informed that unless he discharged the carpenter, he would forfeit his insurance. "I realized vividly then," he told the Minnesota Bar Association years later, "that I had insured myself against my own liability to pay; but that I had done nothing whatever for the benefit of the man who was hurt. On the contrary, . . . in benefitting myself I had injured him; for I was not able to deal as liberally with him as I should have done if I had not been insured."[23]

As a result of this incident, Low became interested in the subject of workman's compensation and made a thorough study of the matter. He favored a state-run insurance system, patterned on the German model, to be financed by payments from employers and employees which would compensate injured workmen according to the seriousness of their injuries. The National Civic Federation pushed for the establishment of such state-run systems, and in 1910 it assisted in the passage of a New York compensation law covering workers in trades deemed unduly dangerous. In the Ives case, the New York Court of Appeals struck down the compensation law on the grounds that it violated "due process of law." The decision stunned Low. "As a layman," he remarked, "I confess myself to have been shocked by the proposition that 'due process of law' means process of law as it was when the Constitution was adopted."[24] Low agitated for an amendment to the state's constitution permitting a state compensation system, and worked for a new liability law. When the state later passed a voluntary compensation plan for farm laborers, Seth Low was the first New York farmer to participate in the program.[25] The Federation's compensation efforts met with indifferent success in New York State, but elsewhere in the Progressive years, Civic Federation-drafted compensation bills were enacted, virtually without change, by many state legislatures, and successfully withstood court assaults.

Aside from personal experience, Seth Low strove to uplift the depressed, for he felt that, in return for the wealth and advantages he had been given at birth, he was obligated to use whatever talents and resources he possessed in the interests of his community. "One has to be constantly on guard," he told his uncle, "lest he forget that everything in the world is not to be tested by its value in dollars and cents."[26] Human needs must not be forgotten in the acquisition of material goods, and with this in mind, Low hoped that he could help the workingman, of whatever nationality, enter the American middle class. He desired to see in the United States the creation of a one-class society, in which all men would have ample means to lead a life of dignity and worth and contribute to the advancement of mankind. Believing that human intelligence, social planning, and remedial legislation could hasten the realization of this society, he hoped that in the National Civic Federation men of trained intelligence and good will could help fashion the future of America. The best way to achieve his dream of a one-class society was to raise the economic standards of labor, not to prevent a socialist revolution, but rather because to exploit labor, "In this day and generation," as he told Judge Gary, "is to come far below that American ideals stand for."[27] In particular, he maintained, it was the function of the churches to promote the welfare of labor, but the churches of America, he lamented, had failed in their duty. "There is a great breach between working men and the Church," he told R.G. Howell, "and this breach is very largely due . . . to a failure on the part of Christian people to approach the problems of the working man sympathetically. Working men . . . are certainly entitled to expect at the hands of Christian people that their claims will be sympathetically considered before they are denied."[28]

To be better able to place his ideas of how labor ought to be treated into operation, Seth Low, in 1914, accepted the presidency of the New York State Chamber of Commerce. "The invitation to become president of the Chamber," he told Columbia President Nicholas Murray Butler:

> came to me like a bolt from the blue, only two days ago
> I thought that my hands were already full, as indeed they
> are; but, nevertheless, I consented to serve at this time, because

I hope, if we are to have a war, that I may be of some service to the Country in that position as well as to the Chamber.

I hope, also, that I may be able to induce the Chamber to take some practical steps looking to the establishment of a local Board of Meditation and Arbitration to serve in industrial crises. Such things as these, together with the fact that my Father once held the same position, led me to think that at least I should try. . . .[29]

He was installed as president of the Chamber of Commerce on May 7, 1914 and urged that the Chamber's Arbitration Committee be greatly expanded to include conciliation and mediation services. He also called upon the Chamber to cooperate with the Central Labor Council in improving working conditions throughout New York. "My Father," he declared upon becoming the Chamber's President, "was fond of saying that commerce is the handmaid of civilization. The Chamber of Commerce . . . may well conceive that it exists not so much to promote the business of this Commonwealth and this community as through the promotion of these interests . . . to advance the standards of civilization of our day."[30] Business, for Seth Low, must serve a better purpose than the mere acquisition of profits, and for the two years that he served as president of the Chamber of Commerce, a new spirit of understanding governed the relationship between capital and labor in New York City.

When Low assumed the presidency of the Chamber, he found that there was considerable opposition to President Wilson's anti-trust legislation then pending in Congress. In the past the Chamber of Commerce had opposed such legislation as that contained in the proposed Federal Trade Commission bill, but Low convinced the businessmen of New York that the measure was in the nation's interest, and no protest was lodged against Wilson's anti-trust program.[31]

With the outbreak of war in Europe, Low and the Chamber became involved with questions of American maritime trade and neutral rights. Through his efforts a War Risk Bureau was established in the Treasury Department to insure American merchant shipping when private insurance companies would no longer assume the risk. He urged upon Congress the necessity of bolstering the American merchant marine through federal subsidies and tax credits, and he took an active lead in fostering measures to improve the facilities and defenses of New York Harbor. Through his friend Lord Bryce, he vigorously protested against Great Britain's Orders in Council and her violation of American maritime rights. In the midst of his activities on behalf of the Chamber of Commerce illness forced him to resign from the presidency of the Chamber in the spring of 1916.[32]

"Poor Mr. Low!" Ralph Easley exclaimed. "I saw him a few minutes last week; he looked very ill."[33] In his sixty-sixth year, Seth Low had cancer, and in the spring of 1916 he entered what was to prove to be a terminal illness. While he was ill, during the summer of 1916, the railroad Brotherhoods, demanding an eight-hour day, threatened a nation-wide railroad strike. Normally, the National Civic Federation would have been in the midst of the controversy seeking to arrange an amicable compromise; but, with its President dying, the organization stood by virtually helpless. "It has been a source of very great grief to me," Low told Easley, "to have been laid on the shelf just at this moment when all of my experience of the past few years might have been exceptionally serviceable. I am sorry too for the N.C.F., because I fear that, in this controversy which is particularly within our field, the N.C.F. may seem to have been helpless."[34] "If," Easley replied:

> you had gone before the 604 brotherhood officials, I am morally certain that you could have gotten them to accept arbitration, because of what you have done for them in the past and of what you, as a citizen, stand for in the community. . . . I know that the brotherhood people, as a whole, would trust anything in your hands. In fact, Cease told me that Lee, his superior, had intended to write to you a letter to that effect, because they always feared you did not realize their appreciation of what you did in the arbitration of other matters.[35]

The strike was averted only by the passage of the Adamson Act, and to many of America's business leaders, the threatened calamity was a vivid foretaste of what might have happened many times over had there been no National Civic Federation to mediate labor settlements. "How is Mr. Low," Henry L. Stimson inquired. "It would be a dreadful calamity to have him incapacitated for long."[36] Six days later, on 17 September, 1916, Seth Low died at his Westchester farm.

His death came as a shock to all who worked for the improvement of America. Seth Low believed, as James E. Russell observed, "that good must finally prevail over the evil in the world." He dedicated his life to a realization of that ideal, and while he was by no means free from making mistakes, "His mistakes were always of the head, never of the heart."[37] The immigrant, the laborer, the Negro knew that in Seth Low they would find a sympathetic friend. Of him, Samuel Gompers declared, "A man endowed with great ability to know, to learn, and to understand not only books, but men, and to deal with mankind in its weakness and its stength and to do the best that could be done in its interest—a just man was Seth Low. . . . His office, his time, his opportunity—all were utilized, not for self, but for his fellowmen. He had the respect and confidence of the men of labor. . . ."[38]

"Mr. Low," businessman J. G. Schmidlapp told Easley, "has been so much to the National Civic Federation that it is going to be very difficult to fill his place."[39] Indeed, it was. With the coming of World War I, the National Civic Federation, caught up in the democratic idealism of Wilsonian rhetoric, became a super-patriotic organization, dedicated to the preservation of traditional American values and the extermination of all subversive movements. The Bolshevik Revolution only served to re-enforce its jingoism, and Ralph Easley—whose rabid anti-socialist bias had been held in check somewhat by Seth Low—now came to the fore as America's number one patriot and declared holy war against all movements which he considered un-American. Under his leadership, the Civic Federation's old idealism and magnanimity were soon forgotten, and it became a reactionary, anti-labor association, quickly losing its once-honored position of importance in American society. Easley became an admirer of Mussolini, and when he died in 1939, the National Civic Federation died with him, totally discredited. Mrs. Harriman, commenting on the post-war Federation declared, "The Civic Federation may be very honest in its convictions; but men are like children, and the wise thing in child-training is to expect the best of children and you will get it. The Civic Federation is much too busy expecting the worst."[40]

In 1924, Sidney Howard began a *New Republic* series on "Our Professional Patriots," and devoted the first installment to Ralph Montgomery Easley, "Dean of the Prodigy." Howard rightly condemned the N.C.F. for being a tool of reactionary business interests, hostile to all liberal and progressive movements, and concluded that the men of the Federation were

"American Fascisti."[41] But this was not the Civic Federation
of which Seth Low was president. In all subsequent treatments
of the Civic Federation, Sidney Howard's passionate indictment,
and the socialist condemnation of the N.C.F. as a capitalist
tool designed to make labor acquiesce in its slavery by throwing
it the crumbs of its economic production, has been seized upon
and accepted wholesale as an explanation of the motivation
behind the Federation's reform program. But even Sidney
Howard acknowledged that, "it [the Federation] has behind it
a record of some worth. [It was] a courageous social
experiment."[42]

Seth Low did not believe in an American society divided
into classes; he felt that America had been established to realize
great things for humanity. America was here to give testimony
to the essential brotherhood of all men, to permit all men to
live with dignity, in freedom, and with material abundance.
He wanted to help the workingman to enter the middle class,
not because he wanted to forestall revolution, but because he
wanted to help America realize its mission in the world, to
redeem its democratic promise.

Under his leadership, the National Civic Federation shielded
the fledgling organized labor movement from the concentrated
and relentless attacks of the anti-union employer's associations.
And we have Samuel Gompers testimony, "that there has never
been an action taken by the Civic Federation that was hostile
to the interests of the working people."[43] Low realized that
large-scale industrial production had come to stay, that modern
industry had to be regulated by the federal government, which
was the only agency capable of exerting effective control, in
the interests of the welfare of the general society. Labor, to
meet the challenge of the new industrial system, must also
organize, for only when the worker could treat with his
employer on a basis of equal strength would he receive his just
share of the wealth he created. America, Low understood, was
entering upon an age in which big industry would have to be
counter-balanced by big government and by big labor. He
did not fear this development, nor did he seek to return to an
earlier social order; rather he accepted this new mode of
production as a logical outgrowth of man's industrial evolution.
In urging that labor's right to organize, to strike, and to engage
in collective bargaining be acknowledged by industry, he was
advocating a program which all responsible labor leaders, and

the vast majority of America's workingmen, wanted implemented. The utopian visions of the socialists never had much of a market in the United States, because the nation's working class desired only to become part of the American middle class. By assisting labor in its quest of middle class status, Seth Low was acting in the best traditions of American liberalism.

If American liberalism can be defined as the effort to spread economic benefits more evenly among the general population, then Seth Low was an American liberal. Conservatives did not generally propose an increase in the positive power of the national government, and a diminution of state sovereignty, nor did they reject *laissez-faire* economic theory and recognize and encourage labor's right to organize, to strike, and to engage in collective bargaining. On the other hand, Low was not a radical who sought to drastically alter the basic structure of American social institutions. Essentially, he believed that the nation's fundamental institutions were sound, and that while there were many abuses to be corrected, all of them could be rectified without destroying the traditional institutions of American democratic society. He was a pragmatist, and as a colleague pointed out, "He was never sentimental, he never made promises that he could not keep, or held out elusive hopes, but always he thought and worked, patiently, unselfishly, sanely and wisely, to extend throughout the whole community the conditions that make for health, intelligence and happiness."[44]

In short, Low was precisely what he called himself—a progressive. A liberal, not a conservative, he wanted to broaden the base of the middle class and to enable the workingman to climb up the social ladder, hoping that one day America would be a one-class—middle class—society. The National Civic Federation has been regarded by historians as being in the extreme right wing of the Progressive movement, but it was not. It was a basically liberal organization with an advanced social program, but because of a fascination with the socialist critique of Progressive reform, historical justice has never been accorded either the N.C.F. or Seth Low.

An idealist, a man of good hope, Seth Low championed the cause of honest municipal government, defended the rights of labor, fought to bring business under the supervision of a democratic government, and stood for the traditonal ideals of America. A scion of Puritan America, he had none of the Puritan's prejudices, but exerted his influence and his labor to helping the Negro, the immigrant and the outcast to become a part of the life of America. He is today largely forgotten because he had an unlovable personality. But this should not deny him his rightful place in American history. As *The Nation* expressed it:

> It has not been the fortune of Seth Low to command the kind of public applause which often goes to citizens whose substantial achievements for the advancement of the general good have been far less than his. . . . He lacked certain personal attributes—personal magnetism was one of them—which go far towards determining the degree in which a man, confronted with so complex and so novel a situation as that with which he had to grapple, shall triumph over the manifold diffiulties and perversities of his environment. But to admit these limitations is not to deny him one of the highest places among the men who, during the past forty years, have greatly served this city and the country. Indeed, it may well be claimed for him that of all the citizens of New York he best represented the ideal of all-round, continuous, and successful devotion to the public good.[45]

CHAPTER XVI

The National Civic Federation, the Progressives, and the Historians

The National Civic Federation performed its best work in the period from 1900–1917, and as such its career can be viewed as a part of the Progressive movement which did so much to alter the life of America in those years. Of course, the Civic Federation was but a small segment of a much larger reform movement, but, nevertheless, it championed and struggled for many of the innovations for which the Progressives as a group worked. It is through study of organizations such as the National Civic Federation that one draws conclusions regarding the nature of the larger movement. It is, thus, important to examine the validity of the interpretations of the Civic Federation which have up to now been brought forth.

Among the first to examine the National Civic Federation in a scholarly manner was Herbert Croly who, in his sympathetic study of Marcus Alonzo Hanna, accepted the Federation's claims at face value. Croly concluded that the Civic Federation was honestly and in good faith seeking to curb the power of big business in the general interest of the larger American society, while preserving the many advantages brought about as a result of large-scale industrial production, and was seeking to secure for labor a larger share of the fruits of the nation's industrial production. Hanna, Croly tells us, gave himself to this movement whole-heartedly and unselfishly, because he earnestly desired to make America a happier land in which to live. Motivated by genuine humanitarian impulses, Hanna wanted to cap his public career by aiding in the solution of the one problem which threatened to tear apart American society—the growing and increasingly more bitter struggle of labor against capital.[1] Indeed, judging by Hanna's performance as chairman of the Civic Federation, Croly's judgment does not seem to have been far off the mark. Certainly the Federation was tireless in its championship of labor's right to organize, strike, and bargain collectively with capital, and it relentlessly sought to place big business under the control of a democratic government. However, considering Croly to be a big business apologist, many historians place little credence in his judgments.

In the decade after Croly's life of Hanna was published, little was written about the Civic Federation by scholars or by serious observers of the contemporary American scene. To be sure, the Federation was mentioned by writers who dealt with contemporary political, social, and economic problems, but the references were brief and uncritical. As a case in point, Charles Edward Merriam—treating New Nationalist economic thought—declared, "many employers, sometimes characterized as 'Civic Federationists' believed that large scale production was inevitable but that strenuous efforts should be put forth to meet all the evils arising from the new situation, while retaining all the benefits of the new type of production."[2] That was the extent of Merriam's treatment of the N.C.F. No effort was made to analyze its program, or to assign it a place in the context of American history and reform. Merriam's brief discussion was typical of the reluctance of many writers to grapple with the ideological premises advanced by the pre-World War I Civic Federation.

In 1922, Clarence E. Bonnett published a substantial volume on American employers' associations. Seeking to understand their goals and aspirations, he presented their platforms, introduced their leadership, and analyzed the membership of such groups as the National Association of Manufacturers, the Anti-Boycott Association, and the Citizens' Industrial Alliance. Bonnett included the National Civic Federation in his list of employers' associations, and devoted a lengthy chapter to the Federation's activities. Reciting its aims and detailing its many and varied activities on behalf of labor and for social reform, Bonnett attempted no critical analysis, and arrived at no conclusions or interpretation of the Civic Federation's program other than to say that its labor policy was much more enlightened than were those of its rivals.[3]

The first critical treatment of the National Civic Federation, as previously noted, came in 1924 in the pages of the liberal *New Republic,* and was colored by the bitter partisan battles of the early 1920s. With the death of Seth Low and the coming of World War I, the Civic Federation, under the leadership of the super-patriotic Ralph Easley, degenerated into a rabidly chauvinistic and anti-foreign organization dedicated to the preservation of true Americanism. Sidney Howard, who, as has already been noted, devoted the first installment in a series of essays entitled *Our Professional Patriots* to Ralph Easley, roundly condemned the Federation, but did so more in sorrow than in anger. Howard freely admitted that the pre-World War Civic Federation was "a courageous social experiment" with a meritorious record of service on behalf of organized labor. "Mr. Easley's Civic Federation," Howard wrote, "with its really visionary platform of bringing capital and labor together about the same table pleased neither the benevolent despots of the Open Shop nor the captious critics of the Socialist party and for all that credit is due."[4] He regretted that the post-war Federation had become so radically different from what it had been in the days of Seth Low, that it was now a reactionary organization dominated by the worst elements of the big business community, and that its chief aim now was to keep labor pacified and satisfied with the *status quo* by raising the frightening spectre of radicalism whenever labor demanded elemental justice. The Civic Federationists of the 1920s, Howard pointed out, were "American Fascisti," and their hero was Benito Mussolini.

While Howard justifiably condemned the post-war Civic Federation as fascistic, he was careful to avoid a wholesale acceptance of the socialist indictment of Progressive reform, and fully praised the pre-war record of the Federation in labor matters. But Howard's series inspired a book edited by Norman Hapgood, published in 1928 when partisan recriminations had hardened into dogmatic bitterness, which deservedly debunked America's professional patriots. Hapgood's treatment of the Civic Federation relied heavily on the critiques advanced by such leading socialists as Eugene V. Debs, Morris Hillquit, and Victor Berger. He accepted without criticism the whole socialist indictment.

"Where organized labor is recognized, as it is in the National Civic Federation," Hapgood wrote, "it is only the conservative leadership that is encouraged and approved."[5] The labor policies of the Federation, he maintained, were designed to strangle labor militancy, suppress class consciousness, and prevent labor from advocating a political program which would alter in any major degree the prevailing social and economic institutions of the United States. To maintain a capitalist form of society, it was willing to grant labor superficial reforms which because it served to improve its lot had the effect of decreasing its militancy. Workman's compensation, unemployment benefits, factory safety measures, trade agreements, and profit-sharing—the stock-in-trade of the Federation's industrial program—while mitigating the condition of labor did nothing to alter the iniquitous and oppressive wage system, which could only be reformed through a radical political reconstruction of the nation's entire social and economic structure. The conservative leadership of the American Federation of Labor acquiesced in the continuation of the unjust capitalist system, and futilely sought to promote the interests of labor in an economic system which was rotten to the core. To the extent that the comforting nostrums of the A.F.L's leadership emasculated the revolutionary fervor of the laboring masses, it was a traitor to its class and was the running dog of the capitalist oppressors. It was, therefore, the natural ally of the capitalist class in the suppression of the working masses, and hence the friendship of the Civic Federation for the A.F.L. becomes readily understandable.

In short, the National Civic Federation was merely the tool of the capitalist exploiters. To the socialists, and to Hapgood, the Civic Federation was labor's most formidable opponent because it passed itself off as labor's friend and held out the hope of reforms which appeared alluring but really did little to help labor. Eugene V. Debs' biographer tells us that "in his search for evil personified," Debs elected to represent the Civic Federation as resulting from the diabolical tactics of the bloated plutocracy.[6] "The National Civic Federation," the socialist-minded Ladies' Garment Workers declared in 1925, "is an organization tending to perpetuate the slavery of the working class. . . . "[7] For the socialists, the Federation was synonymous with the malignant evils of the capitalist economic system, seeking to turn back the clock of human progress and shackle mankind to a new dark age of industrial serfdom. Hapgood in accepting this socialist critique, fell prey to all their historical delusions.

Moreover, as Hapgood observed, the Civic Federation was now closely aligned with the "Black International," the Russian Black Hundred, the Italian Fascist movement, and organized anti-Semitism. The Federation's Department on Subversive

Movements was headed by the notorious Catholic reactionary Condé B. Pallen, and Boris Brasol—one of the heads of the Russian Black Hundred and a vicious anti-Semite—was one of Ralph Easley's proteges.[8] With a membership like that, Hapgood implied, how could the National Civic Federation ever have been "a courageous social experiment?" Its seemingly liberal pre-war program must surely have been a blind to cover a more sinister purpose. Unfortunately, later scholars have been unduly influenced by the rhetorical brilliance of the socialist case against the Civic Federation, and have not sufficiently separated the pre-war Federation from its post-war offspring.

During the 1930's extensive and well-researched histories of American labor began to make their appearance. Spurred by the social struggles of the Great Depression, and the renaissance of hope spawned by the New Deal, these labor histories, written by such outstanding scholars as John Rogers Commons, Selig Perlman, Philip Taft, Norman J. Ware, and Lewis L. Lorwin, all reflected a liberal and humane outlook. All, however, avoided a detailed consideration of organized labor's relations with the National Civic Federation. John R. Commons' monumental four-volume *History of Labor in the United States,* covered the period of the Civic Federation in the last volume, which was co-authored by Selig Perlman and Philip Taft. Professor Commons had been closely associated with the Civic Federation during the first decade and a half of its existence, and it was probably out of respect to their mentor that Perlman and Taft did not hurl down rhetorical judgment and condemn the Federation to historical hell. On the other hand, they had scant praise for the organization and tried their best to ignore it, making only occasional and fleeting references to its work on behalf of organized labor, but concluding that "The Civic Federation vigorously combated the 'open shop' propaganda of the National Association of Manufacturers...."[9] Other than that judgment, Perlman and Taft had little further to say about the Federation's industrial philosophy.

Indeed, the intellectual climate of the 1930s, with its profound contempt for big business, its identification with the economically- and socially-depressed, and its idealization of the early socialists as heroic democratic visionaries, precluded any sympathetic or favorable treatment of the business-dominated National Civic Federation which was now so prominently identified with the fascist cause. It was, therefore, all the more remarkable that the labor historians of the 1930s were able to be as objective as they were, and could resist the temptation to castigate the Federation. Norman J. Ware, for example, in *Labor in Modern Industrial Society,* while acknowledging that the Civic Federation did accomplish some good on behalf of organized labor, nevertheless decided that, "The effect . . . of the National Civic Federation was to cut the claws of aggressive labor leadership."[10] With the socialists, Ware concluded that the long-range effects of the Federation's activities were deleterious to labor in that it acted as a brake on labor's militancy and delayed its achievement of social justice. Organized labor, would have been better off had it shunned the Civic Federation's overtures of friendship. Lewis L. Lorwin, while conceding the usefulness of the Federation's conciliation services, drew no conclusions as to the nature of its industrial program.[11] Considering the social climate of the times, a friendly interpretation of the Civic Federation could not have been expected. In any event, Ralph Easley died in 1939, and the N.C.F.'s career was terminated. Its mortal remains were left with Easley's widow, the former Gertrude Beeks, and it was not long before graduate students, in search of theses topics, were poring over the Federation's remains.[12]

In 1956, two doctoral dissertations on the Civic Federation —one of which was published—made their appearance. In that year, Sister Marguerite Green published her extensive study of the National Civic Federation's labor policies. While recognizing that, "Low brought to the Federation an understanding of the relationship between the existence of power groups in society and the control under law of the forces generated by those groups," she failed to derive the logical conclusions from her own observations.[13] She gave inadequate attention to the Federation's 1907 conference on trusts, its role in the formulation of the 1908 Hepburn bill, or the 1913 Newlands Act, or to the philosophy behind its efforts to secure industry's recognition of labor's right to collective bargaining. Too much time was spent on the personality traits of the Federation's leaders and the examination of specific labor disturbances, and not enough time was devoted to an analysis of the Federation's larger programs and goals. Sister Green declared that the Federation did much to help labor win big business acceptance, but that its motivation in doing so was to steal the thunder of the socialists, keep organized labor pro-capitalist in outlook, and prevent a violent upheaval of the prevailing institutions of American society. As such it was a conservative organization willing to grant only those reforms which were absolutely necessary to keep America a capitalist society.

Gordon Maurice Jensen's *The National Civic Federation: American Business in an Age of Social Change and Social Reform, 1900–1910* was a more subtle analysis of the organization, but it also relied heavily upon the concept of the "status revolution" in its interpretation. Jensen asserted that businessmen in the Progressive era tended to act on the issues of the day much like other Americans, and that they too were interested in reform. But, once making this admission, he quickly returned to the standard interpretation of the patrician reform theory, and declared that the Civic Federation was a businessman's reform organization which sought to meet the challenge of the welfare state by advancing the rise of welfare capitalism.[14] However, he does not define either welfare statism or welfare capitalism, and one wonders if he is not speaking of the same thing: welfare capitalism guided and regulated by a democratically controlled government seeking social justice for all elements of its population. It was Jensen's view that the large capitalists represented in the Civic Federation recognized labor's right to organize, strike, and engage in collective bargaining only because it wanted to win the friendship of labor, gain industrial peace, and influence the working masses to the support of the capitalist social order. Fearing socialism, labor was to be appeased, bought off at the lowest possible cost. But Jensen did not realize that as capital recognized the demands of organized labor to determine its working conditions and wage rates through collective bargaining, it was permitting a basic transformation of the capitalist economic system which was gradually obliterating the very system which the capitalists supposedly were seeking to perpetuate.

Moreover, Jensen argued, by recognizing only conservative union leadership, and by only allowing it to win gains for labor, it corrupted the entire organized labor movement, encouraging those who worked within the framework of the capitalist order while stifling those who wanted basic social reform. As an example of this conservative union leadership, he cited the case of Warren S. Stone, who—abandoning class consciousness and grandiose social reforms—sold out to the capitalists, asserting:

> . . . leaving all questions of sentiment out of it, boiling it
> all down to the basis of dollar and cents—and that is the
> basis we figure on today largely—the Civic Federation has
> enabled the Board of Locomotive Engineers to make two or
> three of the best settlements it ever made, and in doing so
> it has been the means of making settlements that perhaps
> have brought to our individual members over $300,000. The
> Civic Federation has done that for us, and I cannot speak
> in terms too high for the good work it is doing.

Thus did the Civic Federation oppress and degrade the guileless hosts of labor, and—chloroforming labor into a cheerful acceptance of its sad lot—the cunning capitalists continued to dominate American life, and by the 1920s had consolidated their hold over the nation, while providing for the working class a benevolent and paternalistic industrial serfdom. While Progressive reform helped labor, it primarily served to re-enforce business control over America. This, Jensen tells us, was the basic goal of the N.C.F.

In 1957, Philip Taft issued his history of the *A.F. of L. in the Time of Gompers* and devoted six pages to the National Civic Federation. Relying heavily on Sister Green's study, he added nothing new, and concluded that the majority of responsible labor leaders supported the N.C.F. because it "helped to dilute the influence of the militant anti-union employers." He did not deal with the question of the Civic Federation's effect on the militancy of the A.F.L.[16] A year later, Marc Karson brought out his substantial study of *American Labor Unions and Politics* and devoted considerable attention to the ideological conflicts between the American Federation of Labor and the socialists. Much more critical of Gompers and the A.F.L.'s leadership than was Taft, he did not specifically address himself to labor's relationship with the Civic Federation. Noting the battle between the A.F.L. and the socialists over the question of affiliation with the N.C.F. at the Atlanta convention in 1911, he presented the arguments of both sides without comment and gave the Federation no further attention.[17] Finally, Bernard Mandel's recent biography of Samuel Gompers, while giving only cursory attention to Gompers' relation with the Civic Federation, contends that his joining the organization marked the onset of his "conservative middle age" which became increasingly more conservative as the Progressive era wore on.[18] Certainly Gompers can be faulted on many points: his failure to make any major effort to unionize unskilled workers, his support of Chinese exclusion and immigration restriction, and his acquiescence in "Jim Crow" are some of his more glaring weaknesses. However, the decision to join the N.C.F. was in line with the best traditions of American pragmatism. Labor needed help, the Federation promised to provide it, and the humiliation of rubbing shoulders with the businessmen of the N.C.F. was more than offset by the gains which Gompers might secure for labor through such an association.

Two doctoral dissertations, three master's essays, scattered references in general histories of labor, and brief treatment in isolated works constitute the sum total of the work which has so far been done on the National Civic Federation. Everyone who has thus far written on the Federation has been influenced —whether consciously or not—by the wit, charm, and brilliant sarcasm of the socialist critics of Progressive reform; all have been influenced to view the N.C.F. as a conservative organization by the fascinating and extremely plausible concept of patrician reformism. Not one has grappled with the questions raised and the arguments advanced by the Civic Federation's industrial program.

The National Civic Federation was not radical in the sense that it sought fundamental changes in the political, social, or economic institutions of American society, but this is not to imply that its program was, therefore, conservative. In seeking to subject business to the control of a democratic government, in contending for the right of labor to organize, strike, and bargain collectively with management, the Civic Federation was striving to curb the abuses of which unregulated big business was capable, while preserving the many advantages of large-scale economic production, and was attempting to ease labor's path into the American middle class, facilitating its acquisition of its just share of the proceeds of the modern industrial system. The men of the National Civic Federation were believers in the efficacy and validity of American democratic values, they wanted to perfect social as well as political equality because they believed that America had a providential mission to perform for mankind, and they wanted to help in the accomplishment of that mission. They were faithful to their own propaganda, envisioning an America in which everyone would be a member of the middle class, sharing in the benefits of the modern industrial system. Thus, the program advanced by the

National Civic Federation was in the liberal traditio. American reform in that it sought to broaden the base of middle class, curb the unrestrained power of the big busin. community, and uplift the masses. Certainly, the men wh. championed this program were well-to-do, though not all were patricians, and their reformism was motivated not by fear of a socialist revolution, for they were unusually optimistic in their outlook, but rather because as democrats they wanted to share their advantages with their less fortunate fellow citizens. The religious desire to justify their lives through the performance of good works was a key factor motivating their reform efforts. To totally disregard this aspect of the Federation's program is to write history in accordance with a pre-conceived formula which has little or no relation to the actual historical events which they purport to describe. Everyone who has written on the Civic Federation has fallen prey to the fascination of an historical theory and have twisted the facts to fit a dogma.

Organized labor, as represented in the A.F.L., for its part did not seek a drastic reorganization of American society; it was not class-conscious, and did not subscribe to grandiose schemes for re-making America. The American workingman wanted to become a part of middle class society, to earn enough to live comfortably and to enjoy the many advantages of living in an industrial society. He was unashamedly materialistic, imbibing the values of a materialistic American society; he did not want to live in a pre-fabricated socialist paradise. The American Federation of Labor—in pushing "bread and butter" unionism—was manifesting, not subverting, the will of the laboring man, and to the extent that the Civic Federation assisted the A.F.L. in the realization of its goals, it was acting as labor's friend and ally, not as a brake on its militancy. The materialistic nature of the average workingman, and his total aversion to ideology, has scarcely been taken into account by historians of the American labor movement. For the most part, the American workingman was complacently satisfied with American social institutions, and simply wanted to increase his share of what America had to offer.

If the historical profession's interpretation of the National Civic Federation is as remote from the truth as it appears to be, one begins to suspect that our conception of the entire Progressive movement—which is, after all, built upon an analysis of groups such as the N.C.F.—may perhaps be as far from th as is our view of the Civic Federation.[19] Our conceptions ... he motivations and aspirations of Progressive reform have ...n colored too much by the contemporary issues affecting ...he historian's world. In dealing with recent history, it is all the more easy to fall victim to present-mindedness, and in an effort to explain the world in which he lives, the historian has traced its origins back into the Progressive era, and all too often has been reading the present into the past making the historical record fit his intellectual premises.

Historians who were actively engaged in the struggle for Progressive reforms, or who had their intellectual outlook formed in the Progressive era, accepted the Progressives pretty much at their face value. One of the first scholars to deal with the Progressive period, Frederic Austen Ogg, saw the Progressives as concerned with the fundamental question of whether the interests or the people were to rule America, and concluded that the Progressives, through the instrumentalities of the state and federal government, reconciled the great money power with the great democracy by equitably resolving the conflict between property rights and human rights.[20] Similarly, viewing Progressivism as a continuation of Populism, albeit more sophisticated and refined, historians such as Charles A. Beard, Harold U. Faulkner, and John D. Hicks regarded it as an essentially liberal movement to safeguard democratic freedoms against the overweening power of a business elite.[21] As such it was in the finest traditions of America's democratic heritage.

In the same intellectual vein, though on a different theme, Louis S. Reed's brilliant study of *The Labor Philosophy of Samuel Gompers,* first published in 1930, denied the socialist contention that Gompers' industrial program was conservative. Asserting that Gompers' ultimate goal was an America which fulfilled its promise of social and economic justice for all, and which would be organized on lines approaching the socialist conception of societal organization, Reed pointed out that he was pragmatic enough to realize that while men struggled to achieve this utopia, they must still live in the drab present. ... was Gompers' belief that social justice would be achieved ... ugh an evolutionary rather than revolutionary—process, that ... 's condition would constantly improve, and that while ... and capital had conflicting interests they need not abandon ... enities of civilized society in the advancement of their ... e interests. While Gompers was willing to work within the confines of the capitalist system, and employ the tools of democratic politics to achieve his goals, Reed argued that he was basically anti-capitalist and was working for the economy's transformation into a system closer to the socialist ideal.[22] Reed's study has not been given enough attention by historians who have dealt with labor-capital relations. Gompers was willing to work with anyone who shared some of his goals.

The views of Ogg, Beard, Faulkner, and Hicks prevailed, with only one major dissent, until after World War II, when more sophisticated interpretations of Progressive reform began to make their appearance. In 1932, however, John Chamberlain published a caustic and present-minded dissent from the liberal/democratic interpretation of Progressive reform which he subsequently revised in the 1960s. An anti-New Deal reporter, Chamberlain was a nineteenth century liberal of the New Freedom persuasion who viewed Progressivism, in its initial stages, as a democratic movement designed to curb the power of big business, but which, in the guise of the New Nationalism, was captured by big business and ended up as a proto-fascist movement seeking to impose an industrial serfdom upon America. The New Deal, in Chamberlain's view, was a continuation of the New Nationalism by which big business was tightening its control over the life of America. Progressivism, then, was a failure, for beginning as a liberal movement to safeguard the economic freedoms of the American people, it was prostituted to the service of the big business community.[23] Chamberlain's study—written with the issues of the Great Depression consciously in mind—was weak history, and did little to illumine the ideals and goals of the Progressives.

Though Chamberlain was not himself a socialist, many members of the faith would be willing to accept his interpretation without serious quarrel, And, indeed, the socialist condemnation of Progressive reform has its adherents among professional historians who have written since World War II. Perhaps the best example of this "neo-socialist" school was Daniel Aaron's 1951 study, *Men of Good Hope*. Contending that the Progressive movement took place in the last quarter of the nineteenth century, and was championed by such men as Henry George, Thorstein Veblen, Edward Bellamy, Henry Demarest Lloyd, and Williams Dean Howells, Aaron argued that it sought to safeguard the agrarian ideals of human worth and equality by placing the modern industrial system under public control so that it could serve human needs instead of subverting them. The latter-day Progressives, such as Theodore Roosevelt and Woodrow Wilson, were, in Aaron's conception, pseudo-liberals who employed the rhetoric of Progressive reform while being careful to soothe the fears of men of property. Going through the motions of Progressive reform, they—in actuality—permitted big business to consolidate its control over American life and to further exploit the American people. They were "bogus" liberals who were actually serving the ends of the business community.[24] Hence the socialists were correct in arguing that Progressive reform in the version championed by Roosevelt and Wilson was shallow. Likewise, Ray Ginger's *Age of Excess* argued that the intellectual premises of Progressive reform were dredged up from *"McGuffy's Readers,"* and constituted the politics of "make believe," a conscious attempt to produce "self-delusion" in the American people. The White House, under Roosevelt, he tells us, was the nation's chief "flap-doodle" factory.[25] Quite obviously, neither Aaron's nor Ginger's work explain the motivations and nature of Progressive reform.

The concept of the "status revolution" has been among the most influential and fertile of all the interpretations which have been advanced to explain the Progressive movement, but it has been much overworked. One of the first historians to advance the concept, though Richard Hofstadter coined the term, was George E. Mowry whose *California Progressives* appeared in 1951. According to Mowry's "Progressive profile," the typical Progressive was a young man, generally in his thirties, was a college-educated professional coming from a solid middle class family of old-stock, often Puritan, antecedents. Accustomed to social deference and leadership, these middle class Yankee Protestants quickly discovered that the newly-emergent industrial-capitalist class was usurping the social position they once enjoyed exclusively, and a growing spirit of radicalism among new immigrant, working class groups was an added threat to the social order they were seeking to preserve. Mowry saw the Progressives as basically anti-union and anti-monopoly, though not anti-capitalist, who sought to curb big business in order to maintain middle class control of American life, and who were willing to grant labor only those reforms necessary to forestall the threat of lower class upheaval. Since they were seeking to retain the traditional Yankee-Protestant social order, they were conservative reformers who desired no basic changes in the pattern of American society, and generally had limited appeal to the lower classes.[26]

Re-enforced, and given its classic statement by Richard Hofstadter, the concept of the "status revolution" has formed the central theme for the works of John Morton Blum, Samuel P. Hays, and Arthur S. Link to mention only some of the more prominent names in the historical firmament.[27] However, the concept has been over-used. The idea that Progressive reform was an essentially conservative movement of middle class W.A.S.P.s seeking to restore the socio-economic and political patterns of pre-Civil War America and check the growing power of the new capitalist class and the new ethnic groups was spawned as an outgrowth of the liberal disillusionment which followed in the wake of the New Deal and the rise of the McCarthyite insanity. It sought to explain the deadening complacency of contemporary American life by showing that America had always had a conservative consensus whose main aim was to perpetuate the *status quo*.[28] It was, therefore, more an attempt to explain the contemporary state of American life than to understand the Progressive mind. The fact is that the "Progressive profile" becomes increasingly less accurate the further one moves away from California, and there were many Progressives who were neither anti-labor nor anti-immigrant, but were openly pro-labor and their efforts on its behalf were unselfish and sincerely motivated by a desire to be of service to their fellow men. They just do not fit the mold of the conservative, patrician reformer.[29] Moreover, to the extent that they enabled the laboring masses to achieve middle class status, they were working toward liberal ends. In recent years, though, there have been challenges raised to this useful but overly-used conception of Progressive reform.[30]

On the specific subject of business reform, Jack Blicksilver published an illuminating essay on George Gunton's industrial philosophy in *Business History Review* in 1957. Analyzing Gunton's economic program, Blicksilver showed that he accepted large-scale economic production as irrevocable, and believed that it was beneficial because it would result in a higher standard of living for the general society. However, in order for this new economic system to prosper, the consumers—if they were to buy the products of industry—must have a high purchasing power. And, to obtain this high purchasing power, labor must be organized. Hence, labor unions which can strike and bargain collectively with management will promote the interests of the working class, curb the unrestricted power of big business, and—more importantly—by keeping labor prosperous, it will keep industry prosperous. Gunton, Blicksilver tells us, wanted big business and organized labor to form an *entente* and work for the economic advancement of the entire society.Certainly, this in a nutshell was the program of the National Civic Federation. While the program outlined by Gunton was in the ultimate best interest of business, that alone does not make it a conservative course of reform, for the greatest gainers were to have been the masses. Blicksilver implied that many so-called "business" Progressives were, indeed, liberals whose programs had to await the New Deal before being fulfilled. They were, he argued, sincerely trying to promote the interests of all levels of society; and optimism, not fear, altruism, not self-interest, motivated their reform interests.[31]

In line with the view that many business Progressives had a forward-looking view on the issues besetting early twentieth century American society, John A. Garraty found that George W. Perkins welcomed America's new industrial system, confident that it would lead to a better life for all Americans. While feeling that Perkins was paternalistic in his attitude toward labor, Garraty acknowledged that Perkins welcomed labor's organization, and conceded that the workingman had a property right in modern industry. An optimist, Perkins was spurred to champion reform by a strong Puritan ethical heritage.[32]

A year later, John Braeman published a highly perceptive article in *Business History Review* in which he argued that the Progressives were divided into two major groupings which he designated "moderns" and "traditionalists." The "traditionalists" sought to return to a pre-industrial America of small producers, in which the Yankee Protestant middle class dominated the nation's social, economic, and political institutions. Fearing modern industrialism, and labor unionism, they were conservatives compelled by the "status revolution" to seek a return to the tried and true ways of America's past. But, they were not the whole of the Progressive movement.

The "moderns" on the other hand—men like George W. Perkins, Henry L. Stimson, Herbert Croly, Albert J. Beveridge, Theodore Roosevelt, and Seth Low—sought to solve twentieth century problems with the techniques and knowledge of the twentieth, not the nineteenth, century. They accepted the fact of modern industrialism, recognized its many failings, and desired to correct them without losing the many advantages offered by the new industrial system. Genuine Progressives, they believed in the traditional values of American democratic society, and fought for social justice for all segments of the population. They sought to make America a happier, more just, and more prosperous land.[33] Undeniably modernism was as important a factor as traditionalism in the motivation of Progressive reform, and while the "status revolution' may help to explain the inanities of contemporary American life, it is unjust to blame them on the Progressives, who are deserving of a better historical fate.

Treating the business Progressives as a group, Robert H. Wiebe and Gabriel Kolko have produced monographic studies of Progressive economic reform. In *Businessmen and Reform,* Wiebe concluded that business flirtation with Progressivism was brief and half-hearted. Generally, he saw the business reformers of the period as hostile to organized labor, lacking in any real understanding of the needs or aspirations of the working masses, and opposed to any attempts to alter the fundamental institutions of American society. Suspicious of reforms designed to benefit anyone but themselves, they were willing to grant labor only those concessions necessary to keep it pacified. Wiebe concluded that business interest in reform was limited to those innovations which would be of benefit to itself. On the whole, the Progressive movement benefited business more than any other segment of American society, its labor reforms were superficial, and as such, the movement was conservative, designed to help those in power stay there.[34] Continuing in the same stream of thought, Wiebe's recent *Search for Order,* while not breaking sharply with the Mowry-Hofstadter thesis, offers a more sophisticated analysis of Progressive reform. Arguing that the Progressives sought to rationalize and stabilize the American economic and social orders, Wiebe saw them as struggling to understand and control the centralized and complex economic and political institutions arising as an outgrowth of modern industrialism. While seeking to resolve the problems spawned by this new order of things, they wished to retain the fundamental values and conceptions of the older, decentralized and agrarian America. They were, therefore, basically conservative in their orientation.[35]

Gabriel Kolko's *Triumph of Conservatism* is a Marxian analysis turned upside down. Arguing that big business captured control of the Progressive movement, he interpreted the entire sweep of Progressive economic reform as being motivated by the selfish interests of big business and as designed to satisfy its demands.[36] Assuming that all measures favored by businessmen are sinister, Kolko saw Progressivism as a device permitting big business to consolidate its hold over the political life of the American nation. Basically, as a number of his reviewers have pointed out, Kolko's study is a re-statement of the Chamberlain thesis. Clearly, neither Wiebe's nor Kolko's conceptions fit the National Civic Federation.

The concept of the "status revolution" as the motivation for Progressive reform, despite challenges, remains the prevailing orthodoxy in contemporary American historiography. In freeing the historian from the older liberal/democratic view of Progressivism, it served a useful purpose; but, in turn, it has become the new orthodoxy, and to the extent that our conception of the past shapes our future, it is doing us a disservice. The belief in a conservative consensus which has dominated 200 years of American history acts as a brake on social reform, and needlessly so, for American history—especially in the Progressive era—was far more complex than the consensus theory would have us believe. Recent scholars have demonstrated the Progressives genuine concern with liberal social reform. Indeed, liberalism was as strong a motivating force as conservatism in shaping Progressive reform, and it is time that historians took a fresh look at our liberal tradition.

Notes and References

CHAPTER I

1. The early genealogy of the Low family is extracted from William Gilman Low, *A Genealogical Quest and Family Notes* (Privately Printed: 2nd edition, 1928).

2. See Elma Loines, ed., *The China Trade Post-bag of the Seth Low Family of Salem and New York, 1829–1873* (Manchester, Maine: Falmouth Publishing House, 1953), pp. 11ff.

3. Helen Augur, *Tall Ships to Cathay* (Garden City, N.Y.: Doubleday & Co., 1951), p. 56.

4. William Gilman Low, *Some Recollections for His Children and Grandchildren* (Brooklyn, N.Y.: Brooklyn Eagle Press, 2nd edition, 1933), p. 19.

5. Augur, *Tall Ships to Cathay*, pp. 78ff.

6. Abiel Abbot Low to Seth Low, 2 January 1839; in Loines, *China Trade Post-bag.* p. 67.

7. Augur, *Tall Ships to Cathay*, p. 96.

8. Abiel Abbot Low to Harriet Low Hillard, 17 April 1839; in Loines, *China Trade Post-bag*, p. 72.

9. Margaret A. L. Huntington to Josiah O. Low, 26 November 1840; Josiah O. Low Family Letters, 1837–1884, Manuscript Division, New York Public Library, New York, New York.

10. Robert Greenhalgh Albion, *The Rise of New York Port* (New York: Charles Scribner's Sons, 1939), p. 201.

11. Captain Charles P. Low, *Some Recollections* (Boston: George H. Ellis, 1905), p. 84.

12. John Bigelow to A. A. Low, Paris, 6 May 1864; The Seth Low Papers, Spec. Mss. Coll., Special Collections Department: Columbia University Library, Columbia University, New York, New York. (Hereafter cited as Low Papers).

13. A. A. Low, "Address at the Chamber of Commerce" (New York: John W. Amerman, 1866), p. 9.

14. New York Chamber of Commerce, "Entertainment Given to Mr. A. A. Low" (New York: Press of the Chamber of Commerce, 1867), p. 30.

15. Henry R. Stiles, *History of Kings County* (New York: W. W. Munsell, 1884), vol. 1, p. 516.

16. Benjamin R. C. Low, *Seth Low* (New York: G. P. Putnam's, 1925), p. 38.

17. Wm. G. Low, *Some Recollections* p. 52.

18. Seth Low to Harriette Low, 3 July 1862; Low Papers, Spec. Mss. Coll,

19. Seth Low to Harriette Low, 6 October 1863; Low Papers, Spec. Mss. Coll.

20. Seth Low to Harriette Low, 17 May 1863; Low Papers, Spec. Mss. Coll.

21. Seth Low to Harriette Low, 17 October 1863; Low Papers, Spec. Mss. Coll.

22. William M. Sloane, "Seth Low," *Columbia University Quarterly*, 4 (September 1901), p. 3.

23. Oscar S. Straus to Seth Low, 11 August 1916; Low Papers, Speeches: 2.

24. William M. Sloane, "The Life of Seth Low," *American Scenic and Historic Preservation Society, Annual Report*, 22 (1917), p. 708.

25. Sloane, "Seth Low," p. 4.

26. Quoted in Edward Cary, "Seth Low: A Character Sketch," *Review of Reviews*, 16 (July, 1897) p. 34.

27. Seth Low to Harriette Low, 25 April 1869; Low Papers, Spec. Mss. Coll.

28. Seth Low to Harriette Low, 13 April 1869; Low Papers, Spec. Mss. Coll.

29. Sloane, "Life of Seth Low," p. 708.

30. Seth Low to Harriette Low, 28 March 1872; Low Papers, Spec. Mss. Coll.

31. Seth Low to Harriette Low, 23 September 1872; Low Papers, Spec. Mss. Coll.

32. Seth Low to Rev. David H. Greer, 25 November 1910; Low Papers, Spec. Mss. Coll. Carbons.

33. Seth Low to A. A. Low, 30 September 1875; Low Papers, Copybook I.

34. Seth Low to E. H. R. Lyman, 30 December 1878; Low Papers, Copybook I.

35. A. A. Low and Brothers, *Scrapbook of the Far Eastern Trade*, Manuscript Division, New York Public Library, New York, New York. (Hereafter cited as A. A. Low and Brothers, *Scrapbook*).

36. Daniel Van Pelt, ed., *Leslie's History of the Greater New York* (New York: Arkell, 1898), vol. 2, p. 265.

37. Seth Low, *The Problem of Pauperism in the Cities of Brooklyn and New York* (New York: Henry Bessey, 1879), p. 6.

38. National Civic Federation, Minutes, 12 December 1913, p. 4; The National Civic Federation Papers, box 187, Manuscript Division, New York Public Library, New York, New York. (Hereafter cited as N.C.F. Papers).

39. Richard Edwards, *An Historical and Descriptive Review of the City of Brooklyn . . .* (New York: Historical Publishing Co., 1883), p. 65.

40. Low, *Problem of Pauperism*, p. 8.

41. *Ibid.*, p. 9.

42. B. R. C. Low, *Seth Low*, p. 43.

43. *Ibid.*, p. 43.

44. Sloane, "Life of Seth Low," p. 705. " 'Knickerbockers' " in the sense of being one of the City's more prominent families.

CHAPTER II

1. Rush Rhees, "Address in Memory of Seth Low," *Proceedings of the 52nd Convocation of the University of the State of New York, 1916*, p. 34.

2. On the general point see Robert H. Wiebe, *The Search for Order, 1877–1920* (New York: Hill & Wang, 1967), and Seymour J. Mandelbaum, *Boss Tweed's New York* (New York: John Wiley, 1965). The factors making for urban corruption and the remedies proposed by the good government reformers will be more fully explored in chapter four of this book.

3. Seth Low to Harriette Low, 14 October 1880; Low Papers, Spec. Mss. Coll.

4. "Brooklyn Young Republican Club," 16 May 1881; The Brooklyn Young Republican Club Scrapbook, Long Island Historical Society, Brook-

lyn, New York. (Hereafter cited as Brooklyn Young Republican Club Scrapbook).

5. Seth Low to Howard Vernon, 4 January 1909; Low Papers, Spec. Mss. Coll. Carbons.

6. Van Pelt, ed., *Leslie's History of the Greater New York*, vol. 2, p. 273.

7. Harold Coffin Syrett, *The City of Brooklyn, 1865–1898* (New York: Columbia University Press, 1944), p. 90. For an analysis of the charters of 1873 and 1881 see Edward M. Shepard, "The Brooklyn Idea in City Government," *The Forum*, 16 (1893–1894).

8. Syrett, *City of Brooklyn*, p. 107.

9. *New York Times*, 2 October 1881, p. 6.

10. For a spiritely account of Brooklyn's ethnic composition see Ralph Foster Weld, *Brooklyn Is America* (New York: Columbia University Press, 1950).

11. *Brooklyn Eagle Consolidation Number*, 27 January 1898 *(Eagle Library # 22)*, p. 51.

12. *New York Times*, 7 October 1881, p. 2.

13. Syrett, *City of Brooklyn*, p. 103.

14. *Brooklyn Eagle*, 30 August 1881, p. 4.

15. Seth Low to Howard Vernon, 4 January 1909; Low Papers, Spec. Mss. Coll. Carbons.

16. *Brooklyn Eagle*, 10 October 1881, p. 2.

17. *New York Times*, 9 October 1881, p. 2.

18. See "Hon. Ripley Ropes," *Brooklyn Advance*, 6 (April 1882), pp. 41–42.

19. *Brooklyn Eagle*, 13 October 1881, p. 2.

20. *Ibid.*, 16 October 1881, p. 4.

21. *Ibid.*, 15 October 1881, p. 2.

22. *Ibid.*, 16 October 1881, p. 4.

23. *Ibid.*, 18 October 1881, p. 2.

24. Seth Low to Howard Vernon, 4 January 1909; Low Papers, Spec. Mss. Coll. Carbons; *Brooklyn Eagle*, 22 October 1881, p. 2; *New York Times*, 22 October 1881, p. 2.

25. *Brooklyn Eagle*, 22 October 1881, p. 2.

26. *Ibid.*, 23 October 1881, p. 4.

27. *New York Times*, 26 October 1881, p. 2.

28. *Brooklyn Eagle*, 26 October 1881, p. 2.

29. William A. Prendergast, *Oral History Memoir*, Oral History Research Office, Columbia University, New York, New York, pp. 90–91.

30. Quoted in David King Rothstein, "Mayor Seth Low," *Columbia University Quarterly* 32 (December 1940), p. 302.

31. "Men of Brooklyn," 1881; A. A. Low and Brothers, *Scrapbook of the Far Eastern Trade*.

32. Frederick W. Hinrichs, "Seth Low, Mayor of Brooklyn," *Columbia Alumni News*, 8 (20 October 1916), p. 81.

33. Quoted in B. R. C. Low, *Seth Low*, p. 50.

34. *Brooklyn Eagle*, 3 October 1881, p. 2.

35. For recent examinations of Mugwump thought and programs see John G. Sproat, *"The Best Men: "Liberal Reformers in the Gilded Age* (New York: Oxford University Press, 1968), and Geoffrey Blodgett, *The Gentle Reformers: Massachusetts Democrats in the Cleveland Era* (Cambridge, Mass.: Harvard University Press, 1966).

36. McLaughlin did resign, but was quickly restored to the party's leadership after the Kinsella faction was unable to consolidate its hold over the organiaztion.

37. *New York Times,* 2 November 1881, p. 2; and 5 November 1881, p. 5.

38. Mayor of Brooklyn, *Annual Message, 1882* (Brooklyn, 1882), pp. 19–20.

39. Seth Low to the Editor of the *Lafayette Record,* 9 March 1909; Low Papers, Spec. Mss. Coll. Carbons.

40. It would be difficult, if not impossible, to attempt to improve on Harold C. Syrett's two chapters on the administration of Mayor Seth Low, and no effort will be made to do so here. The author will disucss the highlights of Low's administration of Brooklyn's government for the light it throws on the goals, aspirations, and principles of the municipal reformers of the 1880's. By briefly treating Low's administrative accomplishments, the strengths and shortcomings of the "goo-goos" will become apparent. Readers wishing more detailed treatment should consult Syrett's *City of Brooklyn.*

41. Seth Low, "Municipal Home Rule," 6 October 1882, *Addresses and Papers on Municipal Government* (Pamphlet: Place, Publisher, Year not listed), p. 1.

42. George H. Mason to Seth Low, 17 January 1884; Low Papers, box 160.

43. H. A. Barnum to Seth Low, 26 January 1885; Low Papers, box 160.

44. Low, "Municipal Home Rule," p. 7.

45. Extracted from Mayor of Brooklyn, *Annual Message, 1882–1886* (Brooklyn, 1882–1886).

46. Seth Low, "Brooklyn First, Last and All the Time," Address at Masonic Temple, 16 October 1883. The financial aspects of Low's administration are also treated in Demas Barnes, "Municipal Government," *The Brooklyn Magazine,* 2 (June 1885).

47. John A. Heffernan, *Oral History Memoir,* Oral History Research Office, Columbia University, New York, New York, p. 3.

48. In the Low Papers is a file box marked "Brooklyn Board of Education" which contains newspaper clippings, letters, and petitions bearing on the integration of the city's school system.

49. Mayor of Brooklyn, *Annual Message, 1884 & 1885.* See also the reports filed in the *Annual Messages* by the Board of Education.

50. "Our Fire Department," *Brooklyn Advance,* (8 April 1883) details Low's reforms in a typical city department.

51. Frederic W. Hinrichs, "Hon. Seth Low," *Brooklyn Advance,* (9 November 1883), p. 79.

52. B. R. C. Low, *Seth Low,* p. 50.

53. *New York Times,* 19 October 1883, p. 4.

54. Seth Low to William L. Strong, 15 November 1894; Low Papers, Spec. Mss. Coll. Carbons.

55. Shepard, "The Brooklyn Idea in City Government," p. 43.

56. Seth Low to James Larned, 9 September 1882; Low Papers, box 161.

57. Quoted in Rothstein, "Mayor Seth Low," p. 305.

58. Low's excise policy is treated in *Collier's Weekly,* 28 (25 January 1902), p. 3.

59. Syrett, *City of Brooklyn,* p. 134.

60. *New York Times,* 2 September 1883, p. 2.

61. Citizens' Union of New York, *Home Rule in Cities* (New York: Citizens' Union, 1897), p. 8.

62. *New York Times,* 5 November 1883, p. 4.

63. *Brooklyn Advance,* 9 (August 1883), p. 293.

64. *Brooklyn Eagle,* 31 October 1883, p. 4.

65. *Ibid.,* 17 October 1883, p. 2.

66. *Ibid.,* 17 October 1883, p. 2; 22 October 1883, p. 2; and 31 October 1883, p. 4

67. *Ibid.,* 9 October 1883, p. 2; and 17 October 1883, p. 2.

68. See campaign flyers in Brooklyn Young Republican Club Scrapbook.

69. Hinrichs, "Seth Low, Mayor of Brooklyn," p. 81.

70. Raymond E. Dodge to Seth Low, 24 November 1884; Low Papers, box 158.

71. B. R. C. Low, *Seth Low,* pp. 53–54.

72. *Brooklyn Eagle,* 24 October 1885, p. 4.

73. James Bryce to Seth Low, 9 January 1892; Low Papers, Spec. Mss. Coll.

74. Henry W. B. Howard, *The Eagle and Brooklyn* (Brooklyn, N.Y.: Brooklyn Eagle Press, 1893), vol. 1, p. 389.

75. Shepard, "The Brooklyn Idea in City Government," p. 43.

76. Melvin G. Holli, *Reform in Detroit: Hazen S. Pingree and Urban Politics* (New York: Oxford University Press, 1969), pp. 162ff.; and Blodgett, *Gentle Reformers,* p. 104.

CHAPTER III

1. Harry Thurston Peck, "Twelve Years of the University," *Columbia University Quarterly,* 4 (1901), p. 16.

2. John William Burgess, "Reminiscences of Columbia University in the Last Quarter of the Last Century," *Columbia Univ. Quarterly,* 15 (1913), p. 324.

3. Frederick Paul Keppel, *Columbia* (New York: Oxford University Press, 1914), p. 29.

4. Seth Low to Gerard Beckman, 11 November 1881; Low Papers, Copybook I.

5. Background information is extracted from Brander Matthews, *et.al., A History of Columbia University, 1754–1901* (New York: Columbia University Press, 1904); Keppel, *Columbia;* and, Horace Coon, *Columbia: Colosus on the Hudson* (New York: E. P. Dutton, 1947). For a good account of the changes taking place in American higher education in the period from 1870 to 1914 see Walter P. Metzger, "The Age of the University," in Richard Hofstadter and Walter P. Metzger, *The Development of Academic Freedom in the United States* (New York: Columbia University Press, 1955); and, Laurence R. Veysey, *The Emergence of the American University* (Chicago: University of Chicago Press, 1965). Unfortunately, there is no good modern history of Columbia University.

6. Burgess, "Reminiscences of Columbia University . . . ," p. 326.

7. *Ibid.,* p. 326..

8. Roger Howson, *His Excellency a Trustee* (New York: Columbia University Bookstore 1945), p. 19.

9. Seth Low to A. A. Low, 7 October 1889; Low Papers, v. A.

10. William H. H. Beebe to Seth Low, 8 October 1889; Low Papers, v. A.

11. Seth Low to John William Burgess, 9 October 1889; The John William Burgess Papers, Spec. Mss. Coll., Special Collections Department: Columbia University Library, Columbia University, New York. (Hereafter cited as Burgess Papers).

12. Richard T. Ely to Seth Low, 11 October 1889; Low Papers, v. A.

13. Andrew D. White to Seth Low, 17 October 1889; Low Papers, v. A.

14. C. K. Adams to Seth Low, 21 November 1889; Low Papers, v. A.

15. Burgess, "Reminiscences of Columbia University . . . ," "pp. 326–327. Burgess's summary of Low's qualifications for Columbia's presidency has been substantiated by recent scholarship. See especially Veysey, *The Emergence of the American University*, p. 367n.

16. John B. Pine, "King's College: now Columbia University, 1754–1897," *Half-Moon Series*, 1 (1897), p. 51.

17. For a detailed discussion of the American university in the period after 1870 see Veysey, *The Emergence of the American University*.

18. Seth Low to Erastus Wiman, 28 March 1890; Low Papers, Spec. Mss. Coll.

19. Peck, "Twelve Years of the University," pp. 16–17.

20. Munroe Smith, "Seth Low, President of Columbia University," *Columbia Alumni News*, 8 (20 October 1916), p. 71.

21. Coon, *Columbia*, p. 91.

22. Seth Low to the Committee on Education, 31 January 1911; Low Papers, Spec. Mss. Coll. Carbons.

23. Columbia University, *Dedication of the New Site Morningside Heights* (New York: Columbia University Press, 1896), pp. 52–53.

24. Excerpted from Cary, "Seth Low: A Character Sketch," pp. 40–41.

25. Booker T. Washington to Seth Low, 15 November 1913; Low Papers, box 67.

26. Coon, *Columbia*, pp. 91–92.

27. The library cost $1,175,639.32, and Low paid the entire cost over a 10-year period. Moreover, from 1869–1901, he contributed an additional $150,000 to Columbia making for a grand total of $1,325,639.32 in gifts. See Seth Low to Melvil Dewey, 13 February 1903; Low Papers, Spec. Mss. Coll.

28. Frank Diehl Fackenthal, *Oral History Memoir*, Oral History Research Office, Columbia University, New York, New York, pp. 31–32.

29. John William Burgess to Seth Low, 20 July 1912; Low Papers, Spec. Mss. Coll.

30. Regent Byrne, *Proceedings of the 52nd Convocation of the University of the State of New York, 1916*, p. 32.

CHAPTER IV

1. *The Intellectual Versus the City: from Thomas Jefferson to Frank Lloyd Wright* (Cambridge, Mass.: Harvard University Press, 1962), p. 1.

2. A good account of the anti-urban bias can be found in Morton and Lucia White, *The Intellectual versus the City*.

3. Historians have totally misunderstood Low's ideas on municipal government and insist upon labeling him as anti-immigrant. To cite one example of many, John A. Garraty, *The New Commonwealth, 1877–1890* (New York: Harper & Row, 1968) in a footnote on p. 217 declares, "Low . . . also displayed strong prejudices against immigrants." The source for this statement is Low's article in Bryce's *American Commonwealth* which, as we shall show, was in no way anti-immigrant, but which simply asserted that large numbers of unassimilated immigrants made more complicated the task of reforming city governments.

4. Seth Low, "An American View of Municipal Government in the Unit-

ed States," in James Bryce, *The American Commonwealth* (London: Macmillan, 1888), vol. 2, pp. 297–298.

5. Seth Low, "The Problem of Municipal Government in the United States," Address, Cornell University, 16 March 1887, p. 11.

6. Seth Low, "The Problem of City Government," Notes supplementary to the *Johns Hopkins University Studies in Historical and Political Science,* 4, 1889, p. 4.

7. Seth Low, "Municipal Government," Address, Philadelphia Committee of Fifty, 27 January 1892, pp. 12–13.

8. Low, "Municipal Government," p. 11.

9. Seth Low, "Address, American Institute of Civics," undated; Low Papers, Speeches: 1.

10. Seth Low, "Obstacles to Good City Government," *The Forum,* 5 (1888), p. 261.

11. Seth Low, "The Problem of City Government in the United States," *The Outlook,* 53 (4 April 1896), p. 624.

12. Low, "American Institute of Civics;" Low Papers, Speeches: 1.

13. Low, "An American View of Municipal Government in the United States," pp. 309–310.

14. Seth Low, "The Government of Cities in the United States," *The Century Magazine,* 42 (September 1891), p. 730.

15. *Ibid.,* pp. 730–731.

16. Low, "The Problem of City Government," p. 6.

17. Low, "An American View of Municipal Government in the United States," 304–306.

18. *Ibid.,* p. 306.

19. *Ibid.,* p. 306.

20. Low, "Obstacles to Good City Government," p. 262ff.

21. Seth Low, "Civil Service Reform," *The Brooklyn Advance,* 6 (May 1882), p. 90.

22. Seth Low, "Some Questions of the Day," *Harper's Magazine,* 91 (June 1895), p. 143.

23. Low, "The Government of Cities in the United States," p. 734.

24. Seth Low, "Propositions submitted to the Committee on Cities of the Constitutional Convention," 1894 (Pamphlet).

25. In 1915, Seth Low, receiving more votes than any other candidate on the ballot, was elected as a delegate-at-large to the New York State Constitutional Convention, and was appointed Chairman of the Committee on Cities. He brought forth a home rule provision which granted municipalities autonomy in all matters save the granting of franchises and the contraction of debt. The provision, incorporated into the Constitution, displeased those who wanted the cities to have financial as well as political independence from the State. Separate elections and sweeping civil service codes were also provided. For reasons which are many and complex, the voters rejected the Constitution and nothing came of Low's labors.

26. Low, "An American View of Municipal Government in the United States," pp. 298ff.

27. Seth Low, "New York in 1850 and in 1890: A Political Study" (New York: New York Historical Society, 1892), p. 32 (Pamphlet).

28. Low, "An American View of Municipal Government in the United States," pp. 316–317.

29. Low, "Municipal Government," p. 20.

30. Richard Watson Gilder to J. W. Harper, 26 April 1894; Low Papers, Spec. Mss. Coll.

31. J. W. Harper to Richard Watson Gilder, 4 May 1894; Low Papers, Spec. Mss. Coll.

32. Nicholas Murray Butler, *Across the Busy Years: Recollections and Reflections* (New York: Charles Scribner's Sons, 1939), vol. 1, pp. 157–158.

33. Edmond Kelly to Seth Low, 17 May 1894; Low Papers, Spec. Mss. Coll.

34. Charles Stewart Smith to Morgan Dix, 26 July 1894; Low Papers, Spec. Mss. Coll.

35. A. S. Frissel to Seth Low, 27 July 1894; Low Papers, Spec. Mss. Coll.

36. Seth Low to John William Burgess, 2 October 1894; Low Papers, Spec. Mss. Coll. Carbons.

37. Alfred G. Compton to Seth Low, 2 November 1894; Low Papers, Spec. Mss. Coll.

38. Seth Low to Washington Gladden, 12 November 1894; Low Papers, Spec. Mss. Coll. Carbons.

39. Seth Low to William L. Strong, 2 April 1896; Low Papers, Spec. Mss. Coll. Carbons.

40. *The Nursery* (April 1897), p. 2; in The Citizens' Union Papers, W-4, Special Collections Department: Columbia University Library, Columbia University, New York, New York. (Hereafter cited as Citizens' Union Papers).

41. "The Charter for the Greater New York: Supplementary Report by Commissioners Seth Low and W. L. Strong," *Brooklyn Eagle Library*, 12 (February 1897), pp. 166–167.

42. Seth Low to the *New York Evening Post,* undated; Low Papers, box 140. Letter appeared in the issue for 4 February 1897.

43. "The Charter for the Greater New York: Supplementary Report...," p. 166.

44. *The Nursery* (April 1897), p. 2; Citizens' Union Papers, W-4.

45. *New York Times,* 5 February 1897, p. 6.

46. Seth Low to Mrs. F. P. Kinnicut, 23 March 1897; Low Papers, Spec. Mss. Coll. Carbons.

47. Seth Low to Frank S. Black, 17 April 1897; Low Papers, box 142.

48. Seth Low to Charles Stewart Smith, 8 April 1897; Low Papers, box 142.

49. *New York Times,* 11 January 1900, p. 1.

50. Seth Low to George W. Davison, 11 June 1900; Low Papers, Spec. Mss. Coll. Carbons.

CHAPTER V

1. E. L. Godkin, "Business Administration," *The Nation,* 61 24 October 1895), p. 287.

2. The committee consisted of James B. Reynolds, Jacob H. Schiff, Gustav H. Schwab, George M. Cassatt, and Austin G. Fox (Elihu Root and James Carter were *ex-officio* members). The early history of the Citizens' Union is summarized by Walter Tallmadge Arndt, "A Quarter Century of Service," *The Searchlight,* 12 (14 December 1922), pp. 3–15.

3. *New York Times,* 24 February 1897, p. 12. A check of the *City Directory* revealed that of the 165 founders of the Citizens' Union, 40 were lawyers, 28 businessmen, 24 merchants, 20 professional men, 14 bankers,

11 labor union leaders, 6 manufacturers, 2 were classified as workingmen, and 20 were not classified by occupation.

4. *New York Times,* 24 February 1897, p. 12.

5. *New York Times,* 25 February 1897, p. 6.

6. John Jay Chapman, *Practical Agitation* (New York: Charles Scribner's sons, 1900) , p. 17.

7. *New York Times,* 26 February 1897, p. 5.

8. *New York Sun,* 22 March 1897, p. 6.

9. *New York Times,* 16 February 1897, p. 3.

10. *The Nursery* (April 1897) ; in Citizens' Union Papers, W-4.

11. *New York World,* 27 May 1897, p. 6.

12. Seth Low to Mrs. F. P. Kinnicut, 23 March 1897; Low Papers, Spec. Mss. Coll. Carbons.

13. *New York Times,* 13 April 1897, p. 14.

14. *Ibid.,* 16 March 1897, p. 2.

15. *Ibid.,* 7 May 1897, p. 6.

16. *Ibid.,* 16 March 1897, p. 2.

17. Jacob H. Schiff to Seth Low, 25 May 1897; Low Papers, box 47.

18. Richard Watson Gilder to Seth Low, 27 May 1897; Low Papers, box 47.

19. Albert Shaw to Seth Low, 2 June 1897; Low Papers, box 47.

20. Seth Low to R. Fulton Cutting, *et. al.,* 7 June 1897; Low Papers, box 47.

21. *New York News,* 16 June 1897; clipping in Citizens' Union Papers, W-12.

22. Seth Low to Abram S. Hewitt, 12 June 1897; Low Papers, box 47.

23. Thomas Collier Platt, *The Autobiography of Thomas Collier Platt* (Ed. by Louis J. Lang) (New York: B. W. Dodge, 1910) , p. 358.

24. *New York Times,* 14 June 1897, p. 1.

25. *Ibid.,* 9 May 1897, p. 3; 12 May 1897, p. 7; 20 May 1897, p. 2, & 1 June 1897, p. 3.

26. *Ibid.,* 12 June 1897, p. 3.

27. *Ibid.,* 9 June 1897, p. 1.

28. *Ibid.,* 12 May 1897, p. 7.

29. *Ibid.,* 23 May 1897, p. 1. & 3 June 1897, p. 6.

30. "Greater New York and the Citizens' Union," *The Outlook,* 56 (15 May 1897) , pp. 153–154. Statement made on May 8th.

31. *New York Times,* 9 May 1897, p. 3.

32. *Ibid.,* 16 June 1897, p. 1.

33. *Ibid.,* 18 June 1897, p. 1 & 19 June 1897, p. 12.

34. Theodore Roosevelt to Seth Low, 23 June 1897; Low Papers, Spec. Mss. Coll.

35. Theodore Roosevelt to Seth Low, 29 June 1897; Low Papers, Spec. Mss. Coll.

36. *New York Times,* 27 June 1897, p. 1; 30 June 1897, p. 2; 1 July 1897, p. 1, & 18 July 1897, p. 20.

37. Seth Low to Nicholas Murray Butler, 29 July 1897; The Nicholas Murray Butler Papers, Spec. Mss. Coll., Special Collections Department: Columbia University Library, Columbia University, New York, New York. (Hereafter cited as Butler Papers) .

38. *New York Times,* 25 July 1897, p. 1.

39. Platt, *Autobiography,* pp. 262–263.

40. James B. Reynolds to Lemuel E. Quigg, undated; in Arndt, "A Quarter Century of Service," p. 9.

41. *New York Times,* 18 August 1897, p. 2.

42. Seth Low to James McKeen, 10 July 1897; Low Papers, box 49.

43. Seth Low to Charles Stewart Smith, 10 July 1897; Low Papers, box 49.

44. *New York Times,* 31 August 1897, p. 2.

45. *New York Tribune,* 8 September 1897, p. 2.

46. Seth Low to James McKeen, 2 August 1897; Low Papers, box 49.

47. Richard Watson Gilder to Seth Low, 18 August 1897; Low Papers, box 47.

48. *New York Times,* 24 August 1897, p. 1, and *New York Sun,* 25 August 1897, p. 1.

49. Seth Low to Ellen L. Mills, 24 August 1897; Low Papers, Spec. Mss. Coll. Carbons.

50. *New York Sun,* 29 August 1897, p. 6. The *Tribune's* remark was made when Low resigned from the Republican party in protest against its tariff policy.

51. *New York Tribune,* 2 September 1897, p. 1, & 1 September 1897, p. 1.

52. *Ibid.,* 2 September 1897, p. 6, & 3 September 1897, p. 6.

53. Seth Low to William H. H. Beebe, 2 September 1897; Low Papers, box 47.

54. Seth Low to Richard Watson Gilder, 8 September 1897; Low Papers, box 47.

55. Theodore Roosevelt to Seth Low, 11 September 1897; Low Papers, Spec. Mss. Coll.

56. Theodore Roosevelt to Seth Low, 4 September 1897; Low Papers, Spec. Mss. Coll.

57. *New York Tribune,* 13 September 1897, p. 1.

58. Seth Low to Joseph Larocque, *et. al.,* 13 September 1897; in Citizens' Union, *Campaign Book of the Citizens' Union, 1897* (New York: Citizens' Union, 1897) , p. 115.

59. James Bryce, "The Mayoralty Election in New York," *Contemporary Review,* 72 (November 1897) , p. 757.

60. Platt, *Autobiography,* pp. 359–360.

61. *New York World,* 27 October 1897, p. 6, & 6 October 1897, p. 6. See also Gustavus Myers, *History of Tammany Hall* (New York: Boni & Liveright, 1917) , pp. 267–283.

62. "A National Issue," *The Outlook,* 57 (23 October 1897) , p. 461.

63. *Ibid., The Outlook,* 57 (23 October 1897), p. 463.

64. *New York Sun,* 6 September 1897, p. 6.

65. *New York Tribune,* 8 October 1897, p. 6.

66. *New York Sun,* 11 October 1897, p. 6.

67. *Ibid.,* 21 October 1897, p. 6.

68. *Ibid.,* 25 October 1897, p. 6.

69. *New York Times,* 12 October 1897, p. 2.

70. "The Citizen: His Rights and Duties;" Citizens' Union Papers, w-23.

71. "Campaign Card;" Citizens' Union Papers, W-22.

72. Richard Watson Gilder, "The Real Question at Issue in the Municipal Campaign" (New York: Citizens' Union, 1897) , p. 15.

73. "Workingmen as Citizens" (New York: Citizens" Union, 1897), p. 7.

74. "Workingmen as Citizens," p. 2.
75. Citizens' Union, *Campaign Book*, pp. 3–4.
76. *New York Sun*, 16 August 1897, p. 6.
77. *New York World*, 3 September 1897, p. 6.
78. *New York Times*, 10 September 1897, p. 2.
79. Unsigned letter to Seth Low, 20 August 1897; Low Papers, box 47.
80. A. R. Conkling to Seth Low, 21 September 1897; Low Papers, box 48.
81. *New York Times*, 31 August 1897, p. 4.
82. *New York World*, 1 November 1897, p. 9.
83. *Ibid.*, 21 September 1897, p. 1.
84. *Ibid.*, 19 September 1897, p. 5.
85. *New York Sun*, 10 October 1897, p. 6.
86. Chapman, *Practical Agitation*, p. 6.
87. *New York World*, 26 October 1897, p. 3, & 28 October 1897, p. 1.
88. *New York Times*, 27 October 1897, p. 2.
89. *New York World*, 30 October 1897, p. 3.
90. *New York Tribune*, 30 October 1897, p. 2.
91. Walter Hines Page to Seth Low, 3 November 1897; Low Papers, box 51.
92. Richard W. G. Welling, *As the Twig Is Bent* (New York: G. P. Putnam's, 1942), p. 75.
93. Theodore Roosevelt to Seth Low, 13 September 1897; Low Papers, Spec. Mss. Coll.
94. Seth Low to R. Fulton Cutting, 3 November 1897; Low Papers, box 50.
95. James Bryce to Seth Low, 9 November 1897; Low Papers, Spec. Mss. Coll.
96. Seth Low to A. T. Mahan, 13 November 1897; Low Papers, box 51.
97. *Tammany Times*, 9 (3 November 1897) , p. 3.

CHAPTER VI

1. *New York World*, 30 October 1901, p. 4.
2. *New York Vigilant*, 11 December 1900, p. 4.
3. *The Nation*, 73 (5 September 1901) , p. 181.
4. Carl Schurz, "The Task of the Citizens' Union," *Harper's Weekly*, 41 (11 December 1897) , p. 1215.
5. Talcott Williams, "Tammany Hall," *Half-Moon Series*, 2 (February 1898) , pp. 55ff.
6. Arndt, "A Quarter Century of Service," p. 10.
7. John Jay Chapman, "Is a Third Party Necessary in Municipal Reform Work," *Municipal Affairs*, 4 (1900) , p. 330.
8. *Ibid.*, pp. 329–330.
9. John W. Keller, "Municipal Reformers in Party Politics," *Municipal Affairs*, 4 (1900) , p. 343.
10. *Ibid.*, p. 343.
11. A. S. Haight, "Independent Parties," *Municipal Affairs*, 4 (1900) , p. 339.
12. Seth Low to Arthur von Brissen, 30 March 1898; Low Papers, Spec. Mss. Coll. Carbons.
13. Seth Low to Arthur von Brissen, 18 April 1898; Low Papers, Spec. Mss. Coll. Carbons.

14. R. Fulton Cutting, "Objects, Aims and Scope of the Greatest Organization Pledged to Civic Reform in America," in Milo T. Bogard, ed., *The Redemption of New York* (New York: P. F. McBreen, 1902), pp. 49–56.

15. *Ibid.*, p. 56.

16. *Ibid.*, p. 56.

17. City Committee Minutes, 27 June 1898, p. 7; Citizens' Union Papers, K-1.

18. R. Fulton Cutting to John B. Pine, 10 August 1898; Citizens' Union Papers, H-1.

19. City Committee Minutes, 27 March 1899, pp. 1–2; Citizens' Union Papers, K-1.

20. City Committee Minutes, 10 September 1900, pp. 1–2; Citizens' Union Papers, K-1.

21. Cited in Bogard, *The Redemption of New York*, p. 25.

22. Quoted in Platt, *Autobiography*, p. 237.

23. Harold Coffin Syrett, ed., *The Gentleman and the Tiger: The Autobiography of George B. McClellan, Jr.* (Philadelphia: J. B. Lippincott, 1956), p. 158. For a catalog of Croker's corruption see M. R. Werner, *Tammany Hall* (Garden City, N.Y.: Doubleday, Doran & Co., 1928), pp. 303–481, and Myers, *History of Tammany Hall*, pp. 284–289.

24. Homer Folks, *Oral History Memoir*, Oral History Research Office, Columbia University, New York, New York, p. 20.

25. *The City for the People! Campaign Book of the Citizens' Union, 1901* (New York: Citizens' Union, 1901), p. 27. Francis Vinton Greene, Low's Police Commissioner, confirmed in 1903, that Tammany's 1900 take from gambling operations netted $3,095,000. See Francis Vinton Greene, *The Police Department of the City of New York* (New York: City Club, 1903), p. 369.

26. Documentation can be found in any issue of the *New York Vigilant* published by the Society for the Prevention of Crime from December 1900 through October 1901.

27. Lincoln Steffens, *The Autobiography of Lincoln Steffens* (New York: Harcourt, Brace & Co., 1931), p. 245.

28. Bishop Henry C. Potter to Mayor Robert A. Van Wyck, 15 November 1900; in *The City for the People!*, p. 37.

29. Laurence A. Tanzer, *Oral History Memoir*, Oral History Research Office, Columbia University, New York, New York, pp. 14–15.

30. *The City for the People!*, p. 21.

31. *Ibid.*, p. 94.

32. The Mazet Committee's report was summarized in the *New York Times*, 11 January 1900, p. 1, & 15 January 1900, p. 2.

33. *The City for the People!*, p. 87.

34. *Ibid.*, p. 70.

35. *Ibid.*, p. 11.

36. Seth Low to R. R. Bowker, 12 November 1900; Low Papers, box 14.

37. Good accounts of the mechanisms of Tammany's operations can be found in Alexander B. Callow, Jr., *The Tweel Ring* (New York: Oxford University Press, 1966), and in the first chapter of Charles Garrett, *The LaGuardia Years: Machine and Reform Politics in New York City* (New Brunswick, N.J.: Rutgers University Press, 1961). Unfortunately, a good scholarly account of Tammany politics in the period from 1871 to 1914

has yet to be published, and because of the paucity of primary materials probably never will be.

38. *New York Vigilant,* 11 December 1900, p. 4.

39. *World's Work,* 3 (November 1901), p. 1361.

40. Theodore Roosevelt to Seth Low, 9 November 1900; Low Papers, Spec. Mss. Coll.

41. Seth Low to Jacob H. Schiff, 20 November 1900; Low Papers, Spec. Mss. Coll. Carbons.

42. Seth Low to James Bryce, 7 December 1900; Low Papers, Spec. Mss. Coll. Carbons.

43. James Bryce to Seth Low, 20 December 1900; Low Papers, Spec. Mss. Coll.

44. *New York Times,* 4 February 1901, p. 3.

45. *Ibid.,* 28 January 1901, p. 12.

46. *Ibid.,* 22 February 1901, p. 1.

47. "Platform of the Citizens' Union, 1901;" in The E.P. Wheeler Papers, box 4, Manuscript Division, New York Public Library, New York, New York. (Hereafter cited as Wheeler Papers).

48. *New York Times,* 26 April 1901, p. 1, & 27 April 1901, p. 8.

49. John DeWitt Warner, "Municipal Betterment in the New York City Elections," *Municipal Affairs,* 5 (1901), p. 627.

50. Allen F. Davis, *Spearheads for Reform: The Social Settlements and the Progressive Movement, 1890–1914* (New York: Oxford University Press, 1967) reports that the East Side social workers actively and enthusiastically campaigned for Low in his three Mayoral races, pp. 180–187.

51. R. Fulton Cutting, "City Government and the People," *Municipal Affairs,* 5 (1901), p. 883.

52. *New York Vigilant,* 29 June 1901, p. 4.

53. *New York Times,* 5 May 1901, p. 8. The others were: A. J. Boulton, J. Hampton Dougherty, John E. Eastus, M. J. Flaherty, Wallace Macfarlane, Ludwig Nissen, J. Van Vechten Olcott, Gustav M. Schwab, Isaac N. Seligman, Samuel Seabury, and E. P. Wheeler.

54. Committee of 100, Minutes, 14 May 1901; Citizens' Union Papers, H-1.

55. *New York Times,* 17 May 1901, p. 3.

56. Harold F. Gosnell, *Boss Platt and His New York Machine* (Chicago: University of Chicago Press, 1924), p. 294.

57. DeAlva Stanwood Alexander, *Four Famous New Yorkers: The Political Careers of Cleveland, Platt, Hill and Roosevelt* (New York: Henry Holt, 1923), declared on p. 361 that the Citizens' Union was prepared to nominate Edward Morse Shepard, the well-known reform Democrat, for mayor in 1901. This is incorrect. Everett P. Wheeler, a Democrat and a member of the Union's Committee of 12, did sound Shepard out on the possibility of his being the anti-Tammany nominee in the summer of 1901. But Shepard, an ardent anti-imperialist, declared that he did not wish to weaken the national Democratic party, and flatly refused to entertain the idea of a non-partisan nomination, feeling that Tammany could be reformed from within. After Wheeler's visit, Shepard's name never came up in meetings of the Committee of 12. See E. P. Wheeler, *Sixty Years of American Life* (New York: E. P. Dutton, 1917), p. 387.

58. *New York Times,* 25 May 1901, p. 2.

59. Committee of 12, vote of 26 July 1901; Citizens' Union Papers, H-1.

Others listed as acceptable were Charles W. Dayton, George L. Rives, F. Norton Goddard, and Henry E. Tremaine.

60. *New York Times,* 12 June 1901, p. 3.

61. *Ibid.,* 5 August 1901, p. 2.

62. *Ibid.,* 9 August 1901, p. 7.

63. *Ibid.,* 10 August 1901, p. 1, & 13 August 1901, p. 6.

64. Lemuel E. Quigg to Seth Low, 13 August 1901; Low Papers, Spec. Mss. Coll.

65. *New York Telegram,* 6 August 1901, p. 4.

66. *New York Times,* 14 August 1901, p. 2, & 17 August 1901, p. 1.

67. *New York Telegram,* 23 August 1901, p. 1.

68. Lemuel E. Quigg to Seth Low, 27 August 1901; Low Papers, Spec. Mss. Coll.

69. *New York Times,* 28 August 1901, p. 7.

70. *Ibid.,* 23 August 1901, p. 8, & 26 August 1901, p. 1.

71. *New York World,* 30 August 1901, pp. 1–2.

72. *Ibid.,* 27 August 1901, p. 1.

73. *New York Telegram,* 28 August 1901, p. 9 & *New York World,* 29 August 1901, p. 1.

74. Committee of 100, vote of 29 August 1901; Citizens' Union Papers, H-1. George Foster Peaboy received 14 votes as did Charles King, Alexander Orr got 11, R. Fulton Cutting 9, Charles Schieren 8, Wheeler Peckham 6, John DeWitt Warner 5, and F. Norton Goddard 4.

75. Committee of 12, vote of 29 August 1901; Citizens' Union Papers, H-1.

76. *New York Telegram,* 31 August 1901, p. 4, & *New York Times,* 5 September 1901, p. 1.

77. *The Journal of Commerce and Commerical Bulletin,* 4 September 1901, p. 4.

78. *New York World,* 2 September 1901, p. 1.

79. Committee of 100, vote of 4 September 1901; Citizens' Union Papers, H-1.

80. *New York Times,* 6 September 1901, p. 2.

81. *New York World,* 6 September 1901, pp. 2 & 6.

82. John P. Peters to E. P. Wheeler, 11 September 1901; *Shepard-Low Campaign, Fall of 1901,* scrapbook compiled by E. P. Wheeler, Local History Room, New York Public Library, New York, New York. (Hereafter cited as *Shepard-Low Campaign*).

83. *New York Times,* 11 September 1901, p. 1, & 12 September 1901, p. 14.

84. *Ibid.,* 13 September 1901, p. 3.

85. City Committee Minutes, 17 September 1901; Citizens' Union Papers, H-1.

86. *New York Vigilant,* 12 September 1901, p. 4.

87. Nicholas Murray Butler to E. P. Wheeler, 12 September 1901; *Shepard-Low Campaign.*

88. George McAneny, *Oral History Memoir,* Oral History Research Office, Columbia University, New York, New York, p. 32.

89. Syrett, ed., *The Gentleman and the Tiger,* p. 173.

90. *New York World,* 17 September 1901, p. 16.

91. R. Fulton Cutting to Willis L. Ogden, 16 September 1901; Citizens' Union Papers, H-1.

92. *New York World,* 18 September 1901, p. 16.

93. Other groups represented in, or observing, the conference were the Brooklyn Citizens' League, the Brooklyn Municipal League, the City Club, the City Democracy, the German-American Municipal League of Brooklyn, the German-American Municipal League of Manhattan, the German-American Municipal Reform League, the German-American Republican County Committee of New York, the Hungarian-American League, the Independent Democracy, the Italian-American League, the Jeffersonian Democracy, and the New York Municipal League.

94. *New York World,* 19 September 1901, p. 1.

95. Platt, *Autobiography,* p. 411.

96. E. P. Wheeler, letter of 13 October 1901; *Shepard-Low Campaign.*

97. *Tammany Times,* 17 (30 September 1901), p. 11. DeAlva Stanwood Alexander's statement that the second ballot was unanimous is incorrect. Ridder refused to change his vote. Likewise, his statement that "No element had previously advocated him [Low] . . . ," is also erroneous. He was one of the four candidates declared to be acceptable to the Citizens' Union, and the favorite of the Republicans for some weeks before the conference convened. *Four Famous New Yorkers,* pp. 362–363.

98. E. M. Shepard to E. P. Wheeler, 17 February 1902; Wheeler Papers, box 3.

99. E. P. Wheeler to C. D. Wood, 12 October 1901; *Shepard-Low Campaign.*

100. E. P. Wheeler to E. M. Shepard, 6 February 1902; Wheeler Papers, box 3.

101. *New York Telegram,* 20 September 1901, p. 12.

102. John Hay to Seth Low, 21 September 1901; Low Papers, Spec. Mss. Coll.

103. Seth Low to William G. Schermerhorn, 23 September 1901; Low Papers; Spec. Mss. Coll. Carbons.

104. Seth Low to John Hay, 26 September 1901; Low Papers, Spec. Mss. Coll.

105. Alfred Hodder, *A Fight for the City* (New York: Macmillan, 1903), p. 21.

106. Bogard, *Redemption of New York,* pp. 212–215.

107. George Gunton, "Municipal Emancipation," *Lecture Bulletin of the Institute of Social Economics,* 5 (15 October 1901), pp. 60 & 62.

108. *Journal of Commerce and Commercial Bulletin,* 26 September 1901, p. 4.

109. *New York World,* 27 September 1901, p. 6.

110. *New York Times,* 1 October 1901, p. 8.

111. *Tammany Times,* 17 (14 October 1901), p. 8.

112. *New York Telegram,* 28 September 1901, p. 6.

113. Syrett, ed., *The Gentleman and the Tiger,* p. 167.

114. *Journal of Commerce and Commercial Bulletin,* 5 October 1901, p. 4.

115. Richard Watson Gilder to Charles R. Lowell, 11 October 1901; The Richard Watson Gilder Papers, letterbook 16, Manuscript Division, New York Public Library, New York, New York.

116. *The Nation,* 73 (10 October 1901), p. 275.

117. *New York Times,* 30 October 1901, p. 3.

118. George W. Alger, *Oral History Memoir,* Oral History Research Office, Columbia University, New York, New York, p. 328.

119. *New York Times,* 6 October 1901, p. 1.

120. Lindsay Denison, "Scenes from a Great Campaign," *World's Work,* 3 (December 1901) , pp. 1556–1557.

121. Seth Low to John W. Burgess, 5 October 1901; Burgess Papers, Spec. Mss. Coll.

122. "Points made at discussion, East Side House," 26 September 1901; *Shepard-Low Campaign.*

123. *The Nation,* 73 (2 October 1901) , p. 259.

124. *New York Times,* 10 October 1901, p. 1.

125. George Gunton, "New Era in Municipal Government," *Lecture Bulletin of the Institute of Social Economics,* 5 (15 November 1901) , pp. 110–111.

126. *New York World,* 9 October 1901, p. 3.

127. *Tammany Times,* 17 (28 October 1901) , p. 8.

128. *New York Times,* 6 November 1901, p. 8.

129. *Ibid.,* 6 November 1901, p. 8, & Warner, "Municipal Betterment in the New York City Election," p. 625.

CHAPTER VII

1. Gunton, "New Era in Municipal Government," p. 120.

2. Clipping in "Seth Low Scrapbook, #9;" Low Papers.

3. *Greater New York Government, 1902–1903: Father Knickerbocker Adrift* (New York: Fusion Record Publishing Co., 1903) , p. 23.

4. Remarks of Felix Adler, "Dinner to Seth Low, *et. al.,* 14 November 1901, pp. 28–29; The City Club of New York Papers, Manuscript Division, New York Public Library, New York, New York. (Hereafter cited as City Club Papers) .

5. Remarks of Wheeler H. Peckham, "Dinner to Seth Low, *et. al.,*" 14 November 1901; City Club Papers.

6. Clipping in "Seth Low Scrapbook # 9;" Low Papers.

7. *New York Times,* 15 November 1901, p. 1.

8. Remarks of Seth Low, "Dinner to Seth Low, *et. al.,*" 14 November 1901, p. 19; City Club Papers.

9. *Ibid.,* p. 21; City Club Papers.

10. *Ibid.,* p. 23; City Club Papers.

11. John Martin, "A Constructive Program: What the Low Administration Should Do," *Municipal Affairs,* 5 (1901) , pp. 656–657.

12. *New York Times,* 1 January 1902, p. 6.

13. *Ibid.,* 2 January 1902, p. 1.

14. Theodore Roosevelt to Seth Low, 29 October 1902; in Elting E. Morison, ed., *The Letters of Theodore Roosevelt* (Cambridge, Mass.: Harvard University Press, 1951) , vol. 3, p. 371.

15. Sidney Webb to Seth Low, 17 October 1902; Low Papers, Spec. Mss. Coll.

16. Charles C. Burlingham, *Oral History Memoir,* Oral History Research Office, Columbia University, New York, New York, p. 5.

17. Lawrence Veiller, *Oral History Memoir,* Oral History Research Office, Columbia University, New York, New York, p. 39. An excellent account of Tenement House Reform in New York City can be found in Roy

Lubove, *The Progressives and the Slums* (Pittsburgh, Pa.: University of Pittsburgh Press, 1962).

18. Veiller, *Oral History Memoir*, p. 37.
19. *Ibid.*, p. 40.
20. Theodore J. Lowi, *At the Pleasure of the Mayor* (Glencoe, Ill.: The Free Press, 1964), *passim*.
21. *The Nation*, 74 (2 January 1902), p. 5.
22. Seth Low to Theodore Roosevelt, 12 October 1895; Low Papers, Spec. Mss. Coll. Carbons.
23. *The Nation*, 74 (2 January 1902), p. 5.
24. *New York Times*, 7 January 1902, p. 14.
25. *Ibid.*, 25 January 1902, p. 2, & 9 February 1902, p. 2.
26. *Ibid.*, 6 April 1902, p. 1.
27. William C. Lawton to William H. H. Beebe, 11 January 1902; Low Papers, Spec. Mss. Coll.
28. *New York Times*, 4 January 1902, p. 1.
29. *Ibid.*, 5 January 1902, p. 1.
30. Gunton, "New Era in Municipal Government," p. 113.
31. Seth Low to John B. Pine, 26 February 1887; Low Papers, Copybook II.
32. Seth Low to the Rev. Dr. Parkhurst, 20 May 1892; Low Papers, Spec. Mss. Coll.
33. Seth Low to Theodore Roosevelt, 12 October 1895; Low Papers, Spec. Mss. Coll. Carbons.
34. John G. Agar, "The Saloon Problem in New York," *Municipal Affairs*, 5 (1901), p. 289.
35. John DeWitt Warner, "The Raines Liquor Tax Law: State Promotion of Vice," *Municipal Affairs*, 5 (1901), p. 842.
36. Lincoln Steffens, *The Shame of the Cities* (New York: Hill & Wang [American Century Series], 1957), p. 206.
37. Felix Adler, "Social Function of the Saloon," *Municipal Affairs*, 5 (1901), p. 877.
38. *The Outlook*, 69 (26 October 1901), p. 480.
39. *The City for the People!*, p. 133.
40. *The Outlook*, 70 (1 February 1902), p. 345.
41. Agar, "The Saloon Problem in New York," p. 829.
42. *Collier's Weekly*, 28 (25 January 1902), p. 3.
43. *New York Times*, 5 January 1902, p. 3.
44. *Ibid.*, 6 January 1902, p. 1.
45. *Ibid.*, 10 January 1902, p. 1.
46. *Ibid.*, 20 January 1902, p. 1.
47. *Ibid.*, 24 January 1902, p. 14.
48. *The Outlook*, 70 (1 February 1902), p. 346.
49. *New York Times*, 27 January 1902, p. 2.
50. *Review of Reviews*, 25 (February 1902), p. 140.
51. *New York Times*, 28 January 1902, p. 14, & 6 February 1902, p. 2.
52. *Ibid.*, 1 March 1902, p. 3, 10 March 1902, p. 2, & 17 March 1902, p. 2.
53. *Ibid.*, 11 April 1902, p. 1.
54. *Ibid.*, 6 April 1902, p. 1, & 7 April 1902, p. 1.
55. *Ibid.*, 6 April 1902, p. 1.

56. *Ibid.*, 23 June 1902, p. 12.

57. *Ibid.*, 4 January 1903, p. 1; 5 January 1903, p. 1, & 12 January 1903, p. 1. January 1903, p. 1.

58. *Ibid.*, 30 January 1903, p. 3.

59. *Ibid.*, 25 February 1903, p. 1.

60. Seth Low to Gov. Benjamin B. Odell, 13 March 1903; Low Papers, Spec. Mss. Coll. Carbons.

61. W. S. Rainsford to Seth Low, 31 March 1903; Low Papers, Spec. Mss. Coll.

62. *New York Times,* 5 May 1903, p. 2.

63. *Ibid.*, 21 May 1903, p. 6, & 19 June 1903, p. 1.

64. *Acorn,* 18 July 1903, p. 4.

65. Carolyn Flora Schachne, *Some Aspects in the History of the Police Department of the City of New York, 1870–1901,* unpublished Master's essay, Columbia University, 1940, p. 150.

66. *New York Times,* 5 January 1902, p. 3.

67. *Ibid.*, 11 April 1902, p. 1.

68. City Club of New York, "The Police Department of the City of New York" (New York: City Club, 1903), p. 50, & *New York Times,* 6 June 1902, p. 1.

69. *New York Times,* 7 June 1902, p. 16, & 8 June 1902, p. 12.

70. *Ibid.*, 12 July 1902, p. 4.

71. City Club of New York, "The Police Department of the City of New York," p. 52.

72. *New York Times,* 8 August 1902, p. 1.

73. *Ibid.*, 18 September 1902, p. 1.

74. *Ibid.*, 19 September 1902, p. 16.

75. *Ibid.*, 7 October 1902, p. 3.

76. *Ibid.*, 13 December 1902, pp. 1 & 6.

77. *Ibid.*, 2 January 1903, p. 1.

78. Citizens' Union of New York, *The City for the People! The Best Administration New York Ever Had: Campaign Book of the Citizens' Union, 1903* (New York: Citizens' Union, 1903) , p. 43.

79. C. H. Parkhurst to F. V. Greene, 25 May 1903; The Francis Vinton Greene Papers, Manuscript Division, New York Public Library, New York, New York. (Hereafter cited as Greene Papers) .

80. *New York World,* 18 February 1903, p. 6.

81. *New York Tribune,* 28 September 1903, p. 8.

82. City Club of New York, "The Police Department of the City of New York," p. 7.

83. Seth Low, "The Rights of the Citizen," *Scribner's Magazine,* 7 (June 1890) , p. 772. A good administrative history of the Low Mayoralty can be found in Joseph Coviello, *Seth Low as Mayor of New York City,* unpublished Master's essay, Columbia University, 1938.

84. Milo Roy Maltbie, "A Century of Franchise History," *Municipal Affairs,* 4 (1900) , pp. 197–198.

85. *The City for the People! 1903,* p. 130.

86. *The Outlook,* 75 (17 October 1903) , p. 389.

87. *Review of Reviews,* 28 (November 1903) , p. 521.

88. Martin Saxe, *Oral History Memoir,* Oral History Research Office, Columbia University, New York, New York, p. 8.

89. John R. Commons, "Some Taxation Problems and Reforms," *Review of Reviews,* 27 (January 1903) , p. 207.

90. City Committee Minutes, 11 September 1902; Citizens' Union Papers, K-1, & *New York Times,* 10 September 1902, p. 16.

91. *The Outlook,* 75 (24 October 1903) , pp. 425–426.

92. *New York Tribune,* 1 January 1903, p. 8.

93. *Review of Reviews,* 25 (February 1902) , p. 139.

94. *The City for the People! 1903,* p. 79.

95. Open letter of 18 September 1902; Low Papers, Copybook V.

96. See Edward T. Devine, "Municipal Reform and Social Welfare in New York," *Review of Reviews,* 28 (October 1903) .

97. See Robert W. DeForest and Lawrence Veiller, eds., *The Tenement House Problem* (New York: Macmillan, 1903) , 2v.; Devine, "Municipal Reform and Social Welfare in New York;" and Joseph J. Lister, *History of the New York Tenement House Department,* unpublished Master's essay, Columbia University, 1933.

98. *Acorn,* 4 July 1903, p. 1.

99. Devine, "Municipal Reform and Social Welfare in New York," p. 448.

100. *Review of Reviews,* 27 (January 1903) , p. 6.

101. Theodore Roosevelt to Seth Low, 28 March 1903; Low Papers, Copybook VII.

CHAPTER VIII

1. Steffens, *Shame of the Cities,* p. 196.

2. *New York Times,* Fri. Nov. 21, 1902, pp. 1 & 3.

3. *Review of Reviews,* 24 (December 1901) , p. 654.

4. *The Outlook,* 69 (28 December 1901) , p. 1048.

5. Ervin Wardman, "Men and Issues in the New York City Campaign," *Review of Reviews,* 28 (November 1903) , pp. 546–547.

6. *New York Times,* 12 September 1902, p. 1.

7. Platt, *Autobiography,* p. 415.

8. *New York Times,* 2 December 1902, p. 8.

9. Undated public statement; Low Papers, Speeches: 1.

10. *New York Times,* 12 September 1902, p. 1.

11. *Ibid.,* 18 January 1903, p. 8.

12. Reese F. Alsop to Seth Low, 18 April 1903; Low Papers, Spec. Mss. Coll.

13. *Acorn,* 1 August 1903, p. 4.

14. *Ibid.,* 1 August 1903, p. 4.

15. Steffens, *Shame of the Cities,* pp. 200–201.

16. *Acorn,* 1 August 1903, p. 1.

17. *New York Times,* 15 March 1903, p. 10.

18. *Ibid.,* 3 April 1903, p. 1.

19. *Ibid.,* 17 April 1903, p. 1, & 12 May 1903, p. 2.

20. *Ibid.,* 7 May 1903, p. 10, & 12 May 1903, p. 1.

21. *Ibid.,* 25 May 1903, p. 3, & 1 June 1903, p. 4.

22. *Acorn,* 4 July 1903, p. 1.

23. *Ibid.,* 15 August 1903, p. 4.

24. *New York Times,* 14 June 1903, p. 6.

25. Austen G. Fox to Theodore Roosevelt, 30 July 1903; Low Papers, Spec. Mss. Coll.

26. Theodore Roosevelt to Seth Low, 1 August 1903; Low Papers, Spec. Mss. Coll.

27. Seth Low to Theodore Roosevelt, 11 August 1903; The Theodore Roosevelt Papers, Manuscript Division, the Library of Congress, Washington, D.C. (Hereafter cited as Roosevelt Papers).

28. *New York Times*, 3 August, 1903, p. 7; *Acorn*, 8 August 1903, p. 1; and Wardman, "Men and Issues in the New York City Campaign," pp. 546 & 554.

29. William Hepburn Russell to Seth Low, 31 August 1903; Low Papers, Spec. Mss. Coll.

30. *New York Times*, 23 August 1903, p. 12; 24 August 1903, p. 1; & 25 August 1903, p. 3.

31. *Ibid.*, 28 August 1903, p. 5.

32. *Ibid.*, 2 September 1903, p. 1, & 11 September 1903, p. 2.

33. *Greater New York Government, 1902–1903: Father Knickerbocker Adrift*, p. 1.

34. Seth Low to William Hepburn Russell, 21 September 1903; Low Papers, Scrapbook 11.

35. *Acorn*, 8 August 1903, p. 1.

36. Letter to the editor of the *Acorn*, 22 August 1903, p. 2. Low was rumored to be in line for a diplomatic appointment to Europe, but repeatedly declared that he was not interested in diplomatic service.

37. *Acorn*, 29 August 1903, p. 1.

38. *Ibid.*, 5 September 1903, p. 3.

39. *Ibid.*, 11 July 1903, p. 1.

40. *New York Tribune*, 1 September 1903, p. 2.

41. Fusion Conference Minutes, 1 September 1903; Citizens' Union Papers, H-1.

42. *New York World*, 1 September 1903, pp. 1 & 6.

43. A. S. Haight to Seth Low, 1 September 1903; Low Papers, Spec. Mss. Coll.

44. A. S. Haight to Seth Low, 1 September 1903; Low Papers, Spec. Mss. Coll. Low's reply in long-hand at the end of Haight's letter.

45. *New York World*, 2 September 1903, pp. 1–2.

46. *New York Tribune*, 3 September 1903, p. 8; *New York World*, 5 September 1903, p. p; *New York Times*, 3 September 1903, p. 6.

47. *New York Advertiser*, 10 September 1903, p. 6.

48. *New York World*, 4 September 1903, p. 1.

49. *New York Evening Journal*, 4 September 1903, p. 1.

50. Seth Low to R. Fulton Cutting, 7 September 1903; Low Papers, Spec. Mss. Coll. Carbons.

51. *New York World*, 11 September 1903, p. 1.

52. *Ibid.*, 10 September 1903, p. 6.

53. *Ibid.*, 12 September 1903, p. 1, & 22 September 1903, p. 1.

54. Wardman, "Men and Issues in the New York City Campaign," p. 545.

55. *New York Tribune*, 13 September 1903, p. 1.

56. William Travers Jerome to Charles C. Nadal 16 September 1903; *Acorn*, 19 September 1903, pp. 1–2.

57. *New York World*, 16 September 1903, p. 8.

58. Seth Low to Theodore Roosevelt, 23 September 1903; Roosevelt Papers.

59. *New York Times*, 23 September 1903, p. 1.

60. Edward M. Grout to R. Fulton Cutting, 17 September 1903; *Acorn,* 19 September 1903, p. 1.

61. Tammany politics during the period of Low's Mayoral campaigns is well covered in Albert Fein, *New York City Politics from 1897–1903: A Study in Political Party Leadership,* unpublished Master's essay, Columbia University, 1954. See also Myers, *History of Tammany Hall,* pp. 290–323, and Werner, *Tammany Hall,* pp. 482ff.

62. *New York Times,* 27 September 1903, p. 2.

63. Fein, *New York City Politics,* p. 126.

64. Syrett, ed., *The Gentleman and the Tiger,* p. 170.

65. *New York World,* 28 September 1903, p. 6.

66. *New York Times,* 5 October 1903, p. 1.

67. *New York World,* 30 September 1903, p. 2, & 6 October 1903, p. 1.

68. Syrett, ed., *The Gentleman and the Tiger,* p. 169.

69. Jacob Neu to Seth Low, 14 September 1903; Low Papers, Spec. Mss. Coll.

70. *Acorn,* 19 September 1903, p. 4.

71. *New York Tribune,* 10 September 1903, p. 8.

72. Reese F. Alsop to Seth Low, 23 September 1903; Low Papers, Spec. Mss. Coll.

73. Seth Low to E. P. Wheeler, *et. al.,* 9 October 1903; Low Papers, Scrapbook 11.

74. *New York Times,* 14 October 1903, p. 1.

75. Steffens, *Shame of the Cities,* pp. 198–199.

76. Platform of the Citizens' Union, 1903; Citizens' Union Papers, A-26.

77. Elgin R. L. Gould to Richard W. G. Welling, 7 October 1903; The Richard W. G. Welling Papers, box 23A, Manuscript Division, New York Public Library, New York, New York. (Hereafter cited as Welling Papers).

78. *New York Times,* 15 October 1903, p. 2.

79. *Acorn,* 19 September 1903, p. 1.

80. Seth Low to Richard H. Clarke, 28 September 1903; Low Papers, Copybook IV.

81. *New York Times,* 2 November 1903, p. 6; *The Outlook,* 75 (24 October 1903), p. 435; and the *Review of Reviews,* 28 (November 1903), pp. 518–519.

82. *New York Times,* 21 October 1903, p. 2.

83. *New York World,* 26 October 1903, p. 2.

84. Eugene Blumenthal to Richard W. G. Welling, 24 October 1903; *Welling Papers,* box 23A.

85. J. Edgar Leaycraft to Richard W. G. Welling, 28 October 1903; Welling Papers, box 23A.

86. Wardman, "Men and Issues in the New York City Campaign," p. 545.

87. Steffens, *Shame of the Cities,* p. 200.

88. *The Outlook,* 75 (10 October 1903), pp. 343–346.

89. Theodore Roosevelt to Seth Low, 19 October 1903; Low Papers, Spec. Mss. Coll.

90. *New York Tribune,* 2 November 1903, p. 8.

91. *New York Evening Journal,* 2 November 1903, page #'s mutilated.

92. B. R. C. Low, *Seth Low,* p. 71

93. Theodore Roosevelt to Nicholas Murray Butler, 4 November 1903, in Morison, ed., *Letters of Theodore Roosevelt,* vol. 3, p. 641.

CHAPTER IX

1. Steffens, *Shame of the Cities*, p. 205.

2. *Acorn*, 7 November 1903, p. 1.

3. *New York World*, 4 November 1903, p. 6.

4. *The Nation*, 77 (5 November 1903) , p. 1.

5. *Harper's Weekly*, 47 (14 November 1903) , p. 1812; *New York Times*, 5 November 1903, p. 8.

6. *New York Tribune*, 5 November 1903, p. 8.

7. Theodore Roosevelt to Lyman Abbott, 5 November 1903; in Morison, ed., *Letters of Theodore Roosevelt*, vol. 3, pp. 647–648.

8. Theodore Roosevelt to Nicholas Murray Butler, 4 November 1903; in Morison, ed., *Letters of Theodore Roosevelt*, vol. 3, p. 641.

9. Theodore Roosevelt to Seth Low, 3 November 1903; in Morison, ed., *Letters of Theodore Roosevelt*, vol. 3, pp. 640–641.

10. Francis Vinton Greene to Edward Carey, 4 November 1903; Greene Papers, General Correspondence.

11. Herbert Parsons to Seth Low, 4 November 1903; Low Papers, Spec. Mss. Coll.

12. Seth Low to Nevada S. Stranahan, 29 March 1901; Low Papers, Spec. Mss. Coll. Carbons. Actually Low's statement was not quite correct, the Know-Nothings held the Mayoralty for a brief period in the 1840's.

13. Seth Low to J. T. Newcomb, 18 January 1904; Low Papers, Spec. Mss. Coll. Carbons.

14. Seth Low to Benjamin Barker Odell, 14 December 1903; Low Papers, Spec. Mss. Coll. Carbons.

15. Platt, *Autobiography*, pp. 365–366.

16. *Acorn*, 12 December 1903, p. 2.

17. Steffens, *Shame of the Cities*, p. 203.

18. On this general point see Richard Hofstadter, "Idealists and Professors and Sore-Heads: The Genteel Reformers," *Columbia University Forum*, vol. 5, # 2, p. 5.

19. Steffens, *Autobiography*, p. 432.

20. "Why Municipal Reform Succeeds in Chicago and Fails in New York," *The Independent*, 56 (14 April 1904) , pp. 829 & 831.

21. Syrett, ed., *The Gentleman and the Tiger*, pp. 171 & 173.

22. Sydney Brooks, "Tammany Again," *Fortnightly Review*, 80 (December 1903) , p. 923.

23. Carl Carmer, "From Van Wyck to O'Dwyer," in Allan Nevins & John A. Krout, eds., *The Greater City: New York, 1898–1948* (New York: Columbia University Press, 1948) , pp. 68–69. Similarly, Albert Fein, basing his conclusion largely on Democratic sources, considered that, "their reformism [fusion's] was essentially of a conservative nature.... Low's cautious approach to municipal matters reflected the political attitudes of the people who advanced his nomination. He was anxious to avoid attaching a radical reputation to his following. . . . It was important that Low not endanger the support of the conservative reform groups which had contributed so heavily to his election in 1901." *New York City Politics*, pp. 19–20. The middle class and basically conservative nature of the fusion alliance is also emphasized by Richard Skolnik, *The Crystallization of Reform in New York City, 1894–1917*, unpublished Ph.D. dissertation, Yale University, 1964.

24. Steven C. Swett, "The Test of a Reformer: A Study of Seth Low, New York City Mayor, 1902–1903," *New York Historical Society Quarterly,* 44 (January 1960) , p. 39.

25. Robert S. Binkerd, *Oral History Memoir,* Oral History Research Office, Columbia University, New York, New York, p. 83; and Holli, *Reform in Detroit, passim.*

26. *Review of Reviews,* 22 (November 1900) , p. 522.

27. Steffens, *Shame of the Cities,* p. 212. In recent years historians have taken a more critical view of the social role of the political machine. See, for example, James B. Crooks, *Politics and Progress: The Rise of Urban Progressivism in Baltimore, 1895–1911* (Baton Rouge, La.: Louisiana State University Press, 1968) .

28. Circular letter of R. Fulton Cutting, 1902; Citizens' Union Papers, W-24.

29. Brooks, "Tammany Again," pp. 916 & 918.

30. *New York Times,* 11 October 1902, p. 16; *Review of Reviews,* 27 (June 1903) , p. 658.

31. *New York Times,* 19 April 1902, p. 7; *New York Tribune,* 21 September 1903, p. 2.

32. Seth Low to James Bryce, 9 April 1889; Low Papers, Copybook II.

33. Seth Low to George F. Peabody, 31 October 1889, to Edward M. Shepard, 4 November 1892, to C. Augustus Haviland, 4 November 1892; Low Papers, Spec. Mss. Coll. His nephew asserted that he also voted for Cleveland in 1884.

34. Theodore Roosevelt to Seth Low, 29 September 1898; Low Papers, Spec. Mss. Coll.

35. On this point see G. Wallace Chessman, *Governor Theodore Roosevelt: The Albany Apprenticeship, 1898–1900* (Cambridge, Mass.: Harvard University Press, 1965) , *passim.*

36. Theodore Roosevelt to Seth Low, 21 December 1898 & 22 March 1899; Low Papers, Spec. Mss. Coll.

37. Theodore Roosevelt to Seth Low, 23 June 1900, Low Papers, Spec. Mss. Coll.

38. Seth Low to John H. Starin, 9 February 1903; Low Papers, Copybook IV.

39. B. R. C. Low, *Seth Low,* pp. 86–87.

40. Syrett, ed., *The Gentleman and the Tiger,* pp. 172–173.

41. Seth Low to Abbot L. Mills, 12 January 1893; Low Papers, Spec. Mss. Coll.

42. Frederick Tanner, *Oral History Memoir,* Oral History Research Office, Columbia University, New York, p. 124.

43. McAneny, *Oral History Memoir,* p. 13; B. R. C. Low, *Seth Low,* p. 87.

44. Lawson Purdy, *Oral History Memoir,* Oral History Research Office, Columbia University, New York, New York, pp. 6–7.

45. Seth Low to Charles A. Schieren, 3 July 1903; Low Papers, Copybook IV.

46. *New York World,* 27 September 1903, ed. sec., p. 1.

47. Warner, "Municipal Betterment in the New York City Elections," p. 632.

48. Roswell P. Flower, "Is Non-Partisanship in Municipal Government Feasible?" *The Forum,* 23 (July 1897) , p. 533.

49. Hodder, *A Fight for the City,* p. 227.

50. Josephine Shaw Lowell to Seth Low, 18 November 1903; Low Papers, Spec. Mss. Coll.

51. *Review of Reviews,* 27 (January 1903) , p. 6.

52. *The Outlook,* 75 14 (November 1903) , p. 619.

53. Seth Low to Theodore Roosevelt, 5 November 1903; Low Papers, Spec. Mss. Coll.

54. John J. Bealin to Seth Low, 23 December 1903; Low Papers, Spec. Mss. Coll.

55. *The Nation,* 78 (7 January 1904) , p. 6.

56. Jacob Neu to Seth Low, 4 November 1903; Low Papers, Spec. Mss. Coll.

57. Seth Low, "The United States in 1899," Address, University of Pennsylvania, 22 February 1899. Pamphlet.

58. Seth Low, "The International Conference of Peace," *North American Review,* 169 (November 1899) .

CHAPTER X

1. Quoted in *National Civic Federation Monthly Review,* 1 (July 1904) , p. 9. (Hereafter cited as *N.C.F. Review*) .

2. Good accounts of the Chicago Civic Federation can be found in Albion W. Small, "The Civic Federation of Chicago," *American Journal of Sociology,* 1 (1895) ; Graham Taylor, *Pioneering on Social Frontiers* (Chicago: University of Chicago Press, 1930) ; and Douglas Sutherland, *Fifty Years on the Civic Front* (Chicago: the Civic Federation, 1943) . A brief account is to be found in Ray Ginger, *Altgeld's America: The Lincoln Ideal Versus Changing Realities, 1890–1905* (Chicago: Quadrangle Books, 1965) .

3. Taylor, *Pioneering on Social Frontiers,* p. 29.

4. *Ibid.,* p. 30.

5. *Ibid.,* p. 32.

6. Ray S. Baker, "The Civic Federation of Chicago," *The Outlook,* 52 (27 July 1895) , p. 132.

7. *N. C. F. Review,* 1 (April 1903) , pp. 8–9, 15.

8. Small, "The Civic Federation of Chicago," p. 92.

9. Ginger, *Altgeld's America,* p. 253.

10. Small, "The Civic Federation of Chicago," p. 91.

11. Ralph M. Easley to L.L. Loeb, 28 July 1899; *N.C.F. Papers,* box 98.

12. Quoted in *Chicago Conference on Trusts and Combinations, Proceedings of* (Chicago: Civic Federation of Chicago, 1900) , p. 267.

13. Quoted in *Ibid.,* pp. 329–330.

14. Oscar S. Straus, *Under Four Administrations: From Cleveland to Taft* (Boston: Houghton-Mifflin Co., 1922) , pp. 194, 196.

15. For more extensive treatment see Lewis L. Lorwin, *The American Federation of Labor: History, Policies, and Prospects* (Washington, D.C.: The Brookings Institute, 1933), pp. 63ff; Marguerite Green, *The National Civic Federation and the American Labor Movement 1900–1925* (Washington, D.C.: Catholic University of America Press, 1956), pp. 24ff; and Sidney Sass, *The National Civic Federation 1900–1914* (unpublished Masters essay, Columbia University, 1948), pp. 29ff.

16. See the chapter on the 1901 Steel Strike in Samuel Gompers, *Seventy Years of Life and Labor: An Autobiography* (New York: E.P. Dutton, 1925) .

17. *Ibid.*, v. 2, p. 106.

18. Quoted in *N.C.F. Review*, 1 (June 1904), p. 5.

19. Gompers, *Seventy Years of Life and Labor*, vol. 2, pp. 107–109.

20. Quoted in *N.C.F. Review*, 1 (June 1903), p. 6.

21. Quoted in "The Marriage of Capital and Labor," *The Catholic World*, 74 (January 1902), p. 532.

22. Quoted in *N.C.F. Review*, 1 (June 1903), p. 7.

23. See account in John Mitchell, *Organized Labor: Its Problems, Purposes and Ideals* (Philadelphia: American Book and Bible House, 1903), pp. 365ff.

24. *Ibid.*, p. 371.

25. *Ibid.*, p. 373.

26. Walter Wellman, "The Inside History of the Great Coal Strike," *Collier's Weekly*, 30 (18 October 1902), pp. 6–7.

27. Ralph M. Easley, "What Organized Labor Has Learned," *McClure's Magazine*, 19 (October 1902), p. 488.

28. Ralph M. Easley, "The Work of the National Civic Federation," *Harper's Weekly*, 48 (26 November 1904), p. 1808.

29. "The National Civic Federation: Its Methods and Its Aim" (New York: National Civic Federation, 1905), p. 17.

30. Quoted in *N.C.F. Review*, 1 (February 1905), p. 11.

31. Quoted in National Civic Federation, *Industrial Conference, 1902* (New York: Winthrop Press, 1903), p. 165.

32. *N.C.F. Review*, 1 (September 1903), p. 1.

33. *Ibid.*, 1 (September 1903), p. 1.

34. *Ibid.*, 1 (September 1903), p. 1.

35. John Hays Hammond, *The Autobiography of John Hays Hammond* (New York: Farrar and Rinehart, 1935), vol. 2, p. 698.

36. *N.C.F. Review*, 1 (October 1904), p. 8.

37. Ralph M. Easley, "A View of the Labor Question," *Harper's Weekly*, 48 (5 November 1904), p. 1696.

38. Quoted in *N.C.F. Review*, 1 (April 1903), p. 20.

39. Oscar S. Straus, "Results Accomplished by the Industrial Department, National Civic Federation," *Annals of the American Academy of Political and Social Science*, 20 (1902), p. 37.

40. "The National Civic Federation: Its Methods and Its Aim," p. 3.

41. *Ibid.*, p. 9.

42. John Rogers Commons, *Myself* (New York: The Macmillan Co., 1934), p. 73.

43. Quoted in *N.C.F. Review*, 1 (June 1903), p. 8.

44. *Ibid.*, 1 (July 1904), p. 11.

45. Quoted in *American Federationist*, 9 (January 1902), p. 24.

46. Quoted in Easley, "What Organized Labor Has Learned," p. 484.

47. Quoted in Easley, "The Work of the National Civic Federation," p. 1805.

48. Quoted in *N.C.F. Review*, 1 (March 1905), p. 15.

49. *Ibid.*, 1 (September 1904), p. 14.

50. *Ibid.*, 1 (July 1904), p. 10.

51. Theodore Roosevelt to Samuel Gompers, 14 December 1904; *N.C.F. Review*, 1 (January 1905), p. 3.

52. "The National Civic Federation: Its Methods and Its Aim," p. 32.

53. Quoted in *N.C.F. Review*, 1 (January 1905), p. 6.

54. Gompers, *Seventy Years of Life and Labor,* vol. 2, p. 105.

55. Quoted in *N.C.F. Review,* 1 (June 1903) , p. 16.

56. *Ibid.,* 1 (June 1903) , p. 15.

57. *Ibid.,* 1 (June 1904) , p. 2.

58. "Senator Hanna on Labor Unions and Socialism," *Gunton's Magazine,* 26 (March 1904) , pp. 201–202.

CHAPTER XI

1. Seth Low to President Alderman (University of Virginia) , 26 December 1906; Low Papers, Spec. Mss. Coll. Carbons.

2. James Bryce to Seth Low, 6 July 1900; Low Papers, Spec. Mss. Coll.

3. Seth Low to Bishop Henry C. Potter, 19 January 1901; Low Papers, Spec. Mss. Call. Carbons.

4. National Civic Federation, *Industrial Conference, 1902,* pp. 2–4.

5. Seth Low to Abiel Abbot Low, 6 April 1886; Low Papers, Spec. Mss. Coll.

6. Seth Low, "Relation of the Church to the Capital and Labor Question," in James McCosh, *et. al., Problems of American Civilization* (New York: Baker and Taylor, 1888) , pp. 120–121.

7. *Ibid.,* p. 119.

8. *Ibid.,* p. 121.

9. *Ibid.,* p. 122.

10. *Ibid.,* p. 121.

11. Seth Low to Samuel Gompers, 28 September 1889; Low Papers, Spec. Mss. Coll.

12. "Wealth and Character," 1900; Low Papers, Speeches: 1.

13. "Seth Low's Practical Services to Labor" (New York: Citizens' Union, 1897) , p. 5.

14. "Trade Unions," 1896; Low Papers, Speeches: 2.

15. Quoted in *N.C.F. Review,* 3 (September 1907) , p. 20.

16. "Arbiter's Decision in J. J. Little Dispute," Low Papers, box 55.

17. Theodore L. DeVinne to Seth Low, 22 June 1896; Low Papers, Spec. Mss. Coll.

18. Quoted in *N.C.F. Review,* 2 (April 1905) , p. 9.

19. *New York Times,* 4 April 1897, p. 7.

20. "Finding in Arbitration between Typothetae and Franklin Association # 23;" Low Papers, box 55.

21. "Speech," New York, June 1900; Low Papers, Spec. Mss. Coll.

22. "Speech," Brooklyn Young Republican Club, 1900; Low Papers, Speeches: 1.

23. Seth Low to Edward Atkinson, 15 January 1900; Low Papers, Spec. Mss. Coll. Carbons.

24. "Speech," Brooklyn Young Republican Club, 1900; Low Papers, Speeches: 1.

25. Seth Low to G. P. Putnam's Sons, 27 October, 1904; Low Papers, Spec. Mss. Coll. Carbons.

26. "Speech," c. October 1904; Low Papers, Speeches: 2.

27. Quoted in *N.C.F. Review,* 2 (April 1905) , p. 2.

28. Ralph M. Easley to Samuel Gompers, 18 November 1905; N.C.F. Papers, box 16.

29. John Mitchell to Ralph M. Easley, 20 November 1905; Low Papers, box 145.

30. Seth Low to August Belmont, 13 March 1906; Low Papers, box 145.

31. Seth Low to John Mitchell and Francis Robbins, 13 March 1906; Low Papers, box 145.

32. Seth Low to Theodore Roosevelt, 13 March 1906; Low Papers, box 145.

33. Theodore Roosevelt to Seth Low, 14 March 1906; Low Papers, box 145.

34. John Mitchell to Seth Low, 16 March 1906; Low Papers, box 145.

35. Seth Low to Theodore Roosevelt, 24 March 1906; Low Papers, box 145.

36. Seth Low to Theodore Roosevelt, 28 March 1906; Low Papers, box 145.

37. Theodore Roosevelt to Seth Low, 28 March 1906, & 29 March 1906; Low Papers, Spec. Mss. Coll.

38. Letter to the Editor of the *Third Rail,* undated: Low Papers, Spec. Mss. Coll. Carbons.

39. Quoted in *N.C.F. Review,* 2 (March-April 1907) , p. 20.

40. Seth Low to Otto Eidlitz, 23 February 1907; Low Papers, Spec. Mss. Coll. Carbons.

41. Seth Low to Jacob H. Schiff, 23 May 1907; Low Papers, box 145.

42. Jacob H. Schiff to Seth Low, 24 May 1907; Low Papers, box 145.

43. Seth Low to Jacob H. Schiff, 28 May 1907; Low Papers, box 145.

44. Jacob H. Schiff to Seth Low, 29 May 1907; Low Papers, box 145.

45. Seth Low to James R. Garfield, 23 December 1904; Low Papers, Spec. Mss. Coll. Carbons.

46. Seth Low to Theodore Roosevelt, 7 February 1905; Low Papers, Spec. Mss. Coll. Carbons.

47. Of course, Roosevelt had a way of appearing to be all things to all men, and he accepted advice from men like Elbert Gary and Henry Cabot Lodge as readily as from men like Low and Oscar S. Straus. But, on the whole, it is fair to conclude that the main thrust of Roosvelt's economic policy as it evolved during the Progressive years was the establishment of a more equitable and humane socio-economic order. This is the thesis of the most recent and most scholarly biography of the "Rough Rider," William Henry Harbaugh, *Power & Responsibility: The Life and Times of Theodore Roosevelt* (New York: Farrar, Straus & Cudahy, 1961) .

48. Theodore Roosevelt to Seth Low, 8 February 1905; Low Papers, Spec. Mss. Coll.

49. Seth Low to Eugene A. Rowland, 30 March 1906; Low Papers, Spec. Mss. Coll. Carbons.

50. Seth Low to Theodore Roosevelt, 10 July 1906; Low Papers, Spec. Mss. Coll. Carbons.

51. Theodore Roosevelt to Seth Low, 12 July 1906; Low Papers, Spec. Mss. Coll.

52. Theodore Roosevelt to Seth Low, 20 December 1906; Low Papers, Spec. Mss. Coll.

53. Ralph M. Easley to John Mitchell, 18 November 1907; N.C.F. Papers, box 29.

54. Quoted in *N.C.F. Review,* 2 (April 1905) , p. 2.

55. Benjamin Ide Wheeler to Seth Low, 8 January 1908; Low Papers, Spec. Mss. Coll. Carbons.

CHAPTER XII

1. *The Square Deal,* 3 (May 1908) , p. 92.

2. John R. Miller to Ralph M. Easley, 11 December 1906; *N.C.F. Papers,* box 98.

3. National Civic Federation, *Proceedings of the National Conference on Trusts and Combinations, 1907* (New York: National Civic Federation, 1908) , p. 223. (Hereafter cited as N.C.F. *Trusts*) .

4. N.C.F., *Trusts,* pp. 224–226.

5. *Ibid.,* p. 12.

6. *Ibid.,* p. 248.

7. *Ibid.,* pp. 37–38.

8. *Ibid.,* p. 89.

9. *Ibid.,* p. 41.

10. *Ibid.,* pp. 68–69.

11. *Ibid.,* p. 98.

12. *Ibid.,* p. 136.

13. *Ibid.,* pp. 68–69.

14. *Ibid.,* p. 289.

15. *Ibid.,* p. 291.

16. *Ibid.,* p. 110.

17. *Ibid.,* p. 113.

18. *Ibid.,* p. 95.

19. *Ibid.,* p. 175.

20. *Ibid.,* p. 367.

21. *Ibid.,* p. 430.

22. *Ibid.,* p. 127.

23. *Ibid.,* p. 338.

24. Seth Low to Theodore Roosevelt, 26 October 1907; Low Papers, Spec. Mss. Coll. Carbons.

25. Theodore Roosevelt to Seth Low, 30 October 1907; Low Papers, Spec. Mss. Coll. Carbons.

26. Seth Low to Nicholas Murray Butler, 6 February 1908; Butler Papers, Spec. Mss. Coll.

27. *American Federationist,* 15 (March 1908) , p. 190.

28. Robert H. Wiebe's contention that Perkins bore the brunt of responsibility for the drafting of the measure is incorrect. See his *Businessmen and Reform: A Study of the Progressive Movement* (Chicago: Quadrangle Books, 1968) , pp. 80–81.

29. Ralph M. Easley to Samuel Gompers, 12 February 1908; N.C.F. Papers, box 94.

30. Ralph M. Easley to Samuel Gompers, 25 February 1908; N.C.F. Papers, box 33.

31. Samuel Gompers to Seth Low, 6 March 1908; The Samuel Gompers Papers, Manuscript Division, Library of Congress, Washington, D.C. (Hereafter cited as Gompers Papers) .

32. Seth Low to Theodore Roosevelt, 7 March 1908; Roosevelt Papers.

33. Ralph M. Easley to Daniel J. Keefe, 8 March 1908; N.C.F. Papers, box 34.

34. Seth Low to George W. Perkins, 9 March 1908; The George W. Perkins Papers, box 19, Special Collections Department: Columbia University Library,

Columbia University, New York, New York. (Hereafter cited as Perkins Papers).

35. Gompers, *Seventy Years of Life and Labor,* vol. 1, p. 532.

36. *New York Times,* 13 March 1908, p. 1.

37. From draft in Perkins Papers, box 19.

38. *New York Times,* 19 March 1908, p. 1.

39. Seth Low to George W. Perkins, 18 March 1908; Perkins Papers, box 19.

40. Ralph M. Easley to E. A. Bancroft, 21 March 1908; N.C.F. Papers, box 94.

41. *New York Times,* 20 March 1908, p. 4, & 26 March 1908, p. 6.

42. *American Industries,* 7 (1 April 1908) , p. 20.

43. *The Square Deal,* 3 (May 1908) , p. 90; James A. Emery, "Analysis of the Proposed Amendments to the Sherman Anti-Trust Law," *The Square Deal,* 3 (May 1908) , p. 1; James A. Emery, "Hoodwinking Congress and the People," *American Industries,* 7 (15 April 1908) , pp. 5–6.

44. Morefield Storey to Seth Low, 2 April 1908; N.C.F. Papers, box 95.

45. Edgar A. Bancroft to George W. Perkins, 22 April 1908; Perkins Papers, box 19.

46. George W. Perkins to Edgar A. Bancroft, 23 April 1908; Perkins Papers, box 19.

47. Andrew Carnegie to Ralph M. Easley, 24 March 1908; N.C.F. Papers, box 95.

48. Ralph M. Easley to Samuel Gompers, 26 March 1908; N.C.F. Papers, box 95.

49. *New York Times,* 26 March 1908, p. 3.

50. Theodore Roosevelt to Seth Low, 28 March 1908; Low Papers, Spec. Mss. Coll.

51. Samuel Gompers to Ralph M. Easley, 27 March 1908; Gompers Papers.

52. Testimony of Samuel Gompers, House Committee on the Judiciary, 6 April 1908; N.C.F. Papers, box 99. For the published hearings see *United States House of Representatives, Judiciary Committee (Subcommittee 3),* 1908, Hearings on HR 19745.

53. *Ibid.,* N.C.F. Papers, box 99.

54. Testimony of Jeremiah W. Jenks, House Committee on the Judiciary, 6 April 1908; N.C.F. Papers, box 99.

55. Testimony of Seth Low, House Committee on the Judiciary, 6 April 1908; N.C.F. Papers, box 99.

56. *Ibid., N.C.F. Review,* 3 (May 1908), p. 2.

57. *Ibid.,* N.C.F. Papers, box 99.

58. See Burton J. Hendrick, "The Battle Against the Sherman Law," *McClure's Magazine,* 31 (October 1908) .

59. Gabriel Kolko's contention that Roosevelt failed to support the Hepburn bill because it was too favorable to labor is clearly an overstatement, as is his argument that the bill was basically a clever scheme by the House of Morgan to escape anti-trust prosecution. See *The Triumph of Conservatism: A Reinterpretation of American History, 1900–1916* (Chicago: Quadrangle Books, 1967) , pp. 132–138.

60. Ralph M. Easley to Arthur T. Hadley, 23 February 1910; N.C.F. Papers, box 100.

61. Ralph M. Easley to Melville E. Ingalls, 16 July 1908; N.C.F. Papers, box 34.

62. Ralph M. Easley to Arthur T. Hadley, 17 December 1908; N.C.F. Papers, box 34.

63. Theodore Roosevelt to Seth Low, 24 October 1908; Low Papers, Spec. Mss. Coll.

64. Seth Low to Theodore Roosevelt, 27 February 1909; Low Papers, Spec. Mss. Coll. Carbons.

65. Untitled Mss., 30 October 1911; Low Papers, box 106.

66. Untitled Mss., 30 October 1911; Low Papers, box 106.

67. The analysis which follows is drawn from the following addresses delivered by Seth Low in the years, 1909–1911. All are to be found in the Low Papers. "Address at Conference on Uniform Legislation," 1910, box 91; "Remarks at Meeting of Republican Club," 1910, box 63; "Proposition," 1911, box 106; "'Journal of Commerce' essay," 1911, box 107; "'Commercial and Financial Chronicle' essay," 1911, box 92; and "The Necessity for National Incorporation of Companies Doing Interstate Business," 1910, box 92.

68. "Proposition," 1911; Low Papers, box 106.

69. William Howard Taft to Seth Low, 20 February 1910; Low Papers, Spec. Mss. Coll.

70. George W. Wickersham to Seth Low, 24 February 1910; Low Papers, box 92.

71. Frederick P. Fish to Seth Low, 15 March 1910; Low Papers, box 92.

72. R. D. Silliman to Seth Low, 28 March 1910; Low Papers, box 92.

73. John W. H. Crim to Seth Low, 30 November 1910; Low Papers, Spec. Mss. Coll. Carbons.

74. William Howard Taft to Seth Low, 11 January 1911; Low Papers, Spec. Mss. Coll.

75. N.C.F. Review, 3 (February 1912), p. 3.

76. Seth Low to W. S. Taylor, 22 December 1913; Low Papers, box 115.

77. Quoted in National Civic Federation, Eleventh Annual Meeting, 12–14 January 1911, (New York: National Civic Federation, n.d.), pp. 23–24.

CHAPTER XIII

1. New York Call, 21 March 1915, p. 1.

2. Quoted in "Socialism and the National Civic Federation," p. 3; Low Papers, box 104. John Kirby, Jr. was President of the National Association of Manufacturers.

3. Seth Low, "President's Annual Address," National Civic Federation, Ninth Annual Meeting, 1908 (New York: National Civic Federation, 1909), p. 12.

4. Ralph M. Easley to W. G. Lee, 24 February 1910; N.C.F. Papers, box 100.

5. Seth Low, "The Writ of Injunction as a Party Issue," The Century Magazine, 76 (October 1908), p. 914.

6. Low, "Writ of Injunction," p. 911.

7. Quoted in National Civic Federation, Ninth Annual Meeting, p. 203.

8. Quoted in Elsie Glück, John Mitchell Miner: Labor's Bargain with the Gilded Age (New York: John Day Co., 1929), p. 229.

9. Quoted in National Civic Federation, *Ninth Annual Meeting,* p. 23.

10. *Ibid.,* p. 204.

11. *Ibid.,* p. 63.

12. Seth Low to Bishop Chauncey B. Brewster, 22 December 1909; Low Papers, box 92.

13. Seth Low to Elbert H. Gary, 19 April 1911; Low Papers, Spec. Mss. Coll. Carbons.

14. Elbert H. Gary to Seth Low, 20 April 1911; Low Papers, box 43.

15. Gompers, *Seventy Years of Life and Labor,* vol. 2, p. 705.

16. Samuel Gompers, "The American Labor Movement," *American Federationist,* 21 (August 1914), p. 628.

17. *American Federationist,* 15 (January 1908), p. 30.

18. Daniel J. Keefe, untitled speech, 1908; N.C.F. Papers, box 34.

19. Green, *The National Civic Federation and the American Labor Movement,* pp. 138–139.

20. *American Federationist,* 12 (February 1905), p. 79.

21. Quoted in *N.C.F. Review,* 2 (September-October 1905), p. 2.

22. Timothy Healy, "Address" of July 1911; Low Papers, box 151.

23. Gompers, *Seventy Years of Life and Labor,* vol. 1, p. 400.

24. Ralph M. Easley to J. Borden Harriman, 27 October 1908; N.C.F. Papers, box 34.

25. Ralph M. Easley to Seth Low, 25 January 1911; Low Papers, box 90.

26. Seth Low to Ralph M. Easley, 24 June 1911; Low Papers, box 146.

27. Seth Low to Ralph M. Easley, 22 July 1912; Low Papers, box 104.

28. Quoted in Sidney Howard, "Our Professional Patriots,' *The New Republic,* 39 (20 August 1924), p. 350.

29. John Mitchell to Seth Low, 15 February 1911; Low Papers, box 90.

30. Seth Low to John Mitchell, 28 February 1911; Low Papers, box 90.

31. Samuel Gompers, "Organized Labor and the National Civic Federation," *American Federationist,* 18 (March 1911), pp. 188–189.

32. "Socialism and the National Civic Federation," 1911; Low Papers, box 104.

33. Gompers, "Organized Labor and the National Civic Federation," p. 189.

34. *Official Magazine of the International Brotherhood of Teamsters, Chauffers, Stablemen and Helpers,* 8 (March 1911), p. 9.

35. *United Mine Workers' Journal,* 21 (20 April 1911), p. 2.

36. "Socialism and the National Civic Federation," 1911; Low Papers, box 104.

37. *Ibid.,* Low Papers, box 104.

38. *Ibid.,* Low Papers, box 104.

39. Seth Low, "Address 12th Annual Meeting of the National Civic Federation," March 1912; Low Papers, box 151.

40. Quoted in *N.C.F. Review,* 3 (March 1911), p. 2.

41. American Federation of Labor, *Report of the Proceedings of the Thirty-First Annual Convention* (n.p.: American Federation of Labor, n.d.), p. 218.

42. *Ibid.,* p. 25.

43. *Ibid.,* p. 219.

44. Seth Low to R. U. Johnson, 11 April 1911; Low Papers, box 91.

45. Seth Low to "the Editor," 19 May 1911; Low Papers, box 88.

46. Seth Low to Samuel Gompers, 27 April 1911; Low Papers, box 90.

47. Samuel Gompers to Seth Low, 2 June 1911; Low Papers, box 88.

48. Seth Low to Samuel Gompers, 17 June 1911; Low Papers, box 88.

49. Seth Low, "The National Civic Federation as a Factor Making for Industrial Peace," 1912; Manuscript copy in Low Papers, box 94. The article appeared in the *Annals of the American Academy of Political Science,* 44 (November 1912).

50. *Ibid.,* Low Papers, box 94.

51. Seth Low, "Address at Josephine Shaw Lowell Memorial," 21 May 1912; Low Papers, box 150.

52. Low, "The National Civic Federation as a Factor Making for Industrial Peace;" Low Papers, box 94.

53. Low, "Address at Josephine Shaw Lowell Memorial," Low Papers, box 150.

54. Seth Low to G. E. Taylor, 7 June 1912; Low Papers, box 88.

55. Low, "Address 12th Annual Meeting of the National Civic Federation," Low Papers, box 151.

56. Jacob H. Schiff to Seth Low, 14 December 1908; Low Papers, Spec. Mss. Coll.

57. Arthur T. Lyman, to Ralph M. Easley, c. 1910; N.C.F. Papers, box 46.

58. William Green to John Hays Hammond, 19 February 1909; N.C.F. Papers, box 40.

59. Quoted in *The Survey,* 22 (7 August 1909), p. 670.

60. "Socialism and the National Civic Federation," 1911; Low Papers, box 104.

61. Ralph M. Easley to Seth Low, 14 January 1910; Low Papers, box 92.

62. John Kirby to Seth Low, 10 January 1910; Low Papers, box 91.

63. Seth Low to the Rev. John P. Peters, 25 May 1912; Low Papers, box 150.

64. John Kirby, Jr., "A Disloyal and Unpatriotic Organization," *American Industries,* 12 (August 1911), p. 10.

65. Marcus M. Marks to Seth Low, 22 February 1912; Low Papers, box 151.

66. Quoted in National Civic Federation, *Eleventh Annual Meeting,* p. 146.

CHAPTER XIV

1. 4 August 1913; Low Papers, box 94.

2. Seth Low to Theodore Roosevelt, 13 September 1910; Low Papers, Spec. Mss. Coll. Carbons.

3. Seth Low to Theodore Roosevelt, 10 November 1910; Low Papers,

4. Theodore Roosevelt to Seth Low, 16 November 1910; Low Papers, Spec. Mss. Coll. Carbons.

5. Clipping in Low Papers, box 60.

6. Seth Low to Theodore Roosevelt, 16 February 1911; Low Papers, Spec. Mss. Coll. Carbons.

7. Theodore Roosevelt to Seth Low, 21 February 1911; Low Papers, Spec. Mss. Coll.

8. Seth Low to William Howard Taft, 25 January 1912; Low Papers, box 109.

9. Seth Low to Lyman Abbott, 29 February 1912; Low Papers, box 83.

10. Lawrence F. Abbott to Seth Low, 4 March 1912; Low Papers, box 151.

11. Seth Low to John William Burgess, 12 August 1912; Burgess Papers, Spec. Mss. Coll.

12. John William Burgess to Seth Low, undated; Low Papers, Spec. Mss. Coll.

13. Seth Low to John William Burgess, 15 August 1912; Burgess Papers, Spec. Mss. Coll.

14. Murray Nelson to Seth Low, 19 August 1912; Low Papers, box 83.

15. Seth Low to Charles D. Hilles, 16 September 1912; Low Papers, box 60.

16. Seth Low, "The Trusts and the Tariff," 17 October 1912; Low Papers, box 60.

17. Seth Low to *The Outlook*, 15 October 1912; Low Papers, box 120.

18. *Ibid.*, Low Papers, box 120.

19. Seth Low, "The Initiative, the Referendum, and the Recall," 9 October 1912; Low Papers, box 60.

20. Seth Low, "Direct Primaries," 17 June 1913; Low Papers, box 64.

21. Low, "The Initiative, the Referendum, and the Recall;" Low Papers, box 60.

22. Seth Low to "the Editor" of the *New York World,* 6 November 1912; Low Papers, box 120.

23. Seth Low to William Howard Taft, 6 November 1912; Low Papers, box 60.

24. William Howard Taft to Seth Low, 7 November 1912; Low Papers, box 60.

25. Seth Low to J.B. Bishop, 14 March 1913; Low Papers, box 109.

26. Seth Low, "Testimony before Committee on Interstate Commerce, United States Senate," 20 June 1913; Low Papers, box 96. For the published hearings see *United States Senate, Committee on Interstate Commerce,* 1913, pt. 1, *Hearings on S 2517,* and *United States House of Representatives, Judiciary Committee,* 1913, *Hearings on HR 6141.*

27. Ralph M. Easley to W.G. Lee (Bros. R.R. Trainmen), 4 March 1913; N.C.F. Papers, box 50.

28. Seth Low, "Government Mediation in Railroad Labor Disputes," 28 January 1913; Low Papers, box 151.

29. Low, "Testimony before Committee on Interstate Commerce;" Low Papers, box 96.

30. Low, "Government Mediation in Railroad Labor Disputes;" Low Papers, box 151.

31. *Ibid.*, Low Papers, box 151.

32. Seth Low to Woodrow Wilson, 19 March 1913; Low Papers, box 95.

33. J.P. Tumulty to Seth Low, 24 March 1913; Low Papers, box 95.

34. Seth Low to J.P. Tumulty, 27 May 1913; Low Papers, box 95.

35. J.P. Tumulty to Seth Low, 2 June 1913; Low Papers, box 95.

36. Seth Low to Woodrow Wilson, 7 June 1913; Low Papers, box 95.

37. Woodrow Wilson to Seth Low, 10 June 1913; Low Papers, box 95.

38. William C. Redfield to Seth Low, 12 June 1913; Low Papers, box 95.

39. Seth Low to Franklin K. Lane, 17 June 1913; Low Papers, box 94.

40. Low, "Testimony before Interstate Commerce Committee;" Low Papers, box 96.

41. Daniel Willard to Seth Low, 21 June 1913; Low Papers, box 95.

42. Seth Low to William B. Wilson and to Henry D. Clayton, telegram, 22 June 1913; Low Papers, box 94.

43. Seth Low to Francis G. Newlands, telegram, 26 June 1913; Low Papers, box 94.

44. Seth Low to William B. Wilson, 28 June 1913; Low Papers, box 95.

45. Seth Low to William B. Wilson, telegram, 27 June 1913; Low Papers, box 95.

46. William B. Wilson to Seth Low, 30 June 1913, telegram; Low Papers, box 95.

47. Mrs. J. Borden Harriman, *From Pinafores to Politics* (New York: Henry Holt, 1923), pp. 134–135.

48. Gertrude Beeks to Seth Low, 15 July 1913; Low Papers, box 94.

49. Seth Low to Samuel Rea, *et. al.*, 17 July 1913; Low Papers, box 95.

50. Seth Low to Woodrow Wilson, 17 July 1913; Low Papers, box 95.

51. Woodrow Wilson to Seth Low, 21 July 1913; Low Papers, box 95.

52. Seth Low to Andrew Carnegie, 30 July 1913; Low Papers, box 94.

53. Sereno E. Payne to Seth Low, 31 July 1913; Low Papers, box 96.

54. W.G. Lee to Seth Low, 30 July 1913; Low Papers, box 96.

55. Percy S. Grant to Seth Low, 19 July 1913; Low Papers, box 94.

56. Seth Low to Judge W.L. Chambers, 11 November 1913; Low Papers, box 115.

57. By 1916, the Brotherhoods had soured on the efficacy of arbitration as a means of realizing advances for labor, but as D.L. Cease of the Trainmen told Ralph Easley, "I trust that Mr. Low has noticed that in the objections to arbitration that no reference has been made or criticism offered of the Board of Arbitration of which he was Chairman. If he has not noticed this, or referred to it, you might call his attention to my statement." D.L. Cease to Ralph M. Easley, 11 September 1916; N.C.F. Papers, box 53.

58. Seth Low to Talcott Williams, 30 December 1911; Low Papers, box 107.

59. Form letter by Seth Low, 13 February 1913; Low Papers, box 106.

60. A. Leo Weil to Ralph M. Easley, 18 March 1913; N.C.F. Papers, box 98.

61. Seth Low to Woodrow Wilson, 14 January 1914; Low Papers, box 107.

62. Seth Low to Woodrow Wilson, 22 January 1914; Low Papers, box 107.

63. Seth Low, "Memorandum on I.T.C.," undated; Low Papers, box 106.

64. Seth Low to Samuel Gompers, 7 July 1914; Low Papers, Speeches: 2.

65. Seth Low to Edgar A. Bancroft, 11 June 1914; Low Papers, box 107.

66. Seth Low, "Statement before United States Commission on Industrial Relations," New York, 4 February 1915; Low Papers, box 88.

67. Ralph M. Easley to Seth Low, 17 March 1914; Low Papers, box 146.

68. Seth Low to Oswald Garrison Villard, 4 February 1913; Low Papers, box 93.

CHAPTER XV

1. James E. Russell, "Seth Low, Leader of Men," *Columbia University Quarterly*, 19 (December 1916), p. 1.

2. Editorial from *Christian Science Monitor* reprinted in *Columbia Alumni News*, 8 (20 October 1916), p. 94.

3. 1 January 1913; Low Papers, box 70.

4. Emmet J. Scott, "Mr. Low and Tuskegee Institute," *Columbia Alumni News*, 8 (20 October 1916), p. 86.

5. Seth Low, "The Significance of Tuskegee," 1906; Low Papers, Speeches: 2.

6. Seth Low to Frederick A. Goetze, 21 September 1911; Low Papers, box 69.

7. Seth Low to Bishop Charles P. Galloway, 6 September 1904; Low Papers, Spec. Mss. Coll. Carbons.

8. Booker T. Washington to Seth Low, 12 January 1907; Low Papers, Spec. Mss. Coll.

9. Seth Low to Booker T. Washington, 28 July 1907; Low Papers, box 137.

10. Seth Low, et. al., to Woodrow Wilson, undated; Low Papers, box 109.

11. Seth Low to William S. Braithwaite, 16 November 1915; Low Papers, box 69.

12. Andrew Carnegie to Seth Low, 18 January 1915; Low Papers, Spec. Mss. Coll.

13. Seth Low, "Address to Officers of the German Squadron," undated; Low Papers, box 81.

14. Seth Low, "Address at Columbia, S.C.," 27 April 1905; Low Papers, Spec. Mss. Coll. Carbons.

15. *Ibid.*, Low Papers, Spec. Mss. Coll. Carbons.

16. Jacob A. Riis, *How the Other Half Lives* (New York: Hill & Wang (American Century Series), 1957), p. 79.

17. Seth Low to Marlen E. Pew, 30 October 1903; Low Papers, Spec. Mss. Coll. Carbons.

18. Seth Low to J.H. Patten, 31 July 1905; Low Papers, Spec. Mss. Coll. Carbons.

19. Seth Low to Leon Sanders, 20 January 1915; Low Papers, box 82.

20. Seth Low to Huntington Wilson, 20 January 1914; Low Papers, box 82.

21. Seth Low to Theodore Roosevelt, 23 November 1905; Low Papers, Spec. Mss. Coll. Carbons.

22. Seth Low, "Address at Panama-Pacific Exposition," 19 March 1915; Low Papers, box 72.

23. Seth Low, "Address before Minnesota State Bar Association," 20 August 1912; Low Papers, box 72.

24. Seth Low to William J. Moran, 8 May 1911; Low Papers, box 98.

25. John Mitchell (Chairman, N.Y.S. Industrial Commission) to Seth Low, 2 August 1916; Low Papers, box 72.

26. Seth Low to Josiah O. Low, 2 March 1911; Low Papers, box 43.

27. Seth Low to Judge E.H. Gary, 24 March 1909; Low Papers, Spec. Mss. Coll. Carbons.

28. Seth Low to R.G. Howell, 26 April 1909; Low Papers, Spec. Mss. Coll. Carbons.

29. Seth Low to Nicholas Murray Butler, 24 April 1914; Low Papers, box 110.

30. Seth Low, "Address at the New York State Chamber of Commerce," 7 May 1914; Low Papers, box 61.

31. Seth Low to Woodrow Wilson, 29 August 1914; Low Papers, box 61.

32. John Franklin Crowell, "Seth Low's Work as President of the New

York Chamber of Commerce," *Columbia Alumni News*, 8 (20 October 1916), pp. 82–84.

33. Ralph M. Easley to Isaac N. Seligman, 6 May 1916; N.C.F. Papers, box 53.

34. Seth Low to Ralph M. Easley, 23 August 1916; Low Papers, box 146.

35. Ralph M. Easley to Seth Low, 28 August 1916; Low Papers, box 146.

36. Henry L. Stimson to Ralph M. Easley, 11 September 1916; N.C.F. Papers, box 53.

37. Russell, "Seth Low, Leader of Men," p. 3.

38. Quoted in Alfred T. White, "Seth Low," *The Survey*, 36 (30 September 1916), p. 634.

39. J.G. Schmidlapp to Ralph M. Easley, 6 October 1916; N.C.F. Papers, box 53.

40. Harriman, *From Pinafores to Politics*, p. 92.

41. Howard, "Our Professional Patriots," p. 351.

42. *Ibid.*, pp. 348–349.

43. Gompers, "American Labor Movement," p. 628.

44. Franklin H. Giddings, "Mr. Low and the Labor Movement," *Columbia News*, 8 (20 October 1916), p. 80.

45. *The Nation*, 103 (21 September 1916), p. 270.

CHAPTER XVI

1. See the chapter on the National Civic Federation in Herbert Croly, *Marcus Alonzo Hanna: His Life and Work* (New York: Macmillan, 1912).

2. Charles Edward Merriam, *American Political Ideas* (New York: Macmillan, 1920), p. 50.

3. See the chapter on the National Civic Federation in Clarence E. Bonnett, *Employers' Associations in the United States: A Study of Typical Associations* (New York: Macmillan, 1922).

4. Howard, "Our Professional Uatriots," p. 349.

5. Norman Hapgood, ed., *Professional Patriots* (New York: Albert and Charles Boni, 1928), p. 37.

6. Ray Ginger, *The Bending Cross: A Biography of Eugene Victor Debs* (New Brunswick, N.J.: Rutgers University Press, 1949), p. 220.

7. Quoted in Hapgood, *Professional Patriots*, p. 141.

8. *Ibid.*, pp. 46–48.

9. John R. Commons and Associates (Selig Perlman & Philip Taft), *History of Labor in the United States, 1896–1932*, v. 4 *Labor Movements* (New York: Macmillan, 1935), p. 49.

10. Norman J. Ware, *Labor in Modern Industrial Society* (Boston: D.C. Heath, 1935), p. 323.

11. Lorwin, *American Federation of Labor, passim*. Likewise, Foster Rhea Dulles in his *Labor in America: A History* (New York: Crowell, 1955), based his narrative largely on Commons' studied, and added little that was new concerning the N.C.F.

12. In the 1940's, three master's essays were written on the National Civic Federation. The first was completed by Henry D. Gasson in 1940. A brief, general account of the organization's origin, development, and activities, Gasson had access to the Federation's papers as well as the benefit of oral interviews with Easley's widow. He concluded that the Civic Federation was

a basically conservative reaction of the American business community to the challenge of Progressive reform. It was an attempt to keep Progressive reform within suitably conservative bounds. See Henry D. Gasson, *The National Civic Federation*, unpublished master's essay, Catholic University of America, Washington, D.C., 1940.

Seven years later, a Columbia University graduate student made an investigation of the Federation's labor policies. Irving G. Cheslaw examined both the N.C.F. and the Seth Low papers but his 65-page essay made few references to either collection, and totally ignored the Federation's role in the framing of the 1908 Hepburn bill and in the passage of the 1913 Newlands Act, as well as its efforts to establish collective bargaining procedures. With very little evidence he declared that "The National Civic Federation appropriately falls into the Progressive era, but within that context it stood far to the right." See Irving G. Cheslaw, *The National Civic Federation and Labor (a study in conservative reform)*, unpublished master's essay, Columbia University, New York, New York, 1947, p. 64.

A year later, yet another study of the Civic Federation was completed. Sidney Sass went into all aspects of the Federation's activities—labor policies, public utilities regulation, welfare work, and its anti-socialist propaganda—and paid special attention to the organization's sources of revenue. It was the contention of Sass that the Federation was useful in shielding the early labor movement from the relentless attacks of the open shop advocates, but that basically it sought to patch up and gloss over the fundamental economic conflicts in American society, that it sought to preserve traditional American socio-economic institutions while granting organized labor as few reforms as were absolutely necessary to preserve the *status quo*. It was, thus, a conservative organization seeking to keep the conservatives in command of American life. See Sass, *The National Civic Federation, passim*.

All three were greatly, albeit unconsciously, influenced by the socialist critique of the Federation, and by the new concept of patrician reformism which was beginning to sweep the historical profession.

13. Green, *National Civic Federation and the American Labor Movement*, p. 71.

14. Gordon Maurice Jensen, *The National Civic Federation: American Business in an Age of Social Change and Social Reform, 1900–1910*, unpublished Ph.D. dissertation, Princeton University, Princeton, N.J., 1956, p. x.

15. Quoted in *ibid.*, p. 140.

16. Philip Taft, *The A.F. of L. in the Time of Gompers* (New York: Harper Bros., 1957), pp. 225–231.

17. Marc Karson, *American Labor Unions and Politics, 1900–1918* (Carbondale, Ill.: Southern Illinois University Press, 1958).

18. Bernard Mandel, *Samuel Gompers: A Biography* (Yellow Springs, Ohio: Antioch Press, 1963).

19. No effort will be made here to exhaustively cover the extensive literature of Progressive historiography; rather, the emphasis of this discussion will be on the major schools of thought which have arisen since World War II.

20. Frederic Austen Ogg, *National Progress, 1907–1917* (New York: Harper Bros., 1918).

21. Charles A. and Mary R. Beard, *The Rise of American Civilization*,

vol. 2 (New York: Macmillan, 1927); Harold U. Faulkner, *The Quest for Social Justice* (New York: Macmillan, 1931); and John D. Hicks, *The American Nation* (Boston: Houghton-Mifflin, 3rd ed., 1955).

22. Louis S. Reed, *The Labor Philosophy of Samuel Gompers* (Port Washington, N.Y.: Kennikat Press, reprinted 1966).

23. John Chamberlin, *Farewell to Reform: The Rise, Life and Decay of the Progressive Mind in America* (Chicago: Quadrangle Books, reprinted 1965).

24. Daniel Aaron, *Men of Good Hope: A Story of American Progressives* (New York: Oxford University Press, 1951).

25. Ray Ginger, *Age of Excess: The United States from 1877 to 1914* (New York: Macmillan, 1965).

26. George E. Mowry, *The California Progressives* (Chicago: Quadrangle Books, reprinted 1963). The idea that Progressive reform was largely a middle class movement with little following among new immigrant groups has been effectively challenged in recent years. J. Joseph Huthmacher's "Urban Liberalism and the Age of Reform," *Mississippi Valley Historical Review*, 49 (1962), maintained that the immigrant masses were not anti-Progressive, but were interested in reform and acted as a catalyst on the movement's middle class leadership, forcing it to assume more liberal and enlightened positions on socio-economic issues. Arguing that middle class reformism has been overstressed, he saw the lower class as being of equal importance in the reform movements of the Progressive era. Similarly, Irwin Yellowitz's *Labor and the Progressive Movement in New York State, 1897–1916* (Ithaca, N.Y.: Cornell University Press, 1965) demonstrated the crucial, and often independent, role played by organized labor in the New York State reform movement. Finally, Robert F. Wesser's "Charles Evans Hughes and the Urban Sources of Political Progressivism," *New York Historical Society Quarterly*, 50 (1966) has convincingly demonstrated the vital role played by recent immigrants and labor groups in pressing for social welfare legislation and state regulation of economic functions in the New York State Progressive movement.

27. See Hofstader, *Age of Reform* as well as John Morton Blum, *The Republican Roosevelt* (New York: Atheneum, reprinted 1963), and *Woodrow Wilson and the Politics of Morality* (Boston: Little, Brown, 1956); Samuel P. Hays, *The Response to Industrialism, 1885–1914* (Chicago: University of Chicago Press, 1957); Arthur S. Link, *Woodrow Wilson and the Progressive Era, 1910–1917* (New York: Harper Bros., 1954); and also George E. Mowry, *The Era of Theodore Roosevelt and the Birth of Modern America, 1900–1912* (New York: Harper Bros., 1958).

28. John Higham, "The Cult of the 'American Consensus:' Homogenizing Our History," *Commentary*, 27 (1959) offers a biting dissent from the consensus school.

29. A number of recent biographies of prominent Progressives have cast serious doubt on the validity of the "Progressive profile." See especially, E. McClung Fleming, *R. R. Bowker: Militant Liberal* (Norman, Okla.: University of Oklahoma Press, 1952); Harbaugh, *Power and Responsibility*; Richard Lowitt, *George W. Norris: The Making of a Progressive, 1861–1912* (Syracuse, N.Y.: Syracuse University Press, 1963); Charles Forcey, *The Crossroads of Liberalism: Croly, Weyl, Lippman, and the Progressive Era* (New York: Oxford University Press, 1966); Robert F. Wesser, *Charles Evans*

Hughes: Politics and Reform in New York, 1905–1910 (Ithaca, N.Y.: Cornell University Press, 1967); and Jack Tager, *The Intellectual as Urban Reformer: Brand Whitlock and the Progressive Movement* (Press of Case Western Reserve University, 1968).

30. Though not directly concerned with the subjects of this study, a number of recent works have considerably broadened our conception of the motivations behind Progressive reform, and have cast doubt on the "status revolution." Sidney Fine's *Laissez-Faire and the General Welfare State: A Study of Conflict in American Thought, 1865–1901* (Ann Arbor, Michigan: University of Michigan Press, 1956) has thrown new light on the extent of welfare state sentiment in the years just prior to the Progressive era. And, Robert H. Bremner, *From the Depths: The Discovery of Poverty in the United States* (New York: New York University Press, 1956); Lubove, *The Progressives and the Slums;* Holli, *Reform in Detroit;* Crooks, *Politics and Progress;* Davis, *Spearheads for Reform;* and Christopher Lasch, *The New Radicalism in America [1889–1963]: The Intellectual as a Social Type* (New York: Alfred A. Knopf, 1965) have demonstrated the liberal, social welfare orientation of a considerable segment of the Progressive movement.

31. Jack Blicksilver, "George Gunton: Pioneer Spokesman for a Labor-Big Business Entente," *Business History Review,* 31 (1957).

32. John A. Garraty, *Right-Hand Man: The Life of George W. Perkins* (New York: Harper Bros., 1960).

33. John Braeman, "Seven Progressives: A Review Article," *Business History Review,* 35 (1961).

34. Wiebe, *Businessmen and Reform, passim.*

35. Wiebe, *Search for Order, passim.*

36. Kolko, *Triumph of Conservatism, passim.*

Bibliography

PRIMARY SOURCES

I: *Manuscript Collections*

The Brooklyn Young Republican Club Scrapbook, Long Island Historical Society.
The John William Burgess Papers, Columbia University Library.
The Nicholas Murray Butler Papers, Columbia University Library.
The Citizens' Union Papers, Columbia University Library.
The City Club of New York Papers, New York Public Library.
The Richard Watson Gilder Papers, New York Public Library.
The Samuel Gompers Papers, Library of Congress.
The Francis Vinton Greene Papers, New York Public Library.
A. A. Low and Brothers' Scrapbook of the Far Eastern Trade, New York Public Library.
The Josiah O. Low Family Letters, 1837–1884, New York Public Library.
The Seth Low Papers, Columbia University Library.
The National Civic Federation Papers, New York Public Library.
The George W. Perkins Papers, Columbia University Library.
The Theodore Roosevelt Papers, Library of Congress.
Shepard-Low Campaign Scrapbook (Comp. by E. P. Wheeler), New York Public Library.
The Richard W. G. Welling Papers, New York Public Library.
The Everett P. Wheeler Papers, New York Public Library.

II: *Oral History Memoirs,* Oral History Research Office, Columbia University

Memoirs of:

George W. Alger
Robert S. Binkerd
Charles C. Burlingham
Frank Diehl Fackenthal
Lawson Purdy
Martin Saxe
Frederick Tanner

Homer Folks
John A. Heffernan
George McAneny
William A. Prendergast
Laurence A. Tanzer
Lawrence Veiller

III: *Newspapers and Periodicals*

Acorn, 1903.
American Federationist, 1900–1916.
American Industries, 1908.
Brooklyn Advance, 1883.
Brooklyn Eagle, 1881–1885.
Collier's Weekly, 1902.
Columbia Alumni News, 1916.

Harper's Weekly, 1903.
Journal of Commerce and Commercial Bulletin (New York), 1901.
The Nation, 1897, 1901–1904, 1916.
National Civic Federation Monthly Review (became *National Civic Federation Review* with vol. 1, issue #11), 1903–1914.
New York Advertiser, 1903.
New York Call, 1915.
New York Evening Journal, 1903.
New York Sun, 1897.
New York Telegram, 1901.
New York Times, 1881–1885, 1897, 1900–1903, 1908.
New York Tribune, 1897, 1903.
New York Vigilant, 1900–1901.
New York World, 1897, 1901, 1903.
Official Magazine of the International Brotherhood of Teamsters, Chauffers, Stablemen and Helpers, 1911.
The Outlook, 1901–1903.
Review of Reviews, 1900–1903.
The Square Deal, 1908.
The Survey, 1909.
The Tammany Times, 1897–1903 (scattered issues).
United Mine Workers' Journal, 1911.
World's Work, 1901.

IV: *Articles*

ADLER, FELIX. "Social Function of the Saloon," *Municipal Affairs*, 5 (1901).

AGAR, JOHN G. "The Saloon Problem in New York," *Municipal Affairs*, 5 (1901).

BAKER, RAY S. "The Civic Federation of Chicago," *The Outlook*, 52 (27 July 1895).

BARNES, DEMAS. "Municipal Government," *Brooklyn Magazine*, 2 (June 1885).

BROOKS, SYDNEY. "Tammany Again," *Fortnightly Review*, 80 (December 1903).

BRYCE, JAMES. "The Mayoralty Election in New York," *Contemporary Review*, 72 (November 1897).

BURGESS, JOHN W. "Reminiscences of Columbia University in the Last Quarter of the Last Century," *Columbia University Quarterly*, 15 (1913).

CARY, EDWARD. "Seth Low: A Character Sketch," *Review of Reviews*, 16 (July 1897).

CHAPMAN, JOHN JAY. "Is A Third Party Necessary in Municipal Reform Work?" *Municipal Affairs*, 4 (1900).

COMMONS, JOHN R. "Some Taxation Problems and Reforms," *Review of Reviews*, 27 (January 1903).

CROWELL, JOHN FRANKLIN. "Seth Low's Work as President of the New York Chamber of Commerce," *Columbia Alumni News*, 8 (20 October 1916).

CUTTING, ROBERT FULTON. "City Government and the People," *Municipal Affairs*, 5 (1901).

DENNISON, LINDSAY. "Scenes from a Great Campaign," *World's Work*, 3 (December 1901).

DEVINE, EDWARD T. "Municipal Reform and Social Welfare in New York," *Review of Reviews*, 28 (October 1903).

EASLEY, RALPH M. "A View of the Labor Question," *Harper's Weekly,* 48 (5 November 1904).

EASLEY, RALPH M. "What Organized Labor Has Learned," *McClure's Magazine,* 19 (October 1902).

EASLEY, RALPH M. "The Work of the National Civic Federation," *Harper's Weekly,* 48 (26 November 1904).

EMERY, JAMES A. "Analysis of the Proposed Amendments to the Sherman Anti-Trust Act," *The Square Deal,* 3 (May 1908).

EMERY, JAMES A. "Hoodwinking Congress and the People," *American Industries,* 7 (15 April 1908).

FLOWER, ROSWELL P. "Is Non-Partisanship in Municipal Government Possible?" *The Forum,* 23 (1897).

GIDDINGS, FRANKLIN H. "Mr. Low and the Labor Movement," *Columbia Alumni News,* 8 (20 October 1916).

GODKIN, E. L. "Business Administration," *The Nation,* 61 (24 October 1895).

GOMPERS, SAMUEL. "The American Labor Movement," *American Federationist,* 21 (August 1914).

GOMPERS, SAMUEL. "Organized Labor and the National Civic Federation," *American Federationist,* 18 (March 1911).

"Greater New York and the Citizens' Union," *The Outlook,* 56 (15 May 1897).

GUNTON, GEORGE. "Municipal Emancipation," *Lecture Bulletin of the Institute of Social Economics,* 5 (15 October 1901).

GUNTON, GEORGE. "New Era in Municipal Government," *Lecture Bulletin of the Institute of Social Economics,* 5 (15 November 1901).

HAIGHT, A. S. "Independent Parties," *Municipal Affairs,* 4 (1900).

HENDRICK, BURTON J. "The Battle Against the Sherman Law," *McClure's Magazine,* 31 (October 1908).

HINRICHS, FREDERIC W. "Hon. Seth Low," *Brooklyn Advance,* 9 (November 1883).

HINRICHS, FREDERIC W. "Seth Low, Mayor of Brooklyn," *Columbia Alumni News,* 8 (20 October 1916).

KELLER, JOHN W. "Municipal Reformers in Party Politics," *Municipal Affairs,* 4 (1900).

KIRBY, JOHN, JR. "A Disloyal and Unpatriotic Organization," *American Industries,* 12 (August 1911).

LOW, SETH. "Civil Service Reform," *Brooklyn Advance,* 6 (May 1882).

LOW, SETH. "The Government of Cities in the United States," *The Century Magazine,* 42 (September 1891).

LOW, SETH. "Obstacles to Good City Government," *The Forum,* 5 (1888).

LOW, SETH. "The Problem of City Government," *Notes Supplementary to the Johns Hopkins University Studies in History and Political Science,* #4 (1889).

LOW, SETH. "The Problem of City Government in the United States," *The Outlook,* 53 (4 April 1896).

LOW, SETH. "The Rights of the Citizens," *Scribner's Magazine,* 7 (1890).

LOW, SETH. "Some Questions of the Day," *Harper's Magazine,* 91 (June 1895).

LOW, SETH. "The Writ of Injunction as a Party Issue," *The Century Magazine,* 76 (October 1908).

MALTBIE, MILO ROY. "A Century of Franchise History," *Municipal Affairs,* 4 (1900).

"The Marriage of Capital and Labor," *Catholic World*, 74 (January 1902).

MARTIN, JOHN. "A Constructive Program: What the Low Administration Should Do," *Municipal Affairs*, 5 (1901).

"A National Issue," *The Outlook*, 57 (23 October 1897).

"Our Fire Department," *Brooklyn Advance*, 8 (April 1883).

PECK, HARRY THURSTON. "Twelve Years of the University," *Columbia University Quarterly*, 4 (1901).

PINE, JOHN B. "King's College: now Columbia University, 1754–1897," *Half-Moon Series*, 1 (1897).

RHEES, RUSH. "Address in Memory of Seth Low," *Proceedings of the 52nd Convocation of the University of the State of New York*, 1916.

"HON. RIPLEY ROPES," *Brooklyn Advance*, 6 (April 1882).

RUSSELL, JAMES E. "Seth Low, Leader of Men," *Columbia University Quarterly*, 19 (1916).

SCHURZ, CARL. "The Task of the Citizens' Union," *Harper's Weekly*, 41 (11 December 1897).

SCOTT, EMMET J. "Mr. Low and Tuskegee Institute," *Columbia Alumni News*, 8 (20 October 1916).

"Senator Hanna on Labor Unions and Socialism," *Gunton's Magazine*, 26 (March 1904).

SHEPARD, EDWARD M. "The Brooklyn Idea in City Government," *The Forum*, 16 (1893).

SLOANE, WILLIAM M. "The Life of Seth Low," *American Scenic and Historic Preservation Society, Annual Report*, 22 (1917).

SLOANE, WILLIAM M. "Seth Low," *Columbia University Quarterly*, 4 (1901).

SMALL, ALBION W. "The Civic Federation of Chicago," *American Journal of Sociology*, 1 (1895).

SMITH, MUNROE. "Seth Low, President of Columbia University," *Columbia Alumni News*, 8 (20 October 1916).

STRAUS, OSCAR S. "Results Accomplished by the Industrial Department, National Civic Federation," *Annals of the American Academy of Political and Social Science*, 20 (1902).

WARDMAN, ERVIN. "Men and Issues in the New York City Campaign," *Review of Reviews*, 28 (November 1903).

WARNER, JOHN DEWITT. "Municipal Betterment in the New York City Elections," *Municipal Affairs*, 5 (1901).

WARNER JOHN DEWITT. "The Raines Liquor Tax Law: State Promotion of Vice," *Municipal Affairs*, 5 (1901).

WELLMAN, WALTER. "The Inside History of the Great Coal Strike," *Collier's Weekly*, 30 (18 October 1902).

WHITE, ALFRED T. "Seth Low," *The Survey*, 36 (1916).

"Why Municipal Reform Succeeds in Chicago and Fails in New York," *The Independent*, 56 (14 April 1904).

WILLIAMS, TALCOTT. "Tammany Hall," *Half-Moon Series*, 2 (1898).

V: Books

BOGARD, MILO T., ed. *The Redemption of New York*. (New York: P. F. McBreen, 1902).

BUTLER, NICHOLAS MURRAY. *Across the Busy Years: Recollections and Reflections*, vol. 1. (New York: Charles Scribner's Sons, 1939).

CHAPMAN, JOHN JAY. *Practical Agitation.* (New York: Charles Scribner's Sons, 1900).

COMMONS, JOHN ROGERS. *Myself.* (New York: Macmillan, 1934).

DEFOREST, ROBERT W., and LAWRENCE VEILLER, eds. *The Tenement House Problem,* 2 vols. (New York: Macmillan, 1903).

EDWARDS, RICHARD. *An Historical and Descriptive Review of the City of Brooklyn.* . . . (New York: Historical Publishing Co., 1883).

GOMPERS, SAMUEL. *Seventy Years of Life and Labor: An Autobiography.* 2 vols. (New York: E. P. Dutton, 1925).

HAMMOND, JOHN HAYS. *The Autobiography of John Hays Hammond,* vol. 2 (New York: Farrar and Rinehart, 1935).

HARRIMAN, (Mrs.) J. BORDEN. *From Pinafores to Politics.* (New York: Henry Holt, 1923).

HODDER, ALFRED. *A Fight for the City.* (New York: Macmillan, 1903).

HOWARD, HENRY W. B. *The Eagle and Brooklyn.* 2 vols. (Brooklyn Daily Eagle, 1893).

LOINES, ELMA, ed. *The China Trade Post-bag of the Seth Low Family of Salem and New York, 1829–1873.* (Manchester, Maine: Falmouth Publishing House, 1953).

LOW, BENJAMIN R. C. *Seth Low.* (New York: G. P. Putnam's, 1925).

LOW, (Capt.) CHARLES P. *Some Recollections.* (Boston: George H. Ellis Co., 1905).

LOW, SETH. "An American View of Municipal Government in the United States," in James Bryce, *The American Commonwealth,* vol. 2 (London: Macmillan, 1888).

LOW, SETH. "Relation of the Church to the Capital and Labor Question," in James McCosh, *et. al., Problems of American Civilization.* (New York: Baker and Taylor, 1888).

LOW, WILLIAM GILMAN. *Some Recollections for His Children and Grandchildren.* (Brooklyn: Brooklyn Eagle Press, 2nd ed., 1933).

MATTHEWS, BRANDER, *et. al. A History of Columbia University, 1754–1904.* (New York: Columbia University Press, 1904).

MITCHELL, JOHN. *Organized Labor: Its Problems, Purposes and Ideals.* (Philadelphia: American Book and Bible House, 1903).

MORISON, ELTING E., ed. *The Letters of Theodore Roosevelt,* vol. 3. (Cambridge, Mass.: Harvard University Press, 1951).

PLATT, THOMAS COLLIER (ed. by Louis J. Lang). *The Autobiography of Thomas Collier Platt.* (New York: B. W. Dodge, 1910).

RIIS, JACOB A. *How the Other Half Lives.* (New York: Hill & Wang (American Century Series), 1957).

STEFFENS, LINCOLN. *The Autobiography of Lincoln Steffens.* (New York: Harcourt, Brace and Co., 1931).

STEFFENS, LINCOLN. *The Shame of the Cities.* (New York: Hill & Wang (American Century Series), 1957).

STRAUS, OSCAR S. *Under Four Administrations: From Cleveland to Taft.* (Boston: Houghton-Mifflin Co., 1922).

SYRETT, HAROLD C., ed. *The Gentleman and the Tiger: The Autobiography of George B. McClellan, Jr.* (Philadelphia: J. B. Lippincott, 1956).

TAYLOR, GRAHAM. *Pioneering on Social Frontiers.* (Chicago: University of Chicago Press, 1930).

Welling, Richard W. G. *As the Twig Is Bent.* (New York: G. P. Putnam's, 1942).

Wheeler, Everett P. *Sixty Years of American Life.* (New York: E. P. Dutton, 1917).

VI: *Government and Organizational Publications, and Pamphlet Literature*

American Federation of Labor. *Report of the Proceedings of the Thirty-First Annual Convention,* 1911.

Brooklyn Daily Eagle. *Consolidation Number,* 2 January 1898. (*Eagle Library #22*).

Brooklyn, Mayor of. *Annual Messages,* 1882–1886. (Brooklyn: 1882–1886).

The Charter for the Greater New York. (*Brooklyn Eagle Library, #12* (February 1897)).

Chicago Conference on Trusts, 1899. (Chicago: Civic Federation of Chicago, 1900).

Citizens' Union of New York. *The City for the People! Campaign Book of the Citizens' Union, 1897 & 1901.* (New York: Citizens' Union, 1897 & 1901).

Citizens' Union of New York. *The City for the People! The Best Administration New York Ever Had: Campaign Book of the Citizens' Union, 1903.* (New York: Citizens' Union, 1903).

Citizens' Union of New York. *Home Rule in Cities.* (New York: Citizens' Union, 1897).

Citizens' Union of New York. *Seth Low's Practical Services to Labor.* (New York: Citizens' Union, 1897).

Citizens' Union of New York. *Workingmen as Citizens.* (New York: Citizens' Union, 1897).

City Club of New York. *The Police Department of the City of New York.* (New York: City Club, 1903).

Columbia University. *Dedication of the New Site Morningside Heights.* (New York: Columbia University Press, 1896).

Gilder, Richard Watson. *The Real Question at Issue in the Municipal Campaign.* (New York: Citizens' Union, 1897).

Greater New York Government, 1902–1903: Father Knickerbocker Adrift. (New York: Fusion Record Publishing Co., 1903).

Greene, Francis Vinton. *The Police Department of the City of New York.* (New York: City Club, 1903).

Low, Abiel Abbot. "Address at the Chamber of Commerce." (New York: John W. Amerman, 1866).

Low, Seth. *Addresses and Papers on Municipal Government.* (Place: Publisher, Year not given).

Low, Seth. "Brooklyn First, Last and All the Time." (Brooklyn: 1883).

Low, Seth. "Municipal Government." (Philadelphia: Committee of Fifty, 1892).

Low, Seth. *New York in 1850 and in 1890: A Political Study.* (New York: New York Historical Society, 1892).

Low, Seth. "The Problem of Municipal Government in the United States." (Ithaca, N.Y.: Cornell Unuiversity, 1887).

Low, Seth. *The Problem of Pauperism in the Cities of Brooklyn and New York.* (New York: Henry Bessey, 1879).

Low, Seth. "Propositions submitted to the Committee on Cities of the Constitutional Convention [1894]." (Place: Publisher, Year not given).

Low, William Gilman. *A Genealogical Quest and Family Notes.* (Privately printed, 2nd ed., 1928).

National Civic Federation. *Ninth Annual Meeting of the National Civic Federation.* (New York: National Civic Federation, 1909).

National Civic Federation. *Eleventh Annual Meeting of the National Civic Federation.* (New York: National Civic Federation, n.d.).

National Civic Federation. *Industrial Conference Under the Auspices of the National Civic Federation.* (New York: Winthrop Press, 1903).

National Civic Federation. *The National Civic Federation: Its Methods and Its Aim.* (New York: National Civic Federation, 1905).

National Civic Federation. *Proceedings of the National Conference on Trusts and Combinations.* (New York: National Civic Federation, 1908).

New York State Chamber of Commerce. *Entertainment Given to Mr. A. A. Low.* (New York: Press of the Chamber of Commerce, 1867).

SECONDARY WORKS

I: *Articles*

Arndt, Walter Talmadge. "A Quarter Century of Service," *The Searchlight,* 12 (14 December 1922).

Blicksilver, Jack. "George Gunton: Pioneer Spokesman for a Labor-Big Business Entente, *Business History Review,* 31 (1957).

Braeman, John. "Seven Progressives: A Review Article," *Business History Review,* 35.

Higham, John. "The Cult of the 'American Consensus': Homogenizing Our History," *Commentary,* 27 (1959).

Hofstadter, Richard. "Idealists and Professors and Sore-Heads: The Genteel Reformers," *Columbia University Forum,* vol. 5 #2.

Howard, Sidney. "Our Professional Patriots," *The New Republic,* 39 (20 August 1924).

Huthmacher, J. Joseph. "Urban Liberalism and the Age of Reform," *Mississippi Valley Historical Review,* 49 (1962).

Rothstein, David King. "Mayor Seth Low," *Columbia University Quarterly,* 32 (1940).

Swett, Steven C. "The Test of a Reformer: A Study of Seth Low, New York City Mayor, 1902–1903," *New York Historical Society Quarterly,* 44 (1960).

Wesser, Robert F. "Charles Evans Hughes and the Urban Sources of Political Progressism, *New York Historical Society Quarterly,* 50 (1966).

II: *Books*

Aaron, Daniel. *Men of Good Hope: A Story of American Progressives.* (New York: Oxford University Press, 1951).

Albion, Robert Greenhalgh. *The Rise of New York Port [1815–1860].* (New York: Charles Schribner's Sons, 1939).

Alexander, DeAlva Stanwood. *Four Famous New Yorkers: The Political Careers of Cleveland, Platt, Hill and Roosevelt.* (New York: Henry Holt, 1923).

Augur, Helen. *Tall Ships to Cathay.* (Garden City, N.Y.: Doubleday & Co., 1951).

Beard, Charles A. and Mary R. *The Rise of American Civilization,* vol. 2. (New York: Macmillan, 1927).

BLODGETT, GEOFFREY. *The Gentle Reformers: Massachusetts Democrats in the Cleveland Era.* (Cambridge, Mass.: Harvard University Press, 1966).

BLUM, JOHN MORTON. *The Republican Roosevelt* (New York: Atheneum, 1963).

BLUM, JOHN MORTON. *Woodrow Wilson and the Politics of Morality.* (Boston: Little, Brown, 1956).

BONNETT, CLARENCE E. *Employers' Associations in the United States: A Study of Typical Associations.* (New York: Macmillan, 1922).

BREMNER, ROBERT H. *From the Depths: The Discovery of Poverty in the United States.* (New York: New York University Press, 1956).

CALLOW, ALEXANDER B., JR. *The Tweed Ring.* (New York: Oxford University Press, 1966).

CARMER, CARL. "From Van Wyck to O'Dwyer," in Allen Nevins & John A. Krout, eds. *The Greater City: New York 1898–1948.* (New York: Columbia University Press, 1948).

CHAMBERLAIN, JOHN. *Farewell to Reform: The Rise, Life and Decay of the Progressive Mind in America.* (Chicago: Quadrangle Books, 1965).

CHESSMAN, G. WALLACE. *Governor Theodore Roosevelt: The Albany Apprenticeship, 1898–1900.* (Cambridge, Mass.: Harvard University Press, 1965).

COMMONS, JOHN R. and Associates (Selig Perlman & Philip Taft). *History of Labor in the United States, 1896–1932,* vol. 4 *Labor Movements.* (New York: Macmillan, 1935)

COON, HORACE. *Columbia: Colossus on the Hudson.* (New York: E. P. Dutton, 1947).

CROLY, HERBERT. *Marcus Alonzo Hanna: His Life and Work.* (New York: Macmillan, 1912).

CROOKS, JAMES B. *Politics and Progress: The Rise of Urban Progressivism in Baltimore, 1895–1911.* (Baton Rouge, La.: Louisiana State University Press, 1968).

DAVIS, ALLAN F. *Spearheads for Reform: The Social Settlements and the Progressive Movement, 18901914.* (New York: Oxford University Press, 1967).

DULLES, FOSTER RHEA. *Labor in America: A History.* (New York: Crowell, 1955).

FAULKNER, HAROLD U. *The Quest for Social Justice.* (New York: Macmillan, 1931).

FINE, SIDNEY. *Laissez-Faire and the General Welfare State: A Study of Conflict in American Thought, 1865–1901.* (Ann Arbor, Michigan: University of Michigan Press, 1956).

FLEMING, E. McCLUNG. *R. R. Bowker: Militant Liberal.* (Norman, Okla.: University of Oklahoma Press, 1952).

FORCEY, CHARLES. *The Crossroads of Liberalism: Croly, Weyl, Lippmann, and the Progressive Era.* (New York: Oxford University Press, 1966).

GARRATY, JOHN A. *Right-Hand Man: The Life of George W. Perkins.* (New York: Harper Bros., 1960).

GARRATY, JOHN A. *The New Commonwealth, 1877–90.* (New York: Harper & Row, 1968).

GARRATT, CHARLES. *The LaGuardia Years: Machine and Reform Politics in New York City.* (New Brunswick, N.J.: Rutgers University Press, 1961).

GINGER, RAY. *Age of Excess: The United States from 1877–1914.* (New York: Macmillan, 1965).

GINGER, RAY. *Altgeld's America: The Lincoln Ideal versus Changing Realities.* (Chicago: Quadrangle Books, 1965).

GINGER, RAY. *The Bending Cross: A Biography of Eugene Victor Debs.* (New Brunswick, N.J.: Rutgers University Press, 1949).

GLÜCK, ELSIE. *John Mitchell Miner: Labor's Bargain with the Gilded Age.* (New York: John Day Co., 1929).

GOSNELL, HAROLD F. *Boss Platt and His New York Machine.* (Chicago: University of Chicago Press, 1924).

GREEN, MARGUERITE. *The National Civic Federation and the American Labor Movement, 1900–1925.* (Washington, D.C.: The Catholic University of America, 1956).

HAPGOOD, NORMAN, ed. *Professional Patriots.* (New York: Albert and Charles Boni, 1928).

HARBAUGH, WILLIAM HENRY. *Power & Responsibility: The Life and Times of Theodore Roosevelt.* (New York: Farrar, Straus & Cudahy, 1961).

HAYS, SAMUEL P. *The Response to Industrialism, 1885–1914.* (Chicago: University of Chicago Press, 1957).

HICKS, JOHN D. *The American Nation.* (Boston: Houghton-Mifflin, 3rd. ed., 1955).

HOFSTADTER, RICHARD. *The Age of Reform: From Bryan to F.D.R.* (New York: Vintage Books, 1955).

HOFSTADTER, RICHARD, and WALTER P. METZGER. *The Development of Academic Freedom in the United States.* (New York: Columbia University Press, 1955).

HOLLI, MELVIN G. *Reform in Detroit: Hazen S. Pingree and Urban Politics.* (New York: Oxford University Press, 1969).

HOWSON, ROGER. *His Excellency a Trustee.* (New York: Columbia University Bookstore, 1945).

KARSON, MARC. *American Labor Unions and Politics, 1900–1918.* (Carbondale, Ill.: Southern Illinois University Press, 1958).

KEPPEL, FREDERICK PAUL. *Columbia.* (New York: Oxford University Press, 1914).

KOLKO, GABRIEL. *The Triumph of Conservatism: A Reinterpretation of American History, 1900–1916.* (Chicago: Quadrangle Books, 1967).

LASCH, CHRISTOPHER. *The New Radicalism in America [1889–1963]: The Intellectual as a Social Type.* (New York: Alfred A. Knopf, 1965).

LINK, ARTHUR S. *Woodrow Wilson and the Progressive Era, 1910–1917.* (New York: Harper Bros., 1954).

LORWIN, LEWIS L. *The American Federation of Labor: History, Policies, and Prospects.* (Washington, D.C.: Brookings Institute, 1933).

LOWI, THEODORE J. *At the Pleasure of the Mayor.* (Glencoe, Ill.: The Free Press, 1964).

LOWITT, RICHARD. *George W. Norris: The Making of a Progressive, 1861–1912.* (Syracuse, N.Y.: Syrac use University Press, 1963).

LUBOVE, ROY. *The Progressives and the Slums: Tenement House Reform in New York City, 1890–1917.* (Pittsburgh, Pa.: University of Pitsburgh Press, 1962).

MANDEL, BERNARD. *Samuel Gompers: A Biography.* (Yellow Springs, Ohio: Antioch Press, 1963).

MANDELBAUM, SEYMOUR J. *Boss Tweed's New York.* (New York: John Wiley, 1965).

MERRIAM, CHARLES EDWARD. *American Political Ideas*. (New York: Macmillan, 1920).

MOWRY, GEORGE E. *The California Progressives*. (Chicago: Quadrangle Books, 1963).

MOWRY, GEORGE E. *The Era of Theodore Roosevelt and the Birth of Modern America, 1900–1912*. (New York: Harpers Bros., 1958).

MYERS, GUSTAVUS. *History of Tammany Hall*. (New York: Boni & Liveright, 1917).

OGG, FREDERIC AUSTEN. *National Progress 1907–1917*. (New York: Harper Bros. 1918).

REED, LOUIS S. *The Labor Philosophy of Samuel Gompers*. (Port Washington, N.Y.: Kennikat Press, 1966).

SPROAT, JOHN G. *"The Best Men": Liberal Reformers in the Gilded Age*. (New York: Oxford University Press, 1968).

STILES, HENRY R. *History of Kings County*, 2 vols. (New York: W. W. Munsell, 1884).

SYRETT, HAROLD COFFIN. *The City of Brooklyn, 1865–1898*. (New York: Columbia University Press, 1944).

SUTHERLAND, DOUGLAS. *Fifty Years on the Civic Front*. (Chicago: The Civic Federation, 1943).

TAFT, PHILIP. *The A.F. of L. in the Time of Gombers*. (New York: Harper Bros., 1957).

TAGER, JACK. *The Intellectual as Urban Reformer: Brand Whitlock and the Progressive Movement*. (Press of Case Western Reserve University, 1968).

VAN PELT, DANIEL, ed. *Leslie's History of the Greater New York*, vol. 2. (New York: Arkell, 1898).

VEYSEY, LAURENCE R. *The Emergence of the American University*. (Chicago: University of Chicago Press, 1965).

WARE, NORMAN J. *Labor in Modern Industrial Society*. (Boston: D. C. Heath, 1935).

WELD, RALPH FOSTER. *Brooklyn Is America*. (New York: Columbia University Press, 1950).

WERNER, M. R. *Tammany Hall*. (Garden City, N.Y.: Doubleday, Doran & Co., 1928).

WESSER, ROBERT F. *Charles Evans Hughes: Politics and Reform in New York, 1905–1910*. (Ithaca, N.Y.: Cornell University Press, 1967).

WHITE, MORTON and LUCIA. *The Intellectual Versus the City: from Thomas Jefferson to Frank Lloyd Wright*. (Cambridge, Mass.: Harvard University Press, 1962).

WIEBE, ROBERT H. *Businessmen and Reform: A Study of the Progressive Movement*. (Chicago: Quadrangle Books, 1968).

WIEBE, ROBERT H. *The Search for Order, 1877–1920*. (New York: Hill & Wang, 1967).

YELLOWITZ, IRWIN. *Labor and the Progressive Movement in New York State, 1897–1916*. (Ithaca, N.Y.: Cornell University Press, 1965).

III: *Unpublished Works*

CHESLAW, IRVING G. *The National Civic Federation and Labor (a study in conservative reform)*, unpublished master's essay, Columbia University, 1947.

COVIELLO, JAMES. *Seth Low as Mayor of New York*, unpublished master's essay, Columbia University, 1938.

FEIN, ALBERT. *New York City Politics from 1897–1903: A Study in Political Party Leadership,* unpublished master's essay, Columbia University, 1954.

GASSON, HENRY D. *The National Civic Federation,* unpublished master's essay, Catholic University of America, 1940.

JENSEN, GORDON MAURICE. *The National Civic Federation: American Business in an Age of Social Change and Social Reform, 1900–1910,* unpublished doctoral dissertation, Princeton University, 1956.

LISTER, JOSEPH J. *History of the New York Tenement House Department,* unpublished master's essay, Columbia Unuiversity, 1933.

SASS, SIDNEY. *The National Civic Federation 1900–1914,* unpublished master's essay, Columbia University, 1948.

SCHACHNE, CAROLYN FLORA. *Some Aspects in the History of the Police Department of the City of New York, 1870–1901,* unpublished master's essay, Columbia University, 1940.

SKOLNIK, RICHARD. *The Crystallization of Reform in New York City, 1894–1917,* unpublished doctoral dissertation, Yale University, 1964

Index

Abbot, Abiel, 13
Abbott, Lawrence, 305
Abbott, Lyman, 99, 305, 307
Adams, C. K., 53
Addams, Jane, 222
Adler, Felix, 118; comment on 1901 mayoral election, 140–41
Alger, George W., 137–38
Alsop, Reese F., 172, 188
American Federation of Labor, 227; relations with N.C.F., 284–95; 1911 convention of, 294–95
Ankeny, A. T., 260–61
Anthracite Coal Strike, 229–31
Archer, George, 146

Baer, George F., 230, 233
Bancroft, E. A., 268, 270
Bannard, Otto T., 145
Barnard, Frederick A. P., 19, 51–52, 55
Barnum, H. A., 40
Bealin, John J., 212
Beebe, William H. H., 53, 97
Beeks, Gertrude, 316
Belmont, August, 250, 256
Belmont, Perry, 103
Bigelow, John, 17
Binkerd, Robert S., analysis of 1903 mayoral election, 201–2
Black, Frank S., 80, 90
Blaine, James G., 48
Bliss, Cornelius N., 174, 226
Blumenthal, Eugene, 190
Bonaparte, Charles J., 267
Brookfield, William, 92, 94
Brooklyn, arrears problem in, 40–41; charter of 1873, 29; charter of 1880, 30; civil service reform in, 43–44; growth of, 26; home rule in, 39–40; school reform in, 42–43; taxes in, 41–42; village of, 13–14
Brooklyn Association for Improving the Condition of the Poor, 14
Brooklyn Bureau of Charities, 23
Brooklyn Citizens' League, 34
Brooklyn Committee of Fifty, 87, 92, 93, 95–96
Brooklyn Polytechnic Institute, 19
Brooklyn Public Library, 17
Brooklyn Young Republican Club, 27–28, 32–33, 34, 35–36
Brown, William C., 311
Bruce, M. Linn, 193
Bryan, William Jennings, 248, 282–83
Bryce, James, 48, 106, 124, 239
Burgess, John W., 51, 52, 53, 56, 61, 75, 305–6
Burlingham, Charles C., 145
Butler, Nicholas Murray, 57, 60, 61, 93, 132–33, 195, 260, 264–65, 333

Callaway, S. R., 226
Cantor, Jacob A., 164, 171, 174–75, 185
Carnegie, Andrew, 256, 270, 284–85, 317, 327
Carter, James C., 83, 87
Carter, W. S., 311
Castle, Chauncey H., 234
Catlin, Isaac, 48
Chambers, W. L., 317–18
Chapman, John Jay, 78, 79, 85, 103; view of Citizens' Union, 108–9
Charities, N.Y.C. Department of, 167
Chicago Conference on Trusts and Combinations, 224–25

409

Choate, Joseph, 13
Citizens' Industrial Alliance, 269–70, 272
Citizens' Union, 83–85; anger at Low's patronage policy, 147; appeal to labor, 101–2; evaluation of Low administration, 169; fusion with G.O.P., 112–13; 1897 mayoral campaign, 101–2; analysis of 1897 mayoral campaign, 108–13; 1901 mayoral campaign, 121–39; and middle class vote, 103; and organized labor, 84–85; 1897 platform, 84; 1901 platform, 125–26; and police reform, 158, 160; and relations with Republican party, 87, 90–96; and social reform, 123, 126–27
City Club of New York, 83; and police reform, 158, 160, 161
City Vigilance League and police reform, 159–60
Civic Federation of Chicago, 220–24
Clark, Edgar E., 226
Clark, John C., 85
Clayton, Henry, 314–16
Cleveland, Grover, 48, 226
Coler, Bird S., 124, 128, 130, 131, 132, 171
Columbia, 19–20; in the 1870s and 1880s, 51–52; finances, 60; Morningside Heights campus, 60
Committee of Five, 117–18
Committee of Twelve, 127
Committee of Fifteen, 118–19
Committee of Seventy, 75–76
Commons, John R., 230, 233–34
Compton, Alfred G., 76
Conkling, A. R., 103
Conkling, Roscoe E., 89
Cornell, Alonzo B., 44
Crim, John W. H., 278
Crimmins, John D., 125
Croker, Richard, 83, 89, 99, 101, 103, 114–15, 117, 120
Curtis, Anne Wroe Scollay, 23
Curtis, Benjamin Robbins, 23
Cutting, R. Fulton, 85, 92–93, 100, 134, 147, 176, 178, 181, 182, 183, 184, 186, 193, 209; influence in

Citizens' Union, 110–12; as Mayoral choice, 133; on social reform, 126
Cuyler, Theodore L., 39

Danbury Hatters' Case, 204
Debs, Eugene V., 288
Defebaugh, J. E., 263
DeForest, Robert W., 145–46
Delano, Warren, 15–16
Devery, William S., 115, 119, 144
Dix, Morgan, 75
Dow, Ellen Almira, 16
Duncan, James, 235–36
Dutcher, Silas, 42

Easley, Ralph Montgomery, organizes N.C.F., 224–26; 230, 249–50, 256, 258, 265, 268, 270–72,, 282, 284, 289, 292–93, 300, 316, 322, 335–37; on socialism, 289–90
Eidlitz, Otto M., 252
Eliot, Charles W., 226
Ellis, Wade H., 260
Ely, Richard T., 53
Emery, James A., 270
Erdman Act, 310–11
Evarts Bill, 41
Everitt, J. A., 262
Excise issue, 149–57; in 1901 election, 151–52

Fackenthal, Frank Diehl, 61
Fairchild, Charles S., 83, 108, 129, 131, 189
Federal Incorporation, 263–64
Federal Trade Commission, 334
Fenton, Reuben E., 89
Fish, Hamilton, 51
Folks, Homer, 115, 167
Fornes, Charles V., 136, 148, 184, 185, 186
Foulke, William Dudley, 260–61, 262, 280
Fox, Austen G., 175
Fox, Martin, 226
Franchise policy, 80; and reforms, 162–63
Frissel, A. S., 75
Fulton, Thomas A., 184
Fusion alliance, nature and weaknesses of, 209–10

Gage, Lyman J., 222
Galloway, Charles P., 325
Gardiner, Asa Bird, 100
Garfield & Arthur Campaign Club, 27
Garfield, James R., 254
Garretson, A. B., 311, 316
Gary, Elbert H., 264, 286, 333
Gaynor, William J., 103
George, Henry, 99, 101–5
German American Reform Union, 130, 134
Gilder, Richard Watson, 74, 88, 95, 97, 137
Gladden, Washington, 76
Goddard, F. Norton, 131
Godkin, E. L., 83
Goetze, Frederick A., 324–25
Gompers, Samuel, 225–28, 234, 236–37, 244, 249–50, 259–60, 264–71, 284–88, 291–92; 295–96, 313, 336–37
Gould, Elgin R. L., 188
Grant, Percy S., 318
Greater New York, 77–81; charter of, 77–81
Greater New York Democracy, 130, 134, 171, 182–83
Greeley, Horace, 89
Green, William, 299
Greene, Francis Vinton, and excise, 155–57; as Police Commissioner, 160–62, 190; on fusion defeat, 195
Grosscup, Peter S., 259
Grout, Edward M., 136, 139, 172–73, 184–86, 189–90
Gunton, George, 136, 139, 232

Haight, A. S., 110, 179
Hammond, John Hays, 233, 299
Hanna, Marcus A., 226–31, 237, 288
Harper, J. W., 74
Harriman, Mrs. J. Borden, 316, 336
Haskell, Hannah, 12
Hawthorn, Nathaniel, 13
Hay, John, 135–36
Health, N.Y.C. Department of, 166–67
Healy, Timothy, 288
Hearst, William Randolph, 181, 185, 192
Heffernan, John A., 42
Hendrix, Joseph C., 46–47

Hepburn-Warner Bill, 264–73
Hess, Jake, 115
Hewitt, Abram S., 83, 89, 91
Hilles, Charles D., 306
Hillquit, Morris, 292–93
Hinrichs, Frederic W., 43, 186
Holt, Hamilton, 259
Houqua, 15
Howard & Company, 15
Howard, Sidney, 336–37
Howell, James, 32, 38
Howell, R. G., 333
Huntington, Francis C., 193

Immigrants and urban corruption, 64–66
Ireland, Archbishop John, 226

Jefferson Hall movement, 32
Jenks, Jeremiah W., 265, 271
Jerome, William Travers, 118–19, 136, 138–39, 172–73, 179–84, 186, 188, 211; attack on Low, 183, and excise, 153, 154
Johnson, Robert Underwood, 295

Keefe, Daniel J., 226, 235, 287
Keller, John W., on Citizens' Union, 109–10
Kelly, Edmond, 75
Kempner, Otto, 134
Kinsella, Thomas, 32, 34, 38
Kirby, John, 299–301
Knapp, Martin A., 310–11
Knox, Edward M., 130

Lane, Franklin K., 313
Larned, James, 44
Lawton, William C., 147
Lederle, E. J., 145
Lee, W. G., 316–18
Lexow Committee, 113–14
Lin, Commissioner, 15–16
Lindenthal, Gustav, 145
Long Island Historical Society, 17
Lovett, R. S., 311
Low, Abiel Abbot, 13–18, 35
Low, A. A. & Brothers, 16–17; liqui-dation of, 50–51
Low, Ann Davison Bedell, 18
Low, Benjamin Robbins Curtis, 208

Low, Charles Porter, 16
Low, David (I), 12
Low, David (II), 12
Low, David (III), 12
Low, David (IV), 12
Low family, genealogy of the, 12–18
Low, Seth (Sr.), 13–14
Low, Seth, childhood, 18; education, 18–20; religion, 20–21; partner in A. A. Low & Brothers, 21; charitable activities, 22–23; Garfield & Arthur Campaign Club, 27; Young Republican Club, 28; 1881 Brooklyn mayoralty, 32–33, 35–37; and Mugwump analysis of municipal corruption, 37–38; administration as mayor of Brooklyn, 38–45; 1883 Brooklyn mayoralty, 45–47; 1884 presidential election, 48; 1885 New York governorship, 47–48; Columbia Alumni Assaciation, 51; Columbia trustee, 51; president of Columbia, 52–62; administrative reforms at Columbia, 55–58; quota system at Columbia, 57; on the university in American society, 58–60; and office of college president, 61–62; analysis of municipal government, 64–77; reasons for failure of municipal government, 66–68; contrasted with Mugwump's, 73; doctrine of non-partisan government, 44, 68–71; 1894 New York City mayoralty, 74–77; 1897 New York City mayoralty, 86–98; 1897 appeal to labor, 102; reasons for 1897 defeat, 105–6; on the Citizens' Union, 110; 1901 New York City mayoralty, 123–39; view of 1901 election, 141–43; administration as mayor of New York, 143–68; mayoral appointments, 145; charges Aldermanic corruption, 148; excise policy, 44–45, 149, 152–53; fiscal policy, 163–64; franchise reform, 45, 162–63; patronage, 142, 146–47, 169–70; police reform, 157–62; public works, 165; real estate taxes, 164–65; school system, 165; social reform, 142–43, 166–67; 1902 New York governorship, 170–71; 1903

New York mayoralty, 169–92; Democratic opposition to Low, 171–72, 177–78; reluctance to run in 1903, 175–76; on 1903 defeat, 196–97; evaluation as mayor, 193–214; conception of public duty, 206–8; on gold standard, 213; and Hague Arbitration Conference, 213; and imperialism, 213; personality failings, 172–73; relations with G.O.P., 205–6
Low, Seth, joins N.C.F., 239–40; J. J. Little arbitration, 246–47; coal negotiations of 1906, 250–52; telegrapher's strike of 1907, 253; president of N.C.F., 256; effort to amend Sherman Act, 264–73; and Erdman Act, 311–18; and Federal Trade Commission, 319–21; president New York State Chamber of Commerce, 333–35; views on direct primaries, 308–9; immigration, 327–31; industrialism, 240–45; initiative, referendum & recall, 308; Jews, 329; judicial recall, 304–6; labor unions & rights, 244–47, 282–84, 296–99, 321–22; labor violence, 295–96; N.C.F.'s industrial conciliation, 247–57; national incorporation, 273–80; the Negro, 323–27; New Nationalism & 1912 presidential election, 302–9; progressivism, 306–9; regulation of industry, 254–55; restriction of Chinese & Japanese immigration, 329–31; on Roosevelt administration, 255–56; Roosevelt-Taft split, 303–6; social conscience, 331–33; socialism, 289–90; trusts, 248–49, 262–63; death of, 335
Low, Seth & Company, 13, 15
Low, Thomas, 12
Low, Thomas (II), 12
Low, William Henry, 15
Lowell, Josephine Shaw, 146, 211
Lyman, Arthur T., 299

Mahan, A. T., 106
Marks, Marcus M., 226, 301
Martin, John, on Low's prospects, 143
Mason, George H., 40

Mazet Committee, 80–81, 120
McAneny, George, 133, 208
McClellan, George B., Jr., on Van Wyck, 115, 133, 137; on 1903 election, 200; on Low, 207–8; 173, 186, 188–89, 192
McCook, John J., 237
McCullagh, John, 115
McDonald, Duncan, 294–95
McGuire, Edward J., 186
McKeen, James, 94
McKinley, William, 98, 213
McLaughlin, Hugh, 22, 28–32, 38, 46–48, 128, 131, 185
Mitchell, John, 226–27, 230, 234, 237, 250–52, 256, 264, 284–85, 287, 290–92
Morawetz, Victor, 265, 267
Morgan, House of, 270
Morgan, J. P., 227, 231
Morgan, Thomas, 221
Morton, Levi P., 77, 89
Moss, Frank, 118, 126
Murphy, Charles F., 184–86
Murphy, Michael G., 119

Nadal, Charles C., 183–84
National Association of Manufacturers, 236, 269–70, 272; on the N.C.F., 299–300
National Civic Federation (to 1905), 220–38; organization of, 225–26; and labor, 232–34, 281–96; and trusts, 232; and conference on trusts, 259–64; and socialists, 286–95; and U.S. Steel, 286; and Erdman Act, 310–18; and Federal Trade Commission, 319–21; after Low, 336–37; in historiography, 340–49
National Incorporation, 273–80
Neill, Charles P., 310–11
Neu, Jacob, 187
Newlands Act of 1913, 313–18
New Nationalism, 302–9
New York City, Department of Charities, 167; Department of Health, 166–67; excise enforcement in, 149–57; franchise reform in, 162–63; Greater New York, 77–81; Greater New York charter, 77–81;

1894 mayoralty, 74–77; 1897 mayoralty, 86–98; 1901 mayoralty, 123–39; 1903 mayoralty, 169–92; New York under Mayor Low, 143–68; police corruption in, 115–16, 119–20; police reform in, 157–62; prostitution in, 116–18; public works in, 165; schools in, 120–21, 165; taxes in, 163–65; Tenement House Department, 167–68
New York Union Defence Committee, 17
Nixon, Lewis, 118, 226

Odell, Benjamin B., 155, 170–71, 177–79
Ogden, Willis L., 127, 130
Opium Trade, 15–16

Packer Collegiate Institute, 17
Page, Walter Hines, 104–5
Palmer, Mrs. Potter, 222
Parkhurst, Rev. Charles, 116, 153, 161
Parsons, Herbert, 195–96
Partridge, John N., 145, 152, 157–60
Patten, J. H., 329
Payne, Sereno E., 317
Peabody, George Foster, 128, 131, 134
Peck, Harry Thurston, 55
Peckham, Wheeler, on 1901 election, 141
Perkins, George W., 265, 267–68, 270, 284
Peters, John P., 132
Pew, Marlen E., 329
Pfahler, William H., 226
Pine, John B., 54, 60
Pingree, Hazen S., 49, 225
Platt, Thomas C., 83, 89–91, 93, 95, 97–99, 103, 105, 125, 128–29, 131–33, 169–70, 174, 177, 179–80, 183, 186; on 1903 defeat, 197–98
Plunkitt, George Washington, 85
Police corruption, 115–16, 119–20; and excise, 154–55; reform, 157–62
Porter, Mary, 13
Potter, Henry C., 117, 226
Prendergast, William A., 36
Progressivism, historiography of, 349–56
Prostitution, 116–18

Public works, 165
Pullman strike, 222
Purdy, Lawson, 208
Putnam, Israel, 13

Quigg, Lemuel Ely, 90–93, 96, 129

Rabbi Joseph riot, 159
Raines Liquor Tax Law, 86, 150–51
Rainsford, William S., 156
Rea, Samuel, 311
Redfield, William C., 313
Reformers, personality traits of, 210–11
Republican party, and fusion, 125; and patronage, 147, 170
Reynolds, James B., 59, 83, 146
Ridder, Herman, 130, 132, 134, 143, 151, 156, 176, 184
Rives, George L., 131–32, 134, 145, 163
Robbins, Francis L., 234, 250–52
Rogers, Rev. Nathaniel, 11–12
Roosevelt, Theodore, 80–81, 86, 92, 97–98, 105, 123, 144, 149–50, 168, 171, 175, 177–79, 183–84, 191–92, 195, 206, 230, 236, 251–52, 254–56, 263–64, 266–67, 270–73, 302, 303–6, 330
Root, Elihu, 83
Ropes, Ripley, 34–36
Russell & Company, 15
Russell, William E., 49
Russell, William Hepburn, 171, 176–78, 183

Saloon graft under Tammany, 151; social function of saloon, 151
Saxe, Martin, 164
Schieren, Charles A., 128–30, 209
Schiff, Jacob H., 83, 88, 118, 123–24, 253, 299
Schmidlapp, J. G., 336
School reform, in Brooklyn, 42–43; in New York, 165
School system and Tammany, 120–21
Schram, Louis B., 285
Schroeder, Frederick A., 30; "Schroeder" character, 28

Schurz, Carl, on the Citizens' Union, 107
Schwab, Charles M., 226–27
Seligman, Isaac N., 262, 264, 284
Sexton, John B., 120
Shaffer, T. J., 226–27
Shaw, Albert, 88, 265
Sheehan, John C., 99, 134, 171, 174, 183, 185
Shepard, Edward Morse, 44, 49, 104, 134–35, 137–39
Sherman Anti-Trust Act, 258; effort to amend, 264–73
Silliman, R. D., 277
Slocum, Henry W., 32, 34, 38
Small, Albion, 224
Smith, Charles Stewart, 75, 83, 85, 94
Smith, Herbert Knox, 261
Smith, Munroe, 55
Social reform and Low's defeat, 199–205
Socialists and N.C.F., 286–95
Starin, John H., 207
Stead, William T., 221
Steel strike (1901), 226–27
Steffens, Lincoln, 198–99
Stetson, Francis Lynde, 265
Stimson, Henry L., 335
Stone, W. S., 316
Storey, Morefield, 270
Straus, Oscar S., 19, 225–26, 233, 237, 256
Strong, William L., 76–80, 85–86, 91, 113–14, 146–47

Taft, William Howard, 266, 277–78, 303–6, 309
Tanner, Frederick, 208
Taylor, Graham, 221–22
Taylor, Robert, 262
Tenement House Department, New York City, 167–68
Tobin, Daniel J., 292
Tod, J. Kennedy, 85
Tracy, Benjamin Franklin, 33–36, 77, 99–100
Trade agreement, 229, 231, 234–35, 285–86
Tripp, Bartlett, 261
Trumbell, Frank, 311
Tumulty, J. P., 312–13, 316

Tuskegee Institute, 323–24
Twain, Mark, 137, 139

Union League Club (Brooklyn), 91
Unitarian Church of the Saviour
(Brooklyn), 14
United Mine Workers, 229–31, 290-91
University Settlement, 59

Van Cott, Cornelius, 93
Van Wyck, Robert A., 99, 103–4, 114–
21, 143–44
Veiller, Lawrence, 145–46
Villard, Oswald Garrison, 322

Warner, John DeWitt, 92, 126, 128,
131–32, 134, 139, 143, 198
Washington, Booker T., 60, 323–24,
326–27
Webb, Sidney, 144
Weil, A. Leo, 319
Weinstock, Harris, 301
Welling, Richard W. G., 105, 188,
190

Wills, H. E., 311
Wheeler, Benjamin Ide, 257
Wheeler, E. P., 132, 134–35
White, Alfred T., 23, 118
White, Andrew Dickson, 53, 99
White, Harry, 102, 226
Whitney, Daniel D., 48
Wickersham, Charles A., 311
Wickersham, George W., 277
Wilhelm, Kaiser, 144
Willard, Daniel, 311, 314
Williams, Talcott, 107–8, 265
Willis, Theodore, 90, 95
Wilson, Huntington, 329–30
Wilson, John T., 235
Wilson, William B., 313–16
Wilson, Woodrow, 302, 309, 312–13,
316–17, 319–20, 326, 334
Wise, Rev. John, 12
Woodruff, Timothy L., 95, 130, 173
Woodword, John R., 48
Worth, Jacob, 90, 94–95, 103

Ziebold, Charles F., 261